T0300549

This book assembles nine research papers written by leading public-finance economists on the subject of tax progressivity and its relationship to income inequality.

The papers document the changes during the 1980s in progressivity at the federal, state, and local level in the United States. Conceptual issues about how to measure progressivity are investigated, as well as the extent to which declining progressivity contributed to the well-documented increase in income inequality over the past two decades.

Several papers investigate the economic impact and cost of progressive tax systems. Special attention is given to behavioral responses – including portfolio composition – to the taxation of high-income individuals.

The concluding papers address the contentious issue of what constitutes a "fair" tax system. They contrast public attitudes concerning alternative tax systems to economists' notions of fairness, and examine the trade-off between fairness and economic growth.

Each paper is followed by the formal commentary of a conference participant plus a summary of the conference discussion.

Tax progressivity and income inequality

Tax progressivity and income inequality

Edited by

JOEL SLEMROD

University of Michigan

CAMBRIDGE
UNIVERSITY PRESS

CAMBRIDGE
UNIVERSITY PRESS

32 Avenue of the Americas, New York NY 10013-2473, USA

Published in the United States of America by Cambridge University Press, New York

Cambridge University Press is part of the University of Cambridge.

It furthers the University's mission by disseminating knowledge in the pursuit of
education, learning and research at the highest international levels of excellence.

www.cambridge.org
Information on this title: www.cambridge.org/9780521465434

© Cambridge University Press 1996

First published 1994
First paperback edition 1996

A catalogue record for this publication is available from the British Library

ISBN 978-0-521-46543-4 Hardback
ISBN 978-0-521-58776-1 Paperback

Contents

v

Preface

The question of tax progressivity – who should bear the tax burden – has fascinated tax philosophers for over a century, and remains highly controversial in the 1990s. The ultimate answer to this question depends on ethical judgments into which the field of economics offers no insight, but it also depends on some of the bread-and-butter preoccupations of economics, such as the extent and nature of income inequality and the behavioral response of taxpayers to alternative tax systems.

In an effort to contribute to this ongoing policy debate, the Office of Tax Policy Research commissioned nine studies on the economic issues that are relevant for choosing the appropriate degree of tax progressivity. These papers were presented at a conference held at the Michigan Business School on September 11–12, 1992. This volume begins with an overview chapter and then presents the nine commissioned papers, each followed by the remarks delivered at the conference by a formal commentator and a synopsis of the general discussion that followed the conference presentations.

I would like to thank the Bradley Foundation for providing the financial support for this conference. The conference project could not have been successful without the efforts of Mary Molter, who provided all of the logistical support in her usual professional and cheerful manner. Thanks are also due to Marta Diaz, David Hummels, and Alec Rodney, who helped prepare the general discussion synopses.

Contributors

Gary Burtless
The Brookings Institution

Charles Christian
Arizona State University

David M. Cutler
Harvard University

Martin H. David
University of Wisconsin

Amy Dunbar
University of Texas at San Antonio

Daniel Feenberg
National Bureau of Economic Research

William G. Gale
The Brookings Institution

Steven Gold
Center for the Study of the States

Roger H. Gordon
University of Michigan

Jane G. Gravelle
Congressional Research Service

Michael Haliassos
University of Maryland

Peggy Hite
Indiana University

Andrew Hoerner
University of Maryland

Douglas J. Holtz-Eakin
Syracuse University

Robert P. Inman
University of Pennsylvania

Lynn A. Karoly
RAND

Richard Kasten
Congressional Budget Office

Andrew B. Lyon
University of Maryland

Jeff MacKie-Mason
University of Michigan

Michael J. McIntyre
Wayne State University

Paul L. Menchik
Michigan State University

Gilbert E. Metcalf
Princeton University

Kemper W. Moreland
Eastern Michigan University

Richard A. Musgrave
University of California – Santa Cruz

Contributors

George Plesko
Northeastern University

James M. Poterba
Massachusetts Institute of Technology

Michael L. Roberts
University of Alabama

Frank Sammartino
Congressional Budget Office

Richard Sansing
Yale University

John Karl Scholz
University of Wisconsin – Madison

Douglas A. Shackelford
University of North Carolina

Steven M. Sheffrin
University of California – Davis

Joel Slemrod
University of Michigan

Roxanne M. Spindle
Virginia Commonwealth University

C. Eugene Steuerle
The Urban Institute

Eric Toder
Congressional Budget Office

Robert K. Triest
University of California – Davis

Randall Weiss
Deloitte & Touche

Patrick J. Wilkie
George Mason University

CHAPTER 1

Introduction

Joel Slemrod

The question of tax progressivity – who should bear the tax burden – is a central one for tax policy. It has concerned tax philosophers for over a century, and has often dominated political debate over tax-reform options. The issue was certainly prominent in the U.S. presidential campaign of 1992, during which the Democrats proposed tax cuts for the middle class accompanied by tax increases for the wealthy and certain corporations. The Republicans countered by stressing the economic costs of higher taxes and proposed instead tax cuts on capital gains, which are largely received by upper-income individuals, and (at the Republican convention) an across-the-board tax cut for individuals.

The prominence of the tax progressivity issue puts economists in an uncomfortable position, because we know in our heart that progressivity is not solely an economic question. It is equally a matter of ethics, or moral philosophy, because it involves choosing between situations where some people are better off and others worse off. Economics cannot settle which people are more deserving. Economic reasoning cannot determine whether it is a good idea to take one dollar from a wealthy family in order to give one dollar – or, even more problematically, fifty cents – to a poor family.

Lionel Robbins, in his influential book *An Essay on the Nature & Significance of Economic Science* (first published in 1932), argued persuasively that for such issues the role of the economist should be to lay out the implications of various courses of action, and to let the policy-maker decide among these choices. He then added:

> Nor is it in the least implied that economists should not deliver themselves on ethical questions, any more than an argument that botany is not aesthetics is to say that botanists should not have views of their own on the lay-out of gardens. On the contrary, it is greatly to be desired that economists should have speculated long and widely on these matters,

since only in this way will they be in a position to appreciate the implications as regards *given* ends of problems which are put to them for solution. (Robbins 1946, p. 149)

This conundrum explains why, in a conference devoted to tax progressivity, none of the commissioned papers is devoted directly to just how progressive the tax system should be. Rather, most of the papers are devoted to the inputs that a policymaker needs in order to make an informed decision.

Traditionally, economists have used two different principles for evaluating how the tax burden ought to be allocated: the benefit principle and the ability-to-pay principle. Under the benefit principle, taxes are seen as a quid pro quo for the services government provides to its citizens. From this perspective, the problem of assigning tax burden boils down to assessing how much each citizen benefits from government activity.

As a principle to guide tax policy, the benefit principle runs into two problems. The first is an operational problem. For many important government activities, such as national defense, it is impossible to evaluate how the benefit varies from individual to individual or from group to group. In the case of defense, it is plausible that the benefit is higher for people of higher income and wealth, because they have more to be defended, but the precise relationship is elusive. For this reason, the benefit principle does not provide practical guidance with regard to the tax progressivity question. Second, many people would reject the benefit principle on the fundamental ground that it allows no role for the government in redistributing income. Those that accept such a role would want to assign tax burdens not only to mirror the benefits of government activity, but also with an eye toward the resulting distribution of after-tax income. The benefit principle offers no guidance concerning how to do this.

The ability-to-pay principle does offer such guidance. It posits that tax burdens should be assigned, not on the basis of who benefits from government policy, but instead on the basis of who has the "ability to pay." Defining that term precisely becomes the problem. It is plausible, but not provable, that a dollar given up in tax entails less sacrifice, the higher is the taxpayer's income level. Then, if taxing according to ability to pay is interpreted as equalizing the sacrifice due to taxes, taxes should rise with income. However, how fast taxes should rise with income depends on exactly how much sacrifice a dollar of tax causes for people at different income levels, and therein lies the rub. This is impossible to determine, and so the ability-to-pay principle fails as an operational guide to tax progressivity for the same reasons that the benefit principle fails.

The modern approach to evaluating progressivity focuses on the trade-off between the potential social benefit of a more equal distribution of income and the economic costs caused by the disincentive effects of the high marginal tax rates required by a redistributing tax system. As Henry Simons stated so elegantly in *Personal Income Taxation,* "Both progress and justice are costly luxuries – costly, above all, in terms of each other" (1938, p. 24). How that trade-off is resolved depends in part on the value society places on a more equal distribution of income, which is not an economic question. But it also depends on more mundane matters which are the bread and butter of economists, and which are the subject of most of this volume.

One of these matters is how to evaluate exactly who bears the burden of any particular tax, a question which is logically prior to assessing how the actual burden stacks up against what it should be. It is well known that who bears the burden of any given tax need not be the same as the person who writes out the check to the Internal Revenue Service. Taxes can be shifted via their influence on market prices, so assessing the true distribution of the tax burden is a delicate and important matter.

The first two papers of this volume address both how to measure the distribution of the tax burden and how the tax burden, measured appropriately, has changed over the past decade, first for federal taxes and then for state and local taxes.

The volume begins with a paper by Richard Kasten, Frank Sammartino, and Eric Toder, all of the Congressional Budget Office. In it they calculate recent trends in federal effective tax rates (ETRs), and separate the changes in ETRs into those due to changes in the tax law and those due to shifts in the composition of income within income groups. They find that overall ETRs have changed very little in the past decade, going from 23.3% in 1980 to a projected 23.2% in 1993. However, the ETR for the highest income percentile has declined 9% over the same period. There have been important changes in the mix of taxes. The effective income tax rate has fallen from 12.3% to 10.9%, effective social insurance–tax rates have grown from 7.2% to 8.9%, effective corporate income taxes have fallen by 20%, and the effective excise tax has risen by 18%.

In the second paper, Gilbert E. Metcalf of Princeton University computes the lifetime tax incidence of the major state and local taxes used in the United States during the 1980s. Using data from the Consumer Expenditure Survey, he shows that over the life cycle, general sales taxes are equally as progressive as state and local income taxes. He argues that while the progressivity of sales taxes did not change between 1984 and 1989, income taxes became less progressive over that five-year period while property taxes became more progressive. The system of state and local taxes is mildly progressive over the life cycle and became slightly more progressive between 1984 and 1989. Finally, eliminating deductibility for sales taxes in 1986 appears to have had little effect on the overall progressivity of the tax system.

As I have just argued, at what degree of progressivity the marginal economic cost balances the gain of additional redistribution is ultimately not an economic question. Economists can, however, provide policymakers with a kind of spreadsheet, where policymakers can input their views about the social value of a dollar to a family with income X versus a family with income Y, and out pops the appropriate progressivity. Built into the spreadsheet program is an estimate of the cost of redistribution, a (necessarily simple) model of the economy, and some programming code that finds the ideal trade-off between the costs and benefits of redistributive tax policies.

Because the cost of redistribution and the appropriate model of the economy are both still controversial, different economists will offer different spreadsheets. To put it bluntly, we don't know what the right degree of progressivity is. The next four papers in this volume offer insight into what that spreadsheet program would look like.

One important component of the spreadsheet program is the extent of inequality in pre-tax income. Other things equal, more inequality makes a greater degree of progressivity more attractive. There is a broad consensus that income inequality has been increasing in the last two decades. There is evidence of increased dispersion since the mid-1970s in both the lower and upper tails of the distribution for families and for individuals, and in the distribution of labor income for workers. At least since 1979, inequality has grown both between less and more educated workers and also among apparently similar workers. The increase in inequality among workers cannot be explained simply by shifts in the gender, education, or experience of the work force, and is evident even when the sample is restricted to full-time workers.

A variety of alternative explanations have been offered for the increased inequality. Most attention has been paid to labor market factors, as labor market income accounts for about 70% of family income. Among the "supply" explanations offered are shifts in the size of worker age cohorts and the educational distribution of these cohorts. Among the "demand" explanations offered are shifts in the composition of final output, in the occupational mix within industries, and in skill requirements. All of these explanations for the increased inequality boil down to an increased dispersion of the ability to earn income which is exogenous to individual decisions.

There is, however, an alternative explanation that has strikingly different policy implications. Lindsey (1990) has argued that the sharply reduced marginal tax rates initiated in 1981 induced high-income taxpayers to work more hours, report a higher share of their income to the Internal Revenue Service, realize more capital gains, take more compensation in taxable form, and generally substitute taxable income for either nontaxed income or leisure. This argument implies that much of the apparent increase in the dispersion of income in the 1980s does not represent increased dispersion of potential incomes. Instead, it suggests that the high incomes did exist prior to 1981, but in forms that either would not be readily picked up by the standard data sets on income, not be realized income sources, or consisted of potential income consumed in the form of leisure.

If this alternative explanation is correct, the observed increase in inequality does not call for a response of increased tax progressivity. But its validity has not been decisively established. The next two papers add to what we know about this issue.

The paper by Lynn A. Karoly of RAND uses the Census Bureau's Current Population Surveys to examine trends in income inequality, and investigates the role of tax policy, business cycles, family composition, and wage structure. Overall income inequality as measured by the Gini coefficient has risen steadily since a postwar low in 1967–68, with most of the increase occurring in the 1980s.

The paper concludes that tax policy alone cannot explain this trend. Inequality began increasing in the 1970s, whereas tax reforms did not take effect until the early 1980s. Additionally, increased income dispersion occurring in both tails of the distribution cannot be explained solely by high-income taxpayers' supply response to marginal tax–rate cuts. Business cycle explanations also fail because inequality is generally held to be countercyclical, and the increased inequality of the 1980s coincided with business peaks. More convincing explanations are offered by changes in family composition and wage structure. As much as one-third of the rise in inequality may be due to the increasing number of single-parent households; an increasingly divergent wage structure, with rising returns to skilled labor, may also contribute to rising inequality.

The paper by Joel Slemrod of the University of Michigan investigates two related questions – how responsive high-income taxpayers are to changes in tax rates, and whether the recent increase in measured inequality is due to the increased work effort of the rich and greater exposure of their income to taxation. An analysis of both income-tax and wealth data over the past three decades uncovers no evidence that the behavioral responsiveness is large enough to produce an inverse revenue response, and suggests that the growth in inequality is not an illusion caused by behavioral responses to tax changes. A more definitive conclusion will have to wait until the analysis of data from the late 1980s on the labor supply and form of compensation of high-income taxpayers.

Remember that in the spreadsheet program it is the economic cost of the disincentive effect of high marginal tax rates that limits progressivity. The belief that these costs were very high – what I call "elasticity pessimism" – probably reached a high-water mark in 1980, about the time that the Kemp–Roth tax cuts were beginning to be taken seriously as a policy option.

The view that taxes exact a high economic cost was popularized by Arthur Laffer, but at the time many prominent academic economists argued that such key economic variables as saving, investment, and labor supply were highly sensitive to the bite taken out of their return by taxes. Because the cost of high marginal taxes was high, so the reasoning went, it was appropriate that progressivity be restrained.

The two major tax reforms of the 1980s, while playing havoc with long-term planning, provide a wonderful opportunity to re-assess the elasticity pessimism that flourished in 1980. Thus it is important that we carefully assess the record of the past decade. My own reading of this evidence is that the 1980 brand of elasticity pessimism was overstated (Slemrod 1992); the 1980s have strengthened the case that taxes can exert a powerful influence on the timing of economic activity and the financial and legal structuring of economic activity, but have lowered our best estimate of the tax responsiveness of real variables such as labor supply and saving. The best example of the former is the enormous increase in 1986 in long-term capital gains realizations, clearly a response to the increased taxation on capital gains due in 1987. A good example of the latter is the continued decline of the personal savings rate in the face of lower tax rates and special incentives to save. The next paper in this volume reconsiders the evidence on the important question of the responsiveness of labor supply to taxation, and explores its policy implications.

In that paper, Robert Triest of the University of California at Davis uses estimates of labor supply determination to quantify the trade-off between equality and efficiency. He computes the efficiency cost of increased progressivity achieved by increasing top tax rates and either expanding the earned income credit, offering a general refundable tax credit program, or increasing the value of the personal exemption. Although earlier studies suggested large efficiency costs, Triest finds relatively small efficiency costs. For example, a $1 increase in the earned income credit has an efficiency cost of less than $1.20 for the labor supply parameters Triest finds most plausible. Other ways of increasing progressivity have larger efficiency costs, as do estimates based on other labor supply parameters.

Next, John Karl Scholz of the University of Wisconsin uses data from the 1983 and 1989 Survey of Consumer Finances to test the responses of portfolios to the Tax Reform Act of 1986 (TRA). He finds that although overall demand for tax-exempt bonds increased and ownership of these bonds was concentrated in high marginal tax–rate households, there were no sharp changes in ownership patterns after TRA despite the steep reduction in marginal tax rates. Scholz finds evidence to support the "dividend clientele" hypothesis: that high marginal tax–rate households invest in low-dividend equities while low marginal tax–rate households invest in high-dividend equities. He also documents a sixfold increase in home-equity lines of credit, consistent with the fact that TRA removed the tax-deductible status of all but home-equity debt.

The next two papers address perennially vexing issues in progressivity: capital gains and the corporate income tax. Because such a large fraction of the taxable income of affluent taxpayers is capital income, understanding the economic impact of our peculiar way of taxing it is crucial to questions of progressivity.

Michael Haliassos and Andrew B. Lyon, both of the University of Maryland, measure the distribution of capital gains realizations and examine the effects of changes in capital gains tax law using a model that takes a broad view of tax burden, including "lock-in" and risk-sharing effects. Evidence from a five-year panel data set reveals that although those who report capital gains every year constitute only 2.5% of the sample, they account for 42% of the net gains.

Haliassos and Lyon next develop a model to examine the excess burden of capital gains taxation. They note that tax payments understate the burden of taxation if a "lock-in" effect occurs, but that they overstate the burden to the extent that taxation reduces risk. The authors' simulations suggest that tax payments overstate the burden, and that distributional analyses using tax payments as a measure of burden therefore overstate progressivity, since capital gains tax payments are concentrated in high-income brackets.

Steven M. Sheffrin, of the University of California at Davis, employs original survey research and reviews a variety of studies by economists, tax lawyers, accountants, and psychologists in order to examine how tax policy is influenced by perceptions of tax fairness held by the voting public. He begins by asking how well the public understands the tax system, citing evidence that individuals underestimate both their tax liability and marginal tax rate, have perceptions biased by the relative visibility of various taxes, and have difficulty grasping complex tax-law changes or even such concepts as progressivity.

Survey respondents who are asked to give "fair" tax rates suggest schedules that are progressive, but closely related to the income-tax system in place at the time. Respondents overwhelmingly approve of corporate income-tax hikes, but may have difficulty connecting this tax with its incidence on individuals. Finally, the paper discusses the potential link between perceptions of fairness and tax compliance, but notes that this link is difficult to establish empirically.

The volume closes with a paper by Richard Musgrave, who perhaps comes closest of anyone to combining the attributes of an economist and a moral philosopher needed to provide the ultimate answer to how the tax burden should be shared. Musgrave's paper provides a general overview of the theory of tax equity, as well as a look at progressivity as a determinant of tax-structure design. The paper begins by discussing "benefits received" and "ability to pay" as principles of distributive justice, noting that the Anglo-Saxon tradition of tax theory has focused almost entirely on the latter. The history of thought behind the ability-to-pay principle is further examined, discussing how fair patterns of sacrifice, the development of social welfare functions, and excess burden each affect utilitarian calculations. Musgrave also notes the importance of public perception and its relevance to economists' theories of taxation. The paper next turns to the issue of progressivity and tax-structure design. Musgrave argues that the desired degree of progressivity should be determined *before* the tax structure. Complex systems of taxing personal income or personal expenditure can only be justified if progressivity is required.

Thus, while philosophers, theologians and, yes, politicians argue over what is fair, there is much for economists to do. We must understand the nature of the sharp increase in the inequality of pre-tax incomes, and decide how much of it is an exogenous increase in the dispersion of the return to abilities – which increases the value of redistribution – and how much is due to other factors. Second, we must carefully study the evidence from the 1980s in order to sharpen our understanding of the economic cost of redistribution. Finally, we must preserve the integrity of the economics profession by not presuming to know what is fair and what is not. Alas, we must be content with improving the software that generates answers to the burning questions of the day if provided with value-judgment inputs, and admit that we cannot provide the answers themselves.

REFERENCES

Lindsey, Lawrence (1990), *The Growth Experiment.* New York: Basic Books.
Robbins, Lionel (1946), *An Essay on the Nature & Significance of Economic Science,* 2nd ed. London: MacMillan.
Simons, Henry C. (1938), *Personal Income Taxation.* Chicago: University of Chicago Press.
Slemrod, Joel (1992), "Do Taxes Matter? Lessons from the 1980s," *American Economic Review* 82: 250–6.

CHAPTER 2

Trends in federal tax progressivity, 1980–93

Richard Kasten, Frank Sammartino, & Eric Toder

1   Introduction

Since 1980 there have been major changes in federal tax policy. The U.S. Congress enacted five major tax bills: the Economic Recovery Tax Act of 1981 (ERTA), the Tax Equity and Fiscal Responsibility Act of 1982 (TEFRA), the Deficit Reduction Act of 1984 (DEFRA), the Tax Reform Act of 1986 (TRA), and the Omnibus Budget Reconciliation Act of 1990 (OBRA). Congress also had previously enacted the Social Security Amendments of 1977, which increased payroll tax rates throughout the decade, and later enacted the Social Security Amendments of 1983, which accelerated the effective date of those increases and made a portion of social security benefits taxable under the individual income tax. These changes in the law have resulted in a much different tax structure today than the law in effect in 1980. The income-tax rate schedule is lower and flatter, and many tax preferences under the individual income tax have been scaled back or eliminated. The top corporate tax rate is lower, but the investment tax credit has been eliminated and other business investment incentives, which were expanded in ERTA, were subsequently scaled back. The base for payroll taxes is wider and rates are higher. Some excise-tax rates are higher today than at the beginning of the decade, offsetting in part the decline in the real value of excise-tax rates with inflation.[1]

U.S. Congressional Budget Office, Tax Analysis Division. The views in this paper are those of the authors alone and do not necessarily represent the views of the Congressional Budget Office. An earlier version of this paper was presented at the Conference on Tax Progressivity, University of Michigan, September 11, 1992. The authors are grateful for helpful comments from Bruce Davie, William Gale, Jane Gravelle, Rosemary Marcuss, Robert Reischauer, Joel Slemrod, David Weiner, Kenneth Wertz, and conference participants.

[1] For a description of tax changes between 1980 and 1990, see Steuerle (1992).

9

In this paper, we examine the effect of these changes on the distribution of the tax burden among income groups. We report results from simulations of a large micro-database that the Congressional Budget Office (CBO) has developed by combining data files on household income, demographic characteristics, and consumption data from the Census Bureau and the Bureau of Labor Statistics as well as tax-return data from the Internal Revenue Service. We array families by a measure of realized cash income, adjusted for family size; compute income and taxes paid for different income groups for the years 1980, 1985, and 1989; and project income and taxes paid for 1993. We simulate directly the individual income- and payroll-tax liabilities of families under tax laws of different years, and assign corporate and excise taxes according to assumptions about the incidence of these taxes among families. We compute effective tax rates – the ratio of all taxes paid to a measure of pre-tax income that includes all taxes.

There are several ways of measuring changes in tax progressivity over time. One way is simply to compare ratios of taxes paid to pre-tax income for different income groups over time. Using this measure, we find that the sweeping changes in tax policies resulted in virtually no change in either the overall level or the distribution of tax burdens between 1980 and 1993. The total federal effective tax rate (ETR) for all families was 23.3% in 1980 and is projected to be 23.2% in 1993. The distribution of tax burdens became slightly less progressive. The overall ETR changed little for most of the population, but declined by slightly over 10% for families in the top 1 percent of the income distribution. (In 1993, the cutoff level of income for the top 1 percent of families is projected to be $161,000 for a single person, $206,000 for a married couple with no children, and $324,000 for a family of four.)

Changes in observed ETRs over time, however, reflect both changes in tax laws and changes in the income, consumption, and demographic composition of families in different income groups. To isolate the effects of tax-policy changes alone, we must hold income and other characteristics of families fixed. We do this by simulating the effects of 1980, 1985, 1989, and 1993 tax laws on a sample of families from a single year. We perform two separate sets of such "income-fixed" simulations: one comparing the impact of the four tax laws on 1985 families, and another comparing the impact of the tax laws on 1989 families. The income-fixed simulations show that, compared to a small increase in the actual ETR, 1980–93 tax-law changes had no effect on the ETR for 1989 families in the lowest income quintile, while tax-law changes increased the ETR by slightly more than the actual change in the ETR for 1985 low-income families. Tax-law changes measured at both 1985 and 1989 incomes slightly increased the ETRs of families in the middle three quintiles, although actual ETRs declined slightly for families in those quintiles. For families in the top quintile and especially in the top 1 percent, the income-fixed simulations show substantially different results depending on the year to which the tax changes are applied. The 1980–93 tax-law changes increased the ETR only slightly for 1985 families in the top quintile and lowered it only slightly for 1985 families in the top 1 percent. In contrast, the tax-law changes lowered the ETR substantially for 1989 families in the top quintile and especially for families in the top 1 percent. These differences occur because both the share of income of high-income families and its composition (between capital gains and earnings) changed between 1985 and 1989. The following table summarizes changes in effective tax rates (in percentage points) for the period 1980–93.

	Measured at		
	Current incomes	1985 incomes	1989 incomes
Bottom quintile	+0.3	+0.4	0.0
Second quintile	−0.1	+1.2	+1.1
Middle quintile	−0.3	+1.2	+0.9
Fourth quintile	−0.6	+0.7	+0.5
Top quintile	−1.0	+0.4	−2.1
Top 1 percent	−3.5	−0.9	−8.2
All families	−0.1	+0.7	−0.8

The changes that we observe in the distribution of income and its composition by source could to some extent be responses to changes in the tax law. When taxpayers alter their behavior in response to the tax law, reported income, taxes paid, and the total tax burden all can change. A complete measure of the tax burden would include both actual taxes paid and the reduction in utility from behavioral changes to avoid paying tax. We present such a measure of the effect of tax-law changes between 1980 and 1989 on ETRs of different groups, based on assumed responses of cash wages and realized capital gains to changes in marginal tax rates. The results of these simulations show a slightly smaller decline in progressivity over the 1980s than do simulations at fixed 1989 incomes, but with the largest tax reduction still occurring for the top 1 percent of families.

The plan of this paper is as follows. In Section 2, we briefly describe the model CBO uses to simulate the distribution of income and the incidence of taxes. In Section 3, we show how actual ETRs change between

1980 and 1993 for different income groups. Section 4 presents calculations of ETRs between 1980 and 1993, with taxpayer income and demographic characteristics held fixed. We explain why ETRs measured with income held fixed differ from actual changes in ETRs, and also why the results differ depending on whether we apply the tax-law changes to 1985 or to 1989 families. In Section 5 we discuss how to measure ETRs when taxpayers respond to changes in the tax law, and present illustrative computations of changes in ETRs between 1980 and 1989 law using assumed behavioral responses. Section 6 briefly summarizes the findings.

2   The CBO income distribution and tax incidence model

The Congressional Budget Office has estimated distributions of family income for 1980, 1985, and 1989, using reported data for those years, and has projected the distribution for 1993. All these distributions are based on data from three sources. The primary source is the March Current Population Survey (CPS). The CPS is a monthly survey of approximately 60,000 families conducted by the Bureau of the Census. The reported data on income from taxable sources from the CPS files are adjusted for consistency with reported income from Statistics of Income (SOI) samples. The SOI is an extensive annual sample of actual individual income-tax returns. Data on consumer expenditures are taken from the Consumer Expenditure Survey (CEX) Interview Surveys. The CEX Interview Survey is a quarterly panel survey conducted by the Bureau of Labor Statistics; the survey collects detailed data on household expenditures over a 12-month period.

In most analyses CBO does not match data sets, but uses imputations and adjustments to combine micro-data from three separate sources to compute family incomes and to simulate federal taxes.[2] CBO uses a definition of income that closely corresponds to the definition of income used for federal income-tax purposes. Some researchers use a definition of income that measures income when it accrues rather than when it is realized, or that includes noncash income sources, or that adjusts for differences between income reported on tax returns and NIPA (national income and product accounts) measures. These definitions of income require many adjustments to data, often with virtually no information except for the

[2] Matched data sets were used in studies by the Brookings Institution, documented in Pechman and Okner (1974); Minarik (1980); Pechman (1985); and, in a project undertaken by the Office of Tax Analysis in conjunction with its analysis of tax reform in 1984 and 1985, documented in: Treasury Department (1984); Nelson (1987); and Cilke, Nelson, and Wyscarver (1987). CBO analyses that focus on consumption taxes have used matched data; see e.g. Congressional Budget Office (1990, 1992).

aggregate to be allocated. Because CBO uses a definition of income that is close to the definition of income in the federal tax law, the number of required imputations and adjustments is limited.

Measuring family income

The Congressional Budget Office measures family income on a cash receipts basis in a way that is consistent with, but not identical to, the way income is counted by the federal tax system. Major differences from the tax-system definition are that family income includes all cash transfer payments, and that it is measured before all federal taxes. Family income equals the sum of wages, salaries, self-employment income, personal rents, interest and dividends, government cash transfer payments, cash pension benefits, and realized capital gains. To lessen the distortion in measured incomes that results from incentives to realize capital losses but to defer capital gains, the income measure follows the tax code by limiting capital losses in excess of capital gains to $3,000 per return. If gains were measured on an accrual basis, it would be appropriate to net total accrued gains against total accrued losses. Net income from self-employment, rents, interest, dividends, and realized capital gains are not adjusted to remove inflationary gains or losses.

Family income excludes accrued but unrealized capital gains, employer contributions to pension funds, in-kind government transfer payments, and other noncash and implicit income. Because income is measured before reductions for any federal taxes, employer contributions for federal social insurance and federal corporate income taxes are added to family income. Micro-data totals for family incomes are not adjusted to national income aggregates.

Many people incur "paper losses" for tax purposes. To better approximate the economic income of families, rental losses and most partnership losses (but not losses of sole proprietorships) are not subtracted from family income.

Family income is measured over a single year. Income averaged over a number of years would represent the true economic circumstances of families more accurately than would a single year's income, but data available on a multiyear basis for individual taxpayers are inadequate for most analyses. In any particular year, income may be lower than normal because of a period of unemployment, unusually low income from self-employment, or a drop in investment returns. Capital gains realizations are another source of volatility. In any single year, gains will be unusually high if a person sells an asset that has been growing in value for a long time or has changed dramatically in value. If incomes were averaged over a number of years, there would be less dispersion in the distribution of incomes and therefore less dispersion in the distribution of effective tax rates.

Adjusting and aging the data

The Congressional Budget Office uses data from the SOI to adjust CPS family income data. The adjustments correct for top-coding of high incomes and underreporting of certain types of income, and also add missing data on deductions and capital gains realizations. The adjustments are based on imputations from the SOI. CPS families are split into tax-filing units comparable to those on the SOI, and missing or adjusted data are assigned to the CPS based on probability distributions from the SOI. New recipients of certain types of income are created to match SOI totals.

The CBO has created an augmented version of the adjusted CPS file that has extensive information on family expenditures. To construct this augmented file, CEX expenditure records were statistically matched to records from the adjusted CPS. Each CPS unit was assumed to have the same ratio of expenditures to income as the CEX unit to which it was matched.

Extrapolated CPS and SOI data are created using detailed population projections of the Social Security Administration and income and employment projections from the CBO baseline economic forecast. Once population weights are adjusted to reflect population growth, incomes from each source are inflated so that total growth in that source on the file matches CBO's projected aggregate growth rate for income from that source. Itemized deductions are increased at the same projected growth rate as income. Expenditures of different types are inflated by CBO's forecast for components of consumer spending.

Simulating combined federal taxes

Individual income taxes are simulated using constructed CPS tax-filing units, after reported CPS incomes have been adjusted to control totals from SOI data. The entire tax burden from individual income taxes is assumed to fall on families who directly pay the tax, with no shifting of the burden among families.

Social security payroll taxes are simulated using earnings and self-employment income from the adjusted CPS. A similar method is used to simulate the federal part of unemployment taxes. Workers are assumed to bear both the employee and employer shares of payroll taxes.[3]

---

[3] In computing the burden of federal payroll taxes, CBO does not account for any offsetting marginal OASDI (Old-Age, Survivors, and Disability Insurance) benefits employees receive in exchange for higher contributions. For estimates of marginal tax rates on wages that include the offsetting effects of retirement benefits, see Feldstein and Samwick (1992).

Federal excise taxes are simulated using expenditure data from the adjusted CEX. Part of the tax is assigned to families based on their consumption of the taxed items. The remainder of the tax is assumed to fall on intermediate goods; that part is allocated according to total consumption. Federal excise taxes are calculated as a percentage of family income for families in different income categories. Those percentages are then applied to CPS family incomes.

Although the corporate income tax is collected from corporations, families ultimately bear the economic burden of the tax. Economists disagree, however, whether families bear the tax in proportion to their income from corporate shares, income from all capital assets, employee compensation, or consumption. In this study we use the assumption that half of the corporate income tax falls on all income from capital and half falls on labor income. We show in the next section that the method of allocation does not materially affect the main conclusions about how the distribution of the total federal tax burden among income classes has changed over time.

To compute effective tax rates as a fraction of pre-tax income, it is necessary to adjust incomes for taxes that are paid indirectly. Reported pre-tax family incomes are adjusted to include the amount of the employer share of the social security payroll tax, the unemployment insurance payroll tax, and the corporate income tax. The employer share of the social security payroll tax and the unemployment insurance payroll tax are added to family labor incomes. Corporate income taxes are assigned to family incomes in a manner consistent with the incidence assumption that capital and labor bear equal shares of the corporate tax. Capital income is increased by one-half of the amount of the tax, and labor income is increased by the remaining half.

Ranking families

Comparing the distribution of family incomes can present a misleading picture unless some adjustment is made for different family sizes. For example, a single person with income of $40,000 arguably has a much higher standard of living than a family of four with the same income. One alternative is to measure income on a per capita basis. This approach removes all differences among individuals based on family size, including economics of scale from living together. Another alternative is to adjust family income based on some equivalence scale, such as the family-size adjustment used in determining poverty thresholds. This scale assumes, for example, that a family of four needs about twice the income of a single person to maintain the same standard of living. The incomes of families of different sizes are made comparable by dividing each family's income by its poverty threshold. Under this approach, a four-person family with income of about $40,000 – or three times the poverty threshold for a family of four in 1990 – is on a par with a three-person family with an income of about $31,200 – three times the poverty threshold for a three-person family.

To correct for differences in family size, CBO measures family income in terms of multiples of the poverty thresholds for families of different sizes; this measure is called adjusted family income (AFI).[4] CBO defines percentiles of the income distribution based on people, not families. Thus, families in the top quintile of the distribution do not constitute one-fifth of all families but rather one-fifth of the population.[5]

3   Trends in effective tax rates, 1980–93

There were five major tax bills affecting income taxes passed between 1981 and 1990: ERTA in 1981, TEFRA in 1982, DEFRA in 1984, TRA in 1986, and OBRA in 1990. In addition, the social security tax increases enacted in the Social Security Amendments of 1977 were implemented, with the last increase occurring in 1990. Despite these changes, there is little difference between overall effective tax rates (ETRs) in 1980 and 1993, when most of the OBRA changes will be in effect.[6]

The total federal ETR for all families is projected to be approximately the same in 1993 (23.2%) as it was in 1980 (23.3%); see Table 1. The ETR reflects federal individual and corporate income taxes, social insurance taxes, and excise taxes except for the windfall profits tax. The rate will increase slightly for the quintile with the lowest incomes, fall slightly for the second and third quintiles, and fall somewhat more for the two highest quintiles. Within the highest quintile, the top 1 percent will get the largest cut in their ETR – about 11%.

Changes within the period – from 1980 to 1985 and from 1985 to 1993 – are larger than those between 1980 and 1993 overall. ETRs in 1985, after the 1981 ERTA tax cuts and the first round of payroll tax increases, were less progressive than those in either 1980 or 1993. The ETR of the bottom quintile rose 28% between 1980 and 1985, while the ETR of the top 1

---

[4] The CBO has used AFI in a number of published studies and analyses; see e.g. Congressional Budget Office (1988a).

[5] CBO analyses regard individuals not living with relatives as one-person families. In contrast, the Bureau of the Census counts as families only groups of two or more people related by blood, marriage, or adoption.

[6] The simulations for 1993 are based on CBO's economic assumptions of January 1992 and on the tax law as it existed at that time. We assumed that the distribution of income will be the same in 1993 as it was in 1989, adjusted for different rates of growth in income from various sources.

Table 1. *Effective tax rates by income group,*
1980–93

	1980	1985	1989	1993[a]
Income quintile[b]				
Lowest	8.1	10.4	9.3	8.4
Second	15.6	15.9	15.7	15.5
Middle	19.8	19.2	19.4	19.5
Fourth	22.9	21.7	22.0	22.3
Highest	27.6	24.1	25.5	26.6
Total	23.3	21.8	22.5	23.2
Detail on highest quintile				
81%–90%	25.3	23.5	24.2	24.6
91%–95%	26.5	24.3	25.6	26.4
96%–99%	28.1	24.3	26.2	27.2
Top 1%	31.9	24.5	26.2	28.4

[a] Projected.
[b] Ranked by adjusted family income (AFI), equal number of
people per percentile.
Source: CBO.

percent fell by 23%. Some of the change was reversed in the Tax Reform
Act of 1986, and much of the rest was reversed in OBRA.

Effective tax rates by source

Although overall ETRs will change little between 1980 and 1993, there
will be changes for most tax sources. (The ETRs for each source are taxes
from the source divided by total income, not income taxable for that
source. Thus, the ETR for a source reflects not only the ETR on income
taxable by that source but also the fraction of total income represented
by the income it taxes.) The combined ETR from the individual and corporate income tax will drop by 2 percentage points while the social insurance ETR will rise by nearly 2 percentage points; see Table 2.

The ETR due to the individual income tax will fall by about 11%, from
12.3% in 1980 to 10.9% in 1993. Although this progressive source has become relatively smaller since 1980, the individual income tax will be more
progressive in 1993 than it was in 1980. The percentage drop in the ETR
is smaller as income rises: the subsidy as a percentage of income (negative
ETR) for the lowest quintile will more than quintuple; the tax rate of the

Richard Kasten, Frank Sammartino, & Eric Toder

Table 2. *Effective tax rates by income group and tax source, 1980-93*

	1980	1985	1989	1993[a]
Effective individual income-tax rates				
Income quintile[b]				
Lowest	−0.5	−0.2	−1.8	−3.2
Second	4.5	3.8	3.2	2.8
Middle	7.9	6.7	6.5	6.2
Fourth	11.0	9.2	8.9	8.7
Highest	17.2	14.4	15.2	15.5
Total	12.3	10.7	10.9	10.9
Detail on highest quintile				
81%-90%	13.5	11.3	11.3	11.2
91%-95%	15.4	12.7	13.1	13.2
96%-99%	18.5	15.1	16.2	16.1
Top 1%	23.9	19.2	20.4	21.9
Effective social insurance tax rates				
Income quintile[b]				
Lowest	5.2	6.7	7.6	7.6
Second	7.8	9.1	9.4	9.5
Middle	8.6	9.7	10.0	10.1
Fourth	8.6	9.8	10.3	10.5
Highest	6.0	6.8	7.0	7.7
Total	7.2	8.1	8.4	8.9
Detail on highest quintile				
81%-90%	8.3	9.6	10.0	10.4
91%-95%	7.4	8.9	9.6	10.2
96%-99%	5.2	6.2	6.7	7.7
Top 1%	1.5	1.7	1.6	2.1
Effective corporate income-tax rates				
Income quintile[b]				
Lowest	1.3	0.9	1.1	1.1
Second	1.9	1.3	1.5	1.6
Middle	2.2	1.5	1.8	1.8
Fourth	2.4	1.7	1.9	2.0
Highest	3.7	2.4	2.8	2.8
Total	2.9	1.9	2.3	2.3

Table 2 *(cont.)*

	1980	1985	1989	1993[a]
Detail on highest quintile				
81%–90%	2.6	1.8	2.1	2.1
91%–95%	3.0	2.0	2.2	2.2
96%–99%	3.8	2.5	2.9	2.9
Top 1%	6.2	3.4	4.0	4.1
Effective excise-tax rates				
Income quintile[b]				
Lowest	2.1	3.1	2.4	2.8
Second	1.3	1.7	1.5	1.7
Middle	1.1	1.2	1.1	1.3
Fourth	0.9	1.0	0.9	1.1
Highest	0.6	0.6	0.5	0.6
Total	0.9	1.0	0.9	1.1
Detail on highest quintile				
81%–90%	0.8	0.8	0.8	0.9
91%–95%	0.7	0.7	0.7	0.8
96%–99%	0.6	0.5	0.4	0.5
Top 1%	0.3	0.3	0.3	0.3

[a] Projected.
[b] Ranked by adjusted family income (AFI), equal number of people per percentile.
Source: CBO.

second quintile will be cut by nearly 40%; the tax rates of the next two quintiles will be cut by about 20%; and the tax rate of the top quintile will be cut by only 10%.

The added progressivity of the individual income tax did not come until after 1985. Tax rates for the lowest income groups declined, and tax rates for high-income families increased, between 1985 and 1989 and again between 1989 and 1993. In contrast, between 1980 and 1985, the largest percentage cuts had been received by the highest income groups. The net subsidy to the lowest quintile fell as inflation eroded the value of the personal exemptions, standard deductions, and the earned income tax credit.

While the effective individual income tax rate will decline between 1980 and 1993, ETRs imposed by social insurance taxes will increase. The rate for all families will grow by 24%, from 7.2% to 8.9%. Most of the increase in taxes was legislated before the 1980s began. The largest projected increases are at the bottom of the income distribution, where earnings are expected to make up a larger fraction of income in 1993 than in 1980, and in the highest income categories. Because the taxable maximum was raised faster than wages in the early 1980s and because OBRA more than doubled the taxable maximum for hospital insurance (Medicare) payroll taxes, the three groups composing the top 10 percent will have increases in social insurance ETRs ranging from 38% to 48%. Despite these changes, about 10% of earnings will remain exempt from payroll taxes. Because of this exemption and because capital income represents a larger fraction of their income, the social insurance ETR of the top 1 percent will remain much lower than that of any other group.

Corporate income taxes were cut substantially by ERTA, and subsequent tax bills (including TEFRA and TRA, which both raised corporate taxes) have failed to restore the effective corporate income-tax rate to its 1980 level. For all families, the ETR imposed by the corporate income tax was about 35% lower in 1985, and about 20% lower in 1989 and 1993, than in 1980.

Between 1980 and 1993, the ETR imposed by federal excise taxes will rise by about 20%. There was virtually no change in this rate between 1980 and 1989. TEFRA raised some excise taxes in 1982, but then effective excise-tax rates drifted downward because most excise taxes are specific taxes that are not indexed for inflation. The excise ETR will jump between 1989 and 1993 because OBRA raised many excise-tax rates. The tables show larger increases between 1980 and 1993 for low-income families than for families in higher income categories. In part this occurs because the more regressive excise taxes increased faster than others, but a more important factor is that the data show total consumption and consumption of taxed goods – the bases for allocating excise taxes – growing faster than income for low-income families.

In summary, the small changes in overall ETRs between 1980 and 1993 mask a number of offsetting trends. Both individual income taxes and payroll taxes will become somewhat more progressive over the time period. If the relative size of these two sources had stayed constant, the federal tax system would have become more progressive. Instead, the progressive income tax has declined as a fraction of income while payroll taxes have grown, leaving total ETRs almost unchanged, except at the top. The top 1 percent, for whom payroll taxes are a relatively small share of income, will have an 11% lower total ETR in 1993 than in 1980.

The preceding discussion is based on allocating the corporate income tax half to labor and half to capital. Two alternative allocations of the corporate income tax – all to labor or all to capital – alter the level of ETRs but do not alter our conclusions about changes in them; see Table 3.

Table 3. *Effective tax rates by income group,
with alternative assumptions about incidence of
corporate income tax, 1980–93*

	1980	1985	1989	1993[a]
Tax falls on capital income				
Income quintile[b]				
Lowest	7.7	10.2	8.8	7.9
Second	15.0	15.5	15.3	15.1
Middle	19.1	18.8	18.9	19.1
Fourth	22.2	21.3	21.5	21.7
Highest	28.2	24.5	25.9	27.0
Total	23.3	21.8	22.5	23.2
Detail on highest quintile				
81%–90%	24.6	23.1	23.7	24.2
91%–95%	26.4	24.1	25.2	26.1
96%–99%	28.8	24.7	26.7	27.6
Top 1%	34.9	26.2	28.1	30.4
Tax falls on labor income				
Income quintile[b]				
Lowest	8.3	10.6	9.7	8.8
Second	16.0	16.2	16.0	15.8
Middle	20.5	19.6	19.8	19.9
Fourth	23.6	22.1	22.5	22.7
Highest	27.0	23.9	25.1	26.2
Total	23.3	21.8	22.5	23.2
Detail on highest quintile				
81%–90%	25.8	23.9	24.8	25.2
91%–95%	26.7	24.6	25.9	26.7
96%–99%	27.6	24.0	25.9	26.9
Top 1%	28.7	22.8	24.2	26.4

[a] Projected.
[b] Ranked by adjusted family income (AFI), equal number of
people per percentile.
Source: CBO.

Allocating all of the tax to capital income raises the ETR of the top 5
percent, especially the top 1 percent, and lowers the ETR of the other 95
percent. The top 5 percent is the only group that receives a larger share of
their income from capital than the average for all families. The top 1

percent benefits less from the cut in corporate taxes with the all-labor allocation than with the 50/50 allocation used in Table 1, so the percentage cut in the total ETR for the top 1 percent is somewhat smaller (8% instead of 11%), but the result that the top 1 percent gets a larger cut than any other group is unchanged.

4   Effective tax rates at constant incomes

The effective–tax-rate (ETR) measures shown in Tables 1 and 2 reflect shifts in the level and composition of pre-tax income as well as the changes in tax policy that we seek to measure. For example, under a graduated price-indexed income tax, ETRs rise when real incomes rise. Shifts in the composition of income within income groups can change their ETRs, as when the rise in the share of wages in the income of the bottom quintile boosted their ETR owing to social insurance taxes and reduced their benefit from the cut in corporate taxes. Changes in relative tax rates on different types of income (e.g., in relative rates on capital gains and other income) induce changes in income that affect measured ETRs. Shifts in the profitability of corporations that have nothing to do with changes in the tax law may cause shifts in measured ETRs. Shifts in consumption patterns will change relative ETRs from excise taxes.

To isolate the effect of tax-law changes, we apply the tax law from different years to a single year's data. Although this analysis shows how changes in the law affect the relationship between income and taxes, it does not measure the full effect of changes in tax policy because measured pre-tax income in any given year is partly endogenous to that year's particular tax law.

We use these simulated income-constant effective tax rates to re-evaluate how ETRs have changed between 1980 and 1993. While the differences for most income groups are not dramatic, they nonetheless suggest that the overall progressivity of federal taxes decreased by more than what is suggested by changes in actual ETRs.

Simulating income-indexed tax laws

We compare indexed instead of actual tax laws for different years to remove the changes in ETRs produced by growth in nominal incomes. For example, had actual 1980 tax law remained in effect, ETRs would have been much higher in 1993 than in 1980 because both inflation and real-income growth between 1980 and 1993 would have eroded the value of personal exemptions, the standard deduction, and tax-bracket boundaries relative to taxpayers' incomes. An indexed tax system is constructed such that if all forms of income in all parts of the income distribution grew at the same rate, and if the demographic composition of the population remained unchanged, ETRs simulated for income-indexed tax law would be the same as actual ETRs.[7]

We simulate indexed individual income taxes by inflating (or deflating) all dollar tax parameters – such as personal exemption amounts, standard deductions, tax-bracket boundaries, break points for the earned income credit, and others – by the change in per-family pre-tax income between the tax-law year and the income year and then applying tax rates from the tax-law year. (We index by the growth in income instead of by the growth in the consumer price index in order to eliminate the effect on ETRs of both inflation *and* the average growth in real income.) We simulate indexed social security taxes by inflating (or deflating) the maximum taxable earnings amount by the change in per-family earnings between the tax-law year and the income year, applying the payroll tax rates applicable in the tax-law year. Indexed corporate income taxes are simulated by multiplying corporate profits in the income year by the ratio of corporate taxes to corporate profits in the tax-law year. We simulate indexed excise taxes by multiplying per-unit tax rates by the same factor used to index individual income-tax parameters, and applying those indexed tax rates to taxable expenditures in the income year.

When the tax-law year differs from the income year, simulated corporate income taxes and the employer portion of the payroll tax are not equal to actual corporate taxes and employer payroll taxes in the income year. Because pre-tax family income is held constant and measured before all taxes, we must adjust family income net of corporate and employer payroll taxes to keep pre-tax family income constant. We adjust wages and income from capital in proportion to the assumed incidence of corporate income and employer payroll taxes.

---

[7] To illustrate how this works, consider a family of four with adjusted gross income (AGI) and total realized cash income of $25,000 in 1979. If that family had claimed no deductions other than the standard deduction and the personal exemption of $1,000 per family member, it would have been in the 28-percent marginal rate bracket and paid a total income tax of $3,497 or 14% of income. Between 1979 and 1989, income per family increased by about 82%. We simulate the income-indexed 1979 law at 1989 income levels by inflating the personal exemption amount, the standard deduction, and all tax-rate bracket widths by 82% and applying the 1979 tax rates. Under this method, a family of four with the same relative AGI of $45,500 (82% greater than $25,000) would be in the 28-percent marginal rate bracket under income-indexed tax law and pay an income tax of $6,365, which is also 14% of income.

Had we applied actual 1979 tax law instead of indexed 1979 law to 1989 incomes, we would have represented 1979 law as applying much higher tax rates to typical families in 1989 than in 1979. For example, the same 1989 family with an income of $45,500 would have been in the 43-percent marginal rate bracket under actual (unindexed) 1979 law and paid a total income tax of $10,871, or 23% of income.

Table 4. *Effective tax rates by income group:*
1980–93 tax laws applied to 1985 incomes

	Tax law[a]			
	1980	1985	1989	1993[b]
Income quintile[c]				
Lowest	8.6	10.4	9.4	9.0
Second	14.7	15.9	15.9	15.9
Middle	18.8	19.2	19.6	20.0
Fourth	22.0	21.7	22.3	22.7
Highest	26.1	24.1	25.8	26.5
Total	22.5	21.8	22.8	23.2
Detail on highest quintile				
81%–90%	24.4	23.5	24.8	25.1
91%–95%	25.5	24.3	26.0	26.4
96%–99%	26.1	24.3	26.2	26.9
Top 1%	28.8	24.5	26.4	27.9

[a] Tax-law parameters are indexed to 1985 levels of income.
[b] Projected.
[c] Ranked by adjusted family income (AFI), equal number of people per percentile.
Source: CBO.

Effective tax rates: 1980–93

The effect of tax-policy changes on ETRs in the past decade looks different when those changes are evaluated at constant incomes. While the actual total federal ETR was virtually unchanged between 1980 and 1993, tax-law changes for this period increased the total federal ETR by about 3% – from 22.5% to 23.2% – when evaluated at 1985 incomes (Tables 1 and 4). That change is reversed when the ETR is evaluated at 1989 incomes: in this case, the 1980–93 tax-law changes *decreased* the total federal ETR by about 3% – from 23.8% to 23.0%; see Table 5.

The effect of holding income constant differs across income groups. The total ETR for the lowest income quintile increased from 8.1% to 8.4% between 1980 and 1993. Over the same period, changes in the tax law increased the total ETR by about the same amount of 1985 incomes, but tax law changes had no effect on the total ETR at 1989 incomes. The

Table 5. *Effective tax rates by income group:*
1980–93 tax laws applied to 1989 incomes

	Tax law[a]			
	1980	1985	1989	1993[b]
Income quintile[c]				
Lowest	8.5	10.6	9.3	8.5
Second	14.5	15.8	15.7	15.6
Middle	18.7	19.1	19.4	19.6
Fourth	21.8	21.6	22.0	22.3
Highest	28.4	26.1	25.5	26.3
Total	23.8	22.8	22.5	23.0
Detail on highest quintile				
81%–90%	24.2	23.4	24.2	24.5
91%–95%	25.7	24.6	25.6	26.1
96%–99%	28.1	25.9	26.2	26.9
Top 1%	36.0	30.5	26.2	27.8

[a] Tax-law parameters are indexed to 1989 levels of income.
[b] Projected.
[c] Ranked by adjusted family income (AFI), equal number of people per percentile.
Source: CBO.

actual total ETR declined by a small amount for families in the middle three income quintiles between 1980 and 1993, but 1980–93 tax-law changes evaluated at either 1985 or 1989 incomes show an increase in the total ETR for those families. The ETR for the highest income quintile fell from 27.6% in 1980 to 26.6% in 1993, but 1980–93 tax-law changes instead show a small increase at 1985 incomes. At 1989 incomes, 1980–93 tax-law changes show twice as big a decrease in the total ETR for the highest income quintiles as the actual change.

So what did happen between 1980 and 1993? The actual change in the ETR suggests that the tax burden rose in the lowest quintile and fell by varying amounts in all other income quintiles. Yet one set of income-constant results – for 1985 incomes – suggests that the tax burden rose in all income quintiles, whereas the other set of income-constant results – for 1989 incomes – suggests that the tax burden was the same in 1993 as in 1980 in the lowest income quintile, higher in the three middle quintiles, and lower in the highest income quintile.

Explaining the differences

Between 1980 and 1993, average family incomes did not grow at the same rate in all parts of the income distribution. In addition to differential income growth, there were changes in the composition of income for different income groups. These changes are reflected in different estimates of the ETR under the same tax law when those laws are evaluated at 1985 or 1989 incomes, particularly for estimates of the ETR in 1980. For low-income families, the 1980 law ETR is higher with 1985 or 1989 incomes than the ETR with 1980 incomes. For families in the three middle income quintiles, the ETR under 1980 law is significantly lower if 1980 law is simulated with either 1985 or 1989 incomes rather than with actual 1980 incomes.

Low-income families. In the lowest income quintile, the differences between ETR under 1980 law evaluated at 1980 incomes and the ETR under 1980 law evaluated at 1985 or 1989 incomes are almost entirely due to changes in the composition of income. The most notable change is the increased share of income from earnings and the decreased share from transfers (Table 6). Much of this is the result of growth in average social security benefits, which pushed retirees higher up in the income distribution. This is reflected in a declining wage share for the second and middle income quintiles and a small increase in the share of income from transfers (mostly social security benefits) and other income (mostly private pensions).

For the lowest income quintile, the ETR under 1980 law simulated at 1985 and 1989 incomes is 0.4 to 0.5 percentage points higher than the actual ETR in 1980. Part of the increase is due to a higher wage share of total income, which increases the portion of the ETR attributable to payroll and corporate income-tax rates. However, the higher wage share also results in a lower effective individual income-tax rate due to higher subsidies (negative taxes) from the earned income credit, which offset the increase in effective payroll tax rates. The remaining difference between the ETR under 1980 law at 1985 and 1989 incomes and the ETR at 1980 incomes is due to a higher effective excise-tax rate, and reflects an increase in taxable consumption between 1980 and both 1985 and 1989 for low-income families. Using these higher values of consumption raises simulated excise taxes as a share of all income under 1980 law at 1985 and 1989 incomes.

Middle-income families. For families in the three middle income quintiles, the actual ETR fell slightly between 1980 and 1993. The ETR evaluated

Table 6. *Source of family income by income group, 1980–89 (percentage)*

	Wages	Self-employ-ment	Rents, interest, dividends	Capital gains	Transfer	Other	Total
			1980				
Income quintile[a]							
Lowest	42.1	1.7	3.2	0.9	47.0	5.1	100.0
Second	67.2	4.0	4.7	0.7	18.0	5.4	100.0
Middle	77.1	3.6	5.3	0.7	9.0	4.4	100.0
Fourth	80.9	3.0	6.4	0.9	5.2	3.6	100.0
Highest	66.5	6.4	13.9	8.2	2.3	2.6	100.0
Total	70.6	4.3	9.5	4.3	7.7	3.5	100.0
Detail on highest quintile							
81%–90%	81.3	3.6	7.2	1.8	3.2	2.9	100.0
91%–95%	76.7	5.0	9.8	2.9	2.6	3.0	100.0
96%–99%	62.9	8.9	16.4	6.5	2.1	3.2	100.0
Top 1%	34.9	9.7	26.4	27.0	0.8	1.2	100.0
			1985				
Income quintile							
Lowest	46.4	0.9	3.5	0.4	43.4	5.4	100.0
Second	66.4	3.9	5.2	0.4	18.2	5.9	100.0
Middle	74.5	3.0	6.7	0.5	9.6	5.6	100.0
Fourth	78.0	2.9	7.8	0.8	5.7	4.8	100.0
Highest	62.8	5.8	14.6	11.3	2.3	3.2	100.0
Total	68.0	3.7	10.7	6.1	7.3	4.3	100.0
Detail on highest quintile							
81%–90%	79.1	3.0	8.9	1.5	3.6	3.9	100.0
91%–95%	75.6	4.1	11.0	3.2	2.6	3.5	100.0
96%–99%	61.7	7.4	16.1	8.2	2.2	4.3	100.0
Top 1%	30.6	9.3	23.7	35.2	0.6	0.7	100.0
			1989				
Income quintile							
Lowest	51.3	−0.4	3.2	0.4	39.1	6.4	100.0
Second	66.1	3.6	5.3	0.5	17.7	6.8	100.0
Middle	72.9	3.4	6.8	0.6	9.9	6.4	100.0
Fourth	77.0	3.4	7.2	1.1	5.8	5.5	100.0
Highest	62.8	7.8	15.0	7.9	2.3	4.1	100.0
Total	67.6	5.0	10.8	4.5	7.0	5.0	100.0

Table 6 *(cont.)*

	Wages	Self-employ-ment	Rents, interest, dividends	Capital gains	Transfer	Other	Total
Detail on highest quintile							
81%–90%	77.3	3.6	8.5	1.5	4.0	5.1	100.0
91%–95%	75.0	4.9	10.7	2.4	2.5	4.6	100.0
96%–99%	61.9	9.0	16.5	5.6	2.0	4.9	100.0
Top 1%	36.8	14.0	24.7	22.2	0.6	1.7	100.0

[a] Ranked by adjusted family income (AFI), equal number of people per percentile.
Source: CBO.

at 1985 and 1989 incomes increased by about 1 percentage point for the second and middle quintiles and by about half of a percentage point for the fourth quintile.

The difference between the measured changes in actual ETRs and the changes at fixed incomes is again mostly a result of different estimates of the ETR under 1980 law. The simulated 1980 law ETR evaluated at 1985 or 1989 income levels is lower – by about 1 percentage point in most cases – than the 1980 law ETR at 1980 income levels. Almost the entire difference is a difference in effective individual income tax rates. The simulated 1980–law individual income ETR is lower at 1985 and 1989 incomes than at 1980 incomes for two reasons. First, there was a shift between 1980 and 1985 in the composition of pre-tax income from taxable to nontaxable income, as the share of income from wages declined and the share from social security benefits grew. Second, income for the three middle quintiles grew more slowly than did average income between 1980 and either 1985 or 1989. Because indexed law is simulated by indexing all tax parameters by the growth in average income, a graduated tax system makes income-constant effective tax rates lower than actual effective tax rates for groups whose income grows less than the average. This is particularly true for the steeply graduated income-tax schedule in effect in 1980.

Thus, although tax-law changes evaluated at constant incomes increased ETRs for families in the three middle income quintiles, those increases were not observed in actual ETRs because of changes in the income and demographic composition of those quintiles. The increase in the income share from tax-favored retirement benefits (as social security beneficiaries became relatively better off) and the slower-than-average income growth of these quintiles both offset any increase in their ETRs after 1980.

High-income families. For the highest income groups, the story is a combination of changing income composition and relatively high growth in income. This is most clearly illustrated by comparing trends in actual and income-constant ETRs for families in the top 1 percent of the income distribution. For these families, the ETR under 1980 law at 1985 incomes is 10% lower than the ETR under 1980 law at 1980 incomes. About one-third of this difference is due to a lower measured corporate ETR, the result of applying the 1980 ratio (of corporate taxes to corporate profits) to the lower corporate profits of 1985. The remaining two-thirds of the difference is due to a lower ETR under the individual income tax.

The main reason for lower individual income ETRs is a change in the composition of income between capital gains and other sources. Capital gains constituted 27% of the pre-tax income of the top 1 percent in 1980 and 35% of other income in 1985. Because capital gains received favorable treatment under 1980 law (the maximum marginal tax rate on capital gains was 28% in 1980, compared with a maximum rate of 50% on earnings and 70% on other income), the higher capital gains share in 1985 makes the 1980 law ETR with 1985 incomes lower than the 1980 law ETR with 1980 incomes. This lower 1980 law ETR at 1985 incomes makes the decline in the ETR between 1980 law and 1993 law only 3% instead of 11%.

In contrast, the 1980-law ETR for families in the top 1 percent is 13% higher when evaluated at 1989 incomes instead of at 1980 incomes. Income composition changes explain part of the difference. Capital gains in 1989 were 22% of the pre-tax income of the top 1 percent, compared with 27% in 1980. With a smaller gains share, the favorable treatment afforded capital gains under 1980 law has less of an effect, and 1980 effective tax rates are higher when simulated with 1989 incomes. A more important source of the difference, however, is that the income of the top 1 percent increased at a much greater rate than did average income between 1980 and 1989. This results in a much greater portion of 1989 income being taxed at the highest marginal tax rates under 1980 law (indexed to average income growth) compared to the proportion of income of the top 1 percent that was actually taxed at the highest rates in 1980. Slightly offsetting these two effects is the decline in corporate profits in 1989 relative to 1980. As with 1985 incomes, lower corporate profits in 1989 reduce the 1980-law corporate ETR evaluated at 1989 incomes relative to the actual corporate ETR in 1980. This decrease, however, offsets only about a fifth of the higher total 1980 ETR at 1989 incomes attributable to a higher effective individual income-tax rate.

Was TRA a tax cut for high-income families?

Evaluating changes in ETRs with incomes held fixed also gives a different perspective on recent tax legislation. In particular, the effect of TRA on the highest-income families, measured by the change in the effective ETR under the individual income tax, can appear quite different when it is evaluated in different income years.

Measured at current-year income levels (Table 2), the individual income ETR for the top 1 percent rose by 6.3%, from 19.2% under 1985 law to 20.4% under 1989 law. Measured at constant 1985 income levels (Table 7), the individual income for the top 1 percent also rose, but only by 4.7%: from 19.2% under 1985 law to 20.1% under 1989 law. Although the composition of income for the top 1 percent had changed from 1985 to 1989 (partially in response to the tax changes themselves) in ways that offset some of the tax increase, the rapid growth in incomes at the top end of the distribution raised effective tax rates by more than if 1985 incomes had grown at only the average rate.

Measured at constant 1989 income levels, however, the individual income ETR for the top 1 percent *fell* by 20.3%, from 25.6% under 1985 law to 20.4% under 1989 law (see Table 8). The ETR under 1985 law is much higher when that law is evaluated at 1989 incomes (25.6%) instead of at 1985 incomes (19.2%). By 1989, not only had the incomes of the top 1 percent grown more rapidly than average incomes – resulting in a higher ETR when indexed 1985 law is applied to those incomes – but the composition of income had shifted away from sources and activities that previously had been favored under 1985 tax law.

A changing share of income from realized capital gains was part of the shift in the composition of income for the top 1 percent between 1985 and 1989. Because capital gains were taxed at a lower rate than other income under 1985 tax law, applying 1985 law to income in a year in which the top 1 percent received a smaller share of their income from capital gains (1989) yields a higher ETR than applying 1985 law to income in a year in which capital gains were a larger share of income (1985).

The difference also reflects a similar change with respect to passive losses. In 1985, passive losses for the top 1 percent were a much higher percentage of total income than they were in 1989. Because passive losses were deductible under 1985 tax law, applying 1985 law to income in a year in which passive losses were a small percentage of income (1989) yields higher effective tax rates than applying 1985 law to income in a year in which passive losses were a larger percentage of income (1985).

The ambiguity in measuring the effects of TRA on high-income taxpayers is in part a standard index number problem.[8] The effect of changing

---

[8] Another reason TRA may have been less progressive than conventional measures would indicate is that a portion of the increases in the corporate ETR and the ETR on high-income individuals resulted from acceleration of collections from future years. For example, Gravelle (1992) points out that the estimated short-run revenue gains from the inventory capitalization rules and the passive-loss restrictions are unlikely to be permanent.

Table 7. *Effective tax rates by income group and tax source: 1980–93 tax laws applied to 1985 incomes*

	Tax law[a]			
	1980	1985	1989	1993[b]
Effective individual income-tax rates				
Income quintile[c]				
Lowest	−1.1	−0.2	−1.5	−2.8
Second	3.4	3.8	3.3	2.7
Middle	7.0	6.7	6.4	6.3
Fourth	10.2	9.2	9.0	8.9
Highest	16.2	14.4	15.1	15.2
Total	11.8	10.7	10.8	10.7
Detail on highest quintile				
81%–90%	12.8	11.3	11.7	11.5
91%–95%	14.5	12.7	13.5	13.3
96%–99%	16.8	15.1	16.1	15.9
Top 1%	21.9	19.2	20.1	21.2
Effective social insurance tax rates				
Income quintile[c]				
Lowest	5.7	6.7	7.0	7.2
Second	7.9	9.1	9.6	9.8
Middle	8.4	9.7	10.2	10.4
Fourth	8.4	9.8	10.3	10.6
Highest	5.6	6.8	7.2	7.6
Total	6.9	8.1	8.6	8.9
Detail on highest quintile				
81%–90%	8.1	9.6	10.1	10.5
91%–95%	7.3	8.9	9.4	9.9
96%–99%	4.9	6.2	6.6	7.3
Top 1%	1.3	1.7	1.8	2.1
Effective corporate income-tax rates				
Income quintile[c]				
Lowest	1.4	0.9	1.1	1.1
Second	2.1	1.3	1.6	1.6
Middle	2.4	1.5	1.9	1.9
Fourth	2.6	1.7	2.1	2.1
Highest	3.7	2.4	2.9	2.9
Total	3.1	1.9	2.4	2.4

Table 7 *(cont.)*

	Tax law[a]			
	1980	1985	1989	1993[b]
Detail on highest quintile				
81%–90%	2.8	1.8	2.2	2.2
91%–95%	3.1	2.0	2.4	2.4
96%–99%	3.9	2.5	3.0	3.0
Top 1%	5.4	3.4	4.2	4.2
	Effective excise-tax rates			
Income quintile[c]				
Lowest	2.5	3.1	2.7	3.4
Second	1.4	1.7	1.5	1.9
Middle	1.0	1.2	1.1	1.4
Fourth	0.8	1.0	0.9	1.1
Highest	0.5	0.6	0.5	0.7
Total	0.8	1.0	0.9	1.1
Detail on highest quintile				
81%–90%	0.7	0.8	0.7	0.9
91%–95%	0.6	0.7	0.6	0.8
96%–99%	0.5	0.5	0.5	0.6
Top 1%	0.3	0.3	0.3	0.4

[a] Tax-law parameters are indexed to 1985 levels of income.
[b] Projected.
[c] Ranked by adjusted family income (AFI), equal number of people
per percentile.
Source: CBO.

relative prices – in this case, reducing the tax rate on earnings and (the negative rate) on passive losses and increasing the tax rate on capital gains – is sensitive to the quantity weights (the ratios of earnings, gains, and passive losses to total income) used in computing the price effects (tax rates). In the next section we display estimates of changes in effective tax rates assuming that some changes in income are themselves a response to the change in tax laws.

5   Behavioral responses and tax incidence: some illustrative calculations

The calculations of effective tax rates (ETRs) reported in Tables 1–8 do not explicitly represent the effect that tax laws have on taxpayer behavior.

Table 8. *Effective tax rates by income group and tax source: 1980–93 tax laws applied to 1989 incomes*

	Tax law[a]			
	1980	1985	1989	1993[b]
Effective individual income-tax rates				
Income quintile[c]				
Lowest	−1.4	−0.4	−1.8	−3.3
Second	3.5	3.9	3.2	2.6
Middle	7.2	6.8	6.5	6.3
Fourth	10.2	9.3	8.9	8.8
Highest	19.1	16.8	15.2	15.3
Total	13.4	12.0	10.9	10.9
Detail on highest quintile				
81%–90%	12.8	11.5	11.3	11.1
91%–95%	14.9	13.2	13.1	13.0
96%–99%	19.2	17.0	16.2	16.0
Top 1%	29.6	25.6	20.4	21.5
Effective social insurance tax rates				
Income quintile[c]				
Lowest	6.2	7.2	7.6	7.7
Second	7.7	8.9	9.4	9.6
Middle	8.2	9.5	10.0	10.2
Fourth	8.4	9.7	10.3	10.5
Highest	5.4	6.5	7.0	7.5
Total	6.7	7.9	8.4	8.8
Detail on highest quintile				
81%–90%	8.0	9.4	10.0	10.4
91%–95%	7.5	8.9	9.6	10.1
96%–99%	5.0	6.1	6.7	7.5
Top 1%	1.2	1.4	1.6	2.1
Effective corporate income-tax rates				
Income quintile[c]				
Lowest	1.4	0.9	1.1	1.1
Second	1.9	1.2	1.5	1.5
Middle	2.2	1.4	1.8	1.8
Fourth	2.4	1.5	1.9	1.9
Highest	3.4	2.2	2.8	2.7
Total	2.8	1.8	2.3	2.3

Table 8 *(cont.)*

	Tax law[a]			
	1980	1985	1989	1993[b]
Detail on highest quintile				
81%–90%	2.6	1.6	2.1	2.0
91%–95%	2.7	1.7	2.2	2.2
96%–99%	3.6	2.3	2.9	2.8
Top 1%	4.9	3.2	4.0	3.9
Effective excise-tax rates				
Income quintile[c]				
Lowest	2.2	2.9	2.4	3.0
Second	1.4	1.8	1.5	1.8
Middle	1.1	1.3	1.1	1.4
Fourth	0.9	1.1	0.9	1.1
Highest	0.5	0.6	0.5	0.7
Total	0.8	1.1	0.9	1.1
Detail on highest quintile				
81%–90%	0.7	0.9	0.8	1.0
91%–95%	0.6	0.8	0.7	0.8
96%–99%	0.4	0.5	0.4	0.5
Top 1%	0.3	0.3	0.3	0.3

[a] Tax-law parameters are indexed to 1989 levels of income.
[b] Projected.
[c] Ranked by adjusted family income (AFI), equal number of people per percentile.
Source: CBO simulations.

The calculations in Tables 4 and 5, however, indicate that changes in the distribution and composition of pre-tax income can significantly affect static estimates of changes in ETRs. These changes in the composition of income could themselves be a response to changes in the tax law.

In this section, we use an explicit model to calculate changes in tax incidence when reported incomes change in response to changes in the tax law. We display changes in tax incidence under 1980, 1985, and 1989 tax laws evaluated at 1989 incomes, using selected estimates of the responsiveness of cash wages and realized capital gains to changes in marginal tax rates. We compare these estimates to the measured change in tax incidence between 1980 law and 1989 law, at fixed 1989 incomes.

Behavioral responses and tax incidence

Changes in the tax law produce a wide range of taxpayer responses. Changes in effective marginal tax rates on labor and capital income affect the choice between labor and leisure (or nonmarket production) and the choice between present and future consumption, thereby affecting work effort and saving. Changes in the relative effective marginal tax rates among activities affect the allocation of investment, the composition of consumption, and the form in which people receive compensation. Taxpayers can be especially responsive to provisions that enable them to reduce tax liability by altering methods of financing or changing the timing of activities. Based on a review of research on responses to tax-law changes in the 1980s, Slemrod (1990) concludes that the income tax has a significant effect on financial and timing decisions, but only a minor effect on aggregate factor supplies.

Static measures of tax incidence typically measure the taxpayer's gain or loss from tax-law changes as the change in taxes paid at the taxpayer's initial level of income. The behavioral response to this change in tax rates alters both the change in tax payments and the change in the taxpayer's well-being, although not necessarily in opposite directions. If, for example, a taxpayer responds to a reduction in the marginal tax rate on wages by increasing taxable wage income (e.g., by spending more hours in paid work, or bargaining for a higher share of cash wages in total compensation), then this response increases taxes paid and is also associated with an increase in the taxpayer's well-being. Because the response is voluntary, the taxpayer's net utility gain from higher cash-wage income must exceed any utility loss from foregone leisure, lower tax-free fringe benefits, and higher tax payments. The static measure of the tax cut at the taxpayer's initial income overstates the reduction in taxes paid, but understates the increase in the taxpayer's well-being.

If, on the other hand, the taxpayer responds to an increase in marginal tax rates by reducing taxable wage income, then the behavioral response reduces taxes paid and increases well-being. The measured static effect at the initial income level overstates both the increase in taxes paid and the reduction in utility.

Whether the marginal tax rate decreases or increases, the net benefit to the taxpayer is greater than (or the loss is less than) the static estimate of the change in tax payments at the initial level of income. This is because the change in relative prices makes the behavior that produces the initial income suboptimal; the behavioral response always increases utility. On the other hand, the tax-rate change is less beneficial (or more harmful) to the taxpayer than the change in tax payments estimated at the *post-adjustment* level of income. The correct measure of the change in well-being is in between the two static measures of changes in taxes paid.

Effect of 1980–89 tax-law changes on incentives

Economic incentives – including incentives to work, save, invest in assets that produce taxable income, and realize capital gains – are affected by marginal tax rates on earnings, capital gains, and other income from capital (rent, interest, and dividends). The changes in tax law that became effective between 1980 and 1989 (ERTA, TRA, and the Social Security Amendments of 1977 and 1983) altered marginal tax rates substantially for some taxpayers and some forms of income. Both ERTA and TRA reduced marginal income-tax rates on wages, but the Social Security Amendments increased payroll-tax rates.[9] ERTA reduced marginal tax rates on capital gains, but TRA increased them to above pre-ERTA levels. Both ERTA and TRA reduced marginal tax rates on other capital income.

The average marginal tax rate on earnings declined from 35.0% to 31.2%, a reduction of about 11%, when comparing 1980 tax law and 1989 law at 1989 incomes; see Table 9.[10] There were large differences, however, in the change in marginal tax rates among income groups. The marginal tax rate on earnings increased for taxpayers in the bottom two quintiles because the rise in payroll-tax rates more than offset the small decline in marginal income-tax rates. The marginal tax rate declined moderately in the third and fourth quintiles and substantially (by 18%) in the top quintile. For taxpayers in the top 1 percent, the marginal tax rate on earnings dropped by 43% (from over 50% to less than 30%), largely as a result of TRA.

The average marginal tax rate on capital gains increased in all income groups. The proportionate increase in the rate was greatest in the lowest income groups because, for them, there was little decline in marginal tax rates to offset the elimination of the 60% capital gains deduction in TRA. However, the rate increase had relatively little impact on those taxpayers because capital gains account for only a small fraction of their income. The average marginal tax rate on other capital income increased for taxpayers in the bottom three quintiles of the distribution and declined for

---

[9] In our calculations we count both employer and employee contributions when computing the effect of payroll taxes on marginal tax rates. We also assume that employees respond to the tax rates alone, and not to the increase in the present discounted value of higher retirement benefits produced by increases in qualified earnings. For this reason, we may overstate the adverse incentive effect of increases in payroll-tax rates.

[10] The average marginal tax rate on earnings reflects marginal income tax rates, including the phase-in and phase-out of the earned income credit, and both the employee and employer portion of payroll taxes.

Table 9. *Changes in marginal tax rates by income group: 1980–89 tax laws applied to 1989 incomes*

	1980	1985	1989
Marginal tax rates on earnings			
Income quintile			
Lowest	14.7	21.2	19.3
Second	26.2	26.2	28.0
Third	28.7	29.3	27.3
Fourth	32.1	32.8	31.1
Highest	41.2	39.4	33.8
Total	35.0	34.6	31.2
Detail on highest quintile			
81%–90%	35.3	35.9	35.0
91%–95%	39.0	37.6	34.8
96%–99%	45.8	41.3	33.8
Top 1%	51.0	47.5	29.3
Marginal tax rates on capital gains			
Income quintile			
Lowest	0.9	1.4	4.0
Second	2.9	3.0	11.7
Third	4.8	5.1	14.5
Fourth	8.4	8.1	19.1
Highest	21.1	17.5	28.2
Total	19.5	16.3	26.9
Detail on highest quintile			
81%–90%	11.2	11.0	25.0
91%–95%	13.6	12.8	27.6
96%–99%	17.5	15.8	29.7
Top 1%	23.6	19.0	28.2
Marginal tax rates on rent, interest, and dividends			
Income quintile			
Lowest	1.9	3.5	2.9
Second	5.2	7.6	9.0
Third	11.4	13.7	13.4
Fourth	20.0	19.2	18.6
Highest	43.0	36.8	27.9
Total	33.9	29.9	23.8

Table 9 *(cont.)*

	1980	1985	1989
Detail on highest quintile			
81%–90%	25.8	26.3	24.8
91%–95%	31.8	30.7	26.8
96%–99%	42.2	37.5	30.1
Top 1%	56.7	43.8	28.2

the top two quintiles. For the top 1 percent, the marginal tax rate on other capital income was more than halved, dropping from 56.7% to 28.2%.

The changes in marginal tax rates reported in Table 9 do not give a complete picture of the impact of tax-law changes on incentives to work and save. The net tax wedge – between the value of the marginal product of labor and after-tax wages – that affects work effort depends also on excise taxes and tax preferences; the former add to the effective marginal tax rate on the return to paid work by lowering the real wage, while the latter reduce the effective marginal tax rate by allowing some consumption and saving to be financed with pre-tax wages. Because TRA reduced some tax preferences, it is likely that effective marginal tax rates on earnings declined by less than the decline in statutory marginal tax rates. Similarly, the slight decrease over the 1980–90 period in the effective corporate tax rate reduced slightly the total tax on income from capital (or reduced the tax on labor income, if one assumes labor pays the corporate income tax).

Measuring effective tax rates with behavioral responses

To measure the effective tax rate in the presence of behavioral responses, we begin with realized cash income that taxpayers reported in 1989 under 1989 tax law. We use equations that express realized cash income as a function of the marginal tax rate on cash income, and estimate the level of reported income in 1989 as if the marginal tax rate were zero. We call this level of income "potential income." The total effective tax rate is the ratio of taxes to potential income.

Taxes consist of two parts. The first part is the actual amount of taxes paid, including imputations of corporate taxes and employer payroll taxes. We call this amount the "explicit tax." The second amount is an estimate

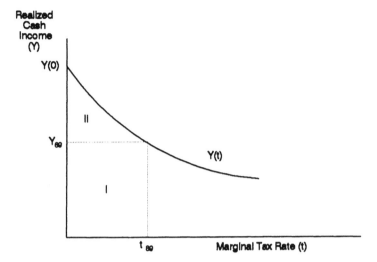

Figure 1. Demand for realized cash income.

of the dollar loss to the taxpayer associated with the realized cash income foregone to reduce tax payments. We call this amount the "implicit tax."[11]

Figure 1 illustrates the method we use to measure tax burdens for each taxpayer. The curve $Y(t)$ represents realized cash income Y as a function of the marginal tax rate t, with $dY/dt < 0$. (The curve conceptually represents an income-compensated demand curve – e.g., how much marginal tax rates on capital gains affect the demand for capital gains realizations with total income held fixed.) The distance Y_{89} is observed realized cash

[11] The incidence assumptions in this paper imply that changes in the individual income tax do not affect pre-tax wage rates or prices of assets. Therefore, the implicit tax that we estimate does not reflect a change in market prices. Instead, it reflects the welfare losses that employees incur from lower cash wages attributable to fewer hours of work and that investors incur from lower realized gains due to fewer sales of assets. Workers and investors voluntarily incur these losses from reduced work effort and fewer asset sales because the cost to them of paying taxes would be even greater.

   Economists have also used the term "implicit tax" to refer to the reduction in pre-tax monetary returns from changes in market prices in response to tax laws. An example is the case of tax-exempt bonds. Financial market equilibration makes the return on tax-exempt bonds lower than the pre-tax return on taxable securities of equal risk; economists have called this reduction in the tax-exempt yield an implicit tax on the owners of tax-exempt bonds. In this sense, the implicit tax reflects a price change that shifts the benefit of tax exemption from lenders to borrowers. See Galper and Toder (1984) and Scholes and Wolfson (1992).

income in 1989, while $Y_{(0)}$ represents potential income in 1989 (i.e., income that the equation projects at a zero marginal tax rate). The explicit tax under 1989 law is represented by area I multiplied by a_{89}, where a_{89} is the ratio of the average tax rate to the marginal tax rate on realized cash income in 1989:

$$T_E = a_{89} t_{89} Y_{89}. \tag{1}$$

The implicit tax (or excess burden) is represented by area II, and measures the loss to the taxpayer from the tax-induced reduction in realized cash income.[12] We can express area II mathematically as

$$T_I = \int_0^{t_{89}} Y(t)\, dt - t_{89} Y_{89}. \tag{2}$$

The total effective tax rate is then:

$$\text{ETR} = (T_E + T_I)/Y_{(0)}. \tag{3}$$

Illustrative responses: capital gains realizations and wages

A complete specification of all potential behavioral responses to tax-law changes would require a complex general equilibrium model that is beyond the scope of this paper.[13] To illustrate how behavioral responses can affect measured changes in effective tax rates, we consider only two possible responses: the response of capital gains realizations to changes in the marginal tax rate on realized gains; and the response of cash earnings from wages to changes in the marginal tax rate on earnings. These responses reflect two income sources whose changing composition had substantial effect on the estimates of changes in ETRs that we report in this paper, especially for high-income families.

---

[12] This is an approximation which assumes that any additional realized cash income under a reduced tax-rate schedule would be taxed at the new (constant) marginal rate. If, for example, current tax rates were reduced across the board by 20% from 15%, 28%, and 31% to 12%, 20%, and 26%, a taxpayer currently in the 15-percent bracket would now face a marginal tax rate of 12%. If the taxpayer increased realized income according to the equation represented in Figure 1, it is possible the increased income could put the taxpayer in the 20-percent bracket. This produces a corner solution where the taxpayer realizes just enough extra income to reach the higher bracket; an explicit utility function would be required to evaluate the reduction in excess burden. For simplicity, we assume in these calculations that induced changes in income do not cause taxpayers to move into different marginal tax brackets.

For use of a similar method to evaluate the efficiency and revenue effects of a capital gains tax in the context of a general equilibrium simulation model, see Hendershott, Toder, and Won (1991).

[13] For a review of the use of general equilibrium models to analyze the 1986 Tax Reform Act, see Henderson (1991).

There have been many econometric studies that have estimated the response of capital gains realizations to changes in the marginal tax rate on gains, but estimates of the size of the response are diverse.[14] We simulate capital gains realizations by using an equation of the form

$$\log(G) = a - bt_g, \tag{4}$$

where G is realized gains, t_g is the marginal tax rate on gains, and a and b are constants.[15] With this functional form, the elasticity of realizations with respect to t_g is directly proportional to t_g. Revenue from capital gains taxes is maximized at the tax rate $t_g^* = 1/b$.[16] We choose values of b to illustrate effects of a lower realizations response ($b = 2.0$ and $t_g^* = 50\%$) and a higher response ($b = 4.0$ and $t_g^* = 25\%$).[17]

We use a similar functional form to relate cash earnings to the marginal tax rate on wages:

$$\log(E) = c - dt_w, \tag{5}$$

where E is cash earnings (including the employer contribution to payroll taxes), t_w is the marginal tax rate on cash wages (including both income tax and the employer and employee contributions to payroll taxes), and c and d are constants.

To be consistent with the assumption that the incidence of individual income taxes falls on recipients of income, we assume the pre-tax wage rate is unaffected by changes in marginal tax rates on earnings. We consider two sources of changes in cash earnings in response to changes in t_w: changes in hours of work, and changes in the proportion of compensation paid in the form of cash wages instead of tax-free fringe benefits. We choose values of L_p, L_s, and F_t, where L_p is the elasticity of labor

[14] For surveys of this research, see Congressional Budget Office (1988b) and Henderson (1989).

[15] The semilog form of the equation for capital gains realizations has been used in several econometric studies. See, for example, Lindsey (1987), Congressional Budget Office (1988b), and Auerbach (1989).

[16] A preferential rate on capital gains can reduce total income-tax revenue by more than it reduces capital gains revenues if it induces people to substitute lightly taxed capital gains for more heavily taxed ordinary income. See Cook and O'Hare (1987) and Hendershott et al. (1991). The examples in this paper do not consider the effects of tax-law changes on the incentive to substitute capital gains for ordinary income.

[17] The high-response assumption implies that the average, gains-weighted elasticities of realizations to marginal tax rates at 1989-law rates were: -0.16 in the bottom quintile, -0.47 in the second quintile, -0.58 in the third quintile, -0.76 in the fourth quintile, and -1.13 for families in the top quintile of the income distribution. Within the top quintile, the implied elasticities are: -1.00 in the 81st–90th percentiles, -1.10 in the 91st–95th percentiles, -1.19 in the 95th–99th percentiles, and -1.13 in the top 1 percent. The low-response elasticities are half as large in absolute value.

supply of primary workers with respect to the after-tax wage, L_s is the elasticity of labor supply of secondary workers with respect to the after-tax wage, and F_t is the elasticity of the fringe-benefit share of compensation with respect to marginal tax rates.[18]

We select values of $L_p = 0$, $L_s = 0.5$, and $F_t = 0$ for the lower-response case, and $L_p = 0.1$, $L_s = 1.0$, and $F_t = 0.2$ for the higher-response case.[19] We then compute values for the percentage change in cash earnings per percentage-point change in the marginal tax rate for primary and secondary workers (d_p, d_s) from the following equations:

$$d_p = -\frac{(f^*)F_t}{(1-f^*)t_w^*} - \frac{(1-f^*)L_p}{(1-t_w^*)(1-f^*)+f^*} ; \qquad (6a)$$

$$d_s = -\frac{(f^*)F_t}{(1-f^*)t_w^*} - \frac{(1-f^*)L_s}{(1-t_w^*)(1-f^*)+f^*} , \qquad (6b)$$

where t_w^* is the 1989 marginal tax rate on wages and f^* is the 1989 ratio of tax-free fringe benefits to total compensation. Equations (6a) and (6b) give the values of d for primary and secondary workers that are implied by the selected values of the labor supply elasticity, the tax-rate elasticity of demand for fringe benefits (at 1989 levels of the marginal tax rate on wages), and the ratio of fringe benefits to total compensation.

The behavioral coefficients we select are illustrative only and do not endorse any particular elasticities estimated in the literature. Two features of the responses that we assume are worth mention. First, the proportional response of capital gains realizations to a percentage-point change in the marginal tax rate is much greater than the corresponding response for cash earnings in both the lower- and higher-response scenarios. Second, the ratio of the response of wages to the response of capital gains realizations is higher in the higher-response scenario.

Illustrative computations of effective tax rates

Implicit tax rates. Implicit tax rates (the ratio of implicit taxes to potential income) declined between 1980 and 1985, reflecting overall reductions in average marginal tax rates on all forms of income; see Table 10. They

---

[18] For discussions of the responsiveness of labor supply to changes in marginal tax rates that raise after-tax wage rates, see Bosworth and Burtless (1992), Hausman (1981), and Hausman and Poterba (1987). Turner (1987) and Long and Scott (1982) have estimated the response of fringe benefits to marginal tax rates.

[19] In a recent book that assesses favorably the economic effects of the tax-policy changes of the 1980s, Lindsey (1990) assumed values of $L_p = 0.1$, $L_s = 1.0$, and (based on Turner 1987) $F_t = 0.18$.

Table 10. *Implicit tax rates: earnings and capital gains,*
1980–89 tax laws applied to 1989 incomes

Lower responses

$d \log(\text{gains})/d(\text{marginal tax rate}) = -2.000$
$d \log(\text{fringe benefit share})/d \log(\text{marginal tax rate}) = 0.0$
$d \log(\text{labor supply})/d \log(\text{net compensation, primary worker}) = 0.0$
$d \log(\text{labor supply})/d \log(\text{net compensation, secondary worker}) = 0.5$

	1980	1985	1989
Income quintile			
Lowest	*	*	*
Second	*	*	0.1
Third	0.1	0.1	0.1
Fourth	0.2	0.1	0.2
Highest	0.6	0.4	0.8
Total	0.4	0.3	0.5
Detail on highest quintile			
81%–90%	0.2	0.2	0.3
91%–95%	0.3	0.3	0.4
96%–99%	0.5	0.4	0.7
Top 1%	1.3	0.9	1.7

Higher responses

$d \log(\text{gains})/d(\text{marginal tax rate}) = -4.000$
$d \log(\text{fringe benefit share})/d \log(\text{marginal tax rate}) = 0.2$
$d \log(\text{labor supply})/d \log(\text{net compensation, primary worker}) = 0.1$
$d \log(\text{labor supply})/d \log(\text{net compensation, secondary worker}) = 1.0$

	1980	1985	1989
Income quintile			
Lowest	0.5	0.8	0.8
Second	1.5	1.4	1.6
Third	1.9	1.9	1.8
Fourth	2.6	2.6	2.5
Highest	4.0	3.6	3.6
Total	3.2	2.9	2.9
Detail on highest quintile			
81%–90%	3.2	3.2	3.3
91%–95%	4.0	3.7	3.5
96%–99%	4.5	3.8	3.5
Top 1%	4.6	3.6	4.0

* Less than 0.05 percent.

increased between 1985 and 1989 (and for the entire 1980–89 period) under the lower-response assumptions, but decreased between 1980 and 1989 under the higher-response assumptions.

These differences reflect the assumed differential responses to changes in marginal tax ra⁺es on wages and capital gains. Under the high-response assumptions, the average implicit tax rate declined from 3.2% in 1980 to 2.9% in 1985 and 1989. For the top 1 percent, the implicit rate declined from 4.6% to 3.6% between 1980 and 1985, and then increased to 4.0% in 1989.

The changes in implicit tax rates reflect offsetting changes in marginal tax rates on earnings and capital gains. As previously discussed, average marginal tax rates on earnings declined between 1980 and 1989, but average marginal tax rates on capital gains, while declining between 1980 and 1985, increased in TRA and were higher in 1989 than in 1980. The assumed percentage response of the tax base to changes in marginal tax rates on earnings is much smaller than the assumed response to capital gains, but the earnings response is applied to a much larger base. Under the lower-response assumptions, the assumed earnings response is so low relative to the capital gains response that the increase in the marginal tax rate on capital gains affects the overall implicit tax more than the cut in the marginal tax rate on earnings. Under the higher-response assumptions, the ratio of the earnings response to the capital gains response is higher; this makes the decline in the implicit tax rate from lower marginal tax rates on earnings greater than the increase from higher marginal tax rates on capital gains for the entire 1980–89 period, although the total implicit tax rate remains constant between 1985 and 1989.

Under the higher-response assumptions, the implicit tax on earnings (as a share of all income) is greater than the implicit tax on capital gains in all years; see Table 11. For the top 1 percent, however, the implicit tax on capital gains under these assumptions is greater than the implicit tax on earnings in 1980 and 1989. The implicit tax on both earnings and capital gains declined between 1980 and 1985 for both the population as a whole and the top 1 percent. Between 1985 and 1989, the implicit tax on earnings declined by 0.4% of income for the population as a whole, and by 1.0% of income for the top 1 percent. This was fully offset by an increase in the implicit tax on gains for the population as a whole, and more than offset by an increase in the implicit tax on capital gains for the top 1 percent.

Overall effective tax rates. When we include the effects of responses of cash wages and realized capital gains to changes in marginal tax rates, the overall ETR declines slightly between 1980 and 1989; see Table 12. For the bottom four quintiles, these results are almost the same as the 1980–89

Table 11. *Implicit tax rates on earnings and capital gains separately: 1980–89 tax laws applied to 1989 incomes (higher responses)*

	Earnings			Capital gains		
	1980	1985	1989	1980	1985	1989
Income quintile						
Lowest	0.5	0.8	0.8	*	*	*
Second	1.5	1.4	1.6	*	*	*
Third	1.9	1.9	1.7	*	*	*
Fourth	2.6	2.6	2.4	*	*	0.1
Highest	3.2	2.9	2.3	0.9	0.7	1.3
Total	2.7	2.5	2.1	0.5	0.4	0.8
Detail on highest quintile						
81%–90%	3.1	3.1	3.0	0.1	0.1	0.3
91%–95%	3.9	3.6	3.2	0.1	0.1	0.4
96%–99%	4.0	3.4	2.4	0.5	0.4	1.1
Top 1%	2.1	1.8	0.8	2.5	1.8	3.2

* Less than 0.05 percent.

changes in ETRs that we measure holding 1989 incomes fixed (Table 5). The similar findings are not surprising, because we use 1989 incomes as the base for both calculations and because behavioral responses produce only minor changes in income in the bottom four quintiles. For families in these quintiles, marginal tax rates changed little except for the marginal tax rate on capital gains. But the latter rate has only a slight effect on the total ETR, because capital gains account for a very small fraction of income of families in the bottom four quintiles. The total ETR increases by about 10% in the bottom quintile and increases slightly for taxpayers in the middle three quintiles.

There are, however, differences in the measured change in ETRs for families in the top quintile, and especially for families in the top 1 percent. The measured ETR declines the most for families in the top 1 percent: 25.3% under the low-response assumptions and 21.5% under the high-response assumptions. (In comparison, the ETR for the top 1 percent at fixed 1989 incomes declined by 27.2% between 1980 and 1989.) For these families, the assumption of large behavioral responses produces lower estimates of the ETR in all years. This occurs because the marginal

Table 12. *Effective tax rates with behavioral responses:*
1980–89 tax laws applied to 1989 incomes

Lower responses

$d \log(\text{gains})/d(\text{marginal tax rate}) = -2.000$
$d \log(\text{fringe benefit share})/d \log(\text{marginal tax rate}) = 0.0$
$d \log(\text{labor supply})/d \log(\text{net compensation, primary worker}) = 0.0$
$d \log(\text{labor supply})/d \log(\text{net compensation, secondary worker}) = 0.5$

	1980	1985	1989
Income quintile			
Lowest	8.5	10.6	9.3
Second	14.5	15.8	15.6
Third	18.6	19.0	19.3
Fourth	21.7	21.5	21.9
Highest	27.5	25.2	24.8
Total	23.4	22.4	22.2
Detail on highest quintile			
81%–90%	23.9	23.2	24.0
91%–95%	25.4	24.3	25.4
96%–99%	27.4	25.2	25.7
Top 1%	32.8	28.0	24.5

Higher responses

$d \log(\text{gains})/d(\text{marginal tax rate}) = -4.000$
$d \log(\text{fringe benefit share})/d \log(\text{marginal tax rate}) = 0.2$
$d \log(\text{labor supply})/d \log(\text{net compensation, primary worker}) = 0.1$
$d \log(\text{labor supply})/d \log(\text{net compensation, secondary worker}) = 1.0$

	1980	1985	1989
Income quintile			
Lowest	8.6	10.6	9.5
Second	14.4	15.5	15.4
Third	17.9	18.3	18.6
Fourth	20.6	20.4	20.8
Highest	24.6	22.9	22.8
Total	21.6	20.9	20.9
Detail on highest quintile			
81%–90%	22.4	21.9	22.7
91%–95%	23.5	22.7	23.6
96%–99%	24.6	23.0	23.6
Top 1%	27.5	23.8	21.6

implicit tax rate on the unrealized portion of projected potential income is less than the average tax rate on both actual realized income under 1989 law and simulated realized income under 1985 and 1980 laws. This occurs even though explicit marginal tax rates are higher than explicit average tax rates. The lower estimates of the ETR reflect in part the ability of tax-payers to avoid the full impact of high marginal tax rates on wages and realized capital gains by working less, converting cash into tax-free fringe benefits, and holding on to assets with accrued capital gains.

Between 1980 and 1989, tax-law changes reduce the ETR in the top 1 percent by a smaller percentage when we assume higher behavioral responses than when we evaluate the tax cut at the post-behavior (1989) level of wages and capital gains realizations. This is because a higher response reduces the 1980 ETR by more than it reduces the ETR in the presence of the lower marginal tax rates on earnings in 1989. Even so, the estimates in Table 12 for high behavioral responses still show that the tax system became less progressive between 1980 and 1989, and still show the changes in TRA reducing the ETR for the top 1 percent.

If we had applied the same method to 1985 incomes, we would have shown a larger cut in taxes for the top 1 percent than the 8% cut between 1980 and 1989 shown in Table 4. However, because our adjustments for earnings and capital gains do not explain all of the differences between 1985 incomes and 1989 incomes, the results based on the 1985 data would have continued to show smaller tax cuts than those based on 1989 data.

6   Summary

Despite major changes in tax laws, total effective tax rates (ETRs) will change little between 1980 and 1993. The total ETR for all families in 1993 will be approximately the same as in 1980. The distribution of ETRs among families in different income groups will be slightly less progressive. The ETR will be slightly higher for low-income families, and slightly lower for middle income families and for most families in the highest quintile. The ETR will be slightly over 10% lower for families in the top 1 percent in 1993 than in 1980. The overall ETR and tax progressivity both declined markedly between 1980 and 1985. However, both the overall ETR and measured progressivity increased between 1985 and 1989, and both are projected to increase again between 1989 and 1993.

The small overall change in the projected distribution of ETRs results mostly from a change in the composition of revenue sources. Between 1980 and 1993, payroll taxes increased as a share of total revenues and individual and corporate income taxes decreased. Although families with higher incomes will pay a larger share of both payroll taxes and individual income taxes in 1993 than they did in 1980, the tax system overall will be slightly less progressive because the distribution of payroll taxes, which increased in importance, is less progressive than the distribution of income taxes, which decreased in importance.

The estimated changes in the distribution of ETRs between 1980 and 1993 result from changes in tax policy and also from changes in the underlying level, distribution, and composition of pre-tax income and consumption. Simulations of how income-indexed tax laws in different years affect a sample of families drawn from a single year show the effect of tax-policy changes alone on ETRs.

The measured effects of tax-policy changes alone, however, depend on the income year for which the tax-policy changes are simulated. Changes in income-indexed tax law between 1980 and 1993 increased the overall ETR when applied to 1985 incomes, but reduced the overall ETR slightly when applied to 1989 incomes. Tax changes increased ETRs for families in the bottom four quintiles at 1985 incomes and the middle three quintiles at 1989 incomes. For families in the top quintile, however, the tax changes increased the ETR by about 3% at 1985 incomes but lowered it about 7% at 1989 incomes. For families in the top 1 percent, tax changes reduced the ETR by about 7% at 1985 incomes and by about 23% at 1989 incomes.

The differences between the two income-fixed measures for 1985 and 1989 tax laws, which reflect the changes in TRA, are particularly striking. For the top 1 percent, the tax-law changes between 1985 and 1989 increased the ETR by 8% at 1985 incomes but reduced the ETR by 14% at 1989 incomes. The difference results mainly from the decline in the ratio of realized capital gains and passive losses to total income between 1985 and 1989. Because TRA reduced the tax rate on ordinary income, increased the tax rate on capital gains, and eliminated deductibility of passive losses, it raised taxes on 1985 incomes but reduced taxes on 1989 incomes, which included relatively fewer capital gains and passive losses.

Changes in the distribution and composition of income could in part reflect responses to changes in the tax law. When people change reported income in response to changes in tax law, the responses alter both tax payments and taxpayer well-being. Because taxpayer responses are voluntary, static estimates of changes in tax payments underestimate the net benefit (or overstate the net cost) to them when measured at initial levels of income. In contrast, static estimates overestimate the net gain (or understate the net cost) to taxpayers when measured at post-adjustment levels of income.

A full measure of tax burdens would include estimates both of explicit taxes paid and of implicit taxes that reflect the cost to taxpayers when they reduce reported income to avoid paying tax. Such measures require assumptions of how taxpayer behavior responds to changes in marginal tax rates. We simulate changes in total tax burdens between 1980 and 1989 using selected values of the responsiveness of earnings and realized capital gains to marginal tax rates. Because marginal tax rate changes in 1980–89 were relatively small for taxpayers in the bottom four quintiles, almost all the difference between the static and full estimates of changes in tax burdens is for high-income taxpayers. The simulations with behavioral response show that ETRs for high-income taxpayers declined for the highest income groups, but by less than the simulated decline between 1980 and 1989 with 1989 incomes held fixed. The decline in ETRs would have been even smaller had we included other sources of income changes in response to the tax law.

In conclusion, our data show little overall change in the level and distribution of federal effective tax rates between 1980 and 1993. There is evidence, however, that tax burdens declined for the very highest-income families and that previous estimates understated their gains from tax-law changes.

REFERENCES

Auerbach, Alan J. (1989), "Capital Gains Taxation and Tax Reform," *National Tax Journal* 42: 391–401.

Bosworth, Barry, and Gary Burtless (1992), "Effects of Tax Reform on Labor Supply, Investment and Saving," *Journal of Economic Perspectives* 6: 3–25.

Cilke, James M., Susan C. Nelson, and Roy A. Wyscarver (1987), "The Tax Reform Data Base," in *1986 Proceedings of the Seventy-Ninth Annual Conference on Taxation.* Columbus, OH: National Tax Association/Tax Institute of America.

Congressional Budget Office (1988a), *Trends in Family Income: 1970–1986.* Washington, DC: Government Printing Office.

(1988b), *How Capital Gains Tax Rates Affect Revenue: The Historical Evidence.* Washington, DC: Government Printing Office.

(1990), *Federal Taxation of Tobacco, Alcoholic Beverages, and Motor Fuels.* Washington, DC: Government Printing Office.

(1992), *Effects of Adopting a Value-Added Tax.* Washington, DC: Government Printing Office.

Cook, Eric W., and John F. O'Hare (1987), "Issues Relating to the Taxation of Capital Gains," *National Tax Journal* 40: 473–88.

Feldstein, Martin, and Andrew Samwick (1992), "Social Security Rules and Marginal Tax Rates," *National Tax Journal* 45: 1–22.

Galper, Harvey, and Eric Toder (1984), "Transfer Elements in the Taxation of Income from Capital," in Marilyn Moon (ed.), *Economic Transfers in the United States,* Studies in Income and Wealth, vol. 49. Chicago: University of Chicago Press.

Gravelle, Jane G. (1992), "Equity Effects of the Tax Reform Act of 1986," *Journal of Economic Perspectives* 6: 27–44.

50   **Richard Kasten, Frank Sammartino, & Eric Toder**

Hausman, Jerry A. (1981), "Income and Payroll Tax Policy and Labor Supply," in Laurence H. Meyer (ed.), *Supply Side Effects of Economic Policy.* Boston: Kluwer-Nijhoff.

Hausman, Jerry A., and James M. Poterba (1987), "Household Behavior and the Tax Reform Act of 1986," *Journal of Economic Perspectives* 1: 101-19.

Hendershott, Patric H., Eric Toder, and Yunhi Won (1991), "Effects of Capital Gains Taxes on Revenue and Economic Efficiency," *National Tax Journal* 44: 21-40.

Henderson, Yolanda K. (1989), "Capital Gains, Rates, and Revenues," *New England Economic Review* (January/February): 3-20.

(1991), "Applications of General Equilibrium Models to the 1986 Tax Reform in the United States," in Henk Don, Theo van de Klundert, and Jarig van Sinderen (eds.), *Applied General Equilibrium Modelling.* Dordrecht: Kluwer, pp. 7-28.

Lindsey, Lawrence B. (1987), "Capital Gains Rates, Realizations, and Revenues," in Martin Feldstein (ed.), *The Effects of Taxation on Capital Accumulation.* Chicago: University of Chicago Press.

(1990), *The Growth Experiment.* New York: Basic Books.

Long, James E., and Frank A. Scott (1982), "The Income Tax and Nonwage Compensation," *Review of Economics and Statistics* 44: 211-19.

Minarik, Joseph J. (1980), "The Merge 1973 Data File," in Robert H. Haveman and Kevin Hollenbeck (eds.), *Microeconomic Simulation Models for Public Policy Analysis.* New York: Academic Press.

Nelson, Susan (1987), "Family Economic Income and Other Income Concepts Used in Analyzing Tax Reform," in *Compendium of Tax Research 1987.* Washington, DC: Office of Tax Analysis, Department of the Treasury.

Pechman, Joseph A. (1985), *Who Paid the Taxes, 1966-85?* Washington, DC: Brookings.

Pechman, Joseph A., and Benjamin A. Okner (1974), *Who Bears the Tax Burden?* Washington, DC: Brookings.

Scholes, Myron S., and Mark A. Wolfson (1992), *Taxes and Business Strategy: A Planning Approach.* Englewood Cliffs, NJ: Prentice-Hall.

Slemrod, Joel (1990), "The Economic Impact of the Tax Reform Act of 1986," in Joel Slemrod (ed.), *Do Taxes Matter?* Cambridge, MA: MIT Press.

Steuerle, C. Eugene (1992), *The Tax Decade.* Washington, DC: Urban Institute Press.

Turner, Robert W. (1987), "Are Taxes Responsible for the Growth in Fringe Benefits?" *National Tax Journal* 40: 205-17.

U.S. Department of Commerce, Bureau of the Census, *Money Income of Households, Families, and Persons in the United States: 1989.* Current Population Reports, Series P-60, No. 168. Washington, DC: Government Printing Office.

U.S. Department of Labor, Bureau of Labor Statistics, *Consumer Expenditure Survey, 1988-1989.* Bulletin 2383. Washington, DC: Government Printing Office.

U.S. Department of the Treasury (1984), *Tax Reform for Fairness, Simplicity, and Economic Growth.* Washington, DC.

U.S. Department of the Treasury, Internal Revenue Service, *Statistics of Income: Individual Income Tax Returns, 1989.* Publication 1304. Washington, DC: Government Printing Office.

Comments

William G. Gale

The succession of major federal tax changes in the 1980s and the simultaneous acceleration of trends toward income inequality have intensified interest in how the federal tax system imposes burdens and redistributes resources across income groups. Despite the tax changes, the authors project virtually no change in the overall "effective tax rate" (ETR)[1] between 1980 and 1993, and a slight decline in the progressivity of the overall federal tax structure, with ETRs for the top 1 percent falling by the largest absolute and relative amount. Within the period, ETRs and progressivity fell between 1980 and 1985 and are projected to rise between 1985 and 1993.

Effective tax rates are affected by shifts in tax law; demographics; the level, distribution, and composition of income; and other factors. To examine the direct effects of changes in tax law (abstracting from incentive effects), the authors apply "indexed tax laws" from different years to the income and demographic data for a given year. This method, contrary to the initial results, suggests that the tax system itself became less progressive in the 1980s. Incorporating estimates of the effects of tax rates on cash earnings and realized capital gains does not significantly alter the results.

The paper provides important information on the distributional aspects of recent federal tax reform. In particular, the findings are inconsistent with the view that tax reforms were the driving force behind the widening income distribution.

The results are based on a model that contains an impressive amount of detail, but of necessity imposes a variety of assumptions, specifications,

Thanks to Drew Lyon, Frank Sammartino, and Eric Toder for helpful comments in preparing these remarks.
[1] The effective tax rates are average tax rates, ratios of a measure of taxes paid over a measure of income. These measures should not be confused with a common alternative use of "effective tax rates" to denote marginal tax rates.

51

and exclusions. This is not unreasonable; one simply can not model everything. Nevertheless, the particular assumptions and exclusions chosen affect the results in a variety of ways. Accordingly, my comments will focus primarily on what I view as the important characteristics of the model, and on how altering them might affect the results.

What should count as a tax?

In a progressive tax system, average tax rates rise with income. This requires defining "taxes" and "income." For example, are social security contributions taxes? Because social security benefits are at least partially related to contributions, it is difficult to consider these contributions on a par with other taxes.

Rising payroll taxes in the 1980s reduced the measured progressivity of the tax system. This may be misleading; when both benefits and contributions are included, social security may well be progressive.[2] Whether social security became more or less progressive over this period is an interesting and open question.

Removing payroll taxes[3] produces a radically different picture of how the federal tax system evolved. Based on projections in Tables 1 and 2, the ETR ignoring payroll taxes will fall by 1.8 percentage points from 1980 to 1993; tax rates in each quintile will fall by at least 1.8 percentage points; and the system will become *more* progressive, with federal tax payments for the lowest quintile falling to 0.8% of income.

What should count as income?

At least two sets of issues arise: the appropriate time frame, and tax-code versus economic measures of income. Both may have important implications for how progressivity has changed.

Lifetime versus annual income measures

Relative to annual income, lifetime income is usually a better measure of ability to pay and is thus the more appropriate measure for progressivity

[2] This is true whether social security is viewed as redistributing funds across people at a given point in time or as redistributing lifetime resources across members of the same cohort. The progressivity of social security is affected by several factors: the benefit formula replaces a higher proportion of wages of lower-income workers and is thus progressive; this is offset to at least some extent by higher-income people tending to live longer and thus collecting benefits for a longer period; finally, lower-income households, with higher death and disability rates, receive a greater share of survivor, dependents, and disability payments (see Aaron 1985).

[3] Other options for treating social security are discussed in what follows.

calculations. Annual income is affected by transitory earnings shocks, the age–earnings profile, large but infrequent capital gains realizations and inheritances, and other factors.[4] Fullerton and Rogers (1993) show the feasibility of analyzing tax reforms in a lifetime income framework.

How would using lifetime income affect the results? As the authors note, a longer time period would reduce the dispersion of tax rates. However, using lifetime income may also change the nature of some taxes. The Congressional Budget Office (1990), Metcalf (1994), and Poterba (1991) have estimated that the incidence of sales, gasoline, and excise taxes based on lifetime incomes is much less regressive than the incidence based on current income, and can be proportional or progressive.[5] A lifetime income framework also makes more compelling the case for including social security benefits as well as contributions. Contributions minus benefits, both properly discounted, would represent the net burden of social security.

A lifetime perspective helps clarify the treatment of deferred income and deferred taxes (i.e., deficits). For example, in an annual income framework, should pension income be recorded when it accrues or when it is received? The former corresponds to economic definitions of income,[6] but would leave elderly people with little "income" but substantial taxes (unless the taxes are assigned when the income accrues as well). In the paper, realized pensions are recorded as income.

The deficit run-up in the 1980s shows that current tax policies have important implications for future tax policies and burdens. These interactions can be captured using lifetime income.

Economic versus tax definitions of income

Economic (Haig-Simons) and tax definitions of income differ substantially. By using a measure similar to the tax definition, the authors have ignored many forms of economic income that happen to be taxed at zero rates. Yet taxing a form of income at a zero rate affects progressivity just as much as taxing it at a positive rate.

---

[4] However, to the extent that households face borrowing constraints, annual income may be the more relevant measure. Survey data indicate that about 20% of households face binding borrowing constraints (Jappelli 1990). For an assessment of the degree to which lifetime incomes differ from annual incomes, see Fullerton and Rogers (1991).

[5] These results are controversial, however. The studies mentioned use a measure of current expenditures to represent lifetime income. In contrast, Lyon and Schwab (1991) construct estimates of lifetime income from multiyear household income data. They find that cigarette taxes are just as regressive, and alcohol taxes somewhat less regressive, in a lifetime framework than in an annual framework.

[6] This suggests an alternative treatment of social security: include the payroll taxes, but add in the implied increase in benefits as well.

The omitted components are significant. The Census Bureau estimates that in 1990 net imputed income on equity in one's own home, employer-provided health benefits, and government noncash benefits raised average household income by $4900 (Bureau of the Census 1991, p. 4). Economic income also includes leisure (or nonmarket time), fringes other than employer-provided health insurance, and imputed income on durables other than housing.

Several issues arise in the treatment of capital income. Realized capital gains are treated as income even though they are not. Realized gains are included at their nominal value, even though part (or in some cases all or more) of the nominal gain is an adjustment for inflation. Real accrued capital gains or losses are omitted even though they are a form of economic income. Most of these issues arise from the use of annual income measures.

Using broader measures of income would raise many new issues in estimation, but is feasible nonetheless. Pechman and Okner (1974) and Pechman (1985) include net imputed rent on owner-occupied dwellings; noncash government benefits such as food stamps, medicare, and medicaid; and measures of accrued rather than realized capital gains.

In any given year, including these and other components of economic income would reduce measured ETRs and, if these items are distributed differently than the tax definition of income, would alter the measured progressivity of the tax system.[7] Over time, the currently omitted components of economic income could affect progressivity even though they continue to be taxed at zero rates. Shifts in nontaxable income as a share of total economic income, and shifts in the distribution of nontaxable income across income groups, will affect how progressivity changes.

Imputations

Developing the data requires a truly impressive amount of work: imputing, matching, and otherwise adjusting data from several different sources with different definitions of the surveying unit, different measures of income, and covering different time periods. Figure 1 compares CBO and Census estimates of income growth for 1977–89. The Census data represent growth of average household money income in each quintile of households, where households are ordered by money income. The CBO data represent growth of adjusted family income in each quintile of persons, where persons are ranked by adjusted family income. Because the

---

[7] For example, Pechman (1985, p. 7) obtains a much flatter distribution of effective federal tax rates in 1980 than do the authors. One of the major differences between that study and the authors' is that Pechman used a broader income definition, as discussed in the text.

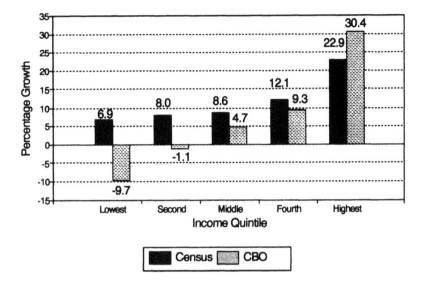

Figure 1. Alternative measures of real income growth by income quintile, 1977–89. *Sources:* Ways and Means Committee, *1992 Green Book*
(p. 1511, table 15); Bureau of the Census, *Money Income of Households, Families, and Persons in the United States: 1990* (p. 216, series
P-60, no. 174).

CBO analysis starts with the Census data, the difference in growth rates
reflects the adjustments made by the authors.

CBO shows income falling in the bottom two quintiles, while Census
shows income rising. The difference in cumulative income growth in the
lowest quintile is 16.6% between 1977 and 1989, or 1.4% per year. In the
second quintile, the difference is 9.1%, or 0.75% per year. During a period when median household income grew by only 0.7% per year, these
differences are large, and could materially affect the trends in ETRs. It
would be useful to understand why such large discrepancies occur.

Adjusting for family size

The authors adjust income for family size on the grounds that, given a
level of income, families with fewer members are better off. However, this
need not always be the case. Consider a couple trying to decide whether
to use their time and money on having and rearing a child or on a series
of extended vacations. Assuming that they choose optimally, they are not
worse off if they choose to have a child. That is, they do not have reduced

ability to pay any more than an otherwise identical couple that chooses to take vacations.

A second issue raised by the family-size adjustment is that the fall in average family size over the last 15 years raises the growth rate of adjusted family income (AFI), but has very different implications than growth in AFI due to increases in the level of income.

Effects of tax-law changes

An interesting application of the results is the effort to isolate changes in tax law from other determinants of changes in ETRs. The fundamental issue is how to define a "constant" tax law. The authors define constant tax law so that if all forms of income in all parts of the distribution rose at the average rate between year 1 and year 2, and there were no demographic change, year-1–indexed tax law applied to year-2 income would give the same tax rate as year-1–actual tax law applied to year-1 income. Put differently, someone whose income level stayed constant relative to the mean income level and whose composition of income did not change would have the same ETR under indexed law as under actual law.

Perhaps the most intriguing finding is the effect of the Tax Reform Act of 1986 on the top 1 percent. Evaluated at current-year tax laws, ETRs for this group rose by 1.8 percentage points from 1985 to 1989. Evaluated at 1985 incomes, ETRs under 1989 indexed tax law were 2.0 percentage points higher than under 1985 tax law, also suggesting a tax increase. However, evaluated at 1989 incomes, ETRs under 1989 tax law were 4.2 percentage points lower than under 1985 indexed tax law. These divergent findings occur mainly because, as the tax rate on capital gains rose from 1985 to 1989, the proportion of income in that form fell.

Conclusion

What do we know about the changing progressivity of the federal tax system? Examining ETRs for all taxes in the paper suggests little change between 1980 and 1993. Removing payroll taxes, for reasons just discussed, suggests that progressivity rose. Indexing tax law, in the manner chosen by authors, suggests that progressivity fell.

These results are based on an income measure that omits a significant fraction of economic income, includes items that do not represent economic income, and uses annual rather than lifetime income. It is unclear how adjusting the income definition would affect the results. Making the adjustments is feasible, however, and would provide a much more complete view of how the progressivity of the tax system has evolved.

While the authors do not resolve these issues, their framework could clearly be adapted to address many of the concerns discussed here and so provide a promising starting point for future work in this area.

REFERENCES

Aaron, Henry (1985), "The Distributional Impact of Social Security: Comment," in David A. Wise (ed.), *Pensions, Labor, and Individual Choice.* Chicago: National Bureau of Economic Research, pp. 215–21.

Bureau of the Census (1991), *Measuring the Effects of Benefits and Taxes on Income and Poverty,* Series P-60, No. 176-RD. Washington, DC: Government Printing Office.

Congressional Budget Office (1990), *Federal Taxation of Tobacco, Alcoholic Beverages, and Motor Fuels.* Washington, DC: Government Printing Office.

Fullerton, Don, and Diane Lim Rogers (1991), "Lifetime versus Annual Perspectives on Tax Incidence," *National Tax Journal* 44: 277–87.

(1993), *Who Bears the Lifetime Tax Burden?* Washington, DC: Brookings.

Jappelli, Tullio (1990), "Who is Credit Constrained in the U.S. Economy?" *Quarterly Journal of Economics* 105: 219–34.

Lyon, Andrew, and Robert Schwab (1991), "Consumption Taxes in a Life-Cycle Framework: Are Sin Taxes Regressive?" Mimeo, Department of Economics, University of Maryland, College Park.

Metcalf, Gilbert E. (1994), "The Lifetime Incidence of State and Local Taxes: Measuring Changes During the 1980s," Chapter 3 in this volume.

Pechman, Joseph A. (1985), *Who Paid the Taxes, 1966–85.* Washington, DC: Brookings.

Pechman, Joseph A., and Benjamin A. Okner (1974), *Who Bears the Tax Burden?* Washington, DC: Brookings.

Poterba, James M. (1991), "Is the Gasoline Tax Regressive?," in David Bradford (ed.), *Tax Policy and the Economy.* Cambridge, MA: MIT Press, pp. 145–64.

General discussion

Gravelle noted the need to realize that the corporate tax–policy changes in TRA were temporary. This reinforced the notion that overall it did not represent an increase in progressivity.

Steuerle commented that when you consider social security taxes and benefits together, the system looks as if it has become more progressive.

Burtless was also concerned about the impact of social security on overall progressivity. However, he questioned whether any legislated changes in the system over the 1980s had actually made the system much more progressive. Some of the apparent change in progressivity was due to the gradual maturation of the system, as opposed to legal changes per se. Concerning the exclusion of various incomes from the paper's definition of income sources, Burtless stated his belief that the untaxed sources grew disproportionately among high-income persons.

Musgrave commented that when measuring changes in tax progressivity, changes in the distribution of pre-tax income are important if we consider progressivity to be a measure of the effect of taxation on income inequality. He also added that the interesting measure of the average tax rate is tax liability divided by the income a person would have had in the absence of taxation.

McIntyre remarked that the corporate incidence assumptions built into the paper are very important when examining short-term changes, because the labor-side incidence of this tax is a very long-term phenomenon. He also questioned the family-size assumptions and adjustments made in the paper, calling them inappropriate and based on wildly incorrect assumptions about the returns to scale in family size.

Menchik noted that including unrealized capital gains in the measure of income would make the income distribution look much more unequal and the average tax burden of upper-middle people much lower.

Wilkie questioned the best method to measure accrued capital gains. Nominal realized gains misrepresent real accrued gains, and these probably represent an upper bound on the true measure. He suggested using zero real gains as an approximation. He noted that these approaches give the bounds within which the "real" result lies.

Shackelford observed that partnership losses are probably most illusory before 1986, but are mostly real after 1986.

Sammartino responded that the authors plan future work considering alternative definitions of income, including a Haig–Simons concept. They will also compare CBO to Census data, but thought that some of the differences pointed out by Gale arise because of different treatments of income and family in the two data sets. He also observed that one might consider social security taxes and benefits together in the context of lifetime income; however, looking at the social security benefits schedule alone isn't enough, as one needs to know about disability incidence, length of life in retirement, and so forth. There is also a need to think about all transfers, not just social security benefits, if we wish to consider the combined progressivity of taxes and transfers.

Toder noted that if an accrual concept of income is used then an accrual concept for taxes must also be used.

CHAPTER 3

The lifetime incidence of state and local taxes: measuring changes during the 1980s

Gilbert E. Metcalf

1   Introduction

The 1980s have been a time of considerable change for state and local tax systems. In particular, the Tax Reform Act of 1986 (TRA) had a substantial effect on state and local taxes, both directly and indirectly. Directly, the deduction for general sales taxes was eliminated and the fall in federal marginal tax rates reduced the value of the remaining deductions for taxpayers. In addition, states that based their tax systems on the federal income tax had unintended windfall revenue gains and losses as the tax base broadened and rates fell. Indirectly, the tax-reform spirit spread, sparking tax-reform efforts in many states. Many of the state tax changes were a combination of an effort to reform taxes to increase progressivity as well as an effort to undo any windfall gains and losses. One goal of this paper is to measure how effective state and local governments were at altering the progressivity of their tax systems.

A second goal of this paper is to re-examine some commonly held beliefs about the relative progressivity of different state and local taxes. The tax-reform debate at the state level has operated from a pair of simple received truths: income taxes are progressive; sales taxes are regressive. The prescription for increasing progressivity, it is thus argued, is to move from sales to income taxation. One consequence of this belief is that politicians who have tried to raise sales taxes to cope with the fiscal crisis facing their states in the early 1990s have been attacked for increasing a regressive tax.

This paper was prepared for the Conference on Tax Progressivity sponsored by the Office of Tax Policy Research at the University of Michigan, September 11-12, 1992. Jeff Nilsen has provided excellent research assistance for this project. I have benefited from comments and suggestions from David Cutler, Jim Poterba, Joel Slemrod, and participants in both the 1992 NBER Summer Institute sessions on State and Local Public Finance and the Conference on Tax Progressivity at Ann Arbor.

In this paper I call into question these beliefs about the relative progressivity of state and local income versus sales taxes. There are three major reasons why income taxes may not be substantially more progressive than sales taxes. First, a lifetime income analysis is likely to make the sales tax look less regressive and the income tax less progressive than will an annual income analysis. This is because the variation in income due to life-cycle effects is eliminated as a cause of variations in tax incidence, which should tend to move taxes toward proportionality.[1] Second, federal tax deductibility of state and local taxes affects their ultimate incidence. After 1986, sales taxes were not deductible at the federal level. This will tend to make sales taxes more progressive and income and property taxes less progressive. Finally, many states exempt items with low income elasticities from sales taxation. For example, the majority of states do not apply the general sales tax to food consumed at home. Again, this will tend to increase the progressivity of this tax.

In this paper I undertake an analysis of the major state and local taxes used in the 1980s, taking these three factors into account. I begin by examining trends in state and local tax collections during the 1980s, with some particular attention paid to the responses to the Tax Reform Act of 1986. I then turn to examining the incidence of three important taxes used at the state and local level: general sales taxes, personal income taxes, and property taxes. I construct distributional tables for the years 1984 and 1989, using both an annual income measure and a measure that proxies for lifetime income for individuals. Finally, I use the results of the incidence analysis to make some comments about the overall progressivity of state and local tax systems and about trends in progressivity during the 1980s.

In brief, I find that if one takes a lifetime perspective for the incidence analysis, the general sales tax is progressive and in fact equally as progressive as the income tax. I also find that the state and local tax system is slightly progressive and became more progressive between 1984 and 1989.

2   Trends in state and local tax collections

Figure 1 graphs aggregate tax shares for different taxes through the 1980s.[2] The main change in tax shares at the state level has been the growth in

---

[1] While this need not be so, most studies of tax incidence using a lifetime income perspective have found that taxes move toward proportionality. See e.g. Davies, St-Hilaire, and Whalley (1984).

[2] I have not corrected for miscategorizing that occurs when tax collections are reported in the Annual Survey of Governments. The size of the necessary correction is small and does not affect the trends illustrated in these graphs. See Metcalf (1993) for a discussion of this issue.

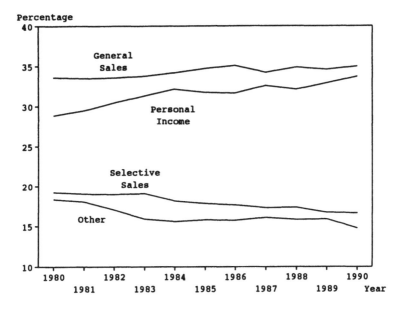

Figure 1. State tax shares. *Source:* Annual Survey of Governments.

the importance of personal income taxes, increasing from 28.9% of tax collections in fiscal year 1980 to 33.7% in 1990. This growth has come largely at the expense of selective sales and corporate income taxes. The linkage of state income taxes to federal income taxes is made clear by observing the sharp increase in importance of the state income tax in 1987. This reflects the windfall that states collected as the federal tax base was broadened, as well as capital gains realizations that occurred in 1986.[3]

Also clear from Figure 1 are the importance of personal income taxes and general and selective sales taxes at the state level. By 1990, these three taxes accounted for 85% of tax collections at the state level. Personal income taxes and general sales taxes alone accounted for over two-thirds of total collections.

Figure 2 shows that property taxes dominate when state and local taxes are combined. Property taxes alone account for over three-quarters of local tax collections. At the local level, there has been a modest increase in the use of local sales taxes and a slight decrease in the importance of personal income taxes. Combining the two levels of government, personal income, general sales, and property taxes are the dominant taxes –

---

[3] These are fiscal-year data. Thus capital gains realized (and subject to tax) in 1986 show up in fiscal-year 1987 data.

Percentage

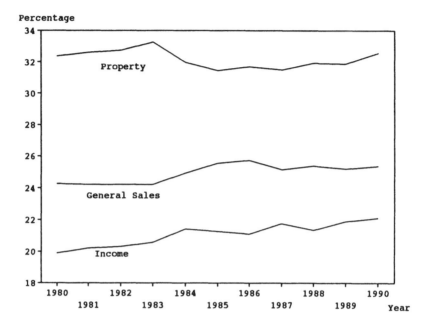

Figure 2. State and local tax shares. *Source:* Annual Survey of Governments.

amounting to 80% of state and local tax collections in 1990. Personal income and general sales–tax shares have grown modestly, while the property-tax share has remained quite stable.

The traditional view of state and local taxes holds that sales and property taxes are regressive and income taxes progressive. For example, a recent report released by the Center for the Study of the States notes that

> the sales tax is the largest generator of state tax revenue, and the property tax accounts for nearly three-quarters of local taxes. Both tax a larger share of income from low-income households than from people at higher income levels. In other words, they are regressive. . . . [M]ost states have at their disposal one major tax that is progressive, the personal income tax. (1991, p. 55)

Based on this perspective, the aggregate tax share numbers suggest a gradual increase in progressivity of state and local tax systems during the 1980s if federal deductibility is ignored. The personal income–tax share rose by about 2.2 percentage points while sales taxes fell by 0.6 percentage points. The fall in the corporate income–tax share might offset the increased progressivity to the extent that this tax is progressive. Note, though, that the corporate income tax collects less than a quarter of the revenue of the personal income tax.

Of course, any statement about the progressivity of a tax system based on shares of tax instruments is inherently very rough. Aggregate figures mask much of the important policy discussion that occurred over the 1980s, as policymakers responded to changes in federal tax policy and in the fiscal condition of their governments. In many states, a stable tax share was only achieved through significant changes in the tax laws.

Looking beyond the aggregate numbers, we can characterize the 1980s by breaking it down into four periods. The first period (1980–82) was a time of fiscal crisis for state and local governments. The combination of the recession and cuts in federal aid created great stress for state and local tax systems. Fiscal year 1983 marked the beginning of the "tax reaction" period, as states began to raise taxes. For the period 1982–83, 27 states increased their use of the personal income tax and 25 their use of the general sales tax (i.e., raised rates or broadened the base). In contrast, only 5 states decreased their use of the income tax and 3 the sales tax.[4] As Gold (1991) has noted, the combination of increased taxes and the economy's recovery led to a surge in tax revenues in 1984. The years 1984–85 were a period of "wait and see," as debate over federal tax reform began in earnest. There was some retrenchment on the income tax (5 states enacted major increases while 25 enacted major decreases) and some growth in the sales tax (16 states enacted increases and 7 decreases).

Finally, the period after TRA (1987–90) was one of budget stability and growth for state and local governments. Gold (1991) has documented the major changes in state taxes during this period. Twenty-eight states had major increases in taxes (revenue increases of at least 5%) while only 3 had major decreases (Gold 1991, table 4); 18 states increased the income tax, while 12 decreased it to some extent. In contrast, 20 states increased their use of the sales tax, while only 1 decreased its use.

Gold also documents the efforts by many state governments to make their income taxes more progressive. States broadened their income bases, increased standard deductions, and eliminated various tax shelters, among other things. Galper and Pollock (1988) analyzed tax reforms in 5 states after TRA and found that the income-tax systems became more progressive after state tax reform.[5] Finally, Greenstein and Hutchinson (1988) document efforts by state governments to reduce the number of low-income families on state tax rolls. They note that 31 of the 41 states with broad-

---

[4] Data on tax changes prior to 1986 come from tables 51 and 52 in ACIR (1986).

[5] Galper and Pollock (1988) analyzed tax systems in California, Colorado, Nebraska, Oklahoma, and Virginia. The Suits index (see Section 3.4) increased from as little as 0.0009 (Nebraska) to as much as 0.0557 (Virginia).

based income taxes raised income-tax thresholds, thereby reducing the tax liability for low-income families.

The efforts by states to make their income-tax systems more progressive, combined with reductions in federal marginal tax rates that reduce the value of deductibility, should combine to increase the progressivity of state taxes. Offsetting these efforts was the need for greater revenue and the resulting tax increases in many states. To see how these different trends ultimately affect the progressivity of state and local tax systems, I now turn to an analysis using data from the Consumer Expenditure Survey.

3   Measuring the incidence of taxes

In this study, I report measurements of the progressivity of various state and local taxes using data from the Consumer Expenditure Survey (CES) for 1984 and 1989. Before discussing the data, let me point out several assumptions that I make in the analysis.[6] First I must decide on an appropriate unit for analysis. Should this be the individual or the household? Because my data are from the CES, it will be convenient to make the household the unit of observation.[7] My second assumption determines the tax liability of each household. As is well known, the statutory and final incidence of a tax can be very different. The final incidence of a tax will depend on relative demand and supply elasticities for the good in question, with purchasers of inelastically demanded goods (elastically supplied goods) bearing the burden of the tax. In addition to measuring the ultimate incidence of a tax, one must take into account federal deductibility of state taxes.[8] But here there is a conceptual issue. Should one attribute the change in tax burden from deductibility of state and local taxes to the federal tax or to state and local taxes? There is no correct answer to this question (in fact, the question becomes immaterial when considering the progressivity of the combined federal–state–local tax system).

I make the following incidence assumptions for the three taxes. For the income tax, I assume that the burden of the tax net of federal deductibility lies with the taxpayer. Put differently, the statutory incidence equals the final incidence. I also assume that the general sales–tax burden lies

---

[6] For a short and elegant treatment of the issues involved in measuring both the incidence of tax systems as well as their progressivity, see Hines (1993).

[7] I have also done much of this analysis using per-capita measures rather than household measures. The results are not significantly altered.

[8] Some states also allow deductibility of federal taxes. I will ignore this complication in this analysis.

with consumers (again net of federal deductibility). These incidence assumptions correspond to the assumptions made by Pechman (1985) and Musgrave, Case, and Leonard (1974) and are standard assumptions made in incidence studies of the sort I am undertaking.

There is less agreement about the incidence of the property tax. Three views of the property tax have been put forward. The first (traditional) view holds that the tax is a combination of a tax on land and a tax on structures. In this case, the tax on land is borne by the landowner and the tax on structures can be shifted to tenants. This suggests that the property tax is borne by homeowners, whereas for tenants some is shifted back to landlords. The second (new) view is that the tax is a combination of a uniform national tax on capital and an excise on local capital. With this assumption, the tax is in large part borne by owners of capital.[9] Finally (the benefit view), Hamilton (1976) has argued that the property tax is in fact a benefit tax – that is, a payment for government services received. In this case, one should properly worry about its incidence no more than we worry about the incidence of the price of a pair of sneakers. However, this view of the property tax depends on strong assumptions about zoning and mobility which are unlikely to be satisfied in practice. Furthermore, to the extent that political interest groups are important at the local level, the link between benefits received and taxes paid is likely to break down.

After eliminating the benefit view, we are left with the traditional and the new view of the property tax. Which view is appropriate in large part depends on what question is being asked.[10] If a single community is considering a reduction in its property tax to be financed by lump-sum aid from the state or federal government, the traditional view is relevant. For questions about the progressivity of the national system of property taxes at some point in time or changes in the progressivity of property taxes over a period of time, the new view is the appropriate one to take. Since this paper deals with the progressivity of the system of state and local taxes over the 1980s, I will take the new view and assume that property taxes are shifted to owners of capital.

My third assumption concerns the time frame for analysis. Traditionally, studies measured tax incidence using an annual measure of income for the analysis (e.g. Musgrave et al. 1974; Pechman 1985). However, recent research has emphasized the importance of fluctuations in annual income and the realization that individuals to a great extent make consumption decisions based on their lifetime income. Individuals who appear to have low income may simply be in a low-income period of their

[9] In fact, as made operational in incidence studies, the new view typically holds that property taxes are entirely borne by owners of capital.

[10] Aaron (1975) makes this point very clearly.

lives (e.g., the elderly and young adults). In fact, it is straightforward to construct models – wherein the population is made up of identical individuals with the same lifetime income and consumption profile – in which the tax system can look sharply progressive *or* regressive on an annual income basis. In this study, I will take lifetime income as the appropriate time period for analysis.

The lifetime frame of reference is of particular importance at the low end of the income distribution. Many households with low annual income are by no means poor. Elderly households drawing down savings and young families at the beginning of their careers may look very different when viewed from a lifetime versus an annual income perspective. Pechman acknowledged the measurement problem in his incidence analyses, and simply dropped the bottom half of the lowest income decile from his study (1985, p. 51, n. 11).

A final issue is the correct measure of income (whatever the time frame). In the context of an annual incidence analysis, the correct measure of income would be a Haig–Simons measure which included all earned and unearned income. As an accounting identity, Haig–Simons income equals consumption plus changes in the stock of wealth. Practically speaking, this is an impossible measure to obtain. Not only must we measure earned income, we must also measure capital income and accrued capital gains and losses in all assets (including any Picasso paintings one might happen to own). In contrast, lifetime income is simply equal to assets held at death plus the sum of consumption over the lifetime in present value. Ignoring bequests, if consumption is smooth over the life cycle then annual consumption provides a good measure of lifetime income.

There have been two approaches to the measurement of lifetime income. The first approach is to find a panel of households or individuals for which income is well measured and then impute the lifetime profile of income (see e.g. Davies et al. 1984; Fullerton and Rogers 1991; Lyon and Schwab 1991). One difficulty with this approach is the inability to measure changes in asset values, which may lead to a systematic mismeasurement of lifetime income.

The second approach is to assume that consumption is relatively smooth over the life cycle and can serve as a proxy for lifetime income. This approach avoids the problem of needing to measure changes in wealth over the life cycle, and has been used by Davies (1959, 1960), Poterba (1989, 1991), and CBO (1990), among others. Following this latter approach, I use current consumption as a proxy for lifetime income. Current consumption is defined by subtracting contributions for life insurance and pensions, housing costs for homeowners, and new-vehicle purchases from total expenditure, and then adding back in the housing-rental value for homeowners and an imputed rental value for automobiles. For the imputed vehicle-rental value, I follow Cutler and Katz (1991) and impute the value of new-car purchases as a function of demographic characteristics of the household (age, nonvehicle spending, spending squared, income, family size, sex and education attainment of the household head). The imputed vehicle value is then multiplied by the number of vehicles owned and depreciated (straight line) over an eight-year period to obtain the rental value. Income, demographic, and expenditure data come from the CES.

The Consumer Expenditure Survey interviews and collects detailed expenditure information on roughly 6,000 households every quarter. Each household is interviewed five times. The first interview collects demographic information and some expenditure information, and is not reported to the public. The second through fifth interviews collect expenditure information during the previous quarter; income information is also collected in the second and fifth interviews. After the fifth interview, the household is dropped from the survey. Households that move during the series of interviews are dropped from the study. I will analyze CES data for 1984 and 1989 to bracket TRA. I include households that begin their second interview in the first or second quarter of the year and have complete income information. For 1984 there are 1,625 observations, with 1,526 observations for 1989. After constructing a gross tax liability for each household, I then use the NBER TAXSIM tax calculator to impute the value of federal deductibility for state and local taxes to construct a net-of-federal-tax state and local tax burden for households. In brief, TAXSIM is a set of FORTRAN routines that can be combined with data sets to compute federal tax liability. Its virtue lies in its flexibility. The value of deductions, for example, can be determined for individual tax returns by computing the tax liability with and without a particular deduction allowed. The difference yields the value of the deduction in lowering tax liability. Both the average and the marginal value of the deduction can be easily calculated.

Table 1 presents information on consumption and income by decile for the two years in the CES. There is considerable variation in consumption within a given income decile. In 1984, for example, 16%–54% of the households have expenditures at least two deciles away from their income decile. On average, 35% of the households are two or more consumption deciles away from their income decile. The differences can be quite substantial. For example, over 6% of the households in the lowest income decile in 1984 had expenditures above the median in that year. The margins of the table report the upper limits for each of the first nine deciles. Not surprisingly, consumption exceeds income in the lowest deciles.

Table 1. *Income and consumption deciles in consumer consumption survey*

Income decile	1984 consumption decile										Income decile cutoffs
	1	2	3	4	5	6	7	8	9	10	
1	61.1	15.3	9.9	4.3	2.5	2.5	2.5	0.6	0.6	0.6	6,105
2	22.8	34.4	19.1	8.6	5.6	4.9	1.9	1.2	0.6	0.6	9,484
3	11.1	21.5	26.5	14.7	8.0	8.0	6.2	3.1	1.2	0.0	12,800
4	3.1	14.7	19.8	21.5	17.3	12.3	7.4	1.8	1.9	0.0	17,200
5	1.2	6.8	11.7	21.5	22.8	11.7	11.1	7.4	4.3	1.8	21,664
6	0.6	5.5	8.0	14.1	14.8	20.3	11.1	12.3	7.4	5.5	26,239
7	0.0	0.0	1.9	9.2	16.7	17.8	25.3	13.5	9.9	6.1	31,300
8	0.0	0.0	1.2	3.7	8.6	16.0	17.9	27.0	15.4	9.8	38,772
9	0.0	0.6	1.9	2.5	3.7	4.3	14.2	23.3	32.1	17.8	48,950
10	0.0	1.2	0.0	0.0	0.0	2.5	2.5	9.8	26.5	57.7	—
Current consumption decile cutoffs	7,763	10,691.1	13,285.6	15,612	18,074.4	20,607.1	23,612.4	27,934.7	34,703.8	—	

Income decile	1989 consumption decile										Income decile cutoffs
	1	2	3	4	5	6	7	8	9	10	
1	63.8	19.6	6.6	4.6	2.0	0.7	1.3	0.0	1.3	0.0	8,603
2	24.3	30.7	21.1	11.8	4.6	3.3	2.0	1.3	1.3	0.0	12,655
3	7.2	26.1	23.7	18.3	7.2	8.6	5.9	2.0	0.0	0.7	17,387
4	2.0	11.8	22.4	17.7	19.6	11.2	7.8	4.6	3.3	0.0	22,500
5	1.3	7.8	12.5	19.6	21.6	11.2	13.7	5.3	5.2	2.0	28,400
6	0.7	0.7	7.2	19.0	12.4	22.4	20.3	11.2	5.2	0.7	35,392
7	0.7	1.3	4.0	3.3	20.9	21.7	15.7	16.5	11.1	5.2	41,763
8	0.0	1.3	1.3	2.6	7.8	11.8	17.7	27.6	19.0	10.5	50,500
9	0.0	0.7	1.3	2.0	3.9	7.2	12.4	21.7	33.3	17.7	65,750
10	0.0	0.0	0.0	1.3	0.0	2.0	3.3	9.9	20.3	63.4	—
Current consumption decile cutoffs	10,158	13,634.4	17,013.1	20,147.5	23,034.7	26,568.9	30,784.6	35,828.9	45,174.1	—	

Notes: There are 1,630 observations for 1984 and 1,526 for 1989. Entries are percentages which add to 100 within rows.
Source: Author's calculations from the CES.

The existence of considerable consumption variation within income deciles indicates the importance of carrying out the lifetime income–tax incidence analysis. I now turn to a distributional analysis of the three most important personal taxes levied at the state and local level: the general sales tax, the personal income tax, and the property tax. In all three cases, I estimate tax liabilities for each household and net out the value of the federal deduction for the tax in question. I then compute average tax burdens by both income and consumption decile.

3.1   *General sales tax*

To estimate the general sales–tax payments made by households in each year, I first construct weighted regional sales-tax rates for six different categories of purchases: general sales, food, clothing, utilities, prescription drugs, and services.[11] I weight the state rates by aggregate income in each state. The rates are taken from the Census Bureau's *Annual Survey of Governments: State Tax Collections,* and are weighted averages of the tax rates at the beginning and end of the year, weighted by the month in which the tax change became effective. Table 2 presents the regional tax rates for the two years. I then categorize expenditures by each of these six categories and apply the appropriate rate to compute a household's sales tax liability.

In 1984, individuals could take a federal deduction for general sales-tax liability. Most households used the "look-up" tables in the tax form which compute the deduction as a function of state of residence, family size, and adjusted gross income. To calculate the deduction for households in the CES, I used a two-step procedure, first estimating a probit model to predict the probability of taking a sales-tax deduction. I compute the inverse Mills ratio from this regression and regress sales-tax deductions on various characteristics of the household and on the inverse Mills ratio for households with positive deductions. I use the 1984 set of tax returns in the University of Michigan tax panel. This panel contains a simple random sample of taxpayers for the years 1979–86 taken from the IRS Statistics of Income data set of individual tax returns.[12] Table 3 presents results from the second-stage regression. The regression results are quite plausible and the fit is reasonable.

Households with high adjusted gross income take larger deductions, as do larger families. While I do not report the probit estimates, the estimated

---

[11] The CES only provides information on the location of households by region for urban households.

[12] There are 9,762 observations in the data set for 1984. I exclude 198 observations either because they have nonpositive adjusted gross income or because their income exceeds $200,000 and therefore their state identifier is deleted for confidentiality reasons.

Table 2. *General sales-tax rates*

	Rural	Northeast	South	Midwest	West
General	4.54	5.11	4.66	4.11	4.41
	4.84	5.12	4.83	4.86	4.49
Food	0.71	0.00	0.50	1.62	0.38
	0.85	0.00	0.60	2.17	0.32
Utilities	0.91	0.00	2.43	0.69	0.48
	1.67	0.00	2.46	1.41	1.13
Prescription	0.00	0.00	0.00	0.00	0.00
drugs	0.00	0.00	0.00	0.00	0.00
Clothing	3.74	2.14	4.22	4.11	4.41
	3.88	1.57	4.38	4.86	4.49
Personal	1.14	2.00	0.88	0.95	0.74
care	1.39	1.99	1.88	1.04	0.76

Notes: Sales-tax rates are weighted averages of state rates for each commodity group, weighted by aggregate income for the states within each region. The top number in each cell is the 1984 rate and the bottom number the 1989 rate.
Source: Author's calculations.

coefficient on the income dummy variables increase sharply as income percentile increases, as do the *t* statistics. In all the probit regressions, I correctly predict (in the sense of the predicted probability exceeding 0.50, indicating that a deduction is taken) 80% of the time.[13]

The estimated coefficients from the sales-tax–deduction regression were applied to data in the CES to generate sales-tax deductions in this data set. If the predicted probability from the probit regression was less than 0.50, I imputed a deduction of zero; otherwise I used the second-stage OLS regression to impute a positive deduction. This method leads to 41% of the households taking a deduction for sales taxes, compared with 38% in the University of Michigan data set for 1984. I then used TAXSIM to compute federal income-tax liabilities, first with the deduction allowed and then without the deduction. The change in the federal tax liability is subtracted from the sales-tax payments to obtain sales-tax liability net of federal tax payments.

Table 4 reports average general sales–tax burdens as a fraction of income and consumption. The first and third columns take annual income

[13] The chi-square statistic (with eight degrees freedom) for the importance of the explanatory variables ranges from 926 to 4,414. Pseudo-R^2s range from 0.326 to 0.366.

Table 3. *Predicting state sales-tax deductions in 1984*

	Rural	Northeast	South	Midwest	West
AGI percentile*					
10%–25%	101.91	238.37	124.94	−30.86	100.79
	(83.14)	(278.61)	(134.81)	(116.73)	(194.72)
25%–50%	217.16	388.11	101.96	230.00	168.52
	(98.65)	(304.03)	(156.66)	(154.07)	(205.44)
50%–75%	635.38	924.12	204.66	855.60	564.63
	(224.98)	(565.71)	(352.56)	(420.53)	(358.69)
75%–90%	1029.03	1497.90	314.24	1461.65	833.18
	(363.24)	(879.40)	(552.39)	(691.24)	(564.57)
90%–95%	1267.89	1894.20	463.52	1685.95	1082.15
	(409.07)	(1010.22)	(589.13)	(796.69)	(629.49)
95%–100%	1477.56	2040.06	618.67	1977.12	1323.53
	(429.27)	(1017.89)	(637.40)	(857.49)	(649.21)
Family size	51.87	58.88	8.04	72.48	46.94
	(13.41)	(29.41)	(23.15)	(16.08)	(30.17)
Elderly*	22.98	7.05	8.40	121.99	−22.02
	(28.31)	(63.64)	(45.12)	(72.39)	(55.92)
Inverse Mills	1847.28	2885.69	−270.25	3311.30	1365.84
	(931.22)	(2135.54)	(1375.42)	(1850.18)	(1430.02)
Intercept	−1339.04	−2203.96	301.07	−2491.70	−887.65
	(748.12)	(1729.31)	(1101.84)	(1477.13)	(1161.60)
R^2	0.174	0.153	0.216	0.217	0.166
Number of observations	3598	806	939	1078	775
Percentage of correct first-stage predictions	80%	80%	80%	80%	80%

Notes: The dependent variable is the sales-tax deduction reported on tax returns in 1984. These regressions are run on all observations with positive deductions. The inverse Mills ratio comes from a first-stage probit regression with the same explanatory variables. Standard errors are reported in parentheses. An asterisk signifies a dummy variable.

as the relevant measure of well-being; in both 1984 and 1989, the general sales tax looks sharply regressive. The ratio of the average tax burden in the first decile to the burden in the tenth decile is 2.7 in 1984 and 1.8 in 1989. These findings corroborate Pechman's results that sales

Table 4. *General sales tax as a fraction of income and consumption*

	1984		1989	
Decile	Income base	Consumption base	Income base	Consumption base
1	1.97	0.82	1.90	1.03
2	1.32	0.94	1.76	1.34
3	1.27	1.00	1.70	1.37
4	1.00	1.06	1.50	1.44
5	1.06	1.15	1.33	1.63
6	1.19	1.30	1.25	1.57
7	0.99	1.31	1.17	1.59
8	0.89	1.14	1.29	1.75
9	0.86	1.14	1.10	1.61
10	0.74	1.31	1.07	1.74

Note: There are 1,625 observations for 1984 and 1,526 for 1989.
Source: Author's calculations from the CES.

and excise taxes are quite regressive in the light of an annual income approach.[14]

However, the story is dramatically changed when consumption is used as the base. Now the sales tax is progressive, with average tax burdens rising in both years (columns 2 and 4). The ratio of the average tax burden in the bottom decile to that in the top decile is 0.6 in both 1984 and 1989. These results suggest that concern over the regressivity of the general sales tax[15] is misplaced, and that the trend toward greater use of sales taxes at the state and local level has not appreciably increased the regressivity of the tax system.[16]

[14] "Sales and excise taxes are clearly regressive throughout the entire income scale. In 1980 they began at almost 18 percent of income at the bottom and declined to less than 1 percent at the top, reflecting the fact that the proportion of family income spent on goods and services subject to tax falls as income rises." (Pechman 1985, p. 55)

[15] Although I do not consider selective sales taxes in this study, previous studies suggest that these taxes are less regressive when consumption is used to measure economic well-being. For example, a Congressional Budget Office study (CBO 1990) found that federal excise taxes for cigarettes and motor fuels are roughly proportional, and that taxes for alcoholic beverages are slightly progressive, when taxes are expressed as a fraction of current expenditures. Cigarette, alcohol, and motor-fuels taxes account for over half of excise-tax collections at the state level.

[16] Of course, to the extent that these taxes replace other, more progressive, taxes, the system becomes more regressive. But the results presented here suggest that reliance on the general sales tax should not in itself make state and local taxes regressive.

What effect has eliminating deductibility had on tax burdens by income groups? Using income as the appropriate measure of well-being, it appears that eliminating deductibility of sales taxes reduced differences in tax burdens across deciles substantially. However, the importance of eliminating deductibility appears to diminish when consumption is used as the base.

To isolate the importance of federal deductibility, I computed distributional tables by income/consumption classes for 1984, gross of the federal tax deduction. While these numbers do not control for any behavioral responses resulting from deductibility, they provide a rough first cut at understanding the role of deductibility in the incidence of sales taxes. Table 5 decomposes the change in average tax burdens between 1984 and 1989 into two components. The first column gives the total change between the two years. The second column measures the effect of eliminating deductibility in 1984.[17] The last column measures the change in tax burdens between 1984 and 1989, assuming no federal deduction in either year. Using either income or consumption as the measure of well-being, eliminating deductibility increased the progressivity of the general sales tax, as average tax burdens rose in the upper deciles. However, this increase in progressivity was offset by increases in average tax burdens in the lower deciles that in most cases exceeded the increases in tax burdens for upper deciles. The consumption analysis suggests that every expenditure group experienced an increase in tax burden and that it was fairly evenly distributed across deciles. Put differently, the increases in progressivity that resulted from the elimination of deductibility were offset in large part by increases in the tax burden for lower consumption deciles.

3.2   *Personal income taxes*

Table 6 presents distributional tables for state and local income taxes. The CES reports state and local income-tax payments in three variables: (1) an annualized amount of taxes withheld from paychecks; (2) any additional payments made; and (3) any refund. In theory, one should be able to add the first two amounts and subtract the third for a measure of income-tax liability. However, there is clearly some misreporting at work here, because – according to this measure – roughly 20% of the households have negative state and local income-tax liabilities.[18] I take two

---

[17] Deductibility for general sales taxes was eliminated in 1986. We are simply considering a hypothetical experiment for 1984.

[18] The CES has notoriously poor income measures. Unfortunately, there is no other data set with extensive expenditure and income information available. Others (e.g. Berliant and Strauss 1993) have used tax data for incidence analysis. These data are marred by severe underreporting at the lower end of the income distribution. One approach that

Table 5. *The role of eliminating deductibility for general sales taxes*

Decile	Total	Eliminating deductibility in 1984	1984 to 1989
	Change in average tax burden		

Decile	Total	Eliminating deductibility in 1984	1984 to 1989
Income base			
1	−0.07	0.00	−0.07
2	0.44	0.00	0.44
3	0.43	0.00	0.43
4	0.50	0.00	0.50
5	0.27	0.00	0.27
6	0.06	0.01	0.05
7	0.18	0.06	0.12
8	0.40	0.13	0.27
9	0.24	0.12	0.12
10	0.33	0.14	0.19
Expenditure base			
1	0.21	0.00	0.21
2	0.40	0.00	0.40
3	0.37	0.01	0.36
4	0.38	0.03	0.35
5	0.48	0.03	0.45
6	0.27	0.08	0.19
7	0.28	0.07	0.21
8	0.61	0.14	0.47
9	0.47	0.18	0.29
10	0.43	0.17	0.26

Source: Author's calculations from the CES.

approaches. I will present one set of results where I drop observations with negative income taxes, as well as another set where I set the negative tax liability to zero. In both cases, I once again use TAXSIM to compute the change in federal tax liability due to eliminating the deduction for

has been taken to the problem of poor income data in the CES has been to combine the CES with the Panel Study and Income Dynamics (PSID); see Lusardi (1991) or Caspersen and Metcalf (1992) for applications of this approach. While this approach may give us a better measure of lifetime income, it will not improve our measure of state and local tax liabilities because the PSID does not report this information.

Table 6. *Income tax as a fraction of income and consumption,
dropping negative tax liabilities*

	1984		1989	
Decile	Income base	Consumption base	Income base	Consumption base
1	0.27	0.54	0.11	0.66
2	0.61	1.87	0.74	1.24
3	0.68	2.15	0.86	2.30
4	1.65	1.98	1.69	1.96
5	1.45	3.01	1.47	2.84
6	2.42	2.61	2.48	2.62
7	2.30	2.94	2.38	2.77
8	2.36	2.98	2.06	3.15
9	2.33	3.27	2.23	2.63
10	2.54	2.92	1.82	2.54

Source: Author's calculations from the CES.

state and local income taxes. This change is then subtracted from state
and local income-tax payments to arrive at a net-of-federal-tax personal
income–tax liability.

With either approach – dropping observations with negative taxes, or
setting negative tax amounts to zero – the state and local income tax is
quite progressive. The consumption-based measure of average tax burden
shows a sharp jump in the average tax burden from the first to second
decile in 1984 and then a more gradual increase through the deciles. The
ratio of the average tax burden in the highest to lowest deciles is 5.4 for
consumption and 9.4 for income. Setting the observations with negative
taxes to zero (Table 7) changes the story only slightly.

No clear picture about progressivity trends in state and local income
tax between 1984 and 1989 emerges from these tables. From Table 6, the
first, third, sixth, and eighth deciles had increases in average tax burdens
(as a fraction of consumption). In contrast, the second, ninth, and tenth
deciles experienced substantial decreases in tax burden. These declines
for the top two deciles took place despite the decreased value of federal
deductibility that occurred as top marginal tax rates fell from 50% to
33% (taking account of the bubble at the top of the tax schedule resulting
from phase-out provisions in the tax code) and despite efforts to make
state income-tax systems more progressive. These declines suggest in fact

Table 7. *Income tax as a fraction of income and consumption, setting negative taxes to zero*

Decile	1984		1989	
	Income base	Consumption base	Income base	Consumption base
1	0.24	0.57	0.16	0.57
2	0.58	1.59	0.67	1.18
3	0.65	1.93	0.83	2.06
4	1.41	1.78	1.33	1.79
5	1.28	2.70	1.23	2.35
6	2.15	2.39	2.17	2.09
7	2.03	2.59	2.03	2.10
8	2.08	2.67	1.80	2.92
9	2.10	2.88	1.89	2.42
10	2.39	2.68	1.66	2.25

Note: There are 1,460 observations for 1984 and 1,445 for 1989.
Source: Author's calculations from the CES.

that state and local income taxes became less progressive between 1984 and 1989, despite reform at the state level.

3.3 Property taxes

In order to compute the burden of local property taxes, I will assume that the property tax is shifted to owners of capital. I proceed by first estimating property-tax burdens on all residential property and then by allocating the aggregate property taxes to owners of capital based on their share of aggregate capital income.

Estimating property-tax burdens is complicated by the fact that we do not observe property taxes for rental housing. I used a two-step estimation procedure to impute property taxes for tenants. In the first step, I ran probit regressions by region for the presence of property taxes for homeowners on a set of housing and demographic variables. This is an important first step, as somewhere between 20% and 35% of the homeowners in different regions reported no property-tax liability. I computed the inverse Mills ratio from this regression and added it to a regression of the property-tax amount for homeowners in a region on the housing and demographic variables, conditional on a positive property tax. Presumably, property

Table 8. *Predicting property taxes in 1984*

	Rural	Northeast	South	Midwest	West
Number of rooms	226.80	304.67	142.79	−44.17	17.71
	(83.31)	(149.78)	(61.90)	(55.51)	(40.54)
Very small lot	—	−17.28	−76.45	−101.17	177.87
		(457.58)	(224.70)	(167.07)	(130.26)
Small lot	176.57	385.71	−101.77	−136.78	430.65
	(265.03)	(416.86)	(191.54)	(171.44)	(172.55)
Large lot	573.40	—	—	−798.14	746.52
	(228.04)			(447.24)	(409.75)
Tennis court or	—	−271.71	445.80	151.04	212.83
swimming pool		(589.07)	(628.91)	(392.98)	(240.18)
Central air	26.13	1452.63	94.59	234.17	365.87
conditioning	(260.65)	(499.51)	(192.87)	(177.03)	(168.84)
Detached home	−70.65	177.14	33.75	112.29	−760.77
	(308.38)	(649.78)	(293.01)	(288.54)	(277.20)
Terrace/patio	−265.70	−633.12	565.90	−291.70	347.86
	(329.30)	(535.38)	(209.03)	(355.24)	(114.05)
Built in:					
1980s	586.65	—	−497.90	−559.02	1475.66
	(509.16)		(611.44)	(311.83)	(526.54)
1970s	432.78	—	−78.33	−52.11	−40.12
	(364.87)		(376.56)	(333.24)	(264.05)
1960s	1479.15	−390.67	−18.17	−93.70	572.28
	(399.48)	(665.61)	(525.64)	(375.59)	(271.52)
1950s	118.33	78.29	−82.92	−16.67	199.96
	(229.19)	(499.75)	(230.82)	(182.19)	(196.80)
1940s	320.94	−455.82	187.35	−68.87	−307.78
	(295.48)	(777.04)	(252.11)	(187.73)	(174.71)
1920s−1930s	361.22	212.73	93.93	−308.51	149.63
	(316.47)	(560.50)	(208.67)	(312.06)	(156.87)
Low income	−133.04	336.21	−20.15	−115.81	−298.60
	(169.92)	(834.43)	(176.73)	(165.35)	(144.29)
High income	—	976.98	—	648.79	18.45
		(1447.44)		(452.18)	(350.81)
Low education	−685.03	313.28	−60.90	−157.71	−601.68
	(227.80)	(426.63)	(335.61)	(179.06)	(232.08)
Some college	−255.28	703.75	226.82	896.37	−484.45
	(271.26)	(715.82)	(184.88)	(434.85)	(169.17)

Table 8 *(cont.)*

	Rural	Northeast	South	Midwest	West
Post-graduate work	−157.29 (379.90)	1132.67 (572.04)	170.38 (249.03)	956.86 (452.18)	−5.92 (149.38)
European background	91.21 (190.19)	65.85 (369.01)	9.97 (168.53)	−51.33 (139.23)	−417.76 (188.76)
Inverse Mills	3945.52 (2480.09)	3342.20 (7610.53)	−947.04 (4143.91)	−7696.04 (3953.85)	−7766.18 (2733.28)
Intercept	−2265.62 (1422.05)	−2667.38 (3035.40)	242.58 (1803.57)	4203.95 (1881.99)	4382.72 (1470.00)
Number of observations	112	141	191	173	170
R^2	0.30	0.28	0.25	0.38	0.34
Percentage of correct first-stage predictions	84%	74%	76%	67%	72%

Notes: These regressions are for owner-occupied housing with positive property taxes in 1984. The inverse Mills ratio comes from a first-stage probit with the same explanatory variables. Estimated coefficients are not reported in cases where the variables would perfectly predict in the first-stage regression.

values (and property taxes) depend on housing characteristics (number of rooms, size of lot, etc.). To the extent that neighborhoods are homogeneous, characteristics of the homeowner should also help explain the level of property taxes. The composition of a neighborhood affects property taxes in large part through the demand for government services imposed by residents. The results of the second-stage regression for 1984 are reported in Table 8. Finally, I imputed property taxes to tenants as the fitted value from the second-stage regression. After computing property-tax payments for rental and owner-occupied housing, I allocate the taxes net of the value of federal deductibility to households based on their share of capital income, which consists[19] of dividends, interest, rents, and pension income.[20]

[19] Also included are royalties, estate and trust income, and annuity income.
[20] I do not pass the value of the property-tax deduction received by landlords forward to tenants in the form of lower rents. Property taxes are a deductible business cost offsetting taxable income; the deduction is already reflected in the rent that the tenant pays. I thank Louis Kaplow for pointing this out.

Table 9. *Property taxes as a fraction of income and consumption*

Decile	1984		1989	
	Income base	Consumption base	Income base	Consumption base
1	1.41	2.17	0.61	3.99
2	2.57	3.93	3.21	2.79
3	3.90	5.13	3.93	3.20
4	3.53	2.69	3.81	4.11
5	3.80	4.31	3.64	3.07
6	2.37	2.83	2.85	2.98
7	2.83	2.66	2.59	3.19
8	2.17	2.55	2.30	3.25
9	2.34	3.25	1.75	3.07
10	1.67	2.92	1.99	3.26

Note: There are 1,584 observations for 1984 and 1,492 for 1989.
Source: Author's calculations using the 1984 and 1989 CES.

The property tax appears to be regressive (Table 9), though less so than if an annual income base is used. With income as the base, the effective tax rates first rise and then fall in both 1984 and 1989. With consumption as the base, rates rise and then fall in 1984 but are relatively flat in 1989. For the consumption-based measure, the ratio of bottom- to top-decile average tax burden is 0.74 in 1984 and 1.22 in 1989. However, there are sharp movements from the first to second deciles which make these ratios less meaningful than for the other taxes.

3.4   *Measuring tax progressivity*

The distributional tables are a useful construct for understanding the incidence of various taxes. However, they are not very helpful as summary statistics for measuring progressivity of the different taxes. Deriving a meaningful summary statistic is very difficult, and a variety of measures have been proposed (see Kiefer 1991 for some discussion and Hines 1989 for a critique of these measures). While acknowledging that any individual summary measure of a tax system's progressivity is flawed, I think these measures can still be helpful in furthering our understanding of the progressivity of a tax system. In this section I report Suits indexes for the different taxes, as well as an aggregate Suits index for the three taxes together (see Suits 1977). The Suits index is a tax-based analog of the Gini coefficient, and is constructed from an income concentration curve – a graph of cumulative tax burden against cumulative income. A strictly proportional tax would have an income concentration curve that follows the 45° line. A progressive tax is likely to fall below the 45° line, whereas a regressive tax would rise above the 45° line. The Suits index equals 1 minus the ratio of the area under the income concentration curve to the area under the 45° line. The index ranges from −1 to 1, with negative values indicating a regressive tax, 0 a proportional tax, and positive values a progressive tax. I compute the Suits index for each tax by approximating the area under the income concentration curve by a series of trapezoids created for each household ordered according to increasing consumption (or income, for an annual measure). A convenient property of the index which I will take advantage of is that for a system of taxes the index can be constructed as the weighted average of the indexes for the individual taxes, with average tax rates serving as weights.

Table 10 reports the Suits index for the three taxes as well as the system of taxes. Using consumption as a proxy for permanent income, the sales tax over the life cycle is progressive in both 1984 and 1989. As suggested by the distributional tables (Section 3.1), the increase in progressivity from eliminating deductibility was offset by changes in sales-tax collections. One can not tell from these calculations whether the increased regressivity is due to changes in expenditure patterns or to changes in tax coverage and tax rates. Moving from an annual income approach to a lifetime approach has a large effect for the sales tax in both years, changing it from a regressive tax to a progressive tax.

The income tax is progressive using either an annual income or an expenditure analysis, though it becomes less progressive under the latter approach.[21] In either case, the income tax has become less progressive between 1984 and 1989. This is in marked contrast to the analysis of Scott and Triest (1992), which shows the income tax becoming more progressive over this period. One possible reason for this difference is their use of federal income-tax returns as the source of information for state tax payments. With the increased standard deduction and more generous exemptions after TRA, many low-income families no longer had to file federal returns. However, they still were required to file state returns in many states. In addition, fewer taxpayers itemize at the federal level and hence do not report deductions for state and local taxes. Therefore, studies using federal tax data will not attribute tax liability to low-income households when in fact they may pay state income taxes.

---

[21] The treatment of observations with negative income-tax liabilities does not make any real difference. The Suits index computed when I set the negative values to zero is unchanged.

Table 10. *The Suits index*

	1984		1989	
	Income base	Consumption base	Income base	Consumption base
Sales tax	−0.11	0.05	−0.07	0.05
Income tax	0.11	0.08	0.06	0.05
Property tax	−0.09	−0.04	−0.11	0.01
Tax system	−0.02	0.02	−0.04	0.03
Effect of eliminating sales tax deductibility in 1984				
Tax system	−0.01	0.02		
Sales-tax Suits index for urban areas				
New York–Philadelphia	−0.07	0.11	0.04	0.18
Chicago–Detroit	−0.23	−0.05	−0.07	0.02
Los Angeles	0.06	0.12	—	—
Combined	−0.10	0.04	−0.01	0.11
Effect of eliminating sales tax deductibility in 1984				
New York–Philadelphia	−0.03	0.13	—	—
Chicago–Detroit	−0.18	−0.02	—	—
Combined	−0.07	0.06	—	—

Note: The income-tax Suits index is computed by dropping observations with negative tax liabilities; see text for further discussion.

Property taxes are regressive when using the income-based measure but less regressive (and, in fact, very slightly progressive in 1989) using the consumption base. Interestingly, the property tax becomes more progressive between 1984 and 1989 when the lifetime income measure is used. The annual income analysis misses this trend and shows the property tax becoming more regressive.

The system of the general sales tax, personal income tax, and property tax is slightly progressive under the lifetime income analysis. Moreover, the tax system has become slightly more progressive over the five-year period. In contrast, the annual income analysis indicates that the tax system is regressive and has become more regressive over the five-year period.

What effect did the elimination of the deduction for sales taxes have on the overall progressivity of this system of taxes? Not much, by this analysis. The Suits index increases slightly, but only by about 0.004 for the lifetime income analysis. There are two reasons for the lack of a large effect. First, sales taxes as a fraction of income (or consumption) are small – on the order of 1%. Income taxes and property taxes take a larger bite out of income (consumption) – on the order of 2%–3%. Therefore, the aggregate Suits index will be less affected by changes in the sales-tax Suits index. Second, the sales-tax deduction was never that large. Eliminating the deduction only increases the sales-tax Suits index in 1984 for the consumption-based analysis from 0.05 to 0.07. We should therefore not be too surprised that there is little change in the overall Suits index as a result of eliminating deductibility of sales taxes.

Perhaps the most surprising result in Table 10 is that by 1989 the sales tax was equally as progressive as the income tax, using consumption as a proxy for lifetime income. This is in marked contrast to the annual income approach, where the Suits indexes differ by 0.13. Any conclusion that the sales tax and income tax are equally progressive deserves further examination. One reason for the large disparity between the annual and the lifetime income results may be due to my use of a national measure of tax progressivity: I might be lumping together wealthy individuals who live in states that impose a sales tax (e.g. New York) and poor individuals who live in states that do not (e.g. New Hampshire). While the *national* system of sales taxes may be progressive, any one state's use of a sales tax might not be. For example, it could be that a sales tax in New York is regressive while the combination of New York and New Hampshire might constitute a progressive tax system.

Although it would be preferable to compute measures for each state separately, I am unable to do so because the CES does not report state of residence. I can, however, narrow down considerably the state of residence of a subset of my sample by using the additional information for urban residents regarding the size of their urban area.[22] For example, there is only one state (California) in the West region with an urban area having a population of more than 4 million. Thus the 49 urban households that live in the West as part of a population greater than 4 million must live in California.[23] There are two urban areas in the Northeast that I can identify (metropolitan New York and Philadelphia) and two in the Midwest (Chicago and Detroit). There are 93 geographically identifiable households in the Northeast urban areas in 1984 and 139 in 1989; there are 60 in the Midwest urban areas in 1984 and 68 in 1989.

[22] Doyle (1992) originally made the observation that additional information within the CES can be used to improve the knowledge of the household's state of residence. My approach is based on her research. I thank Jim Poterba for pointing her paper out to me.
[23] The Bureau of Labor Statistics is obviously aware of this (from their point of view) problem. By the 1989 CES, they no longer report population size for the West region.

Although greater disaggregation improves my ability to measure within-state tax progressivity, the number of observations falls sharply. I therefore also report sales-tax Suits indexes for the urban areas combined, since all the states in which these areas exist rely substantially on sales taxes.[24] This disaggregation is not ideal, but it is a serviceable first cut at identifying states with a considerable dependence on the sales tax.

The bottom part of Table 10 reports sales-tax Suits indexes for these urban areas separately as well as together. The pattern of the national data holds. Focusing on the consumption-based measures, the sales tax in the New York–Philadelphia metropolitan area (as well as in Los Angeles) is progressive in 1984, whereas the Chicago–Detroit measure is regressive. By 1989, both the New York–Philadelphia and the Chicago–Detroit areas had progressive sales taxes. Aggregating the urban areas, the Suits index for 1984 is 0.04 in 1984 and 0.11 in 1989.[25]

The trend between 1984 and 1989 is toward a more progressive sales tax, which suggests that eliminating federal deductibility had more of an effect on progressivity than the national data suggest. The last three rows of Table 10 present the Suits index for 1984 excluding the value of federal deductibility. Federal deductibility matters more when we focus on within-state variation.

The differences in trend results from 1984 to 1989 between the two analyses – total variation in economic well-being versus within-state variation – suggest that further analysis using disaggregated data would be fruitful. However, the essential message of this paper remains unchanged: state sales taxes are progressive in a lifetime tax incidence framework.[26]

4   Conclusion

We can summarize the results of this paper as follows. First, using a lifetime incidence approach, the general sales tax is progressive. Second, despite eliminating deductibility for this tax in 1986, there has been no appreciable change in the progressivity of this tax between 1984 and 1989. However, this result is sensitive to the decomposition of within- versus across-state variance; further research on this point would be valuable.

[24] New York State has a 4% sales tax and Pennsylvania a 6% rate; Illinois has a 5% rate and Michigan a 4% rate; California has a 4.75% rate. In addition, many of these cities impose a local sales tax on top of the state rate. Including these taxes, the city rates would be 8.25% (New York), 6% (Philadelphia), 8% (Chicago), 4% (Detroit), and 6.5% (Los Angeles).

[25] Dropping the Los Angeles observations in 1984 to make the comparison more comparable across years decreases the Suits index in 1984 to 0.01.

[26] Although not reported here, the measures of progressivity for income and property taxes were unchanged when a more disaggregated analysis was undertaken.

Third, as of 1989, the income tax is no more progressive than the sales tax. Fourth, the personal income tax appears to have become *more* regressive between 1984 and 1989. This is in contrast to the anecdotal evidence of Gold (1991) as well as the work by Scott and Triest (1992) and Galper and Pollock (1988). Fifth, using a lifetime income analysis, the property tax shifts from being a regressive tax in 1984 to being a progressive tax in 1989; this shift is undetected by an annual income analysis. Finally, the system of general sales, income, and property taxes is progressive, with a slight increase in progressivity between 1984 and 1989.

In conclusion I mention a few caveats to be considered when interpreting the results. First, a major difficulty with any incidence analysis of state and local taxes is the issue of mobility. If a substantial fraction of households live their working years in low income–tax states and then (upon retirement) move to states with low sales taxes, an incidence analysis based on an individual state will overstate effective tax rates. The problem is mitigated but by no means eliminated by considering the incidence of the state and local tax system as a whole. The problem will also exist whether we use an annual income or a lifetime income measure for economic well-being. One would probably have to undertake fairly elaborate simulations of consumption, income, and mobility over the life cycle to overcome this problem; that task is beyond the scope of this paper.

A second issue to consider is the presence of bequests. Lifetime wealth can be consumed or bequeathed. Menchik and David (1982) estimate that bequests as a function of lifetime earnings fall up to the 80th percentile and then begin to rise again. The bequest/lifetime-earnings ratio at the 95th percentile just exceeds the ratio at the 20th percentile (1982, p. 198, table 4). At face value these numbers suggest that – over most of the income distribution – our proxy for lifetime income is biased downward, with the bias particularly severe at the lowest end of the distribution. This in turn suggests that our measure of the progressivity of taxes over the life cycle is also biased downward.

That the bequest/lifetime–earnings ratio for the lowest decile exceeds that of the 95th percentile is somewhat surprising. Menchik and David compute lifetime earnings as the stream of earnings for a sample of individual taxpayers discounted forward to age 65,[27] but their measure (as they acknowledge) excludes inheritances. As Kotlikoff and Summers (1981) show, inheritances are a major source of wealth transmission between generations. Thus many of the individuals in Menchik and David's lowest decile may not in fact be poor but simply living off their capital. This

[27] They have an average of 14 years of data on individuals in their sample.

illustrates the pitfalls of using longitudinal data to estimate lifetime income in the absence of wealth information.[28]

After correcting for the mismeasure of lifetime income at the bottom of the distribution, it is possible that the bequest/lifetime-income ratio would rise with income. In this case, our measure of tax progressivity over the life cycle would be biased upward. Lacking a good measure of bequests as a ratio of lifetime income (earnings plus inheritances), I simply note the problem and point out that the bias due to ignoring bequests is not clearly a priori.

Finally, I return to the issue of the property tax as a benefit tax. Implicit in this view is the belief that expenditure incidence should be considered hand-in-hand with tax incidence. This is a perfectly reasonable position. The tax incidence analysis conducted in this paper is only half the story. It will remain for future economists to analyze the life-cycle incidence of state and local expenditures.

[28] Menchik and David argue that the exclusion of transfers in income can explain the high bequest/lifetime-earnings ratio in the lowest decile. However, as the authors note, public transfers for the cohort born between 1890 and 1900 (their sample) were small. It seems more plausible that the bias due to the exclusion of inheritances swamps any bias due to excluding transfers.

REFERENCES

Aaron, H. (1975), *Who Pays the Property Tax?* Washington, DC: Brookings.

Advisory Commission on Intergovernmental Relations (ACIR) (1986), *Significant Features of Fiscal Federalism.* Washington, DC: Government Printing Office.

Berliant, M., and R. Strauss (1993), "State and Federal Tax Equity: Estimates before and after the Tax Reform Act of 1986," *Journal of Policy Analysis and Management* 12: 9–43.

Bureau of the Census (various years), *Annual Survey of Governments: State Tax Collections.* Washington, DC: Government Printing Office.

Bureau of Labor Statistics, *Consumer Expenditure Survey,* 1984 and 1989. Washington, DC: Bureau of the Census.

Caspersen, E., and G. Metcalf (1992), "Value Added Taxation: A Progressive Tax?" Mimeo, Department of Economics, Princeton University, Princeton, NJ.

Center for the Study of the States (1991), *The States and the Poor: How Budget Decisions in 1991 Affected Low Income People.* Albany, NY.

Congressional Budget Office (CBO) (1990), *Federal Taxation of Tobacco, Alcoholic Beverages, and Motor Fuels.* Washington, DC: Government Printing Office.

Cutler, D., and L. Katz (1991), "Macroeconomic Performance and the Disadvantaged," *Brookings Papers on Economic Activity* 2: 1–61.

Davies, D. (1959), "An Empirical Test of Sales-Tax Regressivity," *Journal of Political Economy* 67: 72–8.

(1960), "Progressiveness of a Sales Tax in Relation to Various Income Bases," *American Economic Review* 50: 987–95.

Davies, J., F. St-Hilaire, and J. Whalley (1984), "Some Calculations of Lifetime Tax Incidence," *American Economic Review* 74: 633–49.

Doyle, M. (1992), "New Evidence on Government Spending, Tax Policy and Private Charity," Mimeo, Department of Economics, MIT, Cambridge, MA.

Fullerton, D., and D. Rogers (1991), *Who Bears the Lifetime Tax Burden?* Washington, DC: Brookings.

Galper, H., and S. Pollock (1988), "Models of State Income Tax Reform," in S. Gold (ed.), *The Unfinished Agenda for State Tax Reform.* Washington, DC: National Conference of State Legislatures.

Gold, S. (1991), "Changes in State Government Finances in the 1980s," *National Tax Journal* 64: 1–20.

Greenstein, R., and F. Hutchinson (1988), "State Tax Relief for Low-Income People," in S. Gold (ed.), *The Unfinished Agenda for State Tax Reform.* Washington, DC: National Conference of State Legislatures.

Hamilton, B. (1976), "Capitalization of Intrajurisdictional Differences in Local Tax Prices," *American Economic Review* 66: 743–53.

Hines, J. (1989), "Progressive Income Taxes: The Reagan Record, Consistently Measured," Mimeo, Kennedy School of Government, Harvard University, Cambridge, MA.

(1993), "State and Federal Tax Equity: Estimates before and after the Tax Reform Act of 1986: Comment," *Journal of Policy Analysis and Management* 12: 44–6.

Institute for Social Research, "Panel Study of Income Dynamics," University of Michigan, Ann Arbor.

Internal Revenue Service, *Statistics of Income: Individual Income Tax Returns.* Public Use Files, Washington, DC.

Kiefer, D. (1991), "A Comparative Analysis of Tax Progressivity in the United States: A Reexamination," *Public Finance Quarterly* 19: 94–108.

Kotlikoff, L., and L. Summers (1981), "The Role of Intergenerational Transfers in Aggregate Capital Accumulation," *Journal of Political Economy* 89: 706–32.

Lusardi, A. (1991), "Euler Equations in Micro Data: Merging Data from Two Samples," Mimeo, Department of Economics, Princeton University, Princeton, NJ.

Lyon, A., and R. Schwab (1991), "Consumption Taxes in a Life Cycle Framework: Are Sin Taxes Regressive?" Mimeo, Department of Economics, University of Maryland, College Park.

Menchik, P., and M. David (1982), "The Incidence of a Lifetime Consumption Tax," *National Tax Journal* 35: 189–203.

Metcalf, G. (1992), "Tax Exporting, Federal Deductibility, and State Tax Structure," *Journal of Policy Analysis and Management* 12: 109–26.

Musgrave, R., K. Case, and H. Leonard (1974), "The Distribution of Fiscal Burdens and Benefits," *Public Finance Quarterly* 2: 259–311.

Office of Tax Policy Research, "1979–1986 Panel of Individual Returns," University of Michigan, Ann Arbor.

Pechman, J. (1985), *Who Paid the Taxes, 1966–85?* Washington, DC: Brookings.

Poterba, J. (1989), "Lifetime Incidence and the Distributional Burden of Excise Taxes," *American Economic Review* 79: 325–30.

(1991), "Is the Gasoline Tax Regressive?" *Tax Policy and the Economy* 5: 145–64.

Scott, C., and R. Triest (1992), "The Relationship Between Federal and State Individual Income Tax Progressivity," Mimeo, Department of Economics, University of California, Davis.

Suits, D. (1977), "Measurement of Tax Progressivity," *American Economic Review* 67: 747–52.

Comments

Robert P. Inman

Three questions must be addressed in any discussion of tax progressivity. Why do we care? Assuming we do care, what is the empirical evidence on progressivity, both across taxes and over time? Finally, given this evidence, are we concerned by what we see, and if so, what can be done about it? In these comments, I shall offer answers to these three questions using Gib Metcalf's careful, and innovative, look at the progressivity of state and local taxes.

First, why do we care about tax progressivity? Progressivity is a descriptive device to summarize the allocation of the burdens of a tax code. We care about progressivity because we care about the allocation of tax burdens, and tax burdens matter for two reasons: economic efficiency and economic fairness. As a descriptive device, however, the concept of progressivity – and its many numerical realizations – has been focused primarily on the task of describing economic fairness. We use other analytic devices to describe economic efficiency: namely, the logic of "excess burdens." We care about tax progressivity and its measurement because we care about economic fairness.

I raise this all-too-obvious point about tax progressivity as a measure of economic fairness because to me it seems to be of particular relevance to the discussion of tax progressivity in the state and local sector – in particular, how we understand and use progressivity measures for one important state and local tax, the local property tax. Economic fairness, and hence tax progressivity, is a concept fundamentally concerned with the distribution of economic resources. Specifically, what resources do people have available *before* they begin their private consumption of goods and services? Does everyone have a fair and equitable (however defined) opportunity to buy what they personally decide is right for them? From this perspective, the local property tax, *if it is a benefits tax in the sense*

89

of a Tiebout tax "price," is irrelevant to matters of economic fairness and hence to tax progressivity.

In a Tiebout local public-goods economy, the local property tax is simply a means of payment after consumers have shopped for local public goods.[1] Just as we do not concern ourselves with the progressivity of food expenditures (regressive against income) or luxury cars (progressive against income), so too should we not concern ourselves with the progressivity of local property taxation in a Tiebout economy. The tax is regressive, as Metcalf's analysis shows, because lower- and middle-income families choose to devote a larger share of their incomes to local public goods such as protection, education, and recreation than do upper-income families. Lower- and middle-income families also devote a larger share of their incomes to food, clothing, and shelter. If the benefit-tax view of local property taxation is correct as a general description of how the local property tax works, then the measured regressivity of that tax should not be a major concern.

Is the benefits view correct? There are good reasons to suspect that it may be correct, at least for most suburban residents in our major metropolitan areas. The evidence suggests that Tiebout competition is alive and well in these areas. For central-city residents, the benefit-tax view is more controversial. To the extent that city residents are mobile, however, the benefit-tax view would apply here as well. That the property tax is regressive in our central cities – because of assessment-rate variations that favor middle- and upper-income households – is evidence for, not against, the benefit view. It is the regressive tax structure that prevents middle- and upper-income households from paying too much relative to the benefits they receive within the city, thus allowing the central-city fiscal system to be competitive with its surburban alternatives. For residents in rural communities, mobility and fiscal competition are limited, but in such communities preferences for public goods are likely to be very similar. If so, and if there is political competition to control rent seeking, then the local property tax again will operate as a benefits tax. Finally, the mobility of nonhousing capital across jurisdictions will ensure that a local property tax on commercial/industrial property is a benefits tax for firms, and that there will be no cross-subsidy from businesses to residents. As a first approximation, treating the local property tax as a benefits tax has much to recommend it.[2]

---

[1] The argument here applies to renters as well as homeowners, provided the property tax is shifted forward onto renters. This will be the case if the supply of rental housing in central cities is price-elastic. Empirical evidence seems to support this view.

[2] Even if we consider the property tax a benefits tax, there are other important equity issues that affect the local public-goods economy which deserve our attention. First, of course,

Accepting this argument – that the local property tax is in fact a price for government services and thus not relevant to a progressivity calculation – does not mean that a serious discussion of tax progressivity in the state and local sector is inappropriate, or that Metcalf's calculations are wasted effort. What should be a concern from the perspective of economic fairness and tax progressivity are those tax schedules which individuals do not choose for themselves according to the logic of benefit (or individual free-choice) taxation. There are still state taxes, where the mobility and identical-demand assumptions needed for the benefit-tax view are less credible. Relevant state taxes include sales and income taxes.

What then does Metcalf's evidence show about the progressivity of these taxes? It depends. If we measure the progressivity of sales and income taxes by measuring tax rates as the ratio of tax burdens to current annual income, then for an average American (using the CES sampling procedures to define "average") state sales taxes look regressive – rates fall as annual income rises (Metcalf's Table 4) – while state income taxes look progressive – rates rise as annual income rises (Table 6). Together, the two taxes are progressive because the combined tax rates rise with annual income.[3] An important contribution of Metcalf's paper is to show that these results based on annual income are changed, and significantly so, if we use annual consumption (a proxy for lifetime income) as the basis for calculating tax rates. Now the burden of state sales taxation on the average family becomes slightly progressive. The average income-tax burden remains progressive, though slightly less so.[4] Together, the average burdens of the two taxes are more progressively distributed using annual consumption to define the tax base. These general patterns hold in both 1984 and 1989, the two years of Metcalf's sample, though overall progressivity has declined from 1984 to 1989 for two reasons: a shift away

is the overall distribution of income before local taxation is imposed. We may object to the fact that lower-income households receive relatively less local public services, just as they receive less of all goods and services. Second, fairness in the distribution of meritorious local public goods – education being the prime example – may also be important. We might well advocate a more progressive allocation of such goods and services. Both of these issues are separate from the fairness of the burden of the local property tax.

[3] There is a question of exactly whom the CES sample represents as the average taxpayer. If the sampling design is to draw a representative sample of the national population, then the CES data will be weighted toward families in large metropolitan areas in heavily populated states – e.g., New York, California, Ohio, Pennsylvania, and Illinois. Those states typically have higher average tax rates and more progressive income-tax schedules. Although Metcalf's numbers will represent the tax burden on an average U.S. family, they will not represent the tax burden on a family in the average U.S. state. This distinction is important to keep in mind when reading Metcalf's paper.

[4] Metcalf's Table 1 and accompanying discussion explain why the results change with the change in the measure of tax base.

from income taxation and toward sales taxation by states in the last few years, and a slight flattening of the average income-tax rate schedule.

Having discovered that state sales and income taxes are together progressive against both annual and (proxy-measured) lifetime income, we can turn to our third question. Should we be concerned about what we see? Two matters are relevant here: first, what is our sense of economic fairness; second, what is the progressivity of the federal tax-and-transfer system? In a federalist public economy such as ours, the starting distribution of the economic pie is determined by the combined policies of federal, state, and local governments. I have already made the argument that (as a first approximation) the local public sector might best be treated as a "private market" and that, for discussions of economic fairness and tax progressivity, state taxes are therefore of central interest. If so, does the measured progressivity for our state tax system concern me? The answer is no, for two reasons. First, as Metcalf shows, the burden of our state tax system on the average American family is progressive, an outcome that comports with my sense of economic fairness. Second, and more importantly, the central government – not the states – stands as the most appropriate institutional protector of economic fairness in a federalist economy. It is to this level of government, and its ability to control the overall incidence of federal and state taxes, that we must look for economic fairness.

The fact that Metcalf's numbers do not worry me does not mean that the measures of progressivity in the state tax systems which he has provided are irrelevant. On the contrary. I am concerned about the apparent increase in the inequality of the distribution of pre-tax incomes over the past twenty years, and about the failure of the U.S. tax system to moderate these increases. The solution to this problem is not to be found in pronouncements about the progressivity of state taxes, however. The solution lies in increasing the progressivity of central government taxes and transfers, for only the central government has the ability to ensure that all taxpayers participate in the agreed-to re-allocation of pre-tax incomes. In designing central government tax policies, however, consideration must be given to the existing state tax structures and how states are likely to alter these structures in response to federal tax reform.

In other studies, both Metcalf (1992) and Inman (1989) have found strong evidence that state and local governments do alter their tax decisions in response to changes in federal tax policies. Indeed, the recent decisions in the Tax Reform Act of 1986 to lower marginal tax rates and drop the deductibility of state and local sales taxes may have stimulated the increased use of state sales taxes as well as the reduced use, and less progressive rate schedules, now observed for state income taxes. The logic of such a re-allocation involves a balancing of tax-minimizing and redistributive motives. With the loss of deductibility for sales taxation, the tax-mini-mizing motive would argue for reducing the use of sales taxation and increasing the use of other taxes, such as income taxes. The redistribution motive cuts the other way, however. The lowering of federal tax rates and the loss of state sales-tax deductions increases the net burdens of state taxes on upper-income households who itemize. Following the Tax Re-form Act of 1986, upper-income households therefore paid a larger share of the net costs of state government activities. To restore distributional balance – that is, to reduce the upper-income cohort's share of the state's tax burden – the states should increase their use of the less progressive taxes and decrease their use of the more progressive taxes. As Metcalf's results make clear, this means a move toward sales taxes and away from income taxes. Flattening the rate schedule for the income tax would also help restore the distributional equilibrium. Our observation of the move from income to sales taxation and a flattening of the income-tax rate schedule lends some tentative support to the importance of the redistrib-utive motive in setting state taxation.

In this regard, aggregate analyses such as Metcalf's are important data for the design of federal tax policies. We have gained new insights into the existing distribution of state tax burdens, as well as into how changes in federal policies are likely to affect that distribution. In the end, how-ever, we should be looking to the central government, not the states, as the ultimate arbiter of tax progressivity and economic fairness in our fed-eralist public economy.

REFERENCES

Inman, Robert (1989), "Local Decision to Tax: Evidence from Large U.S. Cities," *Regional Science and Urban Economics* 19: 455–91.
Metcalf, Gilbert (1992), "Tax Exporting, Federal Deductibility, and State Tax Structures," *Journal of Policy Analysis and Management* 12: 109–26.

General discussion

Gold observed that this study should be done state-by-state rather than aggregating across states, because otherwise one confounds differential state growth rates with policy changes. He also noted that in response to federal tax reform the progressivity of state income taxes increased rela-tive to the progressivity of the federal income tax, because states did not flatten their tax rate structures as much as the federal government did. Gold also observed that in the 1990s states have been making their tax rates more progressive at high income levels. On the other hand, local taxes have been rising faster than state taxes, which may tend to increase regressivity.

Sheffrin argued that annual consumption is not a good proxy for lifetime income for high-income people. He also noted that the paper reports a large percentage of people that say they pay no property tax. He thought this is because their tax payment is often included along with their mortgage payment in one check to a financial institution and so these individuals may not realize they are paying the tax. He also observed that state taxes have great variability in exemptions for sales taxes on intermediate goods. Finally, Sheffrin noted that property taxes in California are certainly not benefit taxes, as they are capped at 1% of the assessed value.

Menchik agreed that consumption is not a good proxy for lifetime income and, therefore, average tax measures based on consumption overstate progressivity. He also stated that bequests are critically important and that the ratio of bequests to lifetime income increases with income.

Musgrave noted that the impact of taxes and the response to them in terms of incentives and deadweight losses is annual, not lifetime. Because of discounting, it matters when (during a lifetime) that tax is paid. He stated that there is a difference between equity arguments for lifetime taxation, where tax is assessed at the end of life based on lifetime income, and assessing annual liability based on lifetime income.

Hite questioned why wealth is not used as a measure of well-being. She noted that there is a perception among individuals that property tax is the most unfair tax of all.

Poterba commented that the property-tax incidence assumption used in the paper – that tax is shifted forward to renters – is very questionable, and that if one traces the incidence to capital owners the tax looks progressive. He also argued that the mobility of factors constrains the ability of state and local governments to employ a progressive system.

Dunbar questioned where lottery payments fit in. Are they benefit taxes?

Triest thought state income taxes were more progressive than Metcalf's data suggest. He noted that Metcalf based his data on reported state income taxes, and that there could be a lot of measurement error. Triest's own work, based on actual payments, suggests that state income taxes have become more progressive over time.

Metcalf responded that theoretical results concluding that property tax is a benefit tax are quite fragile. He suggested that income-based and consumption-based measures probably bracket the true result, but argued that there are low annual–income people (i.e., the elderly, grad students!) who were not really low-income at all. In response to Triest's comment, he said that using federal tax data (rather than the state survey data) misses those who are taxed at the state but not the federal level.

CHAPTER 4

Trends in income inequality: the impact of, and implications for, tax policy

Lynn A. Karoly

1   Introduction

In the last decade, increased public attention has been drawn to evidence that the distribution of income in the United States has become more unequal. Official Census Bureau data that in the past showed a rather stable level of inequality indicate that the level of inequality in family income reached a post-war peak in 1989 (Bureau of the Census 1989, 1992b). As a result, the 1980s have been characterized as a period where the rich became richer and the poor became poorer. The years between 1981 and 1990 have also been designated the "tax decade" (Steuerle 1992). Eight months after Ronald Reagan became president in 1981, Congress passed the Economic Recovery and Tax Act (ERTA), which dramatically lowered individual and corporate taxes. Five years later, following tax increases in 1982, 1983, and 1984, the Tax Reform Act (TRA) of 1986 became the decade's second hallmark piece of tax legislation. Although total federal, state, and local tax receipts remained relatively constant as a fraction of GNP during the 1980s (at about 26%–27%), changes in tax policy during the decade altered the way taxes were collected (Steuerle 1992). Significant reductions in marginal tax rates for the federal income tax, as well as the shift away from corporate and individual income taxes toward social security and state and local taxes, exemplify the changes that occurred during the decade.

Paper prepared for presentation at the conference on "Tax Progressivity," Office of Tax Policy Research, University of Michigan, September 11–12, 1992. This research was supported by Grant No. P-50-HD-12639 from the Center for Population Research, National Institute of Child Health and Human Development. I would like to thank Joan Keesey and Loretta Verma for excellent programming assistance. I also benefited from comments on an earlier draft by David Cutler, Joel Slemrod, Shlomo Yitzhaki, and the participants at the Tax Progressivity Conference.

The confluence of these two trends – one marking changes in the distribution of income across families, the other signifying shifts in the burden of taxation across families – has led some to suggest a link between changes in the tax code and the distribution of income. Lindsey (1990), for instance, argues that the rise in inequality during the 1980s was caused by the sharp reduction in marginal tax rates for high-income taxpayers, inducing them to work more, report more income to the Internal Revenue Service, shift compensation toward taxable forms, and realize more capital gains. Even without such behavioral effects, changes in the tax structure – by changing the degree of progressivity of the tax system – would be expected to have a direct impact on inequality by altering the shape of the post-tax income distribution. Furthermore, even if changes in tax policy bear no relationship to changing income distribution, the distributional changes in pre-tax incomes have implications for future tax policy.

Within this context, the goal of this paper is to examine the trends in U.S. income inequality and identify the impact, if any, of recent tax changes on income distribution. First, in Section 2 I use micro-data from the annual March Current Population Survey (CPS) to document the changes in the distribution of pre-tax money income in the United States during the past two decades. Although the rise in inequality is identified with the 1980s, it is important to establish a benchmark for comparison. Thus, the analysis of trends in inequality presented in the next section begins with data for 1970 and continues through 1990, the latest year for which CPS data are available. This analysis confirms the findings of a number of recent studies that show a rise in inequality in pre-tax incomes dating back to the 1970s.[1]

In Section 2 I decompose the changes in inequality by income source to determine the relative contribution of different components of pre-tax income to the rise in inequality. The decomposition shows that the rise in inequality cannot simply be identified with one or even a few sources of income. At the same time that inequality in the labor income of the household head increased, the importance of this component in total income declined. Instead, income shifted toward two other components – spouse's earnings, and capital income and other income – which are less equally distributed. The declining importance of inequality-reducing transfers, both those targeted at low-income families and those more evenly distributed, also contributed to the rise in inequality.

Section 3 evaluates the merit of a number of explanations for the rise in inequality, focusing primarily upon the direct and indirect impacts of tax policy. The evidence of the direct impact of the tax system on inequality

---

[1] See e.g. Karoly (1993) and the studies cited therein.

in post-tax income during the last few decades is somewhat mixed. Most analysts conclude that progressivity in the tax system declined in the early part of the 1980s as a result of ERTA and the rise in social security payroll taxes. The 1986 TRA is generally believed to have improved the progressivity of the tax system, although evidence to this effect is far from conclusive. In part, these conclusions depend upon controversial assumptions about who bears the burden of various taxes, in particular the taxation of capital income. In any case, it seems fair to conclude that the rise in pre-tax income inequality dominates any increase in post-tax inequality due to a reduction in the progressivity of the tax system during the 1980s.

The evidence in support of a causal link between tax changes and the rise in pre-tax inequality is also controversial. First, given that inequality began rising in the 1970s, and that dispersion increased in both the lower and upper tails of the distribution, changes in tax policy cannot be the single culprit. Nevertheless, there is some empirical evidence to suggest that aggregate labor supply increased in the period following the 1981 tax cuts. However, the measured effects are not entirely consistent with the changes in marginal tax rates faced by individuals at different points in the income distribution. Instead, a number of other factors have merit as explanations for the rise in inequality, including changes in the demographic composition of families (such as the rise in female-headed households), the increased importance of the earnings of secondary workers (i.e., the spouse), and the rise in wage inequality.

Finally, the paper concludes with a discussion of the implications for tax policy for changes in income distribution. In this section I draw upon the lessons garnered from analyses of behavioral responses to the 1980s tax changes. I also discuss the possible role of the tax system in reducing the growing disparities in pre-tax incomes.

2   Trends in income inequality: 1970 to 1990

The evidence of rising income inequality in the United States has come from a number of fronts. Data from the Census Bureau reveal that inequality among families (defined to exclude single-person families), after reaching a post-war low in 1967–68, began to increase during the 1970s and continued to rise through the 1980s (Bureau of the Census 1989, 1992b). Although the trend toward greater inequality began in the late 1960s, about two-thirds of the absolute increase in the Gini coefficient between 1968 and 1989 occurred between 1980 and 1989. The rise in inequality during this period is further evidenced by a decline in the share of income received by the bottom three quintiles of families and a corresponding increase in the share going to the top two quintiles. The trends in inequality estimated by the Census Bureau are based on data from the annual March Current Population Survey (CPS). One advantage of the CPS is the existence of a relatively long time series of micro-data for a nationally representative cross section of families. The annual survey of about 50,000 to 60,000 households collects information for individuals and families about total income, and income by source, in the previous calendar year. The existence of demographic and labor-force data is also advantageous for distributional analyses. The primary disadvantage of the CPS is that it is difficult to construct a comprehensive measure of post-tax family income. In each survey, the income information is limited to pretax money income, thus excluding federal, state, and local taxes as well as the value of in-kind benefits (e.g., food stamps and health benefits).[2] Other income items such as accrued capital gains are also excluded.

There are a number of different approaches to analyzing changes in the distribution of income. The unit of analysis, income metric, and measure of inequality are the principal methodological differences across income distribution studies. Karoly (1993) provides a recent analysis of trends in income inequality among families and individuals using several methodologies. In the discussion that follows, I update my earlier analysis of trends in inequality by using the March 1971 to March 1991 CPSs, which provide information about income inequality from 1970 to 1990.[3] The unit of analysis is the family, defined to include unrelated individuals (i.e., persons living alone or with nonrelatives).[4] To adjust for differences

[2] The reported cash income data in the CPS suffer from underreporting. In particular, some components of transfer income such as Aid to Families with Dependent Children (AFDC) and Supplemental Security Income (SSI) are underreported. The same is true for property income items such as rent, dividends, and interest income. Using the Urban Institute's TRIM2 micro-simulation model to adjust for underreporting, Michel (1991) shows that the Gini coefficient declines from 0.444 to 0.442. Another problem with the CPS data is the top-coding of income amounts at a constant nominal top code. Top-coding will bias summary measures of inequality downward owing to the truncation of the upper tail of the income distribution (Fichtenbaum and Shahidi 1988). However, trends in percentile points of the distribution will not be affected by top-coding provided that the percentile points remain below the income top code in all years.
[3] Because of a significant change in the CPS processing system introduced in March 1989, which affected the way income and income by sources is measured, the March 1988 survey is available using the old and new processing system. I use both of the March 1988 files in order to adjust for the discontinuity in the time series of inequality. As discussed in Karoly (1993), the new processing system resulted in a slight rise in measured inequality. All time-series plots and tables in the body of the paper adjust for this discontinuity by applying the percentage change between March 1988 (and each successive year) based on the new processing system to the March 1988 data using the old processing system. Tables 1 and 2 contain the results for both March 1988 files.
[4] The income of related subfamilies is included with the income of the primary family.

in family size at a given time and to control for changes in family size over time, I use a measure of adjusted family income (AFI) defined as total family income relative to the appropriate poverty line.[5] In the distribution of AFI among persons, each individual in the family receives a weight of 1.

The income measure is total pre-tax money income, with income disaggregated into eight sources: the family head's wage and salary income; the head's self-employment income; the spouse's earnings (wage and salary income plus self-employment income); the earnings of other family members; means-tested cash transfers (AFDC, SSI, and other public assistance); other cash transfers (social security, unemployment benefits, veteran's benefits, and worker's compensation); capital income (interest, dividends, and rent); and other income (pension income and other miscellaneous sources).[6]

I use two approaches to summarize changes in the distribution of income. First, I rely upon a standard summary measure of inequality, the Gini coefficient.[7] The decomposition of the Gini coefficient by income source will also be exploited in the analysis (cf. Lerman and Yitzhaki 1985). In addition, to further identify just where in the distribution the changes are occurring, I examine trends in the 10th, 25th, 50th, 75th, 90th, and 95th percentiles adjusted for inflation, as well as trends in the various percentiles relative to the median or 50th percentile. Nominal incomes are inflated to 1990 dollars using the CPI-U-XI, the consumer price index that treats housing costs in a consistent manner over time.

Changes in pre-tax income inequality

Figure 1 shows the trend in the Gini coefficient for adjusted family income (AFI) among all persons. For purposes of comparison, the Gini coefficient is also plotted for the distribution of family income (FI) among all

[5] This adjustment implicitly uses the equivalence scales imbedded in the official poverty line to adjust for differences in family needs (Ruggles 1990).

[6] For husband-and-wife families, I define the family head to be the husband while the wife is defined as the spouse. This differs from the CPS public-use files, which starting in 1980 allowed wives to be designated as the family head in married-couple families. In calculating the Gini coefficient, income items that are less than zero are set equal to zero (e.g., self-employment income, capital income). Since at most 2% of all families report negative earnings or capital income, the results are essentially unchanged by this adjustment.

[7] The Gini coefficient ranges from a value of 0 in the case of perfect equality to a value of 1 in the case of perfect inequality. The Gini coefficient has a natural geometric interpretation in terms of the Lorenz curve, a plot of the cumulative percent of the population (ranked from lowest to highest income) against the cumulative share of income. The Gini coefficient is equal to two times the area between the 45% line (the line of perfect inequality) and the Lorenz curve. Algebraically, Lerman and Yitzhaki (1984) show that the Gini

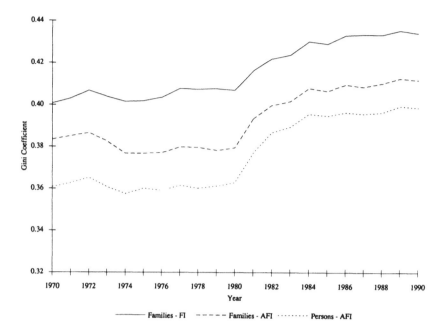

Figure 1. Gini coefficient, 1970–90. *Source:* Author's calculations from March 1971 to March 1991 CPS.

families (where each family receives a weight of 1), and adjusted family income among families. The data plotted in Figure 1 are tabulated in Table 1. For all three distributions, the Gini coefficient shows an unambiguous rise in inequality between 1970 and 1990, with most of the increase occurring between 1980 and 1985. Furthermore, in each case the Gini coefficient continues to rise through 1990 despite the economic recovery.[8] During the 1970s, the Gini coefficient rises until 1972, declines through 1974, and rises through the rest of the decade. The overall flatter trend throughout this period contrasts with the sharper rise during the 1980s.[9]

---

coefficient equals two times the covariance between income and the rank of income divided by the mean. The method described by Lerman and Yitzhaki (1989) for calculating the Gini coefficient with weighted data is used in this analysis.

[8] Michel (1991) also confirms a continued rise in income inequality since the 1982 recession, in both the pre-tax and post-tax distribution of income.

[9] Owing to the use of a constant-dollar nominal top code of $50,000 in the CPS surveys between 1968 and 1981, it is possible that the flat trend during the 1970s is attributable to an increased truncation of the upper tail of the income distribution. Likewise, the discrete jump in the Gini coefficient between 1980 and 1981, and between 1983 and 1984, may result from the increase in the nominal top code for most income items to $75,000 in

Table 1. *Gini coefficients: untrimmed and trimmed distributions*

Year	Family income among families			Adjusted family income among families			Adjusted family income among persons		
	No trim	2%	5%	No trim	2%	5%	No trim	2%	5%
1970	0.401	0.385	0.368	0.384	0.368	0.352	0.361	0.345	0.330
1971	0.403	0.387	0.371	0.385	0.369	0.354	0.363	0.346	0.332
1972	0.407	0.393	0.374	0.387	0.372	0.355	0.365	0.351	0.334
1973	0.404	0.391	0.373	0.383	0.369	0.352	0.361	0.347	0.331
1974	0.401	0.389	0.372	0.377	0.364	0.349	0.358	0.345	0.330
1975	0.402	0.390	0.372	0.377	0.366	0.349	0.360	0.348	0.332
1976	0.404	0.392	0.374	0.377	0.366	0.350	0.359	0.347	0.331
1977	0.408	0.398	0.379	0.380	0.370	0.353	0.362	0.351	0.334
1978	0.407	0.398	0.381	0.380	0.370	0.355	0.360	0.350	0.335
1979	0.408	0.398	0.383	0.378	0.369	0.355	0.361	0.351	0.338
1980	0.407	0.398	0.385	0.379	0.371	0.359	0.363	0.353	0.342
1981	0.416	0.406	0.388	0.393	0.383	0.366	0.377	0.367	0.350
1982	0.422	0.412	0.393	0.400	0.390	0.372	0.387	0.376	0.359
1983	0.424	0.414	0.396	0.402	0.393	0.376	0.390	0.379	0.362
1984	0.430	0.417	0.397	0.408	0.395	0.377	0.396	0.382	0.363
1985	0.429	0.418	0.398	0.407	0.396	0.377	0.395	0.383	0.364
1986	0.433	0.422	0.402	0.410	0.399	0.380	0.397	0.385	0.366

Table 1 *(cont.)*

Year	Family income among families			Adjusted family income among families			Adjusted family income among persons		
	No trim	2%	5%	No trim	2%	5%	No trim	2%	5%
1987[a]	0.434	0.423	0.403	0.409	0.399	0.381	0.396	0.385	0.366
1987[b]	0.435	0.423	0.403	0.409	0.398	0.380	0.396	0.384	0.366
1988	0.434	0.424	0.405	0.411	0.400	0.382	0.397	0.386	0.368
1989	0.436	0.424	0.406	0.413	0.401	0.384	0.400	0.387	0.370
1990	0.435	0.424	0.406	0.412	0.401	0.384	0.399	0.388	0.371

[a] Using old processing system.
[b] Using new processing system introduced in March 1989.
Source: Author's calculations from March 1971 to March 1991 CPS.

A given increase in the Gini coefficient is difficult to interpret. One approach for quantifying the impact of a rise in the Gini coefficient is to perform the following experiment. If the Gini coefficient in year 1 (G_1) is larger than in year 0 (G_0), is there a tax–transfer scheme that can be applied to the base-year distribution to bring about the same rise in inequality? Blackburn (1989) shows that if an equal-sized lump-sum tax from every income unit below the median is transferred to every income unit above the median, then the size of the tax transfer that would cause G_0 to increase to G_1 is equal to $2\mu_0(G_1 - G_0)$, where μ_0 is mean income in the base year. In other words, expressed as a fraction of base-year mean income, the size of the tax levied on the poor and given to the rich would equal twice the increase in the Gini coefficient between the first and second years.

In the case of inequality in FI among families, this hypothetical redistribution scenario implies that the rise in the Gini coefficient between 1970 and 1990 (from 0.401 to 0.435) could have been achieved by transferring 6.8% of 1970 mean income (about $2,070 in 1990 dollars) from every family below the median in 1970 (equal to $26,266 in 1990 dollars) to every family above the median. Over the two decades, the increase in the Gini coefficient, equal to an average of 0.002 per year,[10] implies a redistributive transfer equal to 0.4% of mean income per year. Given that mean income grew an average of 0.5% per year, the redistribution of income among families between 1970 and 1990 is almost equal in magnitude to the shift in the location of the distribution. Since family size declined steadily over the last two decades, however, the relative magnitude of the rise in inequality is smaller when income adjusted for family size is the metric. Real mean AFI among families grew about 1.1% per year, as average family size decreased from 3.0 persons to 2.4 persons. In contrast, the rise in the Gini coefficient of 0.002 per year for AFI also implies a 0.4% redistribution of average AFI per year.

As a summary measure of inequality, the Gini coefficient obscures the location of changes in the distribution. Furthermore, the implicit weighting

March 1982 and to $99,000 in March 1985. One adjustment for the income top-coding is to consistently truncate the upper tail of the distribution over time. In Table 1, the Gini coefficient is shown for the same three samples when the upper tail is trimmed at the 98th and 95th percentile in each year. The lower tail of the distribution is also trimmed at the 2nd and 5th percentiles, respectively. The trends in the 2% and 5% trimmed distributions are similar to the overall trends for the untrimmed Gini coefficients, but they do not show as sharp an increase in inequality between 1980 and 1981 and between 1983 and 1984. In each case, the increase in the Gini coefficient between 1970 and 1980 is higher, by about 0.007 and 0.011 for the 2% and 5% trimmed distributions, respectively. The overall rise in inequality is similar for the 2% and 5% trimmed distributions, although the time series is smoother for the latter, as one would expect.

[10] Based on the slope coefficient in a regression of the Gini coefficient on a time trend.

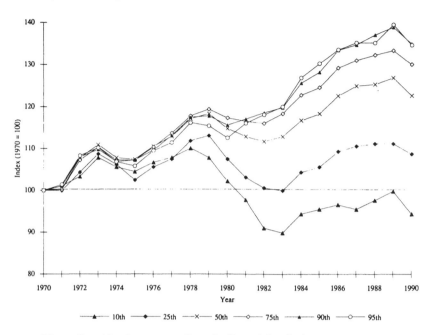

Figure 2a. Absolute percentiles of adjusted family income among persons, 1970–90. *Source:* Author's calculations from March 1971 to March 1991 CPS.

in the Gini coefficient makes it less sensitive to changes at the tails of the distribution compared to some other measures of inequality.[11] For the distribution of AFI among persons, Figure 2a plots the trends in the real absolute percentiles of the distribution at six points – namely, the 10th, 25th, 50th, 75th, 90th and 95th percentiles.[12] The percentiles shown in Figures 2a and 2b are tabulated in Table 2. All percentiles are indexed to equal 100 in 1970, allowing relative comparisons in the real trends over time. Changes in the shape of the distribution are more readily seen in Figure 2b, which plots the trend in each percentile relative to the median, where each relative percentile is again indexed to equal 100 in 1970.

Figure 2a shows that the median individual benefited from an approximate 25% growth in real AFI between 1970 and 1989.[13] Although business

[11] The Gini coefficient violates the transfer principle; i.e., it does not give greater weight to transfers at the lower end of the distribution (Kakwani 1980). In fact, Kakwani shows that the Gini coefficient is most sensitive to transfers at the mode of the distribution.

[12] The trends in the various percentiles through 1989 for the distribution of FI or AFI among families are presented in Karoly (1993).

[13] If no adjustment is made for changes in family size, the trend in real median family income is strikingly different (Karoly 1993). Most notably, there was no real growth over

Table 2. *Absolute percentiles of adjusted family income[a]
among persons*

| | Percentile | | | | | |
| | 10th | 25th | 50th | 75th | 90th | 95th |
Year						
1970	0.89	1.60	2.56	3.86	5.49	6.84
1971	0.90	1.60	2.57	3.87	5.55	6.94
1972	0.92	1.67	2.76	4.14	5.93	7.41
1973	0.96	1.74	2.84	4.26	6.03	7.54
1974	0.94	1.70	2.76	4.14	5.87	7.31
1975	0.93	1.64	2.75	4.14	5.89	7.24
1976	0.95	1.69	2.83	4.26	6.02	7.49
1977	0.96	1.72	2.89	4.39	6.21	7.62
1978	0.98	1.79	3.00	4.55	6.45	7.95
1979	0.96	1.81	3.03	4.61	6.47	7.90
1980	0.91	1.72	2.94	4.53	6.35	7.70
1981	0.87	1.65	2.89	4.50	6.43	7.94
1982	0.81	1.61	2.86	4.48	6.51	8.08
1983	0.80	1.60	2.89	4.57	6.58	8.21
1984	0.84	1.67	2.99	4.74	6.90	8.68
1985	0.85	1.69	3.03	4.81	7.04	8.91
1986	0.86	1.75	3.14	4.99	7.33	9.14
1987[b]	0.85	1.77	3.20	5.06	7.40	9.25
1987[c]	0.87	1.78	3.22	5.09	7.45	9.37
1988	0.89	1.79	3.23	5.14	7.58	9.37
1989	0.91	1.79	3.27	5.18	7.68	9.67
1990	0.86	1.75	3.16	5.05	7.46	9.33

[a] Measured as total family income divided by the poverty line, where the
1967 poverty threshold is inflated using the CPI-X to calculate poverty
lines after 1967.
[b] Using old processing system.
[c] Using new processing system introduced in March 1989.
Source: Author's calculations from March 1971 to March 1991 CPS.

cycle downturns produced declines in real median AFI between 1973 and
1975, and again between 1979 and 1982, the long-run pattern is one of
growth. The steady growth in real income through the end of the 1980s
had been interrupted by the recent recession, which has once again (in
1990) produced a drop in real median income. While the overall picture

the entire 20-year period in median family income. Thus, all of the gains in real income
per equivalent person during the 1970s and 1980s came through declines in average
family size, which may or may not imply gains in economic well-being.

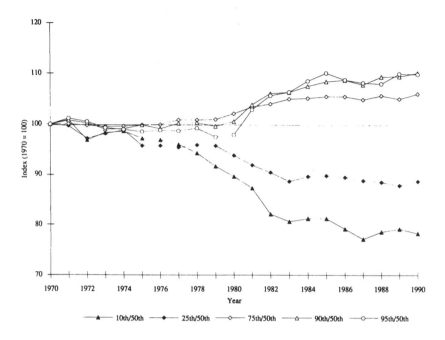

Figure 2b. Relative percentiles of adjusted family income among persons, 1970-90. *Source:* Author's calculations from March 1971 to March 1991 CPS.

is one of growth, the gains at the median were not mirrored at other points in the distribution. Real AFI at the 25th percentile grew barely 10% over the entire period, while the 10th percentile showed no real gains between 1970 and 1990. In contrast, incomes grew even faster at the 75th, 90th, and 95th percentiles.

The rise in inequality summarized in the Gini coefficient is also evident in Figure 2b, which shows gains and losses at the top and bottom of the distribution relative to the median. During the 1970s, the distribution of AFI became more disperse as incomes failed to grow as fast at the lower segments of the distribution (e.g., the 10th and 25th percentiles) compared to the median or upper portions of the distribution. The relative losses at the bottom of the distribution begin about 1974 and accelerate between 1979 and 1983. Despite the economic recovery during the 1980s, the 25th percentile failed to gain relative to the median, while the relative losses continued at the 10th percentile through 1987. In contrast, in the upper segments of the distribution there is evidence of small relative gains at the 75th and 90th percentiles beginning in 1973; the gains at the top accelerated between 1980 and 1985.[14]

It is worth noting that the Gini coefficient, because of its relative insensitivity to changes at the tails of the distribution, does not reflect the rise in dispersion evident in Figure 2b until about 1980. It is also not apparent from the trend in the Gini coefficient that the rise in inequality during the 1980s, especially from 1980 to 1985, is the result of growing dispersion in both the upper and lower tails of the income distribution. In addition, the relative losses at the bottom, ranging from 10% to 20% between 1970 and 1990, are larger than the relative gains at the upper income brackets, which barely reach 10%.

Other studies using CPS data, as well as data from other sources, report similar increases in pre-tax income inequality during the 1970s and 1980s. For example, tabulations by the Congressional Budget Office (CBO) show that the share of AFI going to the lowest quintile declined between 1973 and 1979 (from 5.5% to 5.1%), and then more sharply between 1979 and 1989 (to 4.3%) (Committee on Ways and Means 1991). In contrast, the share of income received by the top quintile remained stable between 1973 and 1979 at 41.7%, and increased to 44.6% by 1989.

Other recent studies, using panel data to study changes in inequality in more permanent measures of income, have generally reached similar conclusions to those based on cross-sectional data. For example, using data from a panel of taxpayers, Slemrod (1992b) shows that the rise in inequality evident in repeated cross-sections is also apparent for income measured over multiple years. Similarly, Sawhill and Condon (1992), in an analysis of data from the Panel Study of Income Dynamics, find evidence of a rise in inequality when income is measured over a 10-year period.

A decomposition of inequality by income source

Family income is derived from a number of sources, any one of which may be responsible for the rise in income inequality. Has family income become less equally distributed because of a rise in inequality of labor incomes or of other sources of income? Or is the increase in inequality the result of a shift toward less equally distributed sources of income?

---

[14] As shown in Karoly (1993), the trends in the relative percentiles shown in Figure 2b are very similar for the distribution of AFI among families (instead of persons). However, when no adjustment is made for family size, the changes in the shape of the distribution are somewhat different. When family income is the income measure, only the 10th percentile shows a sharp relative decline starting in 1974; in addition, relative gains at the top of the distribution begin in 1970 and accelerate at the 90th and 95th percentiles beginning in 1977.

One property of the Gini coefficient is that it is additively decomposable by income source (Lerman and Yitzhaki 1985). This property is useful for determining the relative contribution at a given time of a particular income source to overall inequality, as well as for determining shifts in the relative importance of various income sources over time. If total income is divided into K components, then the Gini coefficient G can be decomposed as

$$G = \sum_{k=1}^{K} S_k G_k R_k,$$

(1)

where S_k is the income component's share of total income, G_k is the component's Gini coefficient, and R_k is a measure of the "Gini correlation" between the income component and total income (Lerman and Yitzhaki 1985).[15] The share of inequality attributable to any one source is measured as

$$I_k = \frac{S_k G_k R_k}{G},$$

(2)

where the I_ks sum to 1. If an income source serves to reduce inequality then the component's I_k will be negative.

Table 3 presents the results for the decompositions of AFI among persons for selected years. Figure 3 plots the full time series for the Gini coefficients G_k, and Figure 4 plots the full time series for the relative shares of overall inequality I_k.[16] The decomposition is conducted for the eight income components listed previously: head's wage and salary income; head's self-employment income; spouse's earnings; other family member earnings; means-tested transfers; other transfers; capital income; and other income, which is composed mostly of pension income.

By far the largest component of income – and the component showing the largest absolute change in its contribution to total inequality – is the wage and salary income of the family head. In 1970, about 61% of family income came from the wages of the head of the family. That portion had fallen to 56% by 1980, and to 52% in 1990. During this period, there was a dramatic rise in the Gini coefficient for this component of income (Figure 3). Inequality in head's wage and salary income rose steadily through the 1970s and sharply accelerated between 1980 and 1983. In the later part of the 1980s the Gini coefficient for this component continued to rise, although to a smaller degree. Despite the sharp rise in inequality for this

[15] The Gini correlation is calculated as the covariance between income source k and the cumulative distribution of total income, divided by the covariance between income source k and the cumulative distribution of income source k.

[16] The results of the decomposition are very similar for the distribution of FI or AFI among families.

Table 3. *Decomposition of Gini coefficient by income source (adjusted family income among persons)*

Income source	Share of income (S_k)	Gini (G_k)	Gini correlation (R_k)	Share of inequality (I_k)
Head's wage and salary				
1970	0.606	0.492	0.721	0.595
1980	0.556	0.527	0.717	0.579
1990	0.515	0.563	0.713	0.517
Head's self-employment				
1970	0.080	0.947	0.521	0.109
1980	0.055	0.954	0.445	0.064
1990	0.054	0.957	0.506	0.065
Spouse's earnings				
1970	0.118	0.812	0.610	0.162
1980	0.134	0.781	0.600	0.173
1990	0.165	0.764	0.648	0.204
Other's earnings				
1970	0.077	0.877	0.458	0.086
1980	0.075	0.877	0.456	0.082
1990	0.068	0.886	0.419	0.063
Means-tested transfers				
1970	0.010	0.958	−0.672	−0.017
1980	0.010	0.946	−0.706	−0.019
1990	0.008	0.947	−0.708	−0.014
Other transfers				
1970	0.057	0.851	−0.038	−0.005
1980	0.071	0.820	−0.073	−0.012
1990	0.064	0.837	0.018	0.002
Capital income				
1970	0.039	0.924	0.638	0.063
1980	0.057	0.891	0.676	0.095
1990	0.068	0.886	0.720	0.108
Other income				
1970	0.015	0.962	0.203	0.008
1980	0.041	0.917	0.351	0.037
1990	0.058	0.892	0.409	0.053
Total income				
1970	1.000	0.361	1.000	1.000
1980	1.000	0.363	1.000	1.000
1990	1.000	0.399	1.000	1.000

Source: Author's calculations from March 1971 to March 1991 CPS.

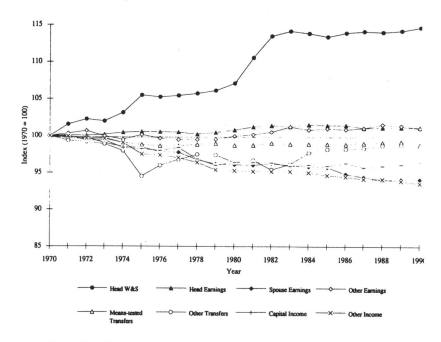

Figure 3. Gini coefficients by income source, 1970–90 (adjusted family income among persons). *Source:* Author's calculations from March 1971 to March 1991 CPS.

component, its share of overall inequality steadily declined, from 60% in 1970 to 58% in 1970 and to 52% in 1990. The contribution of head's wage and salary income declined in absolute terms as well, from 0.215 (out of 0.361) in 1970 to 0.206 (out of 0.399) in 1990.

The earnings of the family spouse (defined to be the wife) served to counteract the declining contribution of head's wages. As a share of income, the spouse's earnings increased slightly between 1970 and 1980. After that time it increased steadily, reaching 17% in 1990. At the same time, inequality in this component of income steadily declined (Figure 3). The combined effect of the three factors in the decomposition – a rising income share and correlation with income, but a falling Gini coefficient – resulted in a steady rise between the mid-1970s and 1990 in the share of overall inequality attributable to this component (Figure 4). By 1990, spouse's earnings, about 17% of total income, contributed 20% to total income inequality.

The reduction in inequality in the spouse's earnings may result from changes in inequality among persons in families with a working wife, or

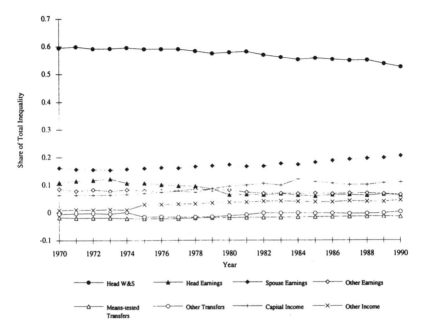

Figure 4. Share of income inequality by income source, 1970–90 (adjusted family income among persons). *Source:* Author's calculations from March 1971 to March 1991 CPS.

changes in the fraction of persons in families with a working wife.[17] Decomposing G_k for spouse's earnings shows that inequality also decreased among the subset of individuals in families with a working wife, falling from 0.507 in 1970 to 0.466 in 1990. Over the same period, the proportion of families with no wife's earnings fell from 62% to 56% because of two countervailing effects. While the proportion of persons in families without a wife rose from 19% to 32%, the fraction of persons in families where the wife had no earnings fell from 43% to 24%. Thus, even though married-couple families became a smaller share of family units, the higher labor-force–participation rate among wives increased the proportion of persons in families with a working wife.

Other sources of labor income declined in importance over the period. The share of both head's self-employment income and earnings from

---

[17] If p is the proportion of persons in families with no earnings from the spouse (or wife), then the Gini coefficient G_k for spouse's earnings among all persons is equal to $p + (1-p)G_{k0}$, where G_{k0} is the Gini coefficient for spouse's earnings among persons in families with working spouses.

other family members fell; the former declined mostly during the 1970s whereas the latter decreased more in the 1980s. At the same time, inequality in the two components among all persons increased, with most of the rise in inequality in head's self-employment income occurring in the 1970s; the rise in dispersion in earnings from other family members is evident only in the 1980s. However, the increase in inequality results from a rise in the fraction of individuals with zero incomes in these two categories. Among persons in families with self-employment income from the head, inequality exhibited a U-shaped pattern, first decreasing between 1970 and 1980, and then increasing through 1990. Over the two decades, the level of inequality remained unchanged. Inequality among persons in families with earnings from other family members decreased during the 1970s, and remained stable in the next decade. Overall, the contribution to total inequality declined for both components, so that they each equaled about 6% in 1990 (Figure 4).

During the period 1970–90, the inequality-reducing effect of transfers declined, both for means-tested transfer payments (e.g., AFDC, SSI) and non–means-tested transfers (e.g., social security, unemployment, worker's compensation). Both types of transfers reduce inequality, as evidenced by the negative I_k terms, but the impact is rather modest. Despite the fact that means-tested transfers are barely a drop in the family income bucket (about 1%), the strong negative correlation of this component with total income means that its inequality-reducing effect exceeds the effect of non–means-tested transfers. These latter transfers constitute about 6% to 7% of total income, but the negative correlation with total income is very small.

The weakening of the inequality-reducing effect of transfers occurred primarily during the 1980s.[18] Both types of transfers had a larger negative impact on inequality in 1980 than they had in 1970. However, by 1990 the inequality-reducing effect of means-tested transfers was less than it had been in 1970, while the other transfer component actually had a slight positive impact on inequality in 1990. In both cases, the share of income received from transfers declined during the 1980s after remaining steady or increasing in the previous decade.

The remaining two income components, capital income and other income, show a pattern of change similar to spouse's earnings. As a share of total income, the two sources combined increased rather dramatically,

[18] Estimates by the Census Bureau, based on the Gini coefficient, also show that cash transfers had a smaller impact on reducing inequality in 1989 compared to 1979, although the decline is small (Bureau of the Census 1992a). Combined with a slight increase in the inequality-reducing impact of noncash transfers, the Census Bureau estimates show no change in the ability of transfers to reduce inequality between 1979 and 1989.

from about 5% in 1970 to nearly 13% in 1990. Although both components are very unequally distributed, the degree of inequality in each source declined throughout the period. However, since inequality among recipients increased for both types of income, this decline was due to the increase in the fraction of people with nonzero capital income and other income. For example, the fraction reporting no capital income fell from 62% in 1970 to 36% in 1980, and remained at that level through 1990. While 91% of individuals reported no income in the "other" category in 1970, that fraction was only 79% in 1980 and 71% in 1990. The net effect is that the contribution to overall inequality increased from 6% to 11% for capital income, and from 1% to 5% for other income, with most of the increase taking place by the mid-1980s (Figure 4).

Table 4 shows the results of decomposing the change in the Gini coefficient between 1970 and 1990 and various subperiods. The change in inequality between year 1 and year 0 is decomposed by income source and the three factors (income shares S_k, correlation with income R_k, and Gini coefficient G_k) in the Gini decomposition as follows:

$$\Delta G = G_1 - G_0 = \sum_{k=1}^{K}(S_{k1} - S_{k0})G_{k1}R_{k1} + \sum_{k=1}^{K}(R_{k1} - R_{k0})S_{k1}G_{k1}$$

$$+ \sum_{k=1}^{K}(G_{k1} - G_{k0})S_{k1}R_{k1} + \text{residual.} \qquad (3)$$

Thus, the total change in inequality can be decomposed along two dimensions: the contribution of each income source due to changes in S_k, R_k, and G_k, and the contribution of changes in S_k, R_k, and G_k across income sources.

Between 1970 and 1990, the Gini coefficient increased by 0.038. Table 4 shows that half of this increase was due to changes in inequality by source. By source, the inequality-reducing effect of declines in the share of income from head's earnings (wages and salaries and self-employment) were more than offset by increases in the share of earnings from the spouse and the rise in the share of capital income and other income. Consistent with Figure 3, the rise in inequality in head's wage and salary income is the dominant effect among income sources in contributing to a rise in inequality.

The decomposition of the change in the Gini coefficient – separately for the periods 1970 to 1980, 1980 to 1985, and 1985 to 1990 – reveals that many of the same trends were at work in all three periods. For instance, the positive impact on inequality of the shift toward earnings from the spouse is evident in the 1970s as well as the 1980s, but the magnitude of the effect is much larger in the second decade. One exception is that, in

Table 4. *Decomposition of change in inequality by income source (adjusted family income among persons)*

	Change in Gini due to income source										
Factor[a]	Head's wages & salary	Head's self-employment earnings	Spouse's earnings	Other's earnings	Means-tested transfers	Other transfers	Capital income	Other income	Total change	Residual	ΔG
1970–80											
S	−0.019	−0.010	0.008	−0.001	0.000	−0.001	0.011	0.008	−0.004		
G	0.014	0.000	−0.003	0.000	0.000	0.000	−0.001	−0.001	0.010		
R	−0.001	−0.004	−0.001	0.000	0.000	−0.002	0.002	0.006	−0.001		
Total	−0.006	−0.014	0.004	−0.001	−0.001	−0.003	0.012	0.013	0.005	−0.0029	0.002
1980–85											
S	−0.007	−0.003	0.007	−0.002	0.001	0.000	0.008	0.001	0.006		
G	0.012	0.000	0.000	0.000	0.000	0.000	0.000	0.000	0.012		
R	0.004	0.002	0.003	−0.001	0.000	0.003	0.002	0.001	0.013		
Total	0.009	−0.000	0.009	−0.002	0.001	0.003	0.010	0.002	0.032	0.0001	0.032

1985–90

S	−0.009	0.002	0.009	0.000	0.000	0.000	−0.002	0.002	0.001		
G	0.002	0.000	−0.001	0.000	0.000	0.000	0.000	0.000	0.001		
R	−0.004	0.000	0.003	−0.002	0.000	0.002	0.001	0.001	0.002		
Total	−0.010	0.002	0.010	−0.002	0.000	0.002	−0.000	0.003	0.004	0.0002	0.004

1970–90

S	−0.035	−0.013	0.024	−0.003	0.001	0.000	0.019	0.012	0.005		
G	0.027	0.000	−0.005	0.000	0.000	0.000	−0.002	−0.001	0.019		
R	−0.001	−0.001	0.004	−0.002	0.000	0.003	0.005	0.009	0.016		
Total	−0.010	−0.014	0.023	−0.005	0.001	0.003	0.022	0.020	0.041	−0.0026	0.038

[a] S = Share of income source; G = Gini coefficient of income source; R = Gini correlation of income source.
Source: Author's calculations from March 1971 to March 1991 CPS.

contrast to the earlier and later periods, head's wage and salary income contributed to a rise in inequality between 1980 and 1985, a period when wage inequality was increasing for both men and women (Karoly 1993). Another difference is that both types of transfers (especially non–means-tested transfers) contributed to a decline in inequality during the 1970s, but added to the rise in inequality during the 1980s. Finally, the contribution of capital income to the rise in inequality was largest during the 1970s and the first half of the 1980s, while other income had the largest impact during the 1970s.

Overall, despite the large rise in inequality in head's wage and salary income, this component served to decrease inequality owing to the decline in its share of total income. Self-employment income of the head and earnings from other family members had a similar overall negative impact. As a result of the shift toward spouse's earnings, capital income, and other income, these components made the largest contribution to the increase in inequality in the last two decades. Transfer income also contributed to the rise in pre-tax income inequality during the 1980s, but the magnitude of the effect is considerably smaller compared to spouse's earnings, capital income, and other income.

3   Explaining changes in income inequality

The rise in inequality in the last two decades raises questions about the factors leading to this divergence from an historical pattern of a more stable income distribution. In this section I review a number of the explanations that have been offered, beginning with the impact of tax policy. The impact of the business cycle, family composition changes, and the labor market are also discussed.

The impact of tax policy

Although the rise in pre-tax income inequality identified in the previous section pre-dates the 1980s "tax decade," it is relevant to consider the impact of tax policy on income distribution. Two major pieces of tax legislation were enacted during the 1980s: the Economic Recovery Tax Act (ERTA) of 1981 and the Tax Reform Act (TRA) of 1986. Tax changes in other years include the Tax Equity and Fiscal Responsibility Act of 1982 (TEFRA), the Social Security Amendments of 1983, the Deficit Reduction Act of 1984, and the Omnibus Budget Reconciliation Act (OBRA) of 1990 (see Steuerle 1992 for a discussion of these various tax measures).

Changes in the tax system could have two effects on income inequality. The first is the direct redistributive effect of taxes on the distribution of income through the progressivity of the tax system. To what extent did changes in tax policy, especially during the 1980s, affect the post-tax distribution of income? Did the major pieces of tax legislation enacted during the 1980s counteract the rise in pre-tax income inequality, or did they further contribute to the trend? Second, changes in tax policy can have dynamic or indirect effects on income distribution by altering the pre-tax distribution of income. Changes in labor supply, savings, and portfolio decisions as a result of revisions in the tax code may have contributed to the rise in pre-tax inequality evident in the previous section. In addition, the overall growth rate of the economy and hence the distribution of pre-tax income may be altered by changes in tax regimes. These two effects of tax policy, direct and indirect, are discussed in turn.

Direct effects of tax policy on post-tax income distribution. Changes in the individual income–tax structure enacted with ERTA and TRA could be expected to have a direct impact on the distribution of post-tax income. ERTA, for example, reduced the top marginal tax rate from 70% to 50% and phased in a 23% reduction in the marginal tax rates in other income brackets. No adjustment was made, however, to the Earned Income Tax Credit (EITC), a benefit targeted to lower-income families. In contrast, TRA specifically targeted changes in the tax code to benefit those at the bottom of the income ladder by expanding the personal exemption, the standard deduction, and EITC. As a result, an estimated 6 million low-income households were removed from the tax rolls (Hausman and Poterba, 1987). At the same time, a 4-bracket tax structure – with rates of 15%, 28%, 33%, and 28% – replaced the existing 14-bracket system and its top marginal tax rate of 50%. The net effect was a reduction in average federal tax liability for the bottom nine deciles, and an increase in the tax liability of the top decile (Pechman, 1987). Other changes in the 1980s include reductions and subsequent increases in corporate taxes, increases in excise taxes, and a 25% increase in social security payroll taxes (Gramlich, Kasten, and Sammartino 1993).

Unfortunately, there is no ideal data source for examining the impact of taxes on the post-tax distribution of income. As noted previously, the CPS does not collect data on taxes paid. Even if individual income tax payments were recorded, it would still be necessary to allocate the incidence of these taxes as well as corporate income taxes, excise taxes, and so on. Instead, researchers have developed methods for allocating tax burdens (including individual income and payroll taxes, consumption taxes, and corporate taxes) to CPS families and imputing other income items (such as capital gains) not recorded in the CPS. Examples of these CPS databases, typically augmented with data from tax returns, include the Urban Institute's TRIM2 model (Webb, Michel, and Bergsman 1990) and the Congressional Budget Office tax-model data (CBO 1987; Gramlich et al. 1993). The alternative to the CPS is data from tax filings such as those maintained by the IRS Statistics of Income Division.

Gramlich et al. (1993), using the CBO tax-model data, provide one of the most recent analyses of post-tax distribution of income using CPS data for 1980, 1985, and 1990.[19] They conclude that, although taxes continued to reduce inequality compared to pre-tax income distribution, the net impact of tax changes in the 1980s was a lessening of the redistributive impact of taxes. In particular, the reduction in inequality (measured by the Gini coefficient) due to the tax system fell from 6.8% in 1980 to 3.2% in 1985. The redistributive impact of taxes was partially restored in the next half of the decade, however, with a 3.9% reduction in inequality due to taxes in 1990. Gramlich et al. conclude that, holding the transfer benefits and tax laws at their 1980 level, the post-tax post-transfer distribution would have been somewhat more equal. About 16% of the rise in post-tax post-transfer inequality is attributable to tax- and transfer-policy changes, with most of the effect occurring in the 1980–85 period. Nevertheless, this means that more than four-fifths of the increase in post-tax post-transfer income inequality is due to changes in incomes before taxes and transfers.

Estimates by the Census Bureau of the impact of taxes on the distribution of income since 1979 confirm an overall decline in progressivity of the tax system during the 1980s (Bureau of the Census 1992a). Measured by the percentage reduction in the Gini coefficient, Census Bureau data show that federal and state income taxes and social security payroll taxes were most progressive in 1980 and 1981 and least progressive in 1986. The conclusion that the tax system became less progressive during the 1980s is also echoed by Slemrod (1992b) and Pechman (1990). Slemrod's analysis, based on data from tax returns maintained by the IRS, shows a decline in the inequality-reducing effectiveness of federal income taxes between 1980 and 1988. Based on results from the Brookings MERGE files, Pechman (1990) estimates that effective rates of federal, state, and local taxes declined between 1980 and 1985 for individuals in the top decile and above, while rates rose or remained stable for most other deciles. The reductions in the effective tax rates at the top 10, 5, and 1 percent of the distribution

---

[19] The later year is based on projections from 1987 CPS data. Their measure of pre-tax post-transfer income does not include the value of in-kind benefits such as food stamps, Medicare, or Medicaid. They also do not include state and local taxes in their post-transfer post-tax measure of income. As with the analysis in Section 2, they also adjust for differences in family size, using the implicit equivalence scales in the official poverty lines and weighting the distribution by persons.

represent the continuation of a trend evident since 1970. As a result of TRA, Pechman estimates that the tax system became somewhat more progressive through a reduction in the effective tax rate faced by the bottom three deciles and increases in the rates faced by all other deciles. Nevertheless, effective tax rates of the top decile and above in 1988 remain significantly below their 1966 levels.

The conclusion that TRA improved the degree of progressivity in the tax system has not been universal. Michel (1991), using the Urban Institute's TRIM2 model, estimates that the inequality-reducing effect of both federal taxes and payroll taxes declined slightly between 1983 and 1987. The differences in his findings compared to those of Pechman (1990) and Gramlich et al. (1993) may be due to the choice of years for comparison or the fact that the incidence of corporate income taxes, which increased with TRA, is not included in Michel's analysis.[20] However, Gravelle (1992) also suggests that the long-run impact of TRA may be more favorable to higher-income individuals. She concludes that many of the provisions affecting corporate taxes, while increasing progressivity in the early years, are likely to have a smaller permanent redistributive impact. In addition, the shift toward equalization in the taxation of different assets could be expected to benefit high-income individuals through a reduction in the risk they bear in equilibrium (Galper, Lucke, and Toder 1988), a factor not accounted for by most studies. Assumptions about the incidence of corporate taxes, typically assigned to owners of capital, can also affect conclusions about the redistributive effect of TRA.

Indirect effects of tax policy. As noted previously, the dramatic changes in tax rates as a result of ERTA and TRA may have also indirectly altered the distribution of income by inducing changes in pre-tax incomes. The tax changes enacted during the 1980s differentially altered the effective tax rates faced by individuals at different points in the income distribution. For example, Gramlich et al. (1993) estimate that between 1980 and 1990, marginal tax rates on earnings (including federal income tax and payroll taxes) increased for the lowest deciles and declined for individuals in the upper half of the distribution, with the largest reductions in marginal rates occurring for individuals in the top decile. Hausman and Poterba (1987) provide a similar estimate, showing that about 40% of taxpayers would experience the same or higher marginal tax rates after TRA, while only 10% would benefit from a rate reduction of more than 10%. In contrast, the marginal tax rate on capital gains increased throughout the distribution between 1980 and 1990 (Gramlich et al. 1993).

---

[20] Pechman (1990) assumes that the corporate income tax is borne by capital, while Gramlich et al. (1993) divide the burden between labor and capital.

The argument for an indirect effect of tax policy on the income distribution is made most strongly by Lindsey (1990). Lindsey contends that inequality in pre-tax incomes rose as a result of the tax cuts of the 1980s (especially ERTA), as higher-income families increased their work effort, converted compensation from nonmonetary to monetary forms, and shifted their portfolios toward taxable assets. Lindsey's conclusions are based on simulations, using the National Bureau of Economic Research (NBER) TAXSIM model, of the revenue effects of ERTA accounting for demand, supply, and pecuniary responses to the 1981 tax cuts. For example, he finds that revenues following the 1981 tax cuts exceeded predictions of the tax simulation model – with most of the excess revenue derived from upper-income taxpayers, suggesting a large supply response.[21]

Evidence in support of Lindsey's hypothesis is mixed. First consider the prima facie case on the basis of the timing of the trends in income inequality. The reduction in tax rates passed with ERTA did not fully become effective in 1981, as the rate reduction was phased in over a three-year period. However, as discussed in the previous section, inequality in total family incomes began to increase in the 1970s, first as a result of relative gains at the top of the distribution and then as a consequence of relative declines in the bottom of the distribution. When an adjustment is made for family size, the relative gains at the top of the distribution begin in the mid-1970s and accelerate in the early 1980s (Figure 2b). Furthermore, the accelerated rise in inequality during the 1980s resulted from increasing dispersion in both tails of the distribution, with absolute declines in incomes at the bottom percentiles. Thus, a supply-side response to changes in tax policy explains neither the rise in inequality prior to 1981 nor the real declines in incomes at the lower segments of the income distribution.

The decomposition analysis in the previous section shows that the rise in inequality between 1980 and 1985 can be attributed both to rising inequality in the wage and salary income of the family head and to an increase in the share of income derived from the spouse's labor earnings and capital income. However, with the exception of the positive contribution of the wage and salary income of the head, these same factors also contributed to a rise in inequality in the previous decade. There is no

---

[21] One problem with Lindsey's simulations, as noted by Bosworth and Burtless (1992), is that he assumes a common growth rate across the income distribution in all income items, including earnings. However, there was a substantial increase in earnings dispersion during this period, with lower-skilled workers experiencing real wage declines; see the review by Levy and Murnane (1992). Thus, the disproportionate rise in earnings of higher-income taxpayers – rather than being a supply response – may be attributable to the rise in wage dispersion, a phenomenon identified with factors other than tax changes.

apparent shift in the underlying factors affecting the rise in inequality beginning with the 1981 tax changes.

The evidence for a labor supply response to the tax changes in the 1980s is far from conclusive. Predictions of the effect of the 1980s tax changes, based on econometric models of male and female labor supply, suggest a larger labor supply response as a result of ERTA compared to TRA, and a larger response for secondary workers (Hausman 1981, 1983; Hausman and Poterba 1987). Bosworth and Burtless (1992), using CPS-based time-series data on annual hours of work by men and women from 1967 to 1989, compare actual labor supply trends before and after the 1980s tax reforms. Their econometric estimates indicate that the average work effort of men in 1989 was about 6% above the level it would have been had the pre-1981 trend in labor supply continued; the effect for women was estimated at 5.4%.

However, even though marginal tax rates fell more for higher-income individuals, Bosworth and Burtless (1992) did not find a consistent pattern of a higher labor supply response for individuals in higher income quintiles. In fact, the largest estimated supply responses occurred for men in the lowest income quintile, a group that experienced either no change or an increase in marginal tax rates. As expected, the labor supply responses were generally larger for women than for men in the high income categories. Due to the decline in real hourly wages, the increased labor supply was not accompanied by an increase in earnings per person, especially at the lower tail of the income distribution.

Another hypothesized supply-side response to the tax changes is the shift in compensation from nonmonetary forms (i.e., fringe benefits such as employer-provided health insurance and pension contributions) to wages. Evidence of this effect is difficult to assemble because the CPS data only began recording the receipt of such benefits in 1980 (and then with no valuation attached to the benefits) and because data from tax filings do not include this information. Data from the National Income and Products Accounts (NIPA) show that supplements to wages and salaries peaked at 17% of total compensation in 1983, after steadily increasing throughout the prior two decades.[22] Since 1983, the share has stabilized at about 16%–17%. The timing of the slowdown in the growth of fringe benefits is consistent with an effect of the 1981 tax cuts, although with a delayed response. However, the NIPA data do not allow a distributional analysis that would measure whether the slowdown in fringe benefits occurred for higher-paid workers, who would have had the most incentive to alter their form of compensation.

---

[22] The data come from the Council of Economic Advisors (1992, table B-22).

In an analysis of the decline in private pension coverage during the 1980s, Bloom and Freeman (1992) do not find evidence in support of a tax-induced substitution away from this fringe benefit. In particular, based on CPS data, they find that the drop-off in pension coverage was smallest for higher-income workers – the group that faced the largest declines in marginal tax rates. They also find no evidence of gains in real wages that offset the declines in pension coverage, as low-skilled workers experienced the largest reductions in real wages and pension coverage rates. Instead, they attribute the decline in this form of compensation to the overall reduction in real wage growth, the decline in union density, and other factors. Thus, the aggregate trend in nonmonetary compensation may be attributable to factors such as changes in the distribution of employment by industry, declines in unionization rates, or an increased use of part-time workers.

Changes in marginal tax rates could also be expected to affect portfolio decisions, such as the timing of capital gains realizations. One effort to measure the total effect of labor supply and portfolio changes is provided by Gramlich et al. (1993). They calculate the impact of tax-induced labor supply changes to tax rates between 1980 and 1990, based on the 1990 distribution of income. Assuming post-tax wage elasticities of 0.2 for the labor supply of primary earners and 1.0 for secondary earners, they estimate that about 14% of the increase in pre-transfer pre-tax income inequality (measured by the Gini coefficient) between 1980 and 1990 is attributable to increased labor supply on the part of high-income individuals. However, they also find an equal and opposite effect on inequality as a result of the rise in marginal tax rates on capital gains. They conclude that the net effect of behavioral responses to changes in marginal tax rates on the distribution of pre-tax pre-transfer income is zero.

The role of other factors

There are a number of other potential explanations for the rise in inequality among families and individuals, including the effect of the business cycle, demographic shifts, and the rise in inequality in wages. Although no systematic analysis of the contribution of various factors has yet, to my knowledge, been undertaken, there is evidence that changes in household composition and labor supply as well as the changing wage structure have contributed to the trend toward greater inequality.

Effect of the business cycle. The conventional wisdom is that inequality is countercyclical (Blank and Blinder 1986). During economic downturns, inequality rises as individuals and families in the lower tail of the distribution are more likely to experience reductions in income compared to those with higher incomes. Periods of economic expansion, in turn, tend to be accompanied by declines in poverty rates and a compression of the income distribution. How much of the rise in inequality in pre-tax incomes can be explained by the series of business cycle downturns in the mid-1970s through the early 1980s?

The time-series evidence suggests that a pure business cycle hypothesis is not sufficient to explain the rise in inequality. In particular, inequality increased in the 1970s between 1973 and 1979, two comparable business cycle peaks. The continued rise in inequality through 1989, despite the sustained economic recovery that began in 1983, also runs counter to the conventional wisdom and to predictions of econometric models of the relationship between macroeconomic activity and the income distribution (Cutler and Katz 1991; Ruggles and Stone 1992). The acceleration in inequality in the early 1980s and the absolute decline in incomes at the lower tail of the distribution may be partially attributable to back-to-back recessions in 1980 and 1981–82. Nevertheless, the absence of a reversal of these trends as the economy expanded suggests that more fundamental factors were at work.

Importance of family composition changes. The period of rising inequality is also marked by a number of significant shifts in the age and headship composition of families (Karoly 1993). For example, in the two decades between 1970 and 1990, the share of families with a head aged 44 years or less and 65 years or more increased, with a corresponding decline in families in the 45–64-year-old bracket. Compositional shifts are also evidenced by the increased representation of unrelated individuals and female-headed families in the count of all family units (including unrelated individuals). Married-couple families with both spouses working, once in the minority, grew to represent more than 70% of husband-and-wife families (Cancian, Danziger, and Gottschalk 1993).

The effects of these demographic and compositional changes are evaluated in a number of studies. Karoly (1993), using a shift-share analysis, finds that the changing age composition of families played no role in the rise in inequality between 1967 and 1987. This follows from the rise in inequality within all groups of families defined by the age of the head, a finding confirmed by Michel (1991). In contrast, Karoly (1993) concludes that about one-third of the rise in inequality can be explained by shifts in household composition toward single-parent families and single individuals.

Analyses of the effect of an increase in the number of working wives have produced mixed results. Cancian et al. (1993) confirm the findings of a number of previous studies showing that wives' earnings tend to equalize the distribution of income among married-couple families. Using CPS data, they also conclude that the equalizing impact has remained stable or increased over time. Ryscavage (1992) reaches a similar conclusion, although he finds that the equalizing impact of wives' earnings among all families (not just married-couple families) declined during the 1980s. Rather than focusing on wives' labor income in married-couple families, Blackburn and Bloom (1987) examine the impact of nonprincipal earners (secondary earners with lower annual earnings than the principal earner) on the distribution of income among all families. They conclude that the earnings from other family members had a positive impact on inequality between 1967 and 1984. Cutler and Katz (1991) also find a positive, but small, contribution of the earnings of secondary earners to the rise in inequality between the 1960s and the 1980s for a sample of nonelderly families.

The decomposition analysis presented in Section 2 also suggests a positive effect of the increase in the share of family income derived from secondary errors, measured as the wife's earnings. Between 1970 and 1990, and in each of the subperiods examined, the earnings of the wife contributed to the rise in inequality, owing to an increase in the share of income from this source. The causes of the increased participation of wives may be a supply-side response to the tax changes that occurred in the 1980s (as discussed previously). However, given that this trend dates back to the 1970s, it may be the result of more fundamental changes, such as the increase in the real wages of women, the declining real wages of men, or changes in women's preferences for work.

Role of changes in the wage structure. Given that about 80% of family income is derived from the labor market, changes in the wage structure are likely to affect the overall distribution of income. Since the 1970s, there has been an increase in dispersion in the wage distribution for men, with an acceleration of the trend during the 1980s (see Karoly 1993 and the review of recent studies by Levy and Murnane 1992). The increased inequality in wages has been accompanied by stagnation in real median wages and falling real wages for workers in the bottom half of the distribution. Another feature of the changing wage structure has been the rising returns to skill evidenced by an increase in the returns to a college education (Levy and Murnane, forthcoming). Wage inequality among women, after declining through the 1970s, also began to rise during the 1980s. However, the changing shape of the wage distribution among women was accompanied by real wage growth throughout the distribution (Karoly 1993). Explanations for these significant changes in the wage structure include shifts in product demand as a result of increased globalization of the economy, the declining role of unions, increased immigration, and technological change.

The decomposition analysis presented in Table 4 can help identify the impact of the rise in wage inequality on overall income inequality. Between 1970 and 1990, the rise in the Gini coefficient for the head's wage and salary income contributed a 0.027 increase in the Gini coefficient (out of an actual increase of 0.038). However, because of the declining share of income and the reduced correlation with income, this component had an overall negative impact. Thus, although inequality in the head's wage and salary income was increasing, the shift away from this source of income contributed to a net decline in inequality. One exception is the 1980–85 period, when the rise in inequality dominated and the overall contribution was to increase inequality. This was a period when inequality was increasing for both men and women. If the level of inequality in the head's wage and salary income were held constant at the 1980 level (with all other components of inequality changing as they did between 1980 and 1985), the increase in inequality would have been about 38% lower; over the entire 1970–90 period, the rise in inequality would have been approximately 65% lower, with no increase in wage inequality among family heads.[23]

4 Implications for tax policy

The rise in income inequality during the last two decades raises two questions regarding the role of tax policy. First, what implications do the recent changes in the income distribution, and our understanding of the causes of these increases, imply for future tax policy? Second, is there a redistributive role for tax policy to counteract the rise in pre-tax inequality?

Motivated by considerations of efficiency and equity, the economics literature offers theoretical guidance regarding the structure of the optimal income tax (Slemrod 1983, 1990b). This literature models the optimal tax rate through the trade-off between the increased social welfare of a more equitable distribution versus the efficiency losses associated with achieving the redistribution. The optimal degree of tax progressivity is dictated by a number of parameters, including the form of the social welfare function, the distribution of endowments, and the wage elasticity of labor supply. For example, a more egalitarian social welfare function, or a less equal distribution of endowments or returns to endowments, implies a more progressive tax system, ceteris paribus. If labor supply is less responsive to changes in the after-tax wage rate, this implies a lower efficiency cost and hence a more highly progressive tax system.

---

[23] Cutler and Katz (1991) also conclude that increased inequality among principal earners contributed to the increase in family income inequality.

One consequence of the "tax decade" has been the opportunity to re-evaluate the impact of changes in marginal tax rates on individual behavior. Studies on the impact of ERTA and TRA have filled a number of edited volumes and special journal symposia.[24] It appears that an emerging consensus of this research is that the behavioral effects of taxes are in fact smaller than previously estimated (Aaron 1990; Slemrod 1992a). In his review of the lessons from the tax changes of the 1980s, Slemrod (1992a) marshals evidence against any strong responsiveness of savings, steady-state capital gains realizations, or investment to changes in the tax structure.[25] And as noted previously, the evidence of a significant labor supply effect is also far from conclusive. These considerations suggest that the efficiency costs of the tax system may not be as large as some have claimed, thereby providing a rationale for placing greater weight on the redistributive role of tax policy. Assuming that the current degree of tax progressivity is at or below the optimum, an argument in favor of a more progressive tax system can also be justified by the increased disparities in the returns to skill in the labor market, which in turn have contributed to the increased inequality in family incomes. The increased dispersion in returns to endowments implies a greater social welfare gain from increasing the progressivity of the tax system.

If there is an increased redistributive role for the tax system, to what extent can changes in the degree of progressivity affect the distribution of income? As noted earlier, the rise in pre-tax inequality is substantial and dominates the effect of reductions in the progressivity of the tax system in the last decade. Nevertheless, can the tax system serve to counteract the trend in pre-tax inequality? One answer is provided by Gramlich et al. (1993): They report the results of simulating a set of progressive changes in the tax system, including a rise in the top marginal tax rate from 28% to 50% and a doubling of the EITC, among other changes. However, the combined set of changes, equivalent to a $50 billion reduction in the 1991 deficit, is estimated to have only a modest impact on post-tax post-transfer inequality. In their simulations, the reduction in the Gini coefficient accounts for about 15% of the rise in the post-tax Gini coefficient since 1980. Gramlich et al.'s estimates of the impact of tax changes introduced in the 1990 Omnibus Reconciliation Act show an extremely small effect, estimated to be less than a 1% reduction in the Gini coefficient.

[24] See e.g. Aaron et al. (1988), Slemrod (1990a), and *The Journal of Economic Perspectives,* Summer 1987 and Winter 1992 issues.

[25] Slemrod's caveats include the possibility that time-series studies of the effect of tax changes will not reveal an impact if the combined changes in the tax system had off-setting effects on individual behavior. In addition, individuals may be slow to respond to the new tax environment, so that the long-run impact is not yet fully evident in the data available to date.

If these estimates are correct, then there may be little opportunity to use the tax system to redress the rise in pre-tax income inequality that has occurred since the 1970s. Although changes in the degree of progressivity of the tax system may be justified on other grounds, it is not clear that they can be used to significantly counteract other factors – such as family composition changes and the changing wage structure – that have contributed to increased disparities in the distribution of income.

REFERENCES

Aaron, Henry J. (1990), "Lessons for Tax Reform," in Slemrod (1990a).

Aaron, Henry J., et al., eds. (1988), *Uneasy Compromise: Problems of a Hybrid Income-Consumption Tax*. Washington, DC: Brookings.

Blackburn, McKinley L. (1989), "Interpreting the Magnitude of Changes in Measures of Income Inequality," *Journal of Econometrics* 42: 21–5.

Blackburn, McKinley L., and David Bloom (1987), "Earnings and Income Inequality in the United States," *Population and Development Review* 13: 575–609.

Blank, Rebecca, and Alan Blinder (1986), "Macroeconomics, Income Distribution and Poverty," in Sheldon Danziger and Daniel Weinberg (eds.), *Fighting Poverty: What Works and What Doesn't*. Cambridge, MA: Harvard University Press.

Bloom, David E., and Richard B. Freeman (1992), "The Fall in Private Pension Coverage in the United States," *American Economic Review* 82: 539–45.

Bosworth, Barry, and Gary Burtless (1992), "Effects of Tax Reform on Labor Supply, Investment and Saving," *Journal of Economic Perspectives* 6: 3–25.

Bureau of the Census (1989), *Money Income of Households, Families, and Persons in the United States: 1987*. Current Population Reports, Series P-60, No. 162. Washington, DC: Government Printing Office.

(1992a), *Measuring the Effect of Benefits and Taxes on Income and Poverty: 1979 to 1991*. Current Population Reports, Series P-60, No. 182-RD. Washington, DC: Government Printing Office.

(1992b), *Money Income of Households, Families, and Persons in the United States: 1987*. Current Population Reports, Series P-60, No. 180. Washington, DC: Government Printing Office.

Cancian, Maria, Sheldon Danziger, and Peter Gottschalk (1993), "Working Wives and Family Income Inequality among Married Couples," in Sheldon Danziger and Peter Gottschalk (eds.), *Uneven Tides: Rising Inequality in America*. New York: Russell Sage Foundation.

Committee on Ways and Means, U.S. House of Representatives (1991), "Trends in Family Income and Income Inequality," in *Background Material and Data on Programs within the Jurisdiction of the Committee on Ways and Means*. Washington, DC: Government Printing Office.

Congressional Budget Office (CBO) (1987), *The Changing Distribution of Federal Taxes: 1975–1990*. Washington, DC: Government Printing Office.

Council of Economic Advisors (1992), *Economic Report of the President*. Washington, DC: Government Printing Office.

Cutler, David M., and Lawrence F. Katz (1991), "Macroeconomic Performance and the Disadvantaged," *Brookings Papers on Economic Activity* 1991: 1–61.

Fichtenbaum, Rudy, and Hushang Shahidi (1988), "Truncation Bias and the Measurement of Income Inequality," *Journal of Business and Economic Statistics* 6: 335-7.

Galper, Harvey, Robert Lucke, and Eric Toder (1988), "A General Equilibrium Analysis of Tax Reform," in Aaron, et al. (1988).

Gramlich, Edward M., Richard Kasten, and Frank Sammartino (1993). "Growing Inequality in the 1980s: the Role of Federal Taxes and Cash Transfers," in Sheldon Danziger and Peter Gottschalk (eds.), *Uneven Tides: Rising Inequality in America*. New York: Russell Sage Foundation.

Gravelle, Jane G. (1992), "Equity Effects of the Tax Reform Act of 1986," *Journal of Economic Perspectives* 6: 27-44.

Hausman, Jerry A. (1981), "Income and Payroll Tax Policy and Labor Supply," in Laurence H. Meyer (ed.), *Supply-Side Effects of Economic Policy*. Boston: Kluwer-Nijhoff.

   (1983), "Stochastic Problems in the Simulation of Labor Supply," in Martin Feldstein (ed.), *Behavioral Simulation Methods in Tax Policy Analysis*. Chicago: University of Chicago Press.

Hausman, Jerry A., and James M. Poterba (1987), "Household Behavior and the Tax Reform Act of 1986," *Journal of Economic Perspectives* 1: 101-19.

Kakwani, Nanak C. (1980), *Income Inequality and Poverty*. New York: Oxford University Press.

Karoly, Lynn A. (1993), "The Trend in Inequality among Families, Individuals, and Workers in the United States: a Twenty-five Year Perspective," in Sheldon Danziger and Peter Gottschalk (eds.), *Uneven Tides: Rising Inequality in America*. New York: Russell Sage Foundation.

Lerman, Robert I., and Shlomo Yitzhaki (1984), "A Note on the Calculation and Interpretation of the Gini Index," *Economic Letters* 15: 363-8.

   (1985), "Income Inequality Effects by Income Source: a New Approach and Applications to the United States," *Review of Economics and Statistics* 67: 151-6.

   (1989), "Improving the Accuracy of Estimates of Gini Coefficients," *Journal of Econometrics* 42: 43-7.

Levy, Frank, and Richard J. Murnane (1992), "Earnings Levels and Earnings Inequality: a Review of Recent Trends and Proposed Explanations." *Journal of Economic Literature* 30: 1333-81.

Lindsey, Lawrence (1990), *The Growth Experience*. New York: Basic Books.

Michel, Richard C. (1991), "Economic Growth and Income Equality Since the 1982 Recession," *Journal of Policy Analysis and Management* 10: 181-203.

Pechman, Joseph A. (1987), "Tax Reform: Theory and Practice," *Journal of Economic Perspectives* 1: 11-28.

   (1990), "The Future of the Income Tax." *American Economic Review* 80: 1-20.

Ruggles, Patricia (1990), *Drawing the Line: Alternative Poverty Measures and Their Implications for Public Policy*. Washington, DC: Urban Institute.

Ruggles, Patricia, and Charles F. Stone (1992), "Income Distribution over the Business Cycle: the 1980s Were Different," *Journal of Policy Analysis and Management* 11: 709-15.

Ryscavage, Paul (1992), "Working Wives and Growing 'Household' Income Inequality," Paper presented at the 1992 Western Economics Association meetings, San Francisco.

Sawhill, Isabel V., and Mark Condon (1992), "Is U.S. Income Inequality Really Growing?" *Policy Bites* (June). Washington, DC: Urban Institute.

Slemrod, Joel (1983), "Do We Know How Progrerssive the Income Tax System Should Be?" *National Tax Journal* 36: 361–9.

ed. (1990a), *Do Taxes Matter? The Impact of the Tax Reform Act of 1986.* Cambridge, MA: MIT Press.

(1990b), "Optimal Taxation and Optimal Tax Systems," *Journal of Economic Perspectives* 4: 157–78.

(1992a), "Do Taxes Matter? Lessons from the 1980s," Working Paper no. 4008, National Bureau of Economic Research, Cambridge, MA.

(1992b), "Taxation and Inequality: a Time-exposure Perspective," in James M. Poterba (ed.), *Tax Policy and the Economy,* vol. 6. Cambridge, MA: MIT Press.

Steuerle, C. Eugene (1992), *The Tax Decade: How Taxes Came to Dominate the Public Agenda.* Washington, DC: Urban Institute Press.

Webb, Randall L., Richard C. Michel, and Anne B. Bergsman (1990), "The Historical Development of the Transfer Income Model (TRIM2)," in G. H. Lewis and R. C. Michel (eds.), *Microsimulation Techniques for Tax and Transfer Analysis.* Washington, DC: Urban Institute.

Comments

David M. Cutler

This paper is a very nice synopsis of the literature on inequality and its implications for tax policy. The paper has three parts. First, it discusses recent trends in inequality, concluding that inequality has grown enormously. Second, it asks whether tax policy has caused the increased inequality, and concludes that it has not. Third, it considers whether there are tax policies that would reduce inequality, and decides that increasing taxes on the rich may make us feel better but would have little effect on inequality.

I mostly agree with the paper. The empirical work in the first half is sensibly done and convincing, and the conclusions about tax policy seem appropriate. I want to comment on the three parts, however, and ultimately suggest that there are some tax policies that may reduce inequality.

1   Trends in income inequality

The best way to think about income distribution, it seems to me, is to divide the population into three groups: the very rich (the top 5 percent of the population); the very poor (the bottom 10 percent of the population); and the middle class (the remaining 85 percent). I make this distinction because I think that policy toward the very top of the distribution must confront issues it does not in the middle of the distribution (substantial business and capital income, greater mobility of resources), and because the problems of the very poor probably go beyond having jobs that don't pay much.

In the tripartite distinction, Karoly's paper is decidedly about the middle class. This is both because surveys have low representation at the top and bottom and because the author focuses on a measure of inequality (the Gini coefficient) which underweights movements at the tails of the distribution and overweights movements in the middle.

The conclusion about middle-class inequality in the paper is that increased inequality is largely due to the trend away from single-earner

130

families and toward multiple-earner families, to the increase in head-of-household income inequality, and to an increase in capital income, particularly interest on the government debt and corporate dividend payments.

Although I think these are the important factors, I would have placed more weight on the increase in head-of-household income inequality and less on the other two. First, one should note that two-thirds of the rise in inequality is accounted for by the increase in head-of-household inequality (Table 4); all the rest together is only one-third of the rise in inequality.

Second, looking at inequality by source of income may be inappropriate in analyzing some changes in the labor force. For example, increased women's labor-force participation will increase the spouse's share of income and thus inequality, as is noted in the paper. However, it will also lower the share of income received by the head of household and thus reduce inequality. Focusing only on the first effect overstates the inequality consequences of increased labor-force participation. These two effects can be weighted in a calculation of the total effect of increased women's labor-force participation on inequality, but that calculation is not reported here. I suspect the true effect of changes in labor-force participation on inequality is smaller than what is claimed.

Finally, one should be more cautious than Karoly is about the rise in capital income. Some of the increased capital income is increased income on government debt, which is generally received by the rich. The true incidence of the public debt, however, depends also on who will ultimately pay for it. If that too is the rich then we are just counting the interest stream now that will be taxed in the future. We may not want to do that.

In a similar vein, the other part of capital income is increased corporate dividend payments. This, it seems to me, is more an issue of bad data than of true increases in inequality. The share of national income accruing to owners of capital has not changed. Instead, more of capital income is being distributed as dividends and less is being retained by corporations. Since dividends show up as income on the CPS but retained earnings do not, this looks like more income for the rich. Correctly measured, however, it is not (for more on this, see Cutler and Katz 1991). Perhaps we should remove capital income entirely when we look at income inequality.

Even with these caveats, the author's conclusions about increased inequality are surely right, as is the conclusion that most of the increased inequality is due to changes in labor market income.

2   Was tax policy responsible?

The second part of the paper asks whether tax policy is the culprit for increased inequality. The most important mechanism in this case would

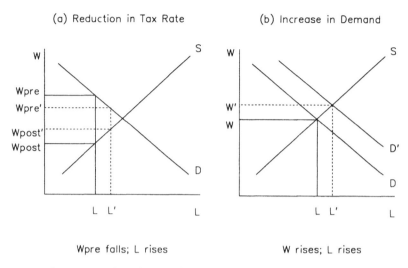

(a) Reduction in Tax Rate   (b) Increase in Demand

Wpre falls; L rises   W rises; L rises

Figure 1. Explanations for increased inequality.

be lower tax rates causing the rich to work harder, thus leading to a greater disparity in income between rich and poor. The paper finds this explanation unconvincing, and again I am in agreement.

The easiest way to address this issue, it seems to me, is with a standard model of tax incidence. Figure 1(a) shows how lower taxes on the rich would produce more inequality. At the initial tax rate, with pre-tax wage W_{pre} and post-tax wage W_{post}, an individual works L hours. If the tax rate falls labor supply would increase, as would post-tax income. Note, however, that the pre-tax wage will fall, because increased hours lower the marginal product of every hour. There is a clear prediction, therefore, that if declining tax rates cause an increase in inequality then people who work more should have lower pre-tax wages. This is in contrast to an explanation of greater demand for the output of rich people, detailed in Figure 1(b). If demand for this group increases, both pre-tax wages and hours of work will increase. We can thus test the demand versus the tax story by looking at the correlation of pre-tax wages and hours across groups of workers.

Such an analysis has been conducted by Lawrence Katz and Kevin Murphy (1992). Katz and Murphy first divide the labor force into 64 groups based on gender, age, education, and experience, and then examine mean wages and employment for each group. They find that, over the 1979–87 period, there is a strong positive correlation of 0.62 between increased wages and increased employment. This clearly suggests that demand is more important than taxes in explaining increased inequality.

An example illustrates how much larger demand shocks must be relative to supply shocks to generate these results. Imagine a simple labor market model (with variables in logarithms) as follows:

$$q_d = Z - w \text{ (demand)}$$

and

$$q_s = w - \theta \text{ (supply)},$$

where Z is exogenous demand and θ is the tax rate.

Some simple algebra shows that in this framework the correlation between the change in wages and the change in employment is

$$\rho = (\Delta Z^2 - \Delta \theta^2)/(\Delta Z^2 + \Delta \theta^2).$$

With the estimated correlation of 0.62, the ratio of the variability of demand shocks to tax shocks ($\Delta Z^2/\Delta \theta^2$) is about 4.26 – that is, demand shocks are over four times more important than tax shocks in explaining increased inequality. Even this is likely to be an underestimate, since the correlation is probably measured with error and since I have assumed unit labor supply and demand elasticities when the true elasticities are surely much smaller.

Much research in the labor literature is directed at sorting out the sources of demand shocks for high-wage earners. That literature has largely ignored the role of tax policy, and it seems to me that decision is substantially correct.

3   Is there a role for tax policy?

The last part of the paper suggests that there is little role for tax policy in addressing issues of increased inequality; this is where I have the most disagreement. Karoly writes about tax policy for the middle class (as I define it) and for the wealthy. It is surely true that the taxes required to offset increased inequality for these groups are far too large to undertake.

However, the author ignores tax policy for the very poor. This, I think, is the issue that we really need to worry about. In the AFDC program, for example, the statutory "tax rate" on earnings (the reduction in benefits for each dollar of earned income) is 100%. The true tax rate is probably even larger, however, since working individuals may lose their benefits for food stamps, housing assistance, or Medicaid.

The consequence of these large tax rates is an extremely low labor supply for welfare recipients. Robert Moffitt (1992) reports that only 6% of women on AFDC work, compared to 54% of all female heads of households with children under 18. That number is an all-time low – about 10 percentage points below the level in the late 1970s.

There are clearly policies that, at the same program cost, could lead to more income for the poor. Policies such as earned income tax credits, which subsidize rather than tax work, are a prime example. This alone would reduce inequality. In addition, if one believes in "neighborhood" or peer-group effects – where people are influenced by the actions of those around them – then policies that encourage work could lead to more work even by those not receiving benefits. The research on these types of policies is only in its infancy. It seems to me, however, that tax policy directed at the lower end of the distribution is more important for inequality than tax policy directed at the middle class or very rich.

REFERENCES

Cutler, David M., and Lawrence F. Katz (1991), "Macroeconomic Performance and the Disadvantaged," *Brookings Papers on Economic Activity* 1991: 1–74.
Katz, Lawrence F., and Kevin Murphy (1992), "Changes in Relative Wages: Supply and Demand Factors," *Quarterly Journal of Economics* 108: 35–78.
Moffit, Robert (1992), "Incentive Effects of the U.S. Welfare System: A Review," *Journal of Economic Literature* 30: 1–61.

General discussion

Shackelford commented that inequality occurs because the brightest marry the brightest.

Burtless remarked that the spouse's income is quite important and that head–spouse correlation drives income inequality. He claimed that the labor demand explanation of growing inequality is much more compelling than the tax explanation.

Slemrod stated that reduced estimates of behavioral response do not imply that taxes should be more progressive than they are now, only more progressive than otherwise; the same holds true for increased inequality in the ability to earn pre-tax income. On the other hand, the increase in international competitiveness means a decreased ability of any one country to tax capital and an overall less progressive system than in a closed economy, other things being equal.

Sheffrin questioned how Karoly's findings compare to earlier periods – in particular, the 1920s – and other countries. He suggested that the results be put into historical perspective.

Hite questioned how the progressivity measure differs if one treats the head of household in isolation versus the household as a whole.

Steuerle remarked that there is more dispersion over time *within* a family in two-earner as opposed to one-earner households. Steuerle questioned the appropriate measure of the poverty line, observing that the adjustment for family size needs to recognize the returns to scale within the family.

Musgrave stated that one can't get away from a high marginal tax rate on low-income individuals if one wants a steep rise in the effective tax rate over the lower–middle range of the income scale.

Slemrod commented that deficits have allowed us to postpone recognizing the personal incidence of government expenditure.

Karoly responded that in order to study female earners, she would like more data on their movements in and out of the labor force.

CHAPTER 5

The efficiency cost of increased progressivity

Robert K. Triest

1   Introduction

In considering the optimal degree of income-tax progressivity, economists and policymakers have long been concerned with the effect of taxation on labor supply. The disincentive effect of taxation on labor supply played a central role in discussions regarding the desirability of introducing a negative income-tax system in the 1970s, and was part of the motivation for the "supply-side" tax cuts in the early 1980s. Most models of optimal income taxation depend critically on the response of labor supply to taxation. Increased income-tax progressivity comes at the cost of increased distortion in individuals' choice of hours of work. Policymakers must decide on what trade-off between equality and efficiency they are willing to accept in determining the progressivity of the tax system. In general, the more responsive labor supply is to economic incentives, the greater will be the efficiency cost of increased progressivity.

Owing to the pivotal role of labor supply in tax-and-transfer policy discussions, a voluminous literature attempting to estimate how labor supply responds to economic incentives grew during the 1970s and 1980s. A much smaller literature has developed that uses labor supply estimates to attempt to quantify the trade-off between equality and efficiency which exists in the United States. In an influential study, Browning and Johnson (1984) estimate that it costs those in the top three quintiles of the income distribution $3.49 in reduced economic well-being when the U.S. tax-and-transfer system is used to increase the welfare of those in the bottom two

This is a revised version of a paper prepared for the Office of Tax Policy Research Conference on Tax Progressivity, University of Michigan, September 11-12, 1992. I would like to thank Charles Ballard, Gary Burtless, Joel Slemrod, Steven Sheffrin, conference participants, participants at the November 1992 National Tax Association/Tax Institute of America annual conference, and several referees for very helpful comments.

137

income quintiles by $1. In other words, there is an efficiency cost equal to $2.49 per dollar transferred to the lower income groups. Their estimate is based on a simulation in which the marginal tax rate on labor income is increased by 1 percentage point for all households (each household faces a linear budget constraint); the resulting increase in revenue is then distributed in the form of equal per-capita cash grants ("demogrants").

Ballard (1988) estimates a much lower efficiency cost of increasing progressivity through the use of a similar tax-increase–demogrant scheme. In the simulations he puts the most emphasis on, the efficiency cost of transferring $1 from the upper-income groups to the lower-income groups is between 50¢ and $1.30. Ballard also investigates the cost of increasing progressivity through use of a "notch grant" program, in which a cash grant for low-income groups is financed by increasing the marginal tax rate faced by higher-income groups (assignment to an income group is exogenous and all individuals face linear budget constraints), and through use of a wage subsidy for low-income workers (again, assignment to the low-income category is exogenous and all individuals face linear budget constraints). Ballard estimates that the efficiency cost of both of these programs is much smaller than for the demogrant policy, and is close to zero for the wage subsidy program.

In this paper, I re-examine the issue of the efficiency cost of increased progressivity. My analysis differs from earlier work on this question in allowing for complex nonlinear tax schedules similar to those which actually exist. I also incorporate the results of recent research on the effect of taxation on labor supply which suggests that labor supply may be less responsive to taxation than had previously been thought. I find that the efficiency cost of increased progressivity varies considerably with the type of tax reform considered. Using the labor supply parameters I consider most reasonable, I find that the efficiency cost of increasing progressivity by expanding the earned income tax credit (EITC) is less than twenty cents per dollar transferred from the upper-income groups to lower-income groups when it is financed by increasing tax rates in the intermediate brackets. Increasing the tax rates that apply only to upper-income taxpayers results in a higher efficiency cost of increased progressivity. Two alternative means of increasing tax progressivity, a general refundable tax-credit program and increasing the value of the personal exemption, also have higher efficiency costs.

The next section reviews recent work analyzing the effect of taxation on labor supply. Section 3 outlines the simulation methodology that I use to investigate the economic cost of increased progressivity. The simulation results are presented and analyzed in Section 4. Section 5 concludes the paper with a brief summary of the findings.

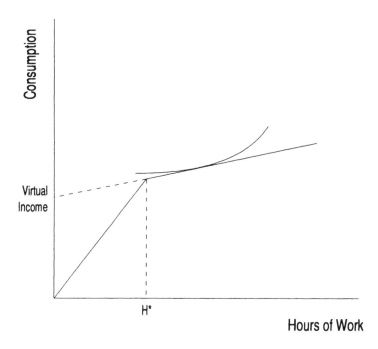

Figure 1. Labor supply with a two-bracket earnings tax.

2   Recent work estimating the effect of taxation on labor supply

Research analyzing the effect of taxation on labor supply has increasingly adopted a methodology, originated by Burtless and Hausman (1978),
which takes full account of the way in which tax-and-transfer programs
affect individuals' budget constraints. A recent exposition of this methodology is provided by Moffitt (1990). An important insight gained from
the development of this method is that an income-tax system with marginal tax rates that vary with taxable income combines a reduction in the
net wage with an implicit lump-sum subsidy equal to the difference between the tax an individual *would* pay, if she faced her current marginal
tax rate over the full range of taxable income, and the tax she actually
does have to pay. Burtless and Hausman (1978) called the sum of non-
earned income and the implicit lump-sum subsidy "virtual income," since
an individual located in a given tax bracket is acting as though she has
unearned income equal to her actual nonlabor income plus the lump-sum
subsidy implicit in the tax system. This is illustrated in Figure 1, which is

an indifference-curve diagram depicting the labor supply decision of an individual who has no unearned income and is subject to a simple two-bracket earnings tax (with the marginal tax rate in the second bracket greater than the marginal tax rate in the first bracket). The individual is in the first tax bracket when she works less than H^* hours. When the individual works H^* hours, her taxable income puts her on the border between the two tax brackets. When she works more than H^* hours, she is in the second tax bracket. Her net wage is then lower than it was in the first bracket, and she acts as though she were receiving an implicit lump-sum subsidy equal to that labeled "virtual income" in the diagram.

In an influential study, Hausman (1981) estimated a fairly large (and negative) income effect for married men. Although Hausman estimated an uncompensated wage effect that was very close to zero, he found that the 1975 U.S. tax system resulted in a large decrease in male labor supply through the virtual income effect. However, more recent work estimating the impact of income taxation on male labor supply has generally tended to find fairly small effects. In a paper (Triest 1990) where I estimated a specification very similar to that of Hausman (1981), I estimated the uncompensated wage elasticity of married American men to be 0.06 when evaluated at sample mean values; this compares to an elasticity of less than 0.01 estimated by Hausman.[1] I estimated an income elasticity of zero, much smaller than Hausman's (1981) estimate of -0.17.[2] MaCurdy, Green, and Paarsch (1990) also found that male labor supply is largely unresponsive to economic incentives. When they imposed parameter restrictions ensuring the nonnegativity of the compensated wage elasticity, both the wage and income elasticities were driven to zero. One interpretation of their results is that male labor supply is completely insensitive to economic incentives.

It is not particularly surprising to find that parameter restrictions need to be imposed to prevent the estimated compensated wage elasticity from being negative. In a recent survey of the male labor supply literature, Pencavel (1986) provides a table summarizing the results of fourteen male labor supply studies using non-experimental U.S. data. Six of the fourteen studies estimate compensated labor supply elasticities that are either zero or negative. However, to some degree this is probably due to the failure of some of these studies to properly account for the effect of taxation. As Hausman (1985) notes, ignoring taxation will induce a downward bias in the estimate of the uncompensated wage elasticity.

---

[1] Elasticity estimates for Hausman (1981) are from Hausman (1985).

[2] The income coefficient was constrained to be nonpositive in this estimation. However, based on a Lagrange multiplier test, I was unable to reject the hypothesis that the true coefficient was zero.

Burtless (1987) reviews the results from labor supply studies using data from the income maintenance experiments of the late 1960s through early 1980s. He reports that male uncompensated wage elasticities estimated using experimental data are clustered tightly around zero; compensated wage elasticities average about 0.08. Overall, data from the income maintenance experiments indicate that male labor supply is not very responsive to economic incentives.

Bosworth and Burtless (1992) construct time series based on microdata from the Current Population Survey in an effort to determine the effect of the Reagan-era tax changes on labor supply. They find that male labor supply is 6% higher in 1989 than it would have been had the trend from 1967–80 continued through 1989. While this provides some support for the view that the decreases in marginal tax rates during the 1980s stimulated labor supply, the distribution of the increase in hours by income quintile does not. Men in the bottom quintile increased their labor supply (relative to trend) more than did those in other quintiles, both in absolute and percentage terms. Bosworth and Burtless note that low-income men faced constant or rising marginal tax rates during most of the 1980s. Thus, it is hard to draw any conclusion from this evidence regarding the effect of the 1981 and 1986 tax changes.

Overall, the bulk of the evidence on male labor supply suggests that there are only minor incentive effects. Although it is important to take any incentive effects into account in analyzing possible tax- or transfer-program changes, one needs to view with some skepticism any efficiency cost calculations that are based on large male labor supply elasticities.

Female labor supply was long thought to be much more elastic than that of men, but this view has changed somewhat in recent years. Mroz (1987) finds that the large wage and income elasticities produced in many previous studies are the result of assumptions that can be statistically rejected: use of a standard tobit specification to control for self-selection into the labor force; treating the wage rate as exogenous; treating prior labor-force experience as exogenous. He concludes (p. 795) that ". . . economic factors such as wage rates, taxes, and nonlabor incomes have a small impact on the labor supply behavior of *working* married women." However, Mroz's results are consistent with economic factors having a large impact on the decision to participate in the labor force.

In estimating a model of married women's labor supply similar to that of Hausman (1981), I found that the estimation method used made a great deal of difference (Triest 1990). Including data on nonparticipants in the estimation resulted in uncompensated wage elasticities (evaluated at the sample means of women with positive hours of work) of approximately 0.9, and virtual income elasticities of about −0.3. Hausman (1981) estimated an uncompensated wage effect of similar magnitude, but a virtual income effect over twice as large. When I estimated the same specification but used only data on women with positive hours of work (with an appropriate statistical adjustment), the uncompensated wage elasticity fell to approximately 0.27 and the virtual income elasticity fell to about -0.16.

The decrease in the magnitude of the wage and income elasticities when one moves from a censored (including observations with zero hours of work) to a truncated (excluding such observations) specification is consistent with Mroz's (1987) work. Mroz similarly finds that wage and income elasticities drop in magnitude when switching from a censored to a truncated tobit specification (in a model without taxes). Moreover, he finds that the elasticities drop by an even larger amount when one switches from a truncated tobit specification to a more general self-selection correction. Mroz is able to reject both the censored and truncated tobit specifications in favor of the more general specification. This implies that even the relatively small elasticities I estimated using the truncated specification may be too high. However, it is important to recall that Mroz's results apply only to working women.

Burtless (1987), in summarizing the literature examining the effect of income maintenance experiments on female labor supply, notes that studies based on experimental data tend to produce much smaller wage elasticity estimates than do studies based on non-experimental data. For wives, the average uncompensated wage elasticity is approximately -0.04 in the experimental studies (0.07 when the studies are weighted to account for differences in sample size). In contrast, the average uncompensated wage elasticity in the non-experimental studies considered by Burtless was nearly 2.

Bosworth and Burtless (1992) attempt to measure the effect of 1980s tax changes on female labor supply in the same manner that they did for men. As with men, labor supply appears to have increased in the 1980s (relative to trend), with the largest increase in the lowest income quintile. However, unlike the case for men, there was a sizeable increase in hours of work for women in the top quintile. Although Bosworth and Burtless claim that "[i]t is likely that part of the estimated change among high-income women is attributable to marginal tax rate reductions" (p. 13), the increase in hours among low-income women casts some doubt on using this type of analysis to make inferences regarding the effect of tax policy. Nonetheless, it would be very surprising if marginal tax-rate decreases had no effect on the labor supply of women in the top quintile.

Overall, recent work on female labor supply has called into question the assumption that women's hours of work are highly responsive to economic incentives. In simulating the efficiency cost of progressivity, using low to moderate wage and income elasticities seems most reasonable.

All of the labor supply research reviewed in this section has taken the overall structure of the tax system as given. Changes in the range of deductible expenditures and other opportunities for tax avoidance have not been considered. However, the Tax Reform Act of 1986 changed much more than just the rate structure of the income tax. The response of labor supply to taxation may vary considerably depending on the opportunities for tax avoidance.[3] For this reason, one must be cautious in using labor supply estimates to analyze the effect of a tax reform that changes the tax base or opportunities for avoidance.

3   Simulation methodology

The main purpose of this paper is to explore the implications of labor supply research described in the previous section for the economic cost of increased progressivity. In order to do this, I first constructed a database using the Panel Study of Income Dynamics (PSID) data (Survey Research Center 1991). A budget constraint relating consumption and leisure was imputed to every PSID sample member. I then assumed a specific functional form for labor supply (which implies a functional form for the underlying preferences), calibrated the labor supply functions given four sets of possible behavioral parameters, and simulated the effects of various possible tax reforms that would tend to increase progressivity. The remainder of this section describes the simulation methodology in greater detail.

The data for the simulations come from wave XXI of the PSID. This wave was collected in 1988, but pertains to calendar year 1987. Family observations were selected if both the family head and spouse (if present) were between 20 and 60 years old. Only the income and labor supply of the family head and spouse are considered in the simulations. While this is restrictive, relatively little is known about the effect of taxation on other family members. The reason for imposing the age restriction is to avoid complications involved in modeling retirement behavior. To the extent that the labor supply of those over sixty is relatively inelastic, or influenced primarily by social security, private pensions, or health status, the omission of the elderly may result in an upward bias in the efficiency cost estimates.

[3] Triest (1992) finds that increasing the marginal tax rate faced by married male itemizers tends to increase their labor supply through the "price of deductible consumption" effect. Heckman (1983) outlines an alternative model of labor supply with endogenous tax avoidance.

For nonworkers, a wage was imputed based on a simple regression.[4] Non-earned taxable income was calculated based on federal tax imputations made by the PSID staff.[5] The PSID tax-payment imputations are fairly sophisticated, and allow itemized deductions to increase with income. In constructing the budget constraints facing potential workers, I treated eligibility for participation in AFDC (Aid to Families with Dependent Children) and food-stamp programs as exogenous. Families receiving any benefits from these programs in 1987 were considered eligible; others were considered ineligible. Given the complex eligibility rules and the fact that not all eligible families participate in these programs, I did not attempt to simulate the program participation decision. The tax reforms I consider do not increase the desirability of program participation, so treating eligibility as fixed should not be a serious problem. I assumed that AFDC benefits would be reduced 70 cents for every dollar earned, and that food stamps would be reduced by 30 cents for every additional dollar of income (including AFDC payments) received.[6] Food stamps were assumed to be valued by recipients at their face value. The eligibility rules and benefit-reduction rates for food stamps and AFDC are not based on an annual accounting period. In reality, families may spend only part of any given year participating in the program. In this case, their effective marginal tax rates would vary considerably over the year. My procedure, which assumes families are either participating or not participating for the entire year, should thus be viewed as a rough approximation.

One explanation of why the participation decision is more sensitive to economic incentives than is hours of work (given participation) is the existence of fixed costs associated with working. I assume that women face fixed monetary costs of working, which vary with family size and the number of young children according to a function estimated by Hausman (1981).[7] Women are assumed to incur this cost with the first hour of work.

---

[4] The natural log of the wage (of labor-force participants) was regressed on a five-part spline based on years of education, a five-part spline based on years of potential labor market experience, and marital status. Separate regressions were run for men and women. The imputed wage was set equal to the exponential of the sum of the predicted log wage plus one-half the variance of the regression error. This is a consistent predictor under the assumption that the error in the log wage regression is homoskedastic and has a normal distribution. No correction was made for possible problems of selection bias. Further details are available on request.

[5] Starting from the PSID variable for federal taxes paid, I calculated taxable income by using the inverse of the statutory federal tax function.

[6] The effective benefit-reduction rate in the AFDC program has been estimated to average 0.7, even though the statutory rate is 1 (Burtless 1990).

[7] Hausman (1981) estimated that married women incur a fixed cost associated with working equal to $1,213 plus $172 times the number of children (less than 6) minus $212 times family size. For female heads of households, fixed costs are estimated to be $1,350 plus

Table 1. *1987 U.S. federal individual income tax*

Gross income range ($)	Marginal tax rate (%)	Implicit lump-sum transfer ($)
0–10,850	0	0
10,850–13,850	11	1,193
13,850–38,850	15	1,747
38,850–55,850	28	6,798
55,850–100,850	35	10,707
Over 100,850	38.5	14,237

Note: This table is accurate only for married couples filing jointly who are eligible for three exemptions and who do not itemize deductions or have other adjustments to income.

Hopefully, incorporation of fixed costs into the simulations results in a realistic model of the participation decision even in scenarios with low assumed wage and income elasticities.

It is difficult to know how to treat the social security payroll tax. To some extent, workers may view the tax as contributions toward the purchase of an annuity they will receive after retiring. The degree to which it is rational for a worker to view social security in this way depends on the worker's age, sex, earnings stream, and expectations of having a dependent spouse after retiring (Feldstein and Samwick 1992). As a crude approximation, I assume that workers treat the employee-paid part of the tax as a true tax, and ignore the employer-paid portion. In 1987, the employee-paid combined social security and Medicare tax rate was 0.0715 on earnings up to $43,800 and zero on earnings above that amount.

The earned income tax credit plays an important role in many of the simulations. In 1987, workers could receive a tax credit equal to 14% of the first $6,080 of their earnings. The credit was reduced by 10 cents for every dollar by which the greater of adjusted gross income (AGI) or earnings exceeded $6,920. The credit was reduced to zero at an earnings or AGI level of $15,432.

The 1987 U.S. federal individual income tax had six brackets, with marginal tax ranging from 0% to 38.5%. Table 1 shows the rate schedule (as a function of gross income) applicable for a married couple filing

$660 times the number of children (less than 6 years old) minus $654 times family size. Since Hausman's estimates are in terms of 1975 dollars, they were inflated to 1987 levels using the consumer price index.

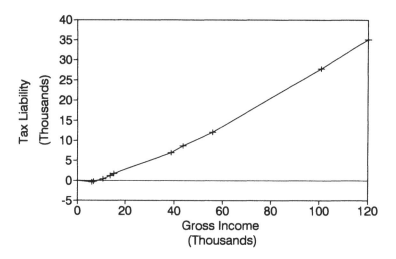

Figure 2. 1987 U.S. federal taxation. *Note:* This figure shows the federal individual income tax liability plus the employee-paid portion of the
social security and Medicare tax for married couples filing jointly who
are eligible for three exemptions and for the earned income tax credit,
who do not itemize deductions or have other adjustments to income,
who have no unearned income, and who have only a single wage earner.

jointly who are eligible for three exemptions, who do not itemize deductions, and who do not have other adjustments to income. The third column in this table displays the implicit lump-sum subsidy (virtual income
adjustment) for each tax bracket. Figure 2 shows how tax liability varies
with gross income (for a couple with the same characteristics assumed
in Table 1, and making the additional assumptions of their having no
unearned income and only a single wage earner), taking into account the
combined effects of the federal individual income tax, the earned income
tax credit, and the employee-paid part of the social security and Medicare tax.

Household heads and spouses are assumed to have preferences (each
spouse with a separate utility function) that result in desired hours of
work h being a linear function of the net wage w and virtual income y:[8]

$$h = \gamma + \alpha w + \beta y.$$

This functional form was chosen because it has often been estimated.
Thus, it is easy to pick α and β values (which are allowed to vary by sex)

---

[8] As noted by Hausman (1981), the indirect utility function implied by this specification is
$v(w, y) = e^{\beta w}[y + (\alpha/\beta)w - \alpha/\beta^2 + \gamma/\beta]$.

that are consistent with previous empirical work. The intercept term γ is allowed to vary over individuals. For each individual (and for each set of assumed α and β values), the intercept is set by finding the value of γ such that the observed value of h is locally optimal.[9] After the γ values are determined, the observed values of h are checked to see if they are consistent with global utility maximization. When a value of h yields higher utility than the observed value, it is substituted for the observed value.[10]

In the case of married couples, each husband was assumed to make his labor supply decision ignoring the hours-of-work decision of his wife. Each wife was assumed to make her labor supply decision taking the hours of work of her husband as fixed.[11] These assumptions are often made in the labor supply literature and simplify the simulations, but they are unlikely to be accurate; future research should incorporate a more realistic model of household decisionmaking.

The simulations consist of specifying a particular tax-policy parameter change (such as increasing the 15% federal rate to 16%) and then allowing another policy parameter (such as the range over which the 14-percent bracket of the earned income tax credit is applicable) to change by the extent necessary to maintain the same total amount of revenue raised as in the original situation.[12] Decreases in transfer payments due to increases in hours worked are counted as tax-revenue increases.

[9] In the case of nonworkers, the maximum value of γ consistent with nonparticipation being optimal is found first. A draw from an assumed distribution for γ (truncated from above at the maximum value consistent with nonparticipation) is then generated. This draw is then used as the nonparticipant's γ value. The assumed distribution for γ is based on parameter estimates in Triest (1990), and varies by sex.

[10] The procedure for picking γ results in the observed value of h being consistent with local (given the segment of the budget constraint) utility maximization but does not ensure that the observed value of h is consistent with global (given the entire budget set) utility maximization, owing to the existence of nonconvex regions of the budget set (which result from the fixed cost of working, AFDC, food stamps, the earned income tax credit, and the social security tax). See Moffitt (1986) for an exposition of the complications caused by nonconvex budget sets. Whenever the observed h value was inconsistent with global utility maximization (given the values of γ, α, and β), I solved for the utility-maximizing value of h and then substituted that for the observed value. For parameter set 1, this was done for 8 (unweighted) men (out of 3,863 total) and for 147 (out of 3,441) women. For parameter set 2, this was done for 73 women but no men; for parameter set 3, this was done for 8 men and 396 women; for parameter set 4, this was done for 126 men and 427 women. The number of observations where the observed value of h must be replaced varies with the parameter set chosen, since the size of the interval around a nonconvex kink point that is inconsistent with utility maximization increases with the magnitude of the compensated wage elasticity.

[11] Although wives are assumed to take their husbands' labor supply as fixed, husbands' earnings are not included in wives' virtual income; this avoids double counting of husbands' earnings in the welfare-change calculations.

[12] The PSID family-level sample weights were used in all tax-revenue calculations.

Table 2. *Parameter sets*

	Parameter set			
	1	2	3	4
Male net wage coefficient	12.4	0	12.4	5.35
Male virtual income coefficient	0	0	0	−0.054
Female net wage coefficient	64.1	32	206.2	218.2
Female virtual income coefficient	−0.0097	−0.0049	−0.019	−0.042

4   Tax progressivity simulations

Table 2 displays the four sets of labor supply parameters used in the simulations; the last lines of Tables 4a (for men) and 4b (for women) display the net wage elasticities and virtual income elasticities (evaluated at the sample means) for the four parameter sets. Set 1 consists of parameters estimated in my 1990 paper, adjusted for the change in the consumer price index. The coefficients for women are from a specification using data only on those with positive hours of work.[13] I take this set of parameters as the base case. The male labor supply parameters in parameter set 2 are those estimated by MaCurdy et al. (1990) in their "Slutsky constrained differentiable budget constraint" specification. The female labor supply parameters are equal to one-half the values in parameter set 1. Parameter set 2 is meant to represent lower-bound estimates of the responsiveness of labor supply to taxation. The male labor supply parameters in parameter set 3 are the same as those in set 1, while the parameters for women are those I estimated using a censored tobit-like specification (using data on both participants and nonparticipants). Parameter set 4 is based on estimates by Hausman (1981), adjusted for changes in the price level. This set of parameters represents an upper bound to plausible estimates of the responsiveness of labor supply to income taxation.

In order to allow for differences by family size in the cost of reaching a given level of economic well-being, I adjust the after–tax-and-transfer income of the family head and spouse using a crude equivalence scale. Based on the federal poverty scales, Cutler and Katz (1992) estimate that the number of equivalent persons per family is equal to $(A + 0.76K)^{0.61}$, where A is number of adults and K is number of children. I use after–tax-

---

[13] The econometric procedure used to estimate these parameters took account of the truncation of the subsample used for estimation.

and-transfer income per equivalent person (calculated using the Cutler and Katz estimates) as the basis for sorting families into deciles of the income distribution. Table 3 presents descriptive statistics by decile of after–tax-and-transfer income per equivalent person. "Selected transfers" in this table is equal to the sum of AFDC, Supplemental Security Income (SSI), food stamps, and social security benefits. Note that the mean marginal tax rate decreases over the first four deciles, and then increases with income thereafter. Families in the bottom two income deciles often face very high benefit-reduction rates (implicit marginal tax rates) in the AFDC and food-stamp programs. The earned income tax credit (EITC) reduces the overall marginal tax rate at very low levels of income, but increases the marginal tax rate by 10 percentage points at slightly higher levels of income as the credit is phased out. Since not all families are eligible for AFDC, food stamps, or the EITC, there is a high degree of heterogeneity in the marginal tax rates faced by lower-income families.

One feature of the linear labor supply specification adopted in this study which merits attention is that the magnitude of the net wage and virtual income elasticities increase with, respectively, the net wage and virtual income. Since the mean net wage and virtual income values increase with adjusted (using the equivalence scale) family income, the labor supply elasticities also tend to increase with adjusted family income. In Tables 4a and 4b, the labor supply elasticities implied by the four parameter sets are displayed by deciles of adjusted family income. The pattern of elasticities increasing with family income implies that the linear labor supply specification is "biased" against tax reforms that increase marginal tax rates on very high-income groups. A constant elasticity specification (with elasticities equal to the mean values of the elasticities from the linear specification) would show a smaller deadweight loss due to increasing the marginal tax rate on upper-income groups.

The first progressivity-increasing reform I consider is using a 1–percentage-point increase in the 1987 15% and 28% federal marginal tax rates to widen the range of earnings over which the earned income tax credit increases (at a rate of 14%); the range of income where the EITC is phased out (at a rate of 10%) is also increased in this reform. The effect of this reform on an individual's budget constraint is shown in Figure 3. The individual (who is assumed to have no unearned income, to be eligible for the EITC, to be ineligible for food stamps and AFDC, and to face no fixed costs associated with working) enjoys the 14% EITC subsidy rate over a longer range of hours of work, but is also subject to the 10% EITC phase-out rate over a wider range of hours. The decreased slope of the budget constraint at higher values of hours of work reflects the increase in the 15% marginal tax rate to 16%, and the increase in the 28% rate to

Table 3. *Mean values by decile*

Decile	Income range ($)	Income per equivalent person ($)	Family income ($)	Percent married	Number of children	Total earnings ($)	Asset income ($)	Selected transfers ($)	Tax payments ($)	Marginal tax rate (%)
1	0–6,868	4,483	7,554	43	1.2	5,775	185	1,413	−522	29
2	6,869–9,324	8,099	14,001	61	1.3	13,896	466	550	1,696	26
3	9,324–11,630	10,515	18,322	68	1.2	19,684	957	143	3,186	24
4	11,631–14,183	12,955	22,965	74	1.2	24,804	1,188	232	4,181	23
5	14,185–16,412	15,349	25,897	73	1.0	28,200	1,374	282	4,949	25
6	16,415–19,005	17,647	30,780	77	1.1	33,744	2,216	189	6,362	29
7	19,005–22,319	20,662	34,314	77	0.8	38,647	2,250	156	7,693	31
8	22,323–26,517	24,335	39,152	73	0.7	44,545	3,312	12	9,627	36
9	26,544–34,192	29,897	46,946	76	0.5	54,533	3,576	41	12,612	38
10	34,244–285,771	50,118	77,135	77	0.4	83,558	16,842	40	24,367	41
Overall		19,417	31,723	70	0.9	34,756	3,242	306	7,421	30

Table 4a. *Male labor supply elasticities*

Decile	Hours of work	Net wage ($/hr)	Virtual income ($)	Parameter set 1		Parameter set 2		Parameter set 3		Parameter set 4	
				Wage	Income	Wage	Income	Wage	Income	Wage	Income
1	1,556	3.52	2,741	0.03	0.00	0.00	0.00	0.03	0.00	0.01	-0.10
2	1,969	5.27	2,997	0.03	0.00	0.00	0.00	0.03	0.00	0.01	-0.08
3	2,212	6.12	3,105	0.03	0.00	0.00	0.00	0.03	0.00	0.01	-0.08
4	2,215	7.75	3,739	0.04	0.00	0.00	0.00	0.04	0.00	0.02	-0.09
5	2,222	8.01	4,235	0.04	0.00	0.00	0.00	0.04	0.00	0.02	-0.10
6	2,265	9.20	5,404	0.05	0.00	0.00	0.00	0.05	0.00	0.02	-0.13
7	2,277	10.13	5,719	0.06	0.00	0.00	0.00	0.06	0.00	0.02	-0.14
8	2,300	10.98	7,385	0.06	0.00	0.00	0.00	0.06	0.00	0.03	-0.17
9	2,344	12.81	9,160	0.07	0.00	0.00	0.00	0.07	0.00	0.03	-0.21
10	2,448	18.96	22,758	0.10	0.00	0.00	0.00	0.10	0.00	0.04	-0.50
Overall	2,210	9.66	7,075	0.05	0.00	0.00	0.00	0.05	0.00	0.02	-0.17

Table 4b. *Female labor supply elasticities*

Decile	Hours of work	Net wage ($/hr)	Virtual income ($)	Parameter set 1		Parameter set 2		Parameter set 3		Parameter set 4	
				Wage	Income	Wage	Income	Wage	Income	Wage	Income
1	1,103	3.43	2,140	0.20	−0.02	0.10	−0.01	0.64	−0.04	0.68	−0.08
2	1,489	3.67	2,015	0.16	−0.01	0.08	−0.01	0.51	−0.03	0.54	−0.06
3	1,578	4.37	1,301	0.18	−0.01	0.09	−0.00	0.57	−0.02	0.60	−0.03
4	1,564	4.95	1,674	0.20	−0.01	0.10	−0.01	0.65	−0.02	0.69	−0.04
5	1,710	5.56	1,820	0.21	−0.01	0.10	−0.01	0.67	−0.02	0.71	−0.04
6	1,660	5.92	2,915	0.23	−0.02	0.11	−0.01	0.74	−0.03	0.78	−0.07
7	1,704	6.36	2,545	0.24	−0.01	0.12	−0.01	0.77	−0.03	0.81	−0.06
8	1,775	6.62	5,023	0.24	−0.03	0.12	−0.01	0.77	−0.05	0.81	−0.12
9	1,819	7.36	5,944	0.26	−0.03	0.13	−0.02	0.83	−0.06	0.88	−0.14
10	1,784	9.05	13,333	0.33	−0.07	0.16	−0.04	1.05	−0.14	1.11	−0.31
Overall	1,647	5.90	4,017	0.23	−0.02	0.11	−0.01	0.74	−0.05	0.78	−0.10

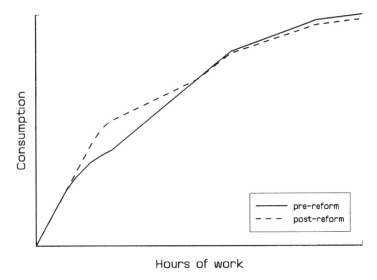

Figure 3. Change in the earned income tax credit financed by increasing the 15% and 28% tax rates.

29%. The last segment of the budget constraint shown, which reflects the 35% marginal tax rate, has an unchanged slope. An individual who is in this bracket (or in the 38.5% bracket) both before and after the reform faces an unchanged marginal tax rate but an increased average tax rate.

Tables 5a and 5b present results from simulating this reform. For each parameter set, the first two columns show the mean (weighted using sample weights) changes in taxes paid and annual hours worked resulting from the policy change. The third column shows the mean equivalent gain (using King's 1983 terminology) associated with the reform. The equivalent gain is the lump-sum transfer that would result in the same change in well-being as the reform being simulated. The fourth column displays the equivalent gain as a percentage of after–tax-and-transfer income. The "efficiency cost of increased progressivity" is equal to the sum of mean equivalent gains over deciles where the equivalent gain is negative, divided by the mean equivalent gains summed over the deciles where they are positive, minus 1. One plus this measure is the same as that which Browning and Johnson (1984) use to quantify the "trade-off between equality and efficiency." My measure is the same as what Ballard (1988) calls the "marginal efficiency cost of redistribution." It indicates the degree to which the welfare losses of those who are made worse off by the policy change of

Table 5a. *Increase in the 14% range of the earned income tax credit funded by 1-percentage-point increases in the 15% and 28% federal tax rates*

	Parameter set 1				Parameter set 2			
	Change in		Equivalent gain ($)	Percentage gain	Change in		Equivalent gain ($)	Percentage gain
Decile	Taxes ($)	Hours			Taxes ($)	Hours		
1	-340	1.8	351	4.6	-338	3.7	341	4.6
2	-693	-0.6	673	4.8	-740	-2.1	735	5.2
3	-405	-4.3	354	1.9	-434	-6.8	420	2.3
4	-104	-6.0	50	0.2	-106	-6.8	92	0.4
5	114	-4.4	-140	-0.5	115	-4	-126	-0.5
6	188	-4.8	-212	-0.7	204	-1.6	-209	-0.7
7	241	-4.0	-264	-0.8	261	-1.6	-266	-0.8
8	282	-2.8	-307	-0.8	304	-1.7	-311	-0.8
9	338	-1.7	-355	-0.8	354	-0.9	-358	-0.8
10	377	-0.7	-377	-0.5	379	0.0	-379	-0.5
Overall	0	-2.8	-23	-0.1	0	-2.2	-6	0.0
Efficiency cost of increased progressivity		0.16				0.04		
Increase in 14% bracket		$7321				$7875		

Table 5b. *Increase in the 14% range of the earned income tax credit funded by 1-percentage-point increases in the 15% and 28% federal tax rates*

	Parameter set 3				Parameter set 4			
	Change in		Equivalent gain ($)	Percentage gain	Change in		Equivalent gain ($)	Percentage gain
Decile	Taxes ($)	Hours			Taxes ($)	Hours		
1	-301	18	320	4.3	-273	5	259	3.5
2	-630	-22.1	589	4.2	-597	-71.2	416	2.9
3	-378	-53.5	261	1.4	-373	-101.5	118	0.7
4	-83	-39.6	-17	-0.1	-102	-67.4	-87	-0.4
5	89	-17.2	-143	-0.6	19	-44.7	-153	-0.6
6	153	-14.4	-213	-0.7	84	-41.4	-210	-0.6
7	197	-15.8	-260	-0.7	170	-25.8	-252	-0.7
8	271	-10.2	-309	-0.8	229	-19.3	-305	-0.8
9	329	-5.9	-356	-0.8	343	-6.5	-349	-0.7
10	351	-0.9	-388	-0.5	498	11	-376	-0.5
Overall	0	-16.2	-52	-0.2	0	-36.2	-94	-0.3
Efficiency cost of increased progressivity	0.44				1.18			
Increase in 14% bracket	$6357				$4866			

redistributing one dollar exceed the welfare gains of those who are made better off by the reform.

For all four sets of parameters considered, sizeable percentage increases in economic well-being are realized by the bottom two deciles, with relatively small percentage decreases in economic well-being realized by those in the upper deciles. When comparing simulations based on different parameters, one should note that the size of the increase in the EITC varies with the parameter set used. This is because the behavioral response to the reform depends on the labor supply parameters. A more elastic labor supply results in less revenue being raised by the tax rate increases, and therefore in a smaller expansion of the EITC being possible.

The efficiency cost of increased progressivity is very small in the base case (parameter set 1). This is well below any of the marginal efficiency-cost estimates of Browning and Johnson (who only consider reforms that increase the value of a demogrant financed by increasing marginal tax rates by 1 percentage point). My estimate of the marginal efficiency cost of expanding the EITC is similar in magnitude to Ballard's (1988) estimates of the marginal efficiency cost associated with what he calls "notch grant" programs, in which a cash grant for low-income groups is financed by increasing the marginal tax rate faced by higher-income groups (assignment to an income group is exogenous, and all individuals face linear budget constraints).

In comparing my estimates to those of Ballard (1988) and Browning and Johnson (1984), one must remember that the policy I am simulating is quite different than those which they considered. In addition, I use a different specification of preferences and use labor supply elasticities that are lower than those they put the most emphasis on.

Predictably, the efficiency cost is lower using parameter set 2 than when basing the simulation on parameter set 1. The simulated efficiency cost rises when the simulations are based on parameter sets 3 and 4. However, the efficiency cost is still relatively low even using parameter set 4, which Browning and Johnson (1984, p. 191) refer to as "implausibly high" for men. Increasing the generosity of the earned income tax credit appears to be an efficient means of increasing progressivity. One reason for the efficiency of this scheme is that it tends to encourage labor-force participation. Although it decreases the marginal net wage for some low-income workers (see Figure 3), it increases the average net wage for those same workers.

The second progressivity-increasing reform which I simulate is using 1-percentage-point increases in the 15% and 28% marginal tax rates to finance an increase in the value of the personal exemption. Figure 4a shows the effect on an individual's budget constraint of increasing the personal

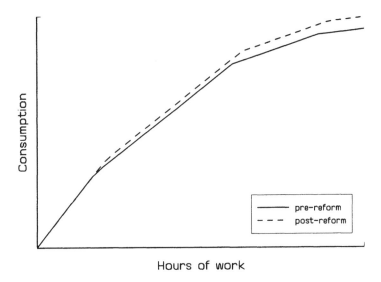

Figure 4a.   Increase in the personal exemption (with no tax-rate increase).

exemption without any tax-rate increases (the individual is assumed to have no unearned income, to be ineligible for the EITC and transfer programs, and to have no fixed costs of working). Hours of work on the first segment of the budget constraint yield earnings that are less than the sum of allowed exemptions and deductions. Hours of work on the second segment of the budget constraint result in the individual being in the 15-percent tax bracket; the third segment of the budget constraint corresponds to the 28-percent bracket; the fourth segment of the budget constraint corresponds to the 35-percent bracket. The kink points in the budget constraint all move to the right as a result of the increase in the exemption. Those who are initially on the first segment of the budget constraint (and therefore have taxable income below the value of their deductions and exemptions) do not realize any decrease in tax payments. Note that the size of the tax decrease (increase in consumption) increases as one moves to successively higher tax brackets. Figure 4b shows the effect on an individual's budget constraint of simultaneously increasing the value of the personal exemption and increasing the 15% and 28% marginal tax rates. Overall, this produces only minor changes in the budget constraint. Consumption (after-tax income) is increased slightly for persons whose hours of work locate them in the low end of the 15-percent tax bracket (the second segment of the budget constraint), and decreases slightly for most hours-of-work values beyond the middle of the 15-percent bracket.

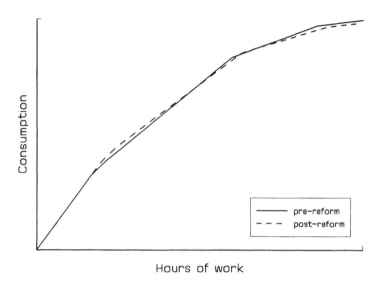

Figure 4b. Increase in the personal exemption financed by increasing the 15% and 28% tax rates.

Tables 6a and 6b display results from simulating the effect of using 1–percentage-point increases in the federal 15% and 28% marginal tax rates to finance an increase in the value of the personal exemption. Perhaps the most striking aspect of these tables is how much less redistribution of the tax burden results from using the increased tax rates to fund increases in the exemption rather than increased generosity of the EITC. This is just another manifestation of what was illustrated in Figure 4b: simultaneously increasing the personal exemption and marginal tax rates results only in fairly minor effects on tax liabilities. The efficiency cost of increased progressivity is fairly low using parameter set 1, but climbs rapidly as parameter sets 3 and 4 are considered. Increasing the personal exemption is a very risky means of increasing tax progressivity if a reasonably high probability is attached to parameter set 4 being "true."

Figure 5 illustrates the effect on an individual's budget constraint of the third type of simulated policy reform: using 1–percentage-point increases in the federal 15% and 28% marginal tax rates to finance the introduction of a "demogrant"-style refundable tax credit.[14] The total credit received by a tax-filing unit is equal to the base amount of the credit multiplied by

---

[14] As in Figures 4a and 4b, the individual is assumed to have no unearned income, to be ineligible for the EITC and transfer programs, and to have no fixed costs of working.

Table 6a. *Increase in the personal exemption funded by 1-percentage-point increases in the 15% and 28% federal tax rates*

	Parameter set 1				Parameter set 2			
	Change in		Equivalent gain ($)	Percentage gain	Change in		Equivalent gain ($)	Percentage gain
Decile	Taxes ($)	Hours			Taxes ($)	Hours		
1	−36	0.8	38	0.5	−37	0.2	37	0.5
2	−95	−2.0	82	0.6	−87	−0.5	86	0.6
3	−60	−2.8	55	0.3	−62	−1.1	61	0.3
4	−29	−2.0	25	0.1	−33	−0.8	32	0.1
5	−2	−3.0	−4	0.0	−3	−1.1	1	0.0
6	−2	−2.1	−4	0.0	−1	−0.4	1	0.0
7	28	−1.2	−42	−0.1	29	0.1	−29	−0.1
8	39	−2.9	−52	−0.1	43	−0.5	−46	−0.1
9	75	−2.3	−85	−0.2	77	−0.4	−78	−0.2
10	83	−0.1	−81	−0.1	73	0.1	−72	−0.1
Overall	0	−1.8	−7	0.0	0	−0.4	−1	0.0
Efficiency cost of increased progressivity			0.30				0.04	
Increase in personal exemption			$333				$344	

Table 6b. *Increase in the personal exemption funded by 1-percentage-point increases in the 15% and 28% federal tax rates*

Decile	Parameter set 3				Parameter set 4			
	Change in		Equivalent gain ($)	Percentage gain	Change in		Equivalent gain ($)	Percentage gain
	Taxes ($)	Hours			Taxes ($)	Hours		
1	−29	1.1	32	0.4	−23	0.0	16	0.2
2	−86	−5.0	65	0.5	−72	−9.9	45	0.3
3	−48	−7.8	36	0.2	−46	−18.7	9	0.1
4	−19	−6.9	6	0.0	−27	−18.2	−20	−0.1
5	8	−7.8	−30	−0.1	−2	−20.7	−54	−0.2
6	8	−7.8	−33	−0.1	−5	−24.0	−58	−0.2
7	23	−8.7	−63	−0.2	13	−18.8	−92	−0.3
8	45	−8.7	−88	−0.2	15	−22.9	−116	−0.3
9	97	−4.8	−120	−0.3	58	−19.9	−149	−0.3
10	1	−8.0	−124	−0.2	88	−4.6	−159	−0.2
Overall	0	−6.4	−32	−0.1	0	−15.8	−58	−0.2
Efficiency cost of increased progressivity			2.32				8.12	
Increase in personal exemption			$288				$236	

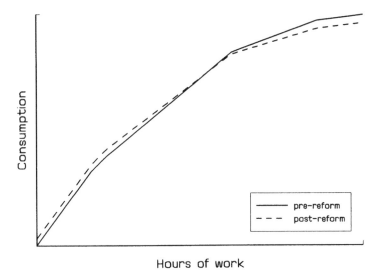

Figure 5. Introduction of a demogrant financed by increasing the 15%
and 28% tax rates.

the number of personal exemptions. The credit is taxable (taxable income
is increased by the amount of the credit), and it enters as income in the
AFDC and food-stamps benefit-reduction formulas.[15] As a result of the
demogrant, the first segment of the budget constraint makes a parallel
shift up; the second and third segments of the budget constraint become
flatter owing to the increase in the 15% and 28% tax rates. Note that –
unlike increasing the value of the personal exemption – introducing a
demogrant increases the after-tax income of an individual located on the
first segment of the budget constraint.

Tables 7a and 7b show results from simulating this policy reform. As
expected (based on a comparison of Figures 5 and 4b), the 1–percentage-
point increase in the 15% and 28% marginal tax rates results in larger
increases in economic welfare for those in the lower income deciles (and
larger decreases in economic welfare in the upper income deciles) when
the revenue increase is used to finance the introduction of a demogrant
rather than an increase in the personal exemption. The demogrant policy
has an efficiency cost roughly the same as that of the increased personal

[15] The policy reform was designed in order to *not* make it more attractive for AFDC and
food-stamps nonparticipants to become participants in response to the reform. This
allows me to avoid modeling the AFDC and food-stamps participation decision (which
depends on very complex eligibility rules).

Table 7a. *Demogrant funded by 1-percentage-point increases in the 15% and 28% federal tax rates*

Decile	Parameter set 1				Parameter set 2			
	Change in				Change in			
	Taxes ($)	Hours	Equivalent gain ($)	Percentage gain	Taxes ($)	Hours	Equivalent gain ($)	Percentage gain
1	-166	-1.5	162	2.1	-172	-0.1	169	2.3
2	-165	-3.6	157	1.1	-172	-0.7	171	1.2
3	-124	-4.1	115	0.6	-132	-1.0	131	0.7
4	-91	-4.0	81	0.4	-100	-1.3	97	0.4
5	-43	-5.4	30	0.1	-45	-1.4	42	0.2
6	-1	-6.5	-20	-0.1	3	-2.1	-9	0.0
7	63	-6.7	-88	-0.3	70	-1.8	-77	-0.2
8	117	-6.2	-143	-0.4	128	-2.0	-136	-0.3
9	183	-4.2	-204	-0.4	192	-1.0	-197	-0.4
10	225	-1.4	-235	-0.3	227	0.0	-227	-0.3
Overall	0	-4.3	-15	0.0	0	-1.2	-4	0.0
Efficiency cost of increased progressivity			0.27				0.06	
Size of demogrant			$88				$93	

Table 7b. *Demogrant funded by 1-percentage-point increases in the 15% and 28% federal tax rates*

	Parameter set 3				Parameter set 4			
	Change in		Equivalent gain ($)	Percentage gain	Change in		Equivalent gain ($)	Percentage gain
Decile	Taxes ($)	Hours			Taxes ($)	Hours		
1	-145	1.9	149	2.0	-126	-8.0	107	1.4
2	-156	-8.0	145	1.0	-151	-21.4	109	0.8
3	-116	-10.7	100	0.6	-107	-26.1	63	0.3
4	-86	-10.8	67	0.3	-86	-27.7	31	0.1
5	-40	-12.0	16	0.1	-50	-29.7	-17	-0.1
6	-7	-14.6	-35	-0.1	-50	-38.1	-59	-0.2
7	30	-18.1	-100	-0.3	16	-29.7	-118	-0.3
8	103	-13.6	-157	-0.4	60	-28.2	-170	-0.4
9	180	-8.2	-215	-0.5	151	-19.1	-209	-0.4
10	236	-1.7	-248	-0.3	343	3.5	-251	-0.3
Overall	0	-9.6	-28	-0.1	0	-22.5	-51	-0.2
Efficiency cost of increased progressivity		0.58				1.66		
Size of demogrant		$80				$65		

exemption policy when the simulations are based on parameter sets 1 and 2, but a lower efficiency cost when the simulations are based on parameter sets 3 and 4. In interpreting this, one must keep in mind that the increased personal exemption policy would have to be financed by larger tax-rate increases than those simulated here to achieve the same redistribution of the tax burden as the demogrant policy. Overall, the demogrant policy seems preferable to increasing the personal exemption as a means of increasing progressivity.

So far, the policy simulations have all been based on increasing only the 15% and 28% federal marginal rates. Table 8 displays results for alternate means of financing an expansion in the range of earnings over which the earned income tax credit increases. Both of the simulations reported in this table are based on parameter set 1. Comparing the effect of increasing the 28% and 35% rates (leaving the 15% and 38.5% rates unchanged) rather than the 15% and 28% rates (as in Table 5a) is instructive. Increasing the higher tax rates results in a sharply higher efficiency cost, and raises less revenue that could be used to increase the generosity of the EITC. However, a potential advantage of increasing the higher marginal tax rates is that proportionately more of the cost of making those in the three lowest deciles better-off is borne by those in the top two deciles.

In some ways, it is "fairer" to compare the effect of using a 1–percentage-point increase in the 15% and 28% marginal tax rates to finance the introduction of a demogrant with using a 1–percentage-point increase in the 28% and 35% marginal tax rates to finance an expansion of the EITC than it is to compare the demogrant policy with using a 1–percentage-point increase in the 15% and 28% marginal tax rates to finance an expansion of the EITC. Comparison of Tables 5a and 8 with Table 6a suggests that the pattern of the redistribution of economic welfare resulting from using increases in the 15% and 28% rates to finance a demogrant is more similar to the pattern of redistribution resulting from using increases in the 28% and 35% tax rates to expand the EITC than it is to the pattern of redistribution resulting from using increases in the 15% and 28% tax rates to finance an expansion of the EITC. Although expanding the EITC has a lower efficiency cost than introducing a demogrant when both are financed by increasing the 15% and 28% marginal tax rates, the demogrant policy has a lower efficiency cost when it is compared with an expansion of the EITC financed by increasing the 28% and 35% marginal tax rates.

One conclusion which can be drawn from this is that a measure such as the efficiency cost of increased progressivity cannot be used to rank the desirability of policy reforms that differ in how they affect the distribution

Table 8. *Increase in the 14% range of the earned income tax credit*

	Financed by 1-percentage-point increases in the 28% and 35% federal tax rates				Financed by a 1-percentage-point increase in the 35% federal tax rate			
	Change in				Change in			
Decile	Taxes ($)	Hours	Equivalent gain ($)	Percentage gain	Taxes ($)	Hours	Equivalent gain ($)	Percentage gain
1	−181	1.6	183	2.4	−77	−0.1	76	1.0
2	−248	−8.4	228	1.6	−65	−2.5	58	0.4
3	−76	−5.9	58	0.3	−16	−1.2	12	0.1
4	−24	−1.4	18	0.1	−4	−0.2	3	0.0
5	−10	−1.4	5	0.0	−5	−0.1	4	0.0
6	8	−2.9	−20	−0.1	−2	−0.1	1	0.0
7	31	−3.9	−50	−0.1	−3	−0.4	−1	0.0
8	72	−5.5	−101	−0.3	2	−1.6	−12	0.0
9	122	−7.5	−181	−0.4	14	−4.7	−48	−0.1
10	305	−7.6	−397	−0.5	154	−7.5	−245	−0.3
Overall	0	−4.3	−26	−0.1	0	−1.8	−15	0.0
Efficiency cost of increased progressivity	0.52				0.96			
Increase in 14% bracket	$3135				$1257			

of economic welfare. When a group of progressivity-increasing tax reforms all have the same effect on the distribution of economic welfare, the one with the lowest efficiency cost of increased progressivity is the most efficient means of achieving that effect. However, comparison of the efficiency cost of increased progressivity for reforms that have varying effects on the distribution of economic welfare merely indicates which reforms have the greatest degree of "leakage" in the redistribution bucket (using Okun's 1975 analogy). One would not necessarily prefer the policy with the smallest degree of leakage if the policies differ in their patterns of redistribution of the tax burden.

Increasing only the 35% marginal rate (Table 8) results in a much higher simulated efficiency cost than when the 28% and 35% rates are both increased. There are two primary reasons for this. First, the excess burden of a tax increases approximately with the square of the tax rate. The increase in excess burden resulting from increasing the marginal tax rate of someone in the 35-percent bracket by 1 percentage point is greater than the increase in excess burden resulting from increasing the marginal tax rate of someone in the 28-percent bracket by 1 percentage point. Second, an increase in the marginal tax rate in the current 28-percent bracket (but not in other brackets) has the effect of creating an implicit lump-sum tax increase for those in higher brackets. Individuals facing 35% and 38.5% marginal tax rates would pay higher taxes as a result of the increase in the 28% rate, but would face unchanged marginal tax rates themselves.

The results in Table 8 suggest that the efficiency cost of redistributing income from the middle class to the poor is much less than that of redistributing income from the very well-off to the poor. However, this conclusion must be treated with some caution. As discussed perviously, the labor supply specification adopted in this study results in wage and income elasticities that increase in magnitude with adjusted family income. This will increase the tendency for marginal excess burden to increase as one moves from increasing the tax rate in a given tax bracket to increasing the tax rate in a higher income-tax bracket.

Perhaps a more important reason for caution is that the rich are neither adequately represented in the data set I use nor adequately treated in the labor supply specification that I employ. High-income filing units are extremely important sources of federal individual income–tax revenue. For example, in 1987 over 10% of federal individual income–tax revenue came from the approximately 1% of returns with adjusted gross income over $500,000 (IRS 1992). Because the data set I draw my sample from – the Panel Study of Income Dynamics – does not oversample high-income households and does not collect information regarding capital gains realizations, I have very little information about high-income filing units.

As Slemrod (1992) notes, behavioral parameters estimated from a sample of the overall population may not accurately predict the behavior of the very rich. The labor supply parameters I use in this study may be more appropriate for predicting the behavior of low- and moderate-income workers (which predominate in the samples used for labor supply estimation) than for predicting the behavior of high-income workers. Slemrod (1992) also notes that capital income makes up a much larger proportion of the total income for very high–income households than it does for the general population, and that those with high earnings may have more flexibility in the form of their employment compensation than do those with lower earnings. Since the only distortion I model in this paper is that of individuals' hours-of-work decisions, I may be missing the most important distortionary effects of taxation affecting very high–income households.

Despite these caveats, the simulations do suggest that the efficiency cost of increasing progressivity by raising the marginal tax rates faced only by very high–income households is likely to be much greater than if the progressivity-increasing reform were instead financed by raising the marginal tax rates faced by moderate income groups. A well-known result appearing in the optimal nonlinear income-tax literature is that, under certain conditions, the optimal marginal tax rate at the highest level of income is *zero,* even if the government is maximizing a very egalitarian social welfare function. Slemrod (1990) provides an intuitive exposition and discussion of this result, which applies only when there is no limit to the number of brackets the income tax may have. Slemrod, Yitzhaki, and Mayshar (1991) find in their simulations that when the income tax is limited to two brackets plus a demogrant, the optimal tax policy is to set the marginal tax rate in the second bracket at a level *lower* than that of the marginal tax rate in the first bracket. The lesson of the optimal income-tax literature is that even if one has a very egalitarian objective, an income tax featuring marginal tax rates that increase sharply with income may not be desirable.

5   Conclusion

In this paper I have investigated the efficiency cost of several possible progressivity-increasing tax reforms. Based on the labor supply parameters I consider to be most reasonable, it appears possible to devise progressivity-increasing tax reforms that have a quite small degree of "leakage" in redistributing after-tax economic welfare from upper-income to lower-income families. The efficiency cost of using an expansion of the earned income tax credit – financed by 1-percentage-point increases in the 15% and 28% federal marginal tax rates – to transfer $1 of economic welfare from upper-income families to lower-income families is only 16¢. When other labor supply parameters are assumed, the efficiency cost of this transfer ranges from 4¢ to $1.18.

When the same simulated changes in tax rates are used to finance a demogrant, the efficiency cost of the transfer is higher, but the pattern of redistribution differs from and may be preferable to that produced by the EITC expansion. While a measure such as the efficiency cost of increased progressivity provides a useful indicator of the degree of leakage involved in redistributing the tax burden, it cannot be used to rank the desirability of tax reforms that differ in their patterns of redistribution.

Further research into the properties of various reforms that increase the progressivity of the tax system is desirable. There may be policies which dominate – in the sense of achieving the same redistribution of the tax burden, with a smaller efficiency cost – those considered in this paper. Horizontal equity also needs to be considered. In 1987, earned income tax credit was available only to those with earned income and dependent children. This property may help to make expansion of the EITC a particularly efficient way of increasing progressivity, since it encourages work effort on the part of those who are likely to be eligible for transfer programs with high benefit-reduction rates. However, some would view as desirable an earnings credit available to a broader group of recipients.

REFERENCES

Ballard, Charles L. (1988), "The Marginal Efficiency Cost of Redistribution," *American Economic Review* 78: 1019–33.

Bosworth, Barry, and Gary Burtless (1992), "Effects of Tax Reform on Labor Supply, Investment, and Saving," *Journal of Economic Perspectives* 6: 3–26.

Browning, Edgar K., and William R. Johnson (1984), "The Trade-off Between Equality and Efficiency," *Journal of Political Economy* 92: 175–203.

Burtless, Gary (1987), "The Work Response to a Guaranteed Income: a Survey of Experimental Evidence," in Alicia H. Munnell (ed.), *Lessons from the Income Maintenance Experiments.* Federal Reserve Bank of Boston.

(1990), "The Economist's Lament: Public Assistance in America," *Journal of Economic Perspectives* 4: 57–78.

Burtless, Gary, and Barry Bosworth (1992), "Effects of Tax Reform on Labor Supply, Investment, and Savings," *Journal of Economic Perspectives* 6: 3–26.

Burtless, Gary, and Jerry A. Hausman (1978), "The Effect of Taxation on Labor Supply: Evaluating the Gary NIT Experiment," *Journal of Political Economy* 86: 1103–30.

Cutler, David M., and Lawrence F. Katz (1992), "Rising Inequality? Changes in the Distribution of Income and Consumption in the 1980s," *American Economic Review* 82: 546–51.

Feldstein, Martin, and Andrew Samwick (1992), "Social Security Rules and Marginal Tax Rates," *National Tax Journal* 45: 1–22.

Hausman, Jerry A. (1981), "Labor Supply," in Henry J. Aaron and Joseph A. Pechman (eds.), *How Taxes Affect Economic Behavior.* Washington, DC: Brookings.
   (1985), "Taxes and Labor Supply," in Alan J. Auerbach and Martin Feldstein (eds.), *Handbook of Public Economics,* vol. 1. Amsterdam: North-Holland.
Heckman, James J. (1983), "Comment" on paper by Jerry A. Hausman, in Martin Feldstein (ed.), *Behavioral Simulation Methods in Tax Policy Analysis.* Chicago: University of Chicago Press.
Internal Revenue Service (IRS) (1992), *Statistics of Income Bulletin,* vol. 12.
King, Mervyn A. (1983), "Welfare Analysis of Tax Reforms Using Household Data," *Journal of Public Economics* 21: 183–214.
MaCurdy, Thomas, David Green, and Harry Paarsch (1990), "Assessing Empirical Approaches for Analyzing Taxes and Labor Supply," *Journal of Human Resources* 25: 415–90.
Moffitt, Robert (1986), "The Econometrics of Piecewise-Linear Budget Constraints: a Survey and Exposition of the Maximum Likelihood Method," *Journal of Business and Economic Statistics* 4: 317–27.
   (1990), "The Econometrics of Kinked Budget Constraints," *Journal of Economic Perspectives* 4: 119–39.
Mroz, Thomas (1987), "The Sensitivity of an Empirical Model of Married Women's Hours of Work to Economic and Statistical Assumptions," *Econometrica* 55: 765–800.
Okun, Arthur M. (1975), *Equality and Efficiency: The Big Tradeoff.* Washington, DC: Brookings.
Pencavel, John (1986), "Labor Supply of Men: a Survey," in Orley Ashenfelter and Richard Layard (eds.), *Handbook of Labor Economics,* vol. 1. Amsterdam: North-Holland.
Slemrod, Joel (1990), "Optimal Taxation and Optimal Tax Systems," *Journal of Economic Perspectives* 4: 157–78.
   (1992), "On the High-Income Laffer Curve," Working Paper, Office of Tax Policy Research, University of Michigan, Ann Arbor. [Chapter 6 in this volume]
Slemrod, Joel, Shlomo Yitzhaki, and Joram Mayshar (1991), "The Optimal Two-Bracket Linear Income Tax," Working Paper no. 3847, National Bureau of Economic Research, Cambridge, MA.
Survey Research Center (1991), *A Panel Study of Income Dynamics: Procedures and Tape Codes, 1988 Interviewing Year.* Ann Arbor, MI: Institute for Social Research.
Triest, Robert K. (1990), "The Effect of Income Taxation on Labor Supply in the United States," *Journal of Human Resources* 25: 491–516.
   (1992), "The Effect of Income Taxation on Labor Supply when Deductions Are Endogenous," *Review of Economics and Statistics* 74: 91–9.

Comments

Gary Burtless

It is always a pleasure to be asked to comment on a paper that treats an interesting subject, is done by a scholar one respects in a defensible way, and reaches conclusions that appear to be valid. Robert Triest has written such a paper. Of course, my pleasure is even greater when I turn to the bibliography and discover more references to my own work than I have ever had the chutzpah to insert into my own papers. Could Bob have known in advance who his discussant would be?

A good economist has applied state-of-the-art techniques to analyze an important topic in empirical public finance: the efficiency losses of increased redistribution. His methods are similar to – but improve upon – those used in other recent articles on this subject, several of which have been published in the best scholarly journals.

One odd thing about this early version of the paper is that it virtually ignores the lessons that can be learned from the most relevant empirical literature, the NIT (negative income-tax) experiments. As I recall, the government spent about $150 million to measure the efficiency costs of an NIT using classical experimentation. So far as I know, this doesn't happen very often in our branch of science. The government then spent additional millions creating data sets and computer software to generalize the experimental responses to the entire population. The experimental results are directly relevant to measuring one of the most important efficiency costs of redistribution: the work-effort and earnings effects of higher transfers on the low-income population, which would receive greater transfers.

Let me remind you (or, more probably, inform you) of one of the most important lessons of this literature: The efficiency cost of transfers depends critically on the specific formulas and eligibility requirements of the proposed reform. Some reforms that yield greater after-tax equality cause large losses in work effort and impose large distortions (and economic losses) in the labor market. Other reforms involve less distortion

170

and economic loss. And still others can actually reduce distortions among the low-wage population – for example, by reducing average and marginal tax rates imposed on poor wage earners.

This conclusion is re-affirmed in the paper, though it was completely missed in some previous contributions to this literature that took far less care in describing the current state of the world or plausible alternatives to it. Let me briefly describe what Triest has done, contrasting it with earlier (and, in my view, weaker) contributions to the literature; summarize his findings; give some modest suggestions for improvements and extensions; and conclude by raising a basic question about this line of inquiry: Are the efficiency-cost estimates in this literature relevant to policymaking?

1   Methodological summary and comparison

Triest starts with a data set that approximately represents the prime-aged population – 20–60 years olds. He uses empirical estimates of the population labor supply function derived from recent work. He develops computer code to calculate tax-and-transfer payments (and tax-and-transfer marginal tax rates) for members of his sample, and then modestly changes the currently predicted tax-and-transfer payments to reflect the effects of small changes in the relevant formulas.

His data set is better than others' – that is, more representative of the variety of U.S. households than some other past work. His labor supply functions are more concrete; they are based on actual recent estimates, rather than "guesstimates" of the average relevant elasticities. His representation of the tax-and-transfer system is much closer to reality than most past work, and his simulated alternatives are fairer and more reasonable than other past attempts. (I should note, however, that Jerry Hausman's work is also an exception to the run-of-the-mill study. Like Triest, Hausman (1981a,b) uses real data about U.S. households and examines relevant policy alternatives. Unlike Triest and other recent analysts, however, Hausman does not calculate the marginal efficiency cost of redistribution.)

Of these differences with past work (e.g., with Browning and Johnson 1984), the most important is the careful representation of the status quo and plausible policy reforms. One reason that Browning and Johnson obtain such implausibly high estimates of the marginal cost of redistribution is that they mischaracterize – oversimplify – the status quo, and propose reforms to the status quo that are very inefficient. For example, they assume that the tax function is essentially a large lump-sum payment to each household which is reduced at a constant (and fairly high) marginal rate. This might be roughly accurate if the population is viewed as 5 or 10 individuals (one in each decile or quintile), but it is emphatically untrue if the population is examined one person at a time, as Triest does.

Some people with high average income do indeed receive substantial transfers, primarily social security and Medicare. But most high-income Americans do not qualify for these transfers, and Triest's representation of their work and income alternatives accurately reflects that fact. Furthermore, Triest has selected reasonable policy alternatives (with one possible exception, as I'll argue shortly). The first of these is liberalization of the earned income tax credit (EITC). This is plausible because Congress has twice liberalized the program since the mid-1980s, and in a way not too different from that proposed here.

However, the policy is reasonable not only because it is "plausible." It is likely a priori to be a comparatively efficient mechanism for increasing progressivity. Why? Because it reduces average *and* marginal taxes paid by the poor, rather than raising them. By contrast, Browning and Johnson characterize a "liberalization" of the system as one that raises the lump-sum component of the formula and the marginal tax imposed on *every* taxpayer and transfer recipient. Triest raises the lump-sum component for some EITC recipients but leaves it unchanged for others (reducing their marginal tax rate); he leaves the lump-sum component unchanged for most high-income taxpayers, and actually *reduces* it for the highest-income taxpayers (who have higher average tax rates but unchanged marginal tax rates). This must be more efficient than Browning and Johnson's proposed reform. Instead of raising transfers to every member of the population and then taxing the transfers back, Triest reduces marginal taxes for some low-income people, raises transfers for some others, and then raises taxes on the remainder of the population to finance the redistribution.

In another simulation, Triest examines the impact of raising exemptions. Though in principle this is much less efficient, it is at least a plausible policy. Many tax reforms involve this kind of liberalization. We do hear proposals for refundable tax credits, I suppose, so perhaps this too is a perfectly plausible policy, though an inefficient one.

My major objection to the simulations is the way positive tax rates are raised. It would be more straightforward to raise every marginal tax rate in the schedule by a fixed proportional amount. By raising rates by a fixed number of percentage *points* at the lower tax rates, Triest is raising lower rates by a proportionately larger amount than high marginal tax rates. In addition, he is leaving marginal rates on high-income taxpayers unchanged. This is one source of his low estimate for marginal efficiency costs.

2   Summary of findings

As expected, liberalization of the EITC is more efficient than other alternatives. Even under the most elastic labor supply functions, the efficiency loss appears to be acceptable. It therefore follows that the devil is in the details of redistribution, even under the most pessimistic estimate of labor supply elasticity.

The marginal cost of redistribution rises rapidly with the elasticity of the assumed labor supply function. Of course, this finding is hardly unexpected. The magnitude of the differences across different functions is startling, however.

Consider the effect of raising the exemption. Under the smallest estimate of efficiency loss, losers give up $1.04 to raise the well-being of low-income gainers by $1. Under Hausman's estimates – the highest ones – losers give up $9.12 to raise the well-being of gainers by $1. Triest sensibly concludes that liberalizing the exemption is a risky proposition if you think Hausman's estimates have even a 20% chance of being true. One thing I would point out is that Triest's estimates of efficiency losses, even for such inefficient policies as increased exemptions, center on numbers that are far below Browning and Johnson's original simulation estimates.

The final conclusion is that efficiency losses appear to rise sharply as tax increases are concentrated on a smaller and smaller portion of population. The reason is not that a 1% tax rise hurts high-income individuals more when they are the only ones facing it. Rather, the tax increase is on top of what is already a higher marginal tax rate. Because losses rise with the square of the tax rate, those with high initial tax rates suffer more than those facing low initial rates.

3   Suggestions

Let me briefly offer a few suggestions for extensions.

1. Is the tax increase a 1–percentage-*point* or a 1-*percent* change? The latter would be more rational, as it would represent an equiproportional marginal tax rise at every income level.

2. Readers should be informed of the labor supply elasticities at the midpoint of data for each specification and gender.

3. Readers could be given a *graphical* exposition of the policy changes simulated. This would make clear that the transfer *policy change* is different under each assumed labor supply parameter set. The positive tax change is the same in each simulation, and the net budgetary *effect* is the same (i.e., zero). But because the same tax change elicits different changes

in tax revenue under different parameters, the EITC liberalization (and the exemption increase, etc.) all change when the parameters change. In addition, a graphical exposition might make clear that under several of the simulations, marginal tax rates (but not average tax burdens) on high-income taxpayers are left unchanged.

4. As one alternative, Triest could *fix* the transfer policy change and permit the positive tax-rate change to vary so that the balanced-budget requirement is met.

4   Conclusions

Let me conclude by making some tentative remarks about the literature on the marginal efficiency costs of redistribution. I say "tentative" because I am not a close student of the economic theory of social welfare, and so may be drawing some incomplete conclusions; I welcome corrections.

Over the past 15 years, there have been significant improvements in our techniques for estimating demand functions in the presence of non-linear budget constraints, and for deriving exact measures of compensating variation for various policy changes. Economists have used these new techniques to derive estimates of aggregate deadweight losses and marginal efficiency losses arising out of small policy changes.

I wonder whether these efficiency-loss estimates have the interpretation they are typically given. Let's look at Triest's estimates – or even better, the estimates obtained by Browning and Johnson, who were much less cautious. Their estimates are based on empirical estimates of a labor supply function, which in some cases can only be obtained by using knowledge about the underlying utility function associated with the supply function. In using these functions, we do not require that the function we write down constitute a literal representation of workers' *cardinal* utility; any monotonic transformation of the functions we write down yielding the same indifference curves would serve equally well.

But when Triest estimates the gains and losses from reform, he calculates population totals by adding and then dividing the "equivalent gains" across individuals. Implicitly, he assigns equal weights to the gains and losses of each individual. If he had assigned different weights to each individual, estimates of marginal efficiency loss would clearly change. It seems to me that lurking somewhere in the background is the unstated assumption that the marginal utility of income is constant across individuals, and also across different income levels for a given individual.

In order to raise the well-being of individual A by $1, it is necessary (under a specific reform proposal) to reduce individual B's well-being by

$1.50. But *B* has high income already, so perhaps that $1.50 is not as valuable to *B* as the $1 is to *A*. Even more significant, perhaps, is that $1.50 is not worth as much to *B* as it would be to *B were his initial income as low as A's!*

The developing literature on the marginal efficiency effects of taxation (or of public spending or redistribution) appears to yield hard numbers about the economic "cost" of such activity. But the "hard" numbers are much softer than they appear. They rest on the unstated, untested, and long-ago *rejected* assumption that a dollar of extra income (or "equivalent gain") obtained by one person can be treated as equivalent (in a welfare sense) to an added dollar received by another person. This proposition was rejected in the 1940s by Paul Samuelson. It's hard to see why today so many public-finance economists are eager to embrace it – without saying so.

Triest's various simulations result in redistribution from individuals who are generally better-off to those who are worse-off. But it makes a big difference to me whether the losses are sustained by individuals in the top 1 percent of the income distribution, by those in the top income quintile, or by those in the middle income quintile. It also matters whether the gains are enjoyed by people in the bottom 5 percent of the distribution (usually they are not), the bottom quintile, or the middle quintile. We should be grateful to Triest for providing tables that help us make this kind of calculation. However, he should explicitly discuss the meaning of the different types of redistribution each of his simulations represents.

The calculations that Triest has performed are well done and interesting. But they do not permit us to make the easy social welfare calculations that some readers of this literature seem to think. Is $9.81 in marginal cost too high? Is $1.04 very low and permissible? If you ask me, it must depend on just who is worse off by $9.81 and who is better off by $1.00. The ratio of losses to gains is by itself a very incomplete (and uncertain) guide to public policymaking.

REFERENCES

Browning, Edgar K., and William R. Johnson (1984), "The Trade-off Between Equality and Efficiency," *Journal of Political Economy* 92: 175–203.

Hausman, Jerry A. (1981a), "Labor Supply," in Henry Aaron and Joseph Pechman (eds.), *The Effect of Taxes on Economic Behavior*. Washington, DC: Brookings, pp. 27–72.

(1981b), "Income and Payroll Tax Policy and Labor Supply," in Laurence H. Meyer (ed.), *Supply-Side Effects of Economic Policy*. Boston: Kluwer-Nijhoff, pp. 173–202.

General discussion

As a policy option, Gale suggested investigating a second-earner deduction. He noted also that progressive income taxes provide an element of insurance against uncertain earnings, which reduces their efficiency cost.

Hoerner wondered whether the result concerning low efficiency cost is driven by women's higher labor supply elasticity, combined with the fact that women are disproportionately represented at the bottom of the income distribution.

Inman remarked that some metric is needed to make social welfare choices, such as the one used in Stern's 1976 paper on optimal taxation. He also commented that Hausman does a good job of mapping labor parameters to an indirect utility function and then goes to efficiency-cost estimates. Inman further noted that if efficiency costs are so low, any redistributive social welfare function will generate steeply progressive optimal tax schedules.

Feenberg suggested considering as a policy option an increase in the standard deduction rather than the personal exemption. A standard-deduction increase will provide no benefit to high-income itemizers, and reduces the compliance cost of itemization.

Musgrave argued that if society assigns identical social welfare weights to all income levels, the only reasonable system is to use a head tax. Society must assign nonneutral weights if progressivity is to be an interesting question.

Poterba commented that, assuming a set of social welfare weights, one could use the same methodology to compute the optimal two-bracket linear income tax.

Hite remarked that a complete policy analysis of the earned income tax credit should consider the fact that it is complicated and therefore prone to error and abuse.

Sheffrin observed that tax policy is currently driven by burden tables that are often misunderstood and misused. It is asking too much of policymakers to expect them to be able to make intelligent use of social welfare functions.

Triest agreed that any analysis that relies on social welfare functions will likely have very little impact on policy. He also noted that, from a public-choice perspective, too much of the transfer to low-income people comes from the middle of the distribution. He also noted that the earned income tax credit goes to those with children at the expense of childless low-income families.

CHAPTER 6

On the high-income Laffer curve

Joel Slemrod

1   Introduction

Should the rich pay more tax? Many in the Democratic party think so, judging by the Democratic-sponsored Congressional proposal of 1992 that featured an increase in the top bracket rate from 31% to 36%, with a 10% surtax on millionaires taking the proposed top rate to 39.6%. So, apparently, do many in the British Labour Party, whose 1992 electoral platform contained an increase in the top marginal income-tax rate from 40% to 50%. As it happened, the U.S. tax bill containing the tax increase was vetoed by President Bush, largely because of the rate increases; the Labour Party was defeated.

Despite the recent lack of success in the United States and the United Kingdom of proposals to tax the rich more heavily, it is unlikely to go away as an issue. A tax increase on those with annual income exceeding $200,000, plus a "millionaire's surtax," is part of the Democratic Party's platform for the 1992 presidential race. Fueling the drive to increase tax progressivity is a sense that the 1980s saw a shift in tax burden away from the high-income class toward the middle-income class, at the same time that the distribution of pre-tax income was becoming substantially more unequal.[1]

Logically prior to the question of whether the rich *should* be taxed more is the question of whether the rich *can* be taxed more. If levying higher rates on the rich yields no increase in revenue then only the envious

Prepared for the Office of Tax Policy Research Conference on Tax Progressivity, held on September 11–12, 1992, in Ann Arbor. I am indebted to Jonathan Parker for providing outstanding research assistance; Shawn Cheng and David Hummels also helped out. Valuable comments on an earlier draft were received from Len Burman, Don Fullerton, Eric Toder, Shlomo Yitzhaki, and the participants in the conference.
[1] For one assessment of these phenomena, see Gramlich, Kasten, and Sammartino (1993).

177

would favor such taxation, for it benefits no one in society. If higher rates yield revenue but cause significant behavioral response, then the economic costs of raising that revenue could be quite high and could exceed the benefits of the revenue gained.

The notion that an increase in tax rates might reduce tax revenue played a major role in the tax-policy debates of the late 1970s and early 1980s, and is most associated with the name of Arthur Laffer. The "Laffer curve" – the inverted-U-shaped plot of revenues against tax rate – encapsulated the idea that because of taxpayer response there would be "leakage" in revenues when tax rates increased, and that tax increases beyond some tax rate would actually cause revenues to fall.

Most economists believe that the economic response to the tax cuts of the 1980s has discredited the idea of an inverse revenue response to tax rates as it applies to an across-the-board cut. Framed as a proposition solely about the highest income classes, however, the Laffer curve is still alive, championed in the work of Lawrence Lindsey (1990), among others. It was Lindsey who first pointed out that the 1981 cut in the top marginal tax rate from 70% to 50% coincided with an unprecedented increase in the income earned by the top 1 percent of the income distribution. The rapid increase in income inequality, and in particular the rising share of income received by the top 1 percent, has since become a widely studied phenomenon, and has been ascribed to increased openness of the economy, technological changes, and an increased return to education due perhaps to changes in the relative supply of skilled and unskilled labor.[2]

The high-income Laffer curve offers a competing, though not necessarily mutually exclusive, explanation for the recent growth in measured inequality. The story goes as follows: Under the pre-1981 tax system, when the top tax rate was 70% (and even higher before 1964), there was a tremendous incentive for high-income individuals to re-arrange their financial affairs and form of compensation to expose less income to taxation; there was also less incentive to expend effort to earn money. Many of these tax responses to high taxation would reduce income as measured by the Census, surveys such as the Panel Study on Income Dynamics, or tax-return data. For example, the imputed income from owner-occupied housing, which is untaxed at the federal level, does not ordinarily enter into measures of income; neither does deferred compensation. To the extent that high taxes before 1981 caused behavior that reduced the *measured* income of high-income individuals, the recent rapid increase in inequality at the top is an illusion. High-income individuals had more

---

[2] See Levy and Murnane (1992) for a useful survey of nontax explanations for the growth of inequality in the past two decades.

income before 1981 than was measured, because much of it came in the form of imputed income, fringe benefits, and leisure.

The answers to both questions – the economic cost of taxing high-income individuals, and the origin of the apparent recent surge in income inequality – depend on the extent of behavioral response to taxation. In other words, we need to know where we are on the high-income Laffer curve. This paper reviews some evidence that may be helpful in evaluating this question and therefore also in understanding the role of taxes in the observed increase in income concentration.

2   Who are the rich?[3]

> F. Scott Fitzgerald: "The rich are different from us."
> Ernest Hemingway: "Yes, they have more money."

2.1   Demographic information

Mr. Hemingway was not quite right, as the demographic information of Table 1 shows. Compared to the overall population, high-income families were (as of 1982) much more likely to be headed by someone between 45 and 74 years old, and to be highly educated. Also true, but not shown in the table, is that high-income families are much more likely to have a household with a working husband and a nonworking wife, and are almost all non-Hispanic Caucasians. Similar demographic patterns are present in the 1962 data that are available, although Wolff (1992) notes that between 1962 and 1983 the share of total wealth accounted for by households headed by someone between 45 and 69 jumped from 60% to 66%.

Table 1 also shows just how different is the occupational breakdown of the rich. While 38% of the total population report their occupation as clerical/sales, craftsman/foreman, or operative/labor/service work, less than 2% of the high-income group do so. For the high-income group there is a preponderance of household heads who are lawyers or accountants (12%), health service professionals (5%), or engaged in banking, insurance, or real estate (24%). For the overall population, these three occupational categories together account for only 4% of the total. More than one-quarter of all heads of high-income families report their occupation as self-employed professional or managerial, compared to only 10% for the overall population.

---

[3] I will use the term "rich" interchangeably with "affluent" and "high-income." The operational definition I employ is those households whose income is in the top 1 percent of all household, or taxpaying, units.

Table 1. *Distribution of age and occupation for high-income and all families, 1982*

	High-income families	All families
Age of head (years)		
Less than 25	0	8
25–34	1.5	23
35–44	15.5	20
45–54	28.5	16
55–64	34.5	15
65–74	17	12
75 or more	3.5	7
	100	100
Education of head		
0–12 years	4.5	60
Some college	12	17
College degree	33	13
Some graduate school	52	10
	100	100
Occupation of head		
Not working	8	31
Clerical or sales	1.5	8
Craftsman or foreman	0	12
Operative, labor, or service work	0	18
Lawyer or accountant	12	1
Health service professional	5	1
Banking, insurance, or real estate	24	2
Other professional or managerial, not self-employed	23	17
Other professional or managerial, self-employed	25.5	10
	100	100

Note: Because of rounding, column totals may not sum to exactly 100.
Source: Computed from table 1 in Avery and Elliehausen (1986, p. 165).

2.2   *Composition of income*

Capital income is a much more important source of income for the affluent, compared to the population as a whole; wages and salaries are correspondingly less important. As Table 2 suggests, (as of 1988) wage and

Table 2. *Composition of gross income for top 1 percent of income earners and all taxpayers, 1988*

	Top 1 percent of taxpayers	All taxpayers
Salaries and wages	43.4	75.9
Taxable interest	7.6	6.1
Dividends	5.8	2.5
Net capital gains	22.1	5.0
Pensions and annuities	1.5	4.5
Rents, royalties, trust, and partnership income	12.6	2.9
Business profit	4.8	4.1

Source: Tabulated from 1988 *Individual Model File* (IRS).

salary income constitutes only 43% of gross income[4] for the rich, but represents 82% of gross income for everyone else. Realized capital gains amount to 22.1% of gross income of the affluent, compared to 1.8% for everyone else. Income from rents, royalties, estates and trusts, and partnerships (schedule E income) is 13% of total income for the rich, compared to 2% for everyone else. The share of reported business profit is, however, not much different for the two groups.

It is important to note that, for the affluent, the averages just mentioned do not describe a typical household. On the contrary, Figure 1 shows that the distribution of the ratio of wages and salaries to gross income is U-shaped, with 17.7% of the rich having no wage income at all and 31.5% having wages and salaries that constitute at least 90% of gross income. The overall average wages-to-income percentage of 43% cited previously is particularly misleading, because the fraction of taxpayers whose wages are between 40% and 50% of gross income is the next-to-lowest of all subsets of the top 1-percent group. In contrast, the bottom panel of Figure 1 shows that, for taxpayers as a whole, 67.7% earn at least 90% of their gross income from wages and salaries; note also that the overall distribution is U-shaped, although a much smaller fraction (15.2% compared to 40.5% for the rich) have positive wage income amounting to less than 90% of gross income.

---

[4] Gross income is defined as adjusted gross income plus the part of long-term capital gains that is excluded from income for tax purposes. This exclusion did not apply in 1988, so that gross income is identical to adjusted gross income for tax purposes, but does matter in the definition for the earlier years discussed in Section 4.

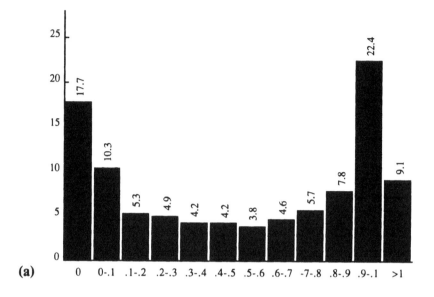

(a)

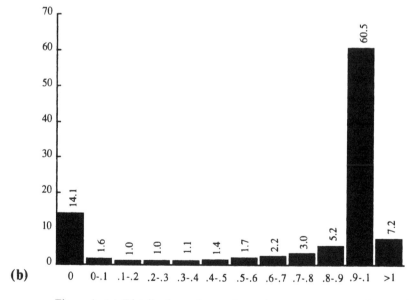

(b)

Figure 1. (a) Distribution of wage/gross-income percentage for top 1 percent of income earners, 1988. (b) Distribution of wage/gross-income percentage for all taxpayers, 1988. *Source:* tabulations from 1988 Individual Model File.

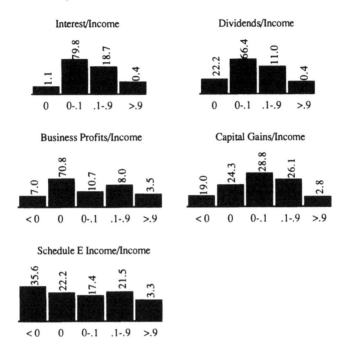

Figure 2. Distribution of the percentage of various income sources to income for the top 1 percent, 1988. *Source:* tabulations from 1988 Individual Model File.

For the other major income sources there is a fairly consistent story for the top 1 percent. Most have some nonzero amount and most receive a small fraction from any particular source, yet some have their income dominated by that source. These patterns are displayed in Figure 2.

2.3   *Important patterns*

The data tell us that the affluent are a diverse group, distributed across all age groups (although concentrated among the 45–74 age classes), occupational groups (although concentrated among professionals and business), and educational classes (although more educated than average). The picture suggested by an average high-income American is particularly misleading with respect to the composition of income, because the income of many of the affluent is dominated by one or two income sources. Although on average 43% of their income is from wage and salaries, deriving half of income in wages and salaries is actually a very atypical situation. Nevertheless, the importance of nonwage income is clear. Figure 1 reveals that 46.1% of the affluent receive at least half of their income from sources other than wages and salaries. Thus, in the analyses that follow we must confront the impact of taxation on nonlabor income.

2.4   *Dimensions of response to high tax rates*

Households can react to high marginal tax rates in a variety of ways. One response is to reduce the amount of time and effort devoted to income-earning activities, via seeking less overtime work, taking more vacation, or choosing lower-paying, less burdensome jobs. This kind of behavior would result in lower wage and salary income as well as less income from self-employment.

Taxes could also affect the form in which compensation to labor effort is paid. Higher tax rates provide an incentive to receive payment in the form of untaxed fringe benefits, to defer compensation until retirement (both to postpone the tax liability and to incur the tax liability in presumably lower-earning, and therefore lower-tax-rate, years), and to receive preferentially taxed stock options rather than salary. For the self-employed, taxes can affect whether firms are incorporated.

Taxes can also affect financial behavior, one aspect of which is portfolio composition. Higher marginal tax rates will induce individuals to favor tax-preferred assets such as owner-occupied housing, tax-exempt bonds, and low-dividend "growth" stocks over fully taxed assets such as taxable bonds and high-dividend stocks. Borrowing (with deductible interest payments) to finance tax-preferred investments becomes especially attractive to people with high tax rates.

A fourth category of response concerns capital gains realization. Because capital gains are taxed upon realization rather than accrual, and because accrued capital gains are excused from taxation upon the bequest of the assets, the decision of when to dispose of assets and thus trigger taxation is potentially quite sensitive to tax law. This is an important issue for the affluent, because capital gains are a significant fraction of their income.

These four dimensions of response to high tax rates, and others not detailed here, apply to both affluent and nonaffluent households.[5] There is, however, reason to suspect that affluent households have more flexibility in arranging their hours of work and form of compensation. Furthermore,

[5] These four categories do not exhaust the ways that individuals can respond to changes in tax rates. One other dimension of response, not treated here for lack of data, is tax evasion. Empirical evidence on the responsiveness of evasion to elements of the tax system is presented in Slemrod (1992b).

because capital income is so important a fraction of their income, portfolio and capital gains–realization responses are more significant than for the rest of the population. For this reason it may not be appropriate to assess the high-income Laffer curve using estimates of behavioral response that are based on evidence and analyses concerning the population as a whole.

Two analytical points are worth making here. The first is that a change in the marginal tax rate applying only to the top bracket of income (or, more generally, to income above a cutoff) is more likely to provoke an inverse revenue response than an across-the-board cut, for a given (uncompensated) elasticity of response. For example, consider a tax system with two brackets yielding a tax liability of $m_1 Y$ if income is less than $\bar{Y}$ and of $m_1 \bar{Y} + m_2 (Y - \bar{Y})$ if Y exceeds $\bar{Y}$, where m_1 and m_2 are the marginal tax rates applicable to each bracket. Now consider an increase in m_2 only, holding m_1 constant. In this case revenue will decline if the (absolute value of the) marginal tax–rate elasticity of income, assumed to be constant for all taxpayers, exceeds $(Y^a - \bar{Y})/Y^a$, where Y^a is the average income level for taxpayers with income over $\bar{Y}$.[6] Of course this trigger elasticity for an inverse revenue response is less than 1, whereas in the simple linear tax case (where $\bar{Y} = 0$) the trigger elasticity is exactly 1. The trigger elasticity is lower because the increase in m_2 does not increase the tax raised on the inframarginal income between 0 and $\bar{Y}$.[7]

The second point is that, for given income and substitution effects, a tax change that applies only to the top tax bracket will produce a more negative uncompensated supply elasticity than would an across-the-board change. This occurs because, compared to an across-the-board tax increase, the decline in income is lower, so that there will be less of a positive income effect on labor supply to offset the negative substitution effect.

3   Tax changes between 1962 and 1988

The best way to judge how high-income people will react to high tax rates is to observe how they actually have reacted in the past. For this purpose the ideal data set would follow the same individuals through periods of tax-rate–regime changes. Unfortunately, there is no panel data set covering

[6] This calculation ignores the fact that it would never be optimal, in response to an increase in m_2, to reduce Y below $\bar{Y}$.

[7] To get a feel for the empirical importance of this point, consider a policy that would impose an increase in the marginal tax rate applying only to the top 1 percent of income earners. In 1988 the cutoff level for the top 1 percent of AGI (adjusted gross income) earners was $156,600, and the mean AGI of taxpayers above this level was $432,110. Thus a tax increase targeted at this group would raise revenue as long as the elasticity of taxable income was less than 0.64.

a long time span which has income and wealth information for a large sample of high-income households. One alternative is to compare the behavior of a nonrepeating sample of individuals under different tax regimes. Fortunately for this kind of exercise, starting in 1988 and peering back over the past three decades, one observes a nondecreasing series of statutory rates on the highest levels of income. In 1988 and 1987 the top rate was 28% and 38.5%, respectively; in the 1981–86 period it was 50%; in the 1965–80 period it was (except for 1968–70) 70%; between 1951 and 1963, the top rate hovered at slightly over 90%.

In Section 4, I begin to analyze data on high-income taxpayers from several years between 1962 and 1988, with a goal of identifying tax-induced changes in behavior that would dampen the revenue otherwise expected from imposing higher rates on high-income individuals. Of course, ascribing differences in behavior across these periods to differences in the tax regimes is a tricky business. Much else changed between 1962 and 1988, including the households for whom data are collected. Nevertheless, the hope is that some illuminating patterns will emerge. Before undertaking this exercise, in this section I briefly review the important changes in taxation between 1962 and 1988.

3.1   *Marginal tax rates on the affluent*

Table 3 presents the tax-rate schedules for a married couple filing jointly for 1962, 1977, 1982, and 1988; all the income brackets are expressed in 1988 dollars. Note first that the notoriously high top marginal taxes of 1962 applied only to very high real-income levels. For example, the top marginal tax rate of 91% applied only to incomes above about $1.5 million (in 1988 dollars). At the real-income level where in 1977 the 70% rate began, in 1962 the marginal tax rate of 78% was higher, but not that much higher, than in 1977. A marginal tax rate as high as 50% began at approximately the same level of real income in 1962 and 1977.

Thus between 1962 and 1977 the marginal tax rate that applied to the top 0.1 percent of families fell significantly; this decline did not, however, occur for the lower nine-tenths of the top 1 percent of taxpayers.[8] However, between 1977 and 1982 there was a significant drop in the marginal tax rate applying to the top 1 percent; another large reduction occurred between 1982 and 1988.

Information concerning the marginal tax rate on taxable income does not, however, complete the picture of how taxes affected high-income

---

[8] In 1988 the cutoff for the top 1 percent of adjusted gross income was $156,000; the cutoff for the top 0.1 percent was $684,900.

Table 3. *Marginal tax rates for married taxpayers filing jointly: 1962, 1977, 1982, and 1988*

	Marginal tax rates (%)			
AGI[a]	1962	1977	1982	1988
5,000	0	0	0	0
10,000	18	0	14	15
20,000	18	17	19	15
35,000	20	25	29	15
50,000	26	32	39	28
75,000	34	42	44	28
100,000	43	50	49	33
150,000	53	55	50	33
250,000	62	64	50	28
500,000	78	70	50	28
1,000,000	89	70	50	28
2,000,000	91	70	50	28

Note: Calculations assume that the couple does not itemize, that they claim two exemptions (for themselves), and that they do not receive the earned income tax credit or use the alternative minimum tax.
[a] Adjusted gross income, in 1988 dollars.
Sources: Individual income tax forms from Internal Revenue Service (various years), Statistics of Income Division, *Individual Income Tax Returns.* Consumer Price Index from Council of Economic Advisers, *Economic Report of the President* (1992, table B-56).

individuals. Throughout this period there was special tax treatment of particular forms of income.

3.2   *Capital gains tax rates*

Capital gains have always received special tax treatment; the basic rate on realized long-term gains has never exceeded 35%, although special provisions (some of which are discussed in what follows) pushed it higher in certain cases. The special tax treatment has several elements. First of all, gains are taxed only upon realization; furthermore, inheritors of capital assets can adjust the taxable basis to the current market price, thus exempting from tax all the gain accrued during the lifetime of the bequeathor. Realized gains are taxed on a nominal basis, with no adjustment for

Table 4. *Average effective marginal tax rates (%) on long-term capital gains for high-income individuals 1965–89*

1965	25.3	1974	34.4	1983	20.0
1966	25.3	1975	34.7	1984	20.0
1967	25.3	1976	37.3	1985	20.0
1968	27.1	1977	41.2	1986	20.0
1969	27.7	1978	39.1	1987	28.0
1970	32.0	1979	26.9	1988	28.0
1971	33.9	1980	27.6	1989	28.0
1972	34.6	1981	24.2		
1973	35.0	1982	20.0		

Source: Lindsey (1987, p. 85, table 3.5). Refers to households with income over $1 million; updated past 1982 by the author.

changes in the price level during the holding period. There is a limit on the amount of losses that can be taken against other income, but losses in excess of that limit can be carried forward without interest to future years.

Since the Revenue Act of 1921, capital gains have been taxed preferentially. Recently, long-term gains (defined as gains on assets held for at least six months or, between 1978 and 1984, for at least one year) were given a 50% exclusion from taxable income. This exclusion was increased to 60% after October 31, 1978, but was eliminated by the Tax Reform Act of 1986.

Several other provisions substantially affected the tax rate on realized capital gains. One such provision was the alternative tax on capital gains. Prior to 1970, this allowed taxpayers the option of paying an effective tax rate of 25% on all long-term capital gains. The Tax Reform Act of 1969 limited the alternative 25% rate to a maximum of $50,000 in net long-term gains per year.

Table 4 presents one estimate of the average marginal tax rate on long-term capital gains for high-income individuals, including all the provisions discussed here and the "poisoning" of the maximum tax on earned income, to be discussed shortly. It shows rates generally rising from 1965 to 1978, falling abruptly in 1979 and still further in 1982, and staying at the low point for the period until 1987, when rates moved up to a level reminiscent of the late 1960s and late 1970s.

3.3   *Maximum tax on earned income*

The maximum tax on personal service income, passed as part of the Tax Reform Act of 1969, was designed to limit the marginal tax rate on

Table 5. *Average marginal tax rates on earned income, 1980*

Marginal rate (%) without maximum tax	Average marginal rate (%) with maximum tax
50–51	50.5
51–52	51.5
52–54	51.6
54–56	53.5
56–60	55.5
60–65	56.5
65–70	58.6
Over 70	59.1

Source: Calculated from Lindsey (1981, table 1), assuming for tax-rate ranges a midpoint of 48% for "under 50%" category and of 72% for "over 70%" category.

noncapital income to be no more than 50%, even though the statutory marginal tax rate could reach 70%.[9] It allowed a qualifying taxpayer to subtract from the ordinary tax liability the difference between the ordinary tax liability on "earned taxable income" and what that liability would have been if the top tax rate were 50%.

This provision did not literally impose a maximum marginal tax rate of 50% on earned income. In fact, the effective marginal tax rate on earned income became $0.50 + (t_0 - \alpha t_E)$, where t_0 is the marginal tax rate on all income, t_F is the (hypothetical) marginal tax rate if there were no unearned income, and α is the fraction of earned income treated as earned taxable income (where the difference is the amount of deductions that had to be apportioned to earned income).[10]

Although the maximum tax did not literally impose a ceiling marginal tax rate of 50% on earned income, it did significantly reduce the marginal tax rate on earned income for high-income taxpayers. Because the maximum-tax provision did not literally impose a top rate of 50%, the subsequent 1981 tax act did provide a further significant cut in the marginal tax rate for affluent taxpayers. As an illustration, Table 5 shows that in 1980 the average marginal tax rate on earned income was below 60%,

[9] This provision was phased in beginning in tax year 1971, and was fully effective in 1972.
[10] This was pointed out by Sunley (1974) and Lindsey (1981); see their papers for further discussion, including a definition of the concept of earned taxable income.

although the top statutory rate in 1980 was 70%; however, a wide dispersion of marginal tax rates existed within any given group. Loosely speaking, the maximum tax was not helpful to taxpayers whose earned income by itself would not put them in a very high tax bracket but whose unearned income did so. In other words, relief was granted in proportion to earned income, regardless of whether the presence of additional unearned income increased the taxpayer's marginal tax rate above 50%.[11]

Between 1971 and 1976 the maximum tax also had an indirect, "poisoning," effect on the marginal tax rate on capital gains, because in some cases additional capital gains reduced the amount of earned income eligible for the maximum-tax preference. Moreover, there was an absolute limit on the amount of income eligible for the maximum tax; this limit was equal to taxable income minus the included portion of capital gains.

3.4   *Other important provisions*

Under the Revenue Act of 1964, taxpayers could average fluctuating income over a five-year period so as to reduce total tax liability compared to that due if the same total income were received in a constant stream; the 1969 Act increased the amount that could be averaged. The 1986 Act eliminated averaging, partly because it is less necessary in an era when the degree of graduation in rates is much less. When in effect, the averaging provisions reduced the effective tax rate on temporarily high income below what it would otherwise be.

The 1969 Act also introduced an "add-on" minimum tax of 10% on a set of "preference" items, including the excluded part of long-term capital gains; the rate was increased to 15% by the Tax Reform Act of 1976. The Revenue Act of 1978 removed from the list of preference items the excluded portion of long-term capital gains; until this time this feature would, in some cases, have increased the tax on capital gains. Starting in 1979, the add-on minimum tax was supplemented by an "alternative" minimum tax whose base included the excluded part of long-term gains and other preference items. For high-income taxpayers the rate has been between 20% and 25% since 1979. The add-on minimum tax was repealed in 1982, although the alternative minimum-tax treatment of capital gains was retained. Because the 1986 Act eliminated the exclusion for long-term capital gains, it is no longer a part of the minimum-tax base.

This discussion does not exhaust all the tax code changes of the past three decades which could affect the economic behavior of the affluent;

[11] This characteristic of the maximum tax on earned income suggests the possibility of an interesting test of the labor supply responsiveness of high-income individuals, since the 1981 act affected different households differently depending on their pre-1981 maximum-tax status.

Table 6. *Composition of gross income for top 1 percent of income earners and all taxpayers, 1962 (billions of 1962 dollars)*

	Top 1 percent of taxpayers		All taxpayers		
	Sum	% of gross income	Sum	% of gross income	Share of top 1 percent
Gross income	33.4	100.0	354.9	100.0	9.4
Salaries and wages	10.2	30.5	282.1	79.5	3.6
Interest	1.2	3.5	7.1	2.0	16.9
Dividends	5.4	16.2	11.3	3.2	47.8
Pensions and annuities	0.1	0.3	2.3	0.6	4.4
Partnership net profit	3.5	10.6	9.5	2.7	36.8
Net capital gain	7.3	21.9	12.3	3.5	59.3
Business or farm net profit	4.4	13.1	24.4	6.9	18.0
Rents, royalties, estate, trust, and other income	1.4	4.2	6.4	1.8	21.9

Note: The first row of each column does not represent the sum of the column, owing to missing categories, elimination of the dividend exclusions, and rounding.
Source: Tabulated from 1962 *Individual Model File* (IRS).

potentially important are the effective tax rate on business income, which was dramatically reduced by the Economic Recovery Tax Act of 1981, and the changing ability to use tax losses to offset other income. These other trends notwithstanding, the overall trend from 1962 to the present has been a decline in the top statutory rate imposed on ordinary income accompanied by a first rising and then falling effective tax rate on capital gains.[12] Because of the large share of capital gains in the income of the affluent, and because of the arguably large tax sensitivity of capital gains realizations, it is important to recognize these two distinct trends.

4   Composition of wealth and income

I begin the search for evidence of tax effects on behavior of the affluent by examining in Tables 6–13 the changes from 1962 to 1988 in the composition of gross income and wealth of the top 1 percent of gross income earners, compared to the population as a whole. The income data in Tables 6–10 are based on the public-use Individual Model Files compiled

[12] The top rate on long-term capital gains rose again in 1987, from 20% to 28%.

Table 7. *Composition of gross income for top 1 percent of income earners and all taxpayers, 1970 (billions of 1970 dollars)*

	Top 1 percent of taxpayers		All taxpayers		
	Sum	% of gross income	Sum	% of gross income	Share of top 1 percent
Gross income	62.2	100.0	689.2	100.0	9.0
Salaries and wages	21.5	34.6	565.2	82.0	3.8
Interest	3.4	5.5	24.2	3.5	14.1
Dividends	7.2	11.6	16.7	2.4	43.1
Pensions and annuities	0.3	0.5	9.7	1.4	3.1
Partnership net profit	9.6	15.4	20.9	3.0	45.9
Net capital gain	15.5	24.9	28.1	4.1	55.2
Business net profit	8.3	13.3	38.7	5.6	21.5
Farm net profit	0.8	1.3	8.7	1.3	9.2
Rents, royalties, estate, and trust income	2.4	3.9	11.0	1.6	21.8

Note: The first row of each column does not represent the sum of the column, owing to missing categories, elimination of the dividend exclusions, and rounding.
Source: Tabulated from 1970 *Individual Model File* (IRS).

by the Statistics of Income Division of the Internal Revenue Service, so that the population is tax-filing units.[13] The wealth data in Tables 11–13 are from the 1962 Survey of Consumer Finances and the 1983 and 1989 Surveys of Financial Characteristics of Consumers, all conducted by the Board of Governors of the Federal Reserve System.

Several characteristics of these tables are worthy of note. First, there is evidence of the recent increased concentration of wealth and, especially, income. Although the share in gross income earned by the top 1 percent gradually fell from 9.4% in 1962 to 8.8% in 1977, it increased to 10.5% in 1982 and rose sharply to 15.4% in 1988. The share of wealth rose slightly from 21.9% in 1962 to 22.8% in 1983, and to 25.3% in 1989.

[13] Because the tax-filing population is a subset of the population as a whole, the concentration of income for tax filers may misrepresent the overall concentration; the direction of the bias is theoretically indeterminate, depending on the precise distribution. Because the real income threshold for filing a return has changed over the past three decades, so has the fraction of all households represented by the tax-filing population; thus, whatever bias exists cannot be assumed to be constant over time. The extent and trend of this bias is being investigated further by the author.

Table 8. *Composition of gross income for top 1 percent of income earners and all taxpayers, 1977 (billions of 1977 dollars)*

	Top 1 percent of taxpayers		All taxpayers		
	Sum	% of gross income	Sum	% of gross income	Share of top 1 percent
Gross income	103.5	100.0	1,180.8	100.0	8.8
Salaries and wages	46.0	44.4	969.4	82.1	4.7
Interest	6.1	5.9	54.6	4.6	11.2
Dividends	11.5	11.1	28.5	2.4	40.4
Pensions and annuities	0.7	0.7	29.2	2.5	2.4
Partnership net profit	5.5	5.3	13.3	1.1	41.4
Net capital gain	21.0	20.3	42.2	3.6	49.8
Business net profit	9.4	9.2	49.5	4.2	19.0
Farm net profit	−0.2	−0.2	0.5	0.0	NA[a]
Rents, royalties, estate, and trust income	2.9	2.8	8.0	0.7	36.3

Note: The first row of each column does not represent the sum of the column, owing to missing categories, elimination of the dividend exclusions, and rounding.
[a] NA = not available.
Source: Tabulated from 1977 *Individual Model File* (IRS).

The composition of income and wealth of the top 1 percent also exhibits some striking trends. The first is the sharp increase in the importance of wages and salaries between 1962 and 1977, increasing from 30.5% in 1962 to 34.6% in 1970 and to 44.4% in 1977; its share remained approximately constant between 1977 and 1988. Offsetting the increased share of wages and salaries were declines between 1962 and 1977 in all major categories of capital income except interest – dividends, net capital gains, rents and royalties, partnership net profit, and business net profit. The declining share of dividends, business net profits, and rent and royalties continued between 1977 and 1988, apparently reflecting a 2½-decade–long trend. Over the entire 1962–88 period the share of dividends fell from 16.2% to 5.8% of income, while the share of business net profits fell from 13.1% to 4.8%.

The approximately constant share of gross income received by the top 1 percent between 1962 and 1977 is thus the net result of two offsetting trends. Wage and salary growth for the top 1 percent far exceeded the overall average: nominal growth of 351% for the top 1 percent compared to 244% overall. The growth of other income (everything but wages and

194   **Joel Slemrod**

Table 9. *Composition of gross income for top 1 percent of income earners and all taxpayers, 1982 (billions of 1982 dollars)*

| | Top 1 percent of taxpayers | | All taxpayers | | |
	Sum	% of gross income	Sum	% of gross income	Share of top 1 percent
Gross income	199.9	100.0	1,903.8	100.0	10.5
Salaries and wages	88.3	44.2	1,565.0	82.2	5.6
Interest	20.3	10.2	157.0	8.2	12.9
Dividends	19.5	9.8	54.0	2.8	36.1
Pensions and annuities	1.6	0.8	60.1	3.2	2.7
Partnership net profit	3.3	1.7	−1.6	−0.1	NA[a]
Net capital gain	57.6	28.8	85.6	4.5	67.3
Business net profit	7.7	3.9	50.6	2.7	15.2
Farm net profit	−1.2	−0.6	−9.8	−0.5	NA
Rents, royalties, estate, and trust income	6.0	3.0	3.6	0.2	166.7

Note: The first row of each column does not represent the sum of the column, owing to missing categories, elimination of the dividend exclusions, and rounding.
[a] NA = not available.
Source: Tabulated from 1988 *Individual Model File* (IRS).

salaries) for the top 1 percent fell short of the overall average – 148% compared to 190%. In contrast, between 1977 and 1988 both the wage and salary income *and* other income of the top 1 percent grew at a much faster rate than for the whole population. The combination of these factors explains the large growth between 1977 and 1988 in the share of total income going to the top 1 percent.

What could be behind the lagging growth of the capital income of the top 1 percent between 1962 and 1977? Two possibilities exist. One is that their share of wealth declined, while the relative rate of return stayed constant. Because no wealth survey exists for 1977, this possibility is impossible to evaluate directly. However, Tables 11 and 12 indicate that wealth became slightly more concentrated between 1962 and 1983. It is therefore unlikely, although not impossible, that wealth was less concentrated in 1977 than in 1962.[14]

[14] Although Wolff (1992), using evidence from estate-tax series, concludes that wealth concentration fell substantially during the mid-1970s and then increased sharply during the late 1970s and early 1980s.

Table 10. *Composition of gross income for top 1 percent of income earners and all taxpayers, 1988 (billions of 1988 dollars)*

	Top 1 percent of taxpayers		All taxpayers		
	Sum	% of gross income	Sum	% of gross income	Share of top 1 percent
Gross income	474.1	100.0	3,082.3	100.0	15.4
Salaries and wages	205.6	43.4	2,338.4	75.9	8.8
Interest	36.0	7.6	187.0	6.1	19.3
Dividends	27.5	5.8	77.6	2.5	35.4
Pensions and annuities	7.3	1.5	138.8	4.5	5.3
Partnership net profit	54.2	11.4	55.6	1.8	97.5
Net capital gain	104.6	22.1	153.0	5.0	68.4
Business net profit	22.6	4.8	125.8	4.1	18.0
Farm net profit	−0.3	−0.1	−1.2	0.0	NA[a]
Rents, royalties, estate, and trust income	5.2	1.1	−4.1	−0.1	NA

Note: The first row of each column does not represent the sum of the column, owing to missing categories, elimination of the dividend exclusions, and rounding.
[a] NA = not available.
Source: Tabulated from 1988 *Individual Model File* (IRS).

The answer thus most likely lies in the second possibility – that the relative nominal rate of return on wealth reported on tax forms by the top 1 percent declined between 1962 and 1977. Part of this could be due to a reshuffling of their portfolios toward assets that yield a lower taxable rate of return. This kind of reaction is inconsistent with a pure tax story, which would imply a re-allocation over time of assets with high taxable rates of return toward high-income individuals, as their marginal tax rate relative to the population as a whole declined. But of course much else had changed between 1962 and 1977, especially the rate of inflation. It stood at 1.3% in 1962, but by 1977 it was 6.7% and had topped 12% just three years before. The fact that the tax system taxes nominal rather than real capital income means that higher inflation intensifies the "clientele" effect: high-tax individuals avoiding (or holding negative positions in) fully taxed assets such as bonds, and instead holding tax-preferred or tax-exempt assets. In periods of inflation, the marginal tax rate under-states the true effective tax rate on real income; higher inflation can offset the clientele effect of compressing marginal tax rates.

Table 11. *Composition of net worth of top 1 percent of income earners and all households, 1962 (billions of 1962 dollars)*

	Top 1 percent of households		All households		
	Sum	% of net worth	Sum	% of net worth	Share of top 1 percent
Net worth[a]	259.9	100	1,188.0	100	21.9
Gross asset values					
Principal residence	24.6	9.5	460.2	38.7	5.4
Other real estate	29.2	11.2	128.2	10.8	22.8
Stocks	99.9	38.4	222.6	18.7	44.9
U.S. government bonds	2.5	1.0	26.6	2.2	9.4
State and local bonds	10.8	4.2	12.7	1.1	85.0
Other marketable securities	4.3	1.7	12.6	1.1	34.1
Checking accounts	5.6	2.2	23.7	2.0	23.6
Savings accounts	6.1	2.3	104.8	8.8	5.8
Net business profession	81.1	31.2	224.8	18.9	36.1
Net business not managed by family	4.5	1.7	43.9	3.7	10.3
Automobiles	1.7	0.7	55.0	4.6	3.1
Liabilities					
Debt on principal residence	4.2	1.6	143.8	12.1	2.9
Debt on real estate	6.8	2.6	26.0	2.2	26.2
Other debt	8.8	3.3	52.2	4.4	16.9

Note: Columns do not sum to totals owing to excluded categories.
[a] Net worth includes all assets less all debt in the survey, except the value of pensions and life insurance (which are excluded from the survey's definition of wealth because of misreporting and nonresponse).
Source: Tabulated from 1962 *Survey of Financial Characteristics of Consumers*, Board of Governors of the Federal Reserve System.

The declining importance of dividends for the top 1 percent is mirrored in the data on the composition of wealth (Tables 11–13) by the decline in the share of wealth held in stock for this group. In 1962 stocks amounted to 38% of the net worth of the top 1 percent, but had fallen to 22% by 1983 and only 8% by 1989.[15] Thus, the income and wealth data consistently reflect a decline in the role of stocks for high-income individuals.

[15] The share of stocks in net worth for the whole population was also sharply declining over this period, from 17% to 6%. But the portion of all stock that was held by the top 1 percent fell from 51% to 44%.

Table 12. *Composition of net worth of top 1 percent of income earners and all households, 1983 (billions of 1983 dollars)*

	Top 1 percent of households		All households		
	Sum	% of net worth	Sum	% of net worth	Share of top 1 percent
Net worth[a]	2,240.1	100	9,820.5	100	22.8
Gross asset values					
Principal residence	252.9	11.3	3,738.5	38.1	6.8
Other real estate	331.9	14.8	1,687.5	17.2	19.7
Stocks	500.7	22.4	1,041.1	10.6	48.1
U.S. government bonds	2.0	0.1	27.3	0.3	7.3
State and local bonds	93.3	4.2	204.6	2.1	45.6
Other marketable securities	49.7	2.2	162.4	1.7	30.6
Checking and money market accounts	84.3	3.8	395.6	4.0	21.3
Savings accounts and CDs	33.4	1.5	581.4	5.9	5.7
Net business/profession	581.0	25.9	1,924.4	19.6	30.2
Net business not managed by family	117.2	5.2	360.0	3.7	32.6
Automobiles	10.8	0.5	373.3	3.8	2.9
Liabilities					
Debt on principal residence	40.1	1.8	864.6	8.8	4.6
Debt on other real estate	58.7	2.6	324.1	3.3	18.1
Other debt	29.8	1.3	260.6	2.8	11.4

Note: Columns do not sum to totals owing to excluded categories. Income data are 1982 earnings, while wealth is current wealth at the time of the interview (between February and July, 1983).
[a] Net worth includes all assets less all debt in the survey, except the value of pensions and life insurance (which are excluded for comparability with the 1962 survey data).
Source: Tabulated from 1983 *Survey of Consumer Finances,* Board of Governors of the Federal Reserve System.

For business assets and real estate, however, the wealth and income data do not tell a consistent story. The wealth data show that the portion of the net worth of high-income individuals held in business assets first dropped from 33% in 1962 to 31% in 1983, and then rose sharply to 38% in 1989. Recall that over this same period the business-income fraction of capital income declined for this group. Trends in real estate ownership of the top 1 percent are also mixed. While the fraction of net worth

Table 13. *Composition of net worth of top 1 percent of income earners and all households, 1989 (billions of 1989 dollars)*

	Top 1 percent of households		All households		
	Holdings	% of net worth	Holdings	% of net worth	Share of top 1 percent
Net worth	4,155.3	100	16,459.2	100	25.3
Gross asset values					
Homes	470.9	11.3	6,391.3	38.8	7.4
Other real estate	1,057.1	25.4	2,983.6	18.1	35.4
Stocks	332.4	8.0	918.6	5.6	36.2
Taxable bonds	152.2	3.7	286.8	1.7	53.1
Nontaxable bonds	206.1	5.0	407.4	2.5	50.6
Trusts	124.8	3.0	350.3	2.1	35.6
Life insurance	40.6	1.0	350.7	2.1	11.6
Checking and money market accounts	207.5	5.0	859.8	5.2	24.1
Savings accounts and CDs	80.5	1.9	864.8	5.3	9.3
Business	1,576.4	37.9	3,511.0	21.3	44.9
Vehicles	40.5	1.0	754.0	4.6	5.4
Liabilities					
Mortgages	89.8	2.2	1,615.9	9.0	5.6
Debt on other real estate	323.8	7.8	745.7	4.5	43.4

Note: Columns do not sum to totals owing to excluded categories.
Source: Tabulations of 1989 *Survey of Consumer Finances* data provided by John Karl Scholz.

represented by the principal residence shows no trend, the portion of net worth held in other real estate increased sharply from 11% in 1962 to 15% in 1983 and 25% in 1989. However, the share of other real estate in total net worth of all households rose similarly over this period, so that there was no marked move toward concentration of other real estate.

One of the striking aspects of Tables 6–13 is the comparative evolution of business assets and income of the top 1 percent. According to the wealth surveys, net business and professional assets of the top 1 percent rose from $85.6 billion in 1962 to $698.2 billion in 1982, more than an eightfold nominal increase. Yet the sum of business, farm, and partnership incomes reported on the tax returns of the top 1 percent rose from

$7.9 billion in 1962 to only $9.8 billion in 1982, an increase of just 24%. Part of the explanation is that 1982 was a recession year, but almost certainly another important part of the explanation is that the combination of generous investment incentives (accelerated depreciation and investment tax credits) and favorable tax-shelter provisions reduced the effective tax rate on business operations. Notably, by 1988 the partnership, business, and farm income of the top 1 percent had rebounded to $76.5 billion; of course, by 1988 the recession had passed and the ability to offset other income with partnership losses had been sharply curtailed.

Are the differences in portfolio composition between 1962 and the 1980s consistent with the story that lower tax rates induced high-income taxpayers to shift from tax-preferred to taxable assets? This question is difficult to answer with this impressionistic look at highly aggregated data, comparing time periods for which much more than relative tax rates have changed, including inflation rates and the supply of various assets. It is also very difficult to assess the "taxability" of assets – ranging from fully tax-exempt to fully taxed on nominal income – because the structure of marginal individual tax rates changed in addition to the tax rules governing business and real estate income. Beyond presenting some helpful data, only a few broad conclusions are possible.

Consider first the two types of completely federal-tax–exempt assets, the principal residence and state and local bonds; they should become less attractive to the rich as their relative marginal tax rate declines. In fact, neither shows a clear downward trend over the period as a share of the net worth of the affluent. However, the fraction of all state and local bonds held by the top 1 percent did decline from 85% to 51% between 1962 and 1989, a reduced concentration of holdings predicted by the tax clientele story. Such bonds constitute only 4.2% of the net worth of the rich in 1962, and only 3.0% in 1989.

Another interesting, but not decisive, calculation supports the view that the portfolio composition of the affluent has not changed in a way that has significantly increased the amount of income that is exposed to taxation. According to the 1962 wealth survey, the top 1 percent of income earners had $279.7 billion of net worth plus debt; in that year, the top 1 percent of taxpaying income earners had $19.5 billion of taxable capital income (defined to include interest, dividends, partnership net profit, half of net capital gains, business or farm net profit, and rents, royalties, estate, trust, and other income). The nominal rate of taxable return was thus 7.0%. The comparable calculation for the other 99 percent of income earners yields a nominal rate of taxable return equal to 4.0% (45.3 divided by 1,130.3). Repeating the same calculation for 1989 yields 5.4%

for the top 1 percent and 2.6% for the other 99 percent.[16] Thus both the absolute and relative difference in rate of return remained roughly constant between these two periods.

5   Capital gains and rank reversals

The data on income composition in Tables 6-10 makes it clear that realized capital gains are a significant part of the income of the well-to-do, amounting to more than 20% of their gross income in each of the years studied. For this reason alone, it is important to clarify their role in the high-income Laffer curve and how taxes affect the distribution of income. A key issue here is the responsiveness of capital gains realizations to the tax rate imposed on realized gains, and to the differential between the tax rate on capital gains and the tax rate on ordinary income. A high value of the capital gains tax rate provides the incentive to postpone realizing gains, perhaps until the gain is relieved from taxation upon the demise of the holder. A high value of the differential increases the incentive to convert ordinary income into realized capital gains, so as to take advantage of the preferential rate accorded to the gains.

I will not wade far into the large and contentious literature on the tax elasticity of capital gains realizations. I will, though, get my feet wet by characterizing the findings of what, in my opinion, are the two best kinds of empirical studies: aggregate time-series and longitudinal analyses.[17] The first finding is that the timing of realizations is highly sensitive to anticipated changes in capital gains tax rates. The second is that there is also a significant long-run sensitivity of capital gains realizations to a permanent change in capital gains rates; however, this elasticity is less than 1, so that in the long run a reduction in rates lowers the revenue collected on realizations.

The data surrounding the recent episodes of anticipated changes in rates - 1969-70, 1978-79, and 1986-87 - illustrate well the first proposition. In the 1969-70 and 1986-87 cases, an anticipated increase in tax rates led to a huge increase in realizations in the year before the rate increase was to take place. An anticipated decrease in tax rates as of 1979 led to a large amount of postponement of gains from 1978 until 1979.

Assessing the magnitude of the relationship between a steady rate of tax and the volume of realizations is a more subtle task, and a perusal of

[16] This calculation is based on 1989 income data, not 1988 data as in Table 10. Note that the definition of taxable capital income includes all of net capital gains for 1989.

[17] For an aggregate analysis, see Auerbach (1988). For longitudinal analyses, see Auten and Clotfelter (1982), Auten, Burman, and Randolph (1989), and Slemrod and Shobe (1990).

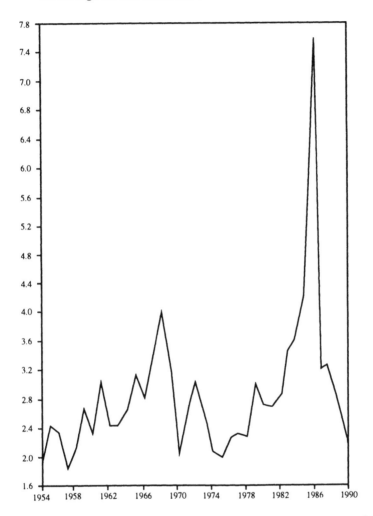

Figure 3. Long-term capital gains realizations as a percentage of GNP, 1954–90.

the time series is instructive, though not decisive. Figure 3 shows nominal long-term realizations as a fraction of nominal GNP for the period 1954–90. This figure suggests dividing 1954–90 into three periods: an upward trend characterizing the period until 1968; large declines in 1969 and 1970 followed by no growth until 1978; and rapid growth beginning in 1979, pushing the 1985 ratio to a high for the period. The 1986 ratio was nearly twice as high as the previous record level set in 1985, but post-1986 ratios fell back to below their pre-1986 levels.

It has been duly noted that these periods roughly correspond to eras of capital gains taxation as illustrated in Table 4, with the rate on long-term gains being highest in the period 1970 through 1978, when gains were generally low. There are, of course, other reasons why realized gains would be low during this period, including stagnant common stock prices.[18]

Although Figure 3 shows that aggregate capital gain realizations were relatively low in the 1970s, Tables 6–10 show it is also true that the share of total gains received by the top 1 percent of income earners fell during this period. This decline is one of the reasons that the share of the top 1 percent in total income did not begin to rise until the 1980s.

That the share of total gains of the top 1 percent fell in the 1970s is no doubt partially due to the tax rate on capital gains for high-income taxpayers rising much more than for low-income taxpayers. But part of the apparent decrease in the concentration of capital gains in the 1970s could also be due to the phenomenon of rank reversals. Because the top 1 percent is defined by income (which includes capital gains), if for any reason capital gains decrease – *even proportionately* – then individuals with relatively high capital gains will tend to drop out of the top 1 percent and be replaced by others with lower capital gains. This can be a quantitatively important phenomenon, as the example in Slemrod (1989) shows. There I simulate a 61.2% equiproportionate increase in all taxpayers' capital gains, in addition to a 19.5% equiproportionate increase in other income (the actual aggregate increase in capital gains and other income, respectively, between 1980 and 1983). When taxpayers are ranked by gross income before the equiproportionate increases, 46% of gains are received by the top 1 percent of gross income earners. With the equiproportionate increases and attendant reranking by (the new) gross income, 62% of gains are received by the top 1 percent. This increased share occurs even though the distribution of capital gains is completely unchanged.

One lesson of this example is that the decline in the share of gains received by the top 1 percent is not necessarily a reflection of a flattened distribution of the gains themselves. In fact, Slemrod (1992a) shows that the own-Gini coefficient of gains did not change much during the 1970s and 1980s. But the methodological caveat of rank reversals applies much more broadly. For example, an equiproportionate reduction in capital gains realizations could reduce the apparent concentration of wage and salary income, as measured by the share of wages earned by the top 1 percent of income earners. This could occur because when capital gains are of lesser importance, ranking by income becomes closer to ranking by non–capital gains income, which is largely wages and salaries. By necessity,

---

[18] Some have argued that high capital gains taxes are a principal *cause* of low equity prices.

the concentration of any source of income will look larger when ranked by itself or something highly correlated with itself.

Although the phenomenon of rank reversals potentially clouds the interpretation of trends in the 1970s, it apparently does not overturn the characterization that the concentration of wages began about 1970 rather than 1980. The own-Gini coefficient for wages began rising as early as 1972, as shown by Slemrod (1992a); see also the findings of Feenberg and Poterba (1992) discussed in Section 6.1.

6   Taxes and the increasing concentration of labor income

According to data based on tax returns, the income of the top 1 percent of American income earners rose appreciably during the period 1977–89, while the average real income of the rest of the population stagnated. One measure of this phenomenon, due to Gramlich et al. (1993), is that the share of the top 1 percent in total income rose from 8.4% in 1977 to 12.4% in 1989, an extraordinary increase by the standards of usually glacial demographic trends. The evidence presented in the previous sections suggests that this trend is really the net result of at least three distinct phenomena: a growing concentration of wages and salaries beginning earlier than 1977; a decline in the volume of capital gain realizations in the 1970s, and a decline in the nominal capital income of the affluent in the 1970s. Only in the 1980s was there a concurrent increase in the concentration of wages and salaries coupled with an increase in the measured importance of capital income, and thus only in the 1980s did the concentration of overall income become apparent.

In this section I focus on the increasing concentration of labor income, and attempt to distinguish nontax and tax explanations for this trend. In the former category are a wide range of hypotheses, including technological change, globalization of commerce, cohort supply changes, and an increasing return to education. All of these nontax explanations share one common element: a prediction of a relative increase in the pre-tax return per unit of effort to the types of human capital possessed by high-income individuals. An increased pre-tax return to labor could induce changes in labor supply, depending on the relative strength of the income and price effects. The pure tax explanation is that reduced marginal tax rates have, by increasing the after-tax return to effort, increased both the amount of effort and the fraction of compensation paid in taxable form.

The challenge to the researcher is to identify empirical phenomena that are consistent with one story but not the other. Of course, these two explanations need not be mutually exclusive; it is certainly possible that there has been both an increase in the pre-tax return to high-income occupations and a substantial behavioral response to lower marginal tax rates.

There are, though, some differences in the predictions that accompany the pure versions of these two explanations. Unfortunately, data are not always available to distinguish the two. For example, in the nontax explanation, the total pre-tax compensation per unit of effort increases; in the tax explanation, it does not. But because there is no reliable data on hours of effort of the affluent across time periods, this explanation cannot be pursued.[19] Lacking that critical set of data, in what follows I look at three possible ways to distinguish the two explanations.

6.1   *Timing*

If the tax story predominates, and if the behavioral response to taxes happens quickly, then the timing of changes in the concentration of income should correspond to the timing of the tax changes in the last 15 years. If the nontax story predominates, then only by coincidence would changes in pre-tax income match up with changes in the tax law. Note, though, that most affluent taxpayers are likely to have considerable flexibility regarding the timing of income recognition, not only of capital gains but of labor income as well. For this reason one must be cautious about data both from years immediately before anticipated tax changes and from years immediately after tax changes.

The principal changes of the last three decades were the 1964 Revenue Act, which dropped the top rate from 91% to 70% (77% in 1964) but also featured across-the-board cuts of approximately equal proportions; the 1969 Act, which lowered the maximum rate on labor income to between 50% and 60%; the 1981 Act, which dropped the top rate on all income to 50%; and the 1986 Act, which dropped the top rate from 50% to 28% (38.5% in 1987).[20] Tables 6–10 suggest that the concentration of wages began in earnest between 1970 and 1977, just as the 1969 Act was becoming effective. Of course, the precise timing is difficult to judge from snapshots taken every few years. More revealing is a graph from Feenberg and Poterba (1992), reproduced here as Figure 4, which plots the fraction

[19] Of course there is a large literature on labor supply responsiveness to taxes which is not focused on the affluent. See e.g. Burtless (1990) and MaCurdy, Green, and Paarsch (1990). But this literature generally does not address whether high-income households' elasticity is different from the nonaffluent population. However, as noted in Section 2, for a tax cut that applies only to the top bracket, a lower elasticity is required for an inverse revenue response to be generated.

[20] There were several other changes along the way. See Pechman (1987, table A-3) for a chronology.

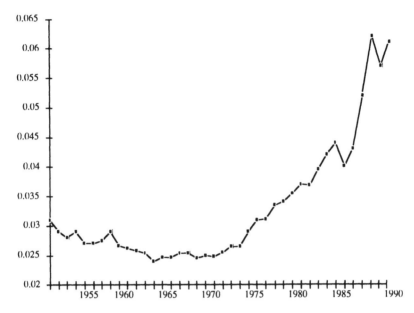

Figure 4. Share of wages received by top 0.25 percent of adult population, 1951–90. *Source:* Feenberg and Poterba (1992, fig. 6), reproduced by permission.

of total wages received by those in the top 0.25 percent of the adult population (by adjusted gross income), based on interpolations from published IRS Statistics of Income data. This graph shows a steady increase beginning in 1970, from 2.5% in that year to 3.7% in 1980. The proportion continues to grow beyond 1980, rising to 4.4% by 1984, but falls back to 4.0% in 1985. After that it is buffeted about by the timing effects of the 1986 Act, but jumps to 6.2% in 1990. Their graph reveals no break in wage concentration around 1981, although it is certainly consistent with a steadily increasing amount of concentration that begins about when the maximum tax on earned income is introduced. Of course, these are impressions and not a decisive analysis by any means. Furthermore, because taxpayers are ranked by income rather than wages, the analysis is subject to the bias introduced by rank reversals caused by changes in nonwage income sources.

A rising concentration of wages beginning about 1970 would also correspond with the start of the increase in inequality within groups of similar educational attainment, as discussed in Levy and Murnane (1992). Beginning in the 1980s, the return to education also began to grow rapidly, thus adding a compounding increase to the within-educational-group inequality. That the concentrated earnings of the top 0.25 percent (or 1 percent) began around 1970 rather than 1980 may reflect something other than increased returns to education. Such an hypothesis would undoubtedly be uncontroversial when applied to baseball players and other entertainers, whose earning power is generally accepted to be unrelated to their educational achievement, but would be controversial when applied to investment bankers and CEOs.

6.2   *Other countries*

Finding that other countries – whose top tax rates did not fall as in the United States – had a similar increase in income growth at the top would undermine the tax explanation. Unfortunately, data are not available to make a precise cross-national comparison that focuses on the top 1 percent of income earners. What cross-national evidence does exist, though, suggests that the United States was not alone in experiencing increased inequality in wages. Gottschalk and Joyce (1991) examined the eight industrial countries of the Luxembourg Income Study[21] and concluded that inequality in the earnings of male family heads rose in almost all of them, and that there were "important changes in the upper end of the distribution. The rich were getting richer in every country except France" (p. 16).

Although suggestive, these conclusions need to be qualified in at least two ways. First, because of the problem of top-coding of income measures from surveys, Gottschalk and Joyce excluded the top 5 percent of the distribution in every country and every year. The resulting data are thus not helpful in assessing income distribution questions specifically referring to the top 1 percent. Second, in the 1980s some of the seven other countries also flattened the dispersion of their marginal tax rates, though none did so to the extent that occurred in the United States.[22]

6.3   *Trends in composition of the compensation of the rich*

One distinguishing characteristic of the tax explanation for the increasing concentration of labor income is its prediction that, as marginal tax rates fall, high-income individuals would reduce the fraction of compensation received in nontaxable or tax-preferred form. This would imply a lower fraction of compensation received as fringe benefits, deferred

---

[21] Besides the United States, the countries included were Australia, Canada, France, Germany, the Netherlands, Sweden, and the United Kingdom.

[22] See Whalley (1990) for a cross-national chronology of income-tax changes in the 1980s.

compensation, and stock options and other forms of preferentially taxed executive compensation.

If this actually happened, and concomitantly the share of wages and salaries in the compensation of the affluent increased, then it would almost certainly show up in the data as an increased concentration of wages and salaries. Of course, there should be an offsetting decrease in the concentration of non–wage-and-salary compensation, but that is much less likely to show up in the available data on annual incomes (given its nature as fringe benefits and deferred compensation).

I can find no evidence that high-income American households have significantly increased the fraction of their labor compensation received as wages and salaries.[23] I have chosen the wording of the last sentence carefully, because neither have I found definitive evidence to rule out such a trend. Although there are data on the recent trends in average compensation in such high-paying occupations as physicians and professional athletes, there is very little breakdown of compensation into immediately taxable salaries and other types of compensation.

There is some sketchy evidence on trends in the composition of executive compensation. The portion of top executives from the largest 1,000 American corporations that have some stock-option plan was constant in the early to mid-1970s; fell in the late 1970s, when the tax advantages were sharply curtailed; and has risen continuously in the 1980s to 77% in 1990, the highest level in two decades.[24] *Forbes* magazine annually publishes information on the compensation packages of the top 500 firms in the United States. These data show no change between 1982 and 1991 in the portion (23%) of total compensation that is fully taxable salary or

---

[23] There is empirical support for the contention that, for the population as a whole, higher marginal tax rates are associated with a higher fraction of compensation received as fringe benefits. See e.g. Turner (1987), who concludes from an analysis of time-series data that the tax elasticity of the fringe share is about 0.2. Taken literally, an elasticity of 0.2 implies that a 60% decline of the marginal tax rate, from 0.7 to 0.28, would reduce the share of fringes by about 12%, which in turn would raise the share of nonfringe compensation by about 1%. However, it should be noted that Turner's data pertained to the entire population and so did not include observations of tax rates over 0.4; hence a simple extrapolation of results to high-income individuals may be unwarranted.

Bloom and Freeman (1992) document that during the 1980s the proportion of workers covered by pension plans and the proportion of total employee compensation taking the form of employer contributions to retirement plans both fell significantly. They dismiss the role of tax changes in this development, mainly because the 1980s fall in pension coverage was smallest among high-income workers, for whom marginal tax rates declined the most.

[24] This data is taken from selected editions of *Top Executive Compensation,* published by the Conference Board.

bonus for the 50 highest-compensated CEOs. The problem with these and similar data is that compensation via stock options is valued at the realized sales price at the time of the *exercise* of the option, rather than as the expected value of the option at the time it is granted. Thus the data are biased toward including CEOs that did exercise their stock options, and thus overstates the average importance of such options. The apparent importance of stock options will also depend on how well the stock market has performed in the recent past. All these caveats notwithstanding, I can offer no evidence that the relative importance of fully taxable wages and salaries for the affluent has increased in recent decades, even as their marginal tax rates have fallen.

7   Summary and conclusions

In this paper I set out to shed light on two possibly related issues – the high-income Laffer curve, and the apparently increasing concentration of income. The research has been more successful in highlighting the scarcity of information needed to reliably address these issues than it has in providing definitive answers. Nevertheless, some tentative conclusions can be offered.

A prime lesson of this paper is that, because the rich have relatively more capital income and perhaps more flexibility in both financial matters and in the form of labor compensation, it is dangerous to rely on behavioral elasticities estimated from the population as a whole. Comparing portfolios of the affluent in the 1980s to the higher-tax era of the early 1960s reveals no noticeable shift out of tax-exempt securities and in to taxable securities, and no increase in the relative nominal rate of taxable return of the affluent. I can thus find no evidence that taxable capital income falls sharply in response to higher tax rates. Capital gains realizations, which are largely a phenomenon of the affluent, were noticeably lower in the 1970s – a decade that featured, among other characteristics such as a falling stock market, relatively high capital gains taxation. The increasing concentration of wage and salary income appears to have begun around 1970, about the time of the introduction of the maximum tax on earned income and pre-dating the cuts in top tax rates that began in 1981. I could find no indication that the fraction of compensation of the affluent that is received in the form of wages and salaries has increased as their marginal tax rate has declined.

In sum, with respect to two aspects that differentiate the rich from the nonrich – the importance of capital income, and the flexibility of the form of compensation – I have uncovered no evidence of a significant behavioral response to the marginal tax rate. There is, however, evidence of a significant response of capital gains realizations to the tax on capital gains; exactly how substantial is the long-run elasticity of this response remains a controversial issue. Thus, in assessing the behavioral response of the affluent, it is important to consider separately the marginal tax rate on ordinary income and the effective tax rate on capital gains.

An important lesson is that the effect of changing tax rates on revenue must be kept conceptually distinct from its effect on the measured distribution of income. This is especially important with regard to capital gains. While capital gains realizations may be the most tax-responsive element of taxable income, they definitely should not be included in any measure of income used to assess year-to-year changes in income concentration. If (for whatever reason) capital gains realizations increase, the resulting increase in the tax concentration of measured income does not necessarily reflect an increase in the concentration of economic welfare. This problem is understood by researchers who avoid analyzing years of extraordinary capital gains activity such as 1986, but the problem is more general. Because of rank reversals, inclusion of capital gains in a measure of income will also bias measures of the concentration of other sources of income such as wages.

The same caveat applies, to a lesser extent, to capital income other than capital gains. The relationship between real capital income and nominal taxable capital income is a tenuous one, influenced by inflation, taxation, and other factors. Discarding taxable capital income as a reliable measure of real income leaves the distribution of wealth and the distribution of labor income as the building blocks of a proper distributional analysis. Future research on how these have changed, and the role of taxation in their evolution, will require both better data and that more attention be devoted to the life-cycle structure of savings and capital accumulation.

REFERENCES

Auerbach, Alan (1988), "Capital Gains Taxation in the United States: Realizations, Revenue, and Rhetoric," *Brookings Papers on Economic Activity* 2: 595–637.

Auten, Gerald, Leonard Burman, and William Randolph (1989), "Estimation and Interpretation of Capital Gains Realization Behavior: Evidence from Panel Data," Working Paper no. 67, U.S. Department of the Treasury, Office of Tax Analysis, Washington, DC.

Auten, Gerald, and Charles Clotfelter (1982), "Permanent versus Transitory Tax Effects and the Realization of Capital Gains," *Quarterly Journal of Economics* 97: 613–32.

Avery, Robert B., and Gregory E. Elliehausen (1986), "Financial Characteristics of High-Income Families," *Federal Reserve Bulletin* 72: 163–75.

Bloom, David E., and Richard B. Freeman (1992), "The Fall in Private Pension Coverage in the United States," *American Economic Review* 2: 539–45.

Burtless, Gary (1990), "Supply Side Legacy of the Reagan Years: Effects on Labor Supply," in A. Sahu and R. Tracy (eds.), *The Economic Legacy of the Reagan Years: Euphoria or Chaos*. New York: Praeger.

Feenberg, Daniel, and James Poterba (1992), "Income Inequality and the Incomes of Very High Income Households: Evidence from Tax Returns," Unpublished manuscript, Department of Economics, MIT, Cambridge, MA.

Gottschalk, Peter, and Mary Joyce (1991), "Changes in Earnings Inequality – an International Perspective," Unpublished manuscript, Department of Economics, Boston College, Chestnut Hill, MA.

Gramlich, Edward M., Richard Kasten, and Frank Sammartino (1993), "Growing Inequality in the 1980s: the Role of Federal Taxes and Cash Transfers," in S. Danziger and P. Gottschalk (eds.), *Uneven Tides: Rising Inequality in America*. New York: Russell Sage Foundation.

Internal Revenue Service (IRS) (various years), Statistics of Income Division, *Individual Model Files*.

Levy, Frank, and Richard J. Murnane (1992), "U.S. Earnings Levels and Earnings Inequality: a Review of Recent Trends and Proposed Explanations," *Journal of Economic Literature* 30: 1333–81.

Lindsey, Lawrence B. (1981), "Is the Maximum Tax on Earned Income Effective?" *National Tax Journal* 34: 349–55.

(1987), "Capital Gains Rates, Realizations, and Revenues," in M. Feldstein (ed.), *The Effects of Taxation on Capital Accumulation*. Chicago: University of Chicago Press, pp. 69–97.

(1990), *The Growth Experiment*. New York: Basic Books.

MaCurdy, Thomas, D. Green, and H. J. Paarsch (1990), "Assessing Empirical Approaches for Analyzing Taxes and Labor Supply," *Journal of Human Resources* 25: 415–90.

Pechman, Joseph (1987), *Federal Tax Policy*, 5th ed. Washington, DC: Brookings.

Slemrod, Joel (1989), "Rank Reversals and the Tax Elasticity of Capital Gains Realizations," *National Tax Journal* 4: 503–7.

(1992a), "Taxation and Inequality: a Time-Exposure Perspective," in J. Poterba (ed.), *Tax Policy and the Economy*, vol. 6. Cambridge, MA: MIT Press.

ed. (1992b), *Why People Pay Taxes: Tax Compliance and Enforcement*. Ann Arbor: University of Michigan Press.

Slemrod, Joel, and William Shobe (1990), "The Tax Elasticity of Capital Gains Realizations: Evidence from a Panel of Taxpayers," Working Paper no. 3237, National Bureau of Economic Research, Cambridge, MA.

Sunley, Emil M., Jr. (1974), "The Maximum Tax on Earned Income," *National Tax Journal* 27: 543–52.

Turner, Robert (1987), "Are Taxes Responsible for the Growth in Fringe Benefits?" *National Tax Journal* 40: 203–21.

Whalley, John (1990), "Foreign Responses to U.S. Tax Reform," in J. Slemrod (ed.), *Do Taxes Matter? The Impact of the Tax Reform Act of 1986*. Cambridge, MA: MIT Press, pp. 286–314.

Wolff, Edward N. (1992), "Changing Inequality of Wealth," *American Economic Review* 2: 552–8.

Comments

C. Eugene Steuerle

In his paper Joel Slemrod quotes F. Scott Fitzgerald and Ernest Hemingway as musing that the rich are those who have more money than themselves. This anecdote is interesting not only for its humor, but because both Fitzgerald and Hemingway would have been classified as relatively rich on a lifetime basis, even if not for every year of their lives under an annual basis. It warns us to be cautious with almost all measures of well-being, income, and wealth.

Although Slemrod's paper is entitled "On the High-Income Laffer Curve," in truth it turns out to be a broad discussion of various data sets on income and wealth distribution, together with some interpretations of what those data sets do and do not tell us. Some economists disdain research that involves wide-ranging efforts at trying to glean what we know from different empirical observations. I would like to applaud the effort as being refreshingly honest.

The disadvantage as a commentator on this type of research, however, is that there is no one theme on which I can concentrate. Therefore, I must instead join Joel on this journey by heading down a few of the paths he has pointed out and wandering a bit further into the thicket.

One overall observation must be made at the start. It is quite clear that financial or portfolio behavior is much more controllable, especially over the short run, than changes in the provision of real resources: what I invest in, rather than how much; whether I work off the books, as opposed to not working at all. Much of what the data reveal over time simply reflects those financial or portfolio shifts; they tell us little about the supply of labor, capital, and invention in an economy.

My remaining observations can be divided into four sections, in reverse of the author's order: capital gains, other portfolio behavior, the form of labor compensation, and time and effort.

211

1   Capital gains

Of all the analyses of high-income individuals, capital gains realizations needs to be separated almost totally. Capital gains taxes are discretionary. At best, they should be compared to toll charges – charges that apply mainly to portfolio shifts designed to diversify, increase liquidity, or consume. Look, for instance, at the following tabulation – based on data of the Treasury Department – regarding capital gains realizations in recent years:

Year	Realized capital gains ($)
1978	50,526
1979	73,443
1980	74,132
1981	80,938
1982	90,153
1983	122,773
1984	139,765
1985	171,448
1986	326,334
1987	144,173
1988	161,871
1989	153,513
1990	123,783

No one can explain these variations in capital gains realizations by changes in the amount of individual savings. In fact, a lower rate of tax makes consumption out of existing savings cheaper, which discourages saving over the short run.

The data mainly reflect changed incentives to re-allocate assets in one's portfolio, although not simply in response to tax rates. For instance, while the falloff in 1987 reflects a shifting of gains to 1986, when capital gains tax rates were low, I would argue that part of the decline between 1989 and 1990 was influenced greatly by a drop in short-term interest rates. This shift in rates of return reduced the extent to which individuals decided to move out of the stock market and into more liquid assets. Still, whatever one's belief concerning the effect of the tax rate on gains realizations, that effect tells us almost nothing about the Laffer curve with respect to real work and real output.

2   Portfolio behavior

The opportunities for sheltering one's capital income go beyond capital gains. Indeed, in 1983 over 80% of individuals' assets were in a form for which some or all related income could be excluded or deferred from taxation. Net income from capital reported on individual income-tax returns represented only 32% of the real capital income in the economy. This doesn't mean that it isn't taxed: capital income is taxed mainly through corporate and property taxes, not the individual income tax.[1]

Opportunities for tax shelters can easily dominate a pure tax-rate effect, although there are important interactions between the two. For instance, the drying up of the formal tax-shelter market after 1986 is due both to the lower tax rate and to the very strict rules on passive losses. In turn, the growth in the tax-shelter market in the years immediately following 1981 (when rates actually fell) was due partly to increased investment incentives and the increased abilities of money managers and lawyers to manipulate the tax laws.

The power to manipulate portfolios was revealed in another study I performed on the income and wealth of top wealthholders. For deaths in 1976 or 1977, income in the full calendar year prior to death varied significantly by wealth class, as shown in the following table.

Size of wealth	Gross capital income as a percentage of wealth
$100,000 to $250,000	6.1
$250,000 to $500,000	5.9
$500,000 to $1,000,000	5.1
$1,000,000 to $2,500,000	4.8
$2,500,000 or more	2.2

The average gross capital income reported as a percentage of wealth was only 2.2% in the class of those with $2,500,000 or more in wealth. Of these 57 individuals, 9 reported zero or negative capital income, while 23 reported less than 3%.[2]

---

[1] C. Eugene Steuerle (1985), *Taxes, Loans, and Inflation* (Washington, DC: Brookings).

[2] C. Eugene Steuerle (1985), "Wealth, Realized Income, and the Measure of Well-Being," in Martin David and Timothy M. Smeeding (eds.), *Horizontal Equity, Uncertainty, and Well-Being,* vol. 50 of National Bureau of Economic Research, *Studies in Income and Wealth* (Chicago: University of Chicago Press).

In tracking inheritors, I found that 437 out of 1,451 showed less capital income after receiving a sizeable inheritance than before. These results almost assuredly came from portfolio allocations to assets with low rates of current realization of income.

Portfolio effects, by the way, are also affected by interactions between taxes and economic variables. For instance, if the interest rate falls and all else stays the same, then there is more capital income realized on net. Why? Most interest income is received by zero- or low-rate taxpayers, most interest deductions by high-income taxpayers. In sum, tax rates have significant effects on portfolio re-allocations, but they again tell us little about the Laffer curve.

3   Form of labor compensation

Slemrod is probably right about the mixed effect of taxes on the form of labor compensation, although the empirical data here are poor. Individual choices are also influenced importantly by opportunities, other economic variables, and by tax provisions other than the tax rate. The rising cost of health care, for instance, must have had an impact on the distribution of income if the cost of that care, as assumed in most economic analyses, is paid by the worker. Similarly, tax provisions allowing employee benefits to be excluded from tax affect the extent to which cash income can be transferred to nontaxable benefits.

For very high executive salaries and the incomes of the top 1 percent, however, most nontaxable employee benefits (other than consumption on the job of fancy offices, good food, and so forth) are fairly restricted. Recent rises in executive salaries, I believe, probably have little to do with changes in the tax rate. Census Bureau data, moreover, show that relative incomes of the top quintile (and probably of the top 1 percent) may have been falling during the late 1980s and early 1990s. The timing on all of these measurements, as the paper notes, is also critical: stock options realized by executives reflect both past labor compensation and past growth in the value of stock.

4   Time and effort

Finally, we must turn to time and effort, or (more narrowly) to labor input. If we really want to examine Laffer-curve effects, however, I'm not sure why we would focus on those with the highest incomes. After all, the Laffer curve is supposed to reflect reaction to *marginal* tax rates. Despite the progressive nature of the income tax by itself, the highest marginal tax rates – combining tax, earned income credit, and welfare programs – are faced by low-income workers.

One should also worry about the timing of tax-rate effects. Suppose that substitution effects are initially stronger, but that income effects start to dominate later. For example, entrepreneurs may accumulate income, but their inheritors may tend to favor higher rates of consumption. Since the children of entrepreneurs are likely on average to have fewer special abilities than their parents, they cannot sustain their former lifestyles by relying as much upon returns to labor. Hence, they may be more likely to consume out of their capital.

On this subject, the author cites some revealing data of Daniel Feenberg and James Poterba on the wages of the top ¼ of 1 percent, but again we have no indication that these increases in income are due to additional work effort. More likely, it reflects such causes as the temporary ability to create individual monopolies or oligopolies of information, and the recognition of certain types of income due to past performance.

By the way, if I were to believe that increases in the relative income of the very highest-paid workers were due to changes in work habits, then I should probably be able to prove it by surveys on hours worked or by evidence that American executives work much harder than some of their more poorly paid international counterparts, as in Japan. No such evidence, as far as I know, has ever been produced.

5   Conclusion

After examining the importance of capital income and the flexibility of the form of labor compensation, the paper concludes that no evidence has been found of a significant behavioral response to the marginal tax rate. So far, only capital gains realizations seem to have a significant short-term response, but the long-term response remains controversial. Capital gains realizations, however, have little to do with Laffer claims anyway.

Slemrod's conclusions, I believe, are right on the mark. These results, however, do not prove that there is no Laffer curve or that there is no point at which increases in tax rates reduce revenues. This paper indicates, instead, that such effects are not likely to operate at the tax rates we have observed recently in the United States. Examination of the data, moreover, makes clear that simple correlations of changes in tax rates with changes in measured income are misleading. We must also examine closely related changes in the tax base, opportunities for shifting income to nontaxable forms, and the basic economic factors affecting overall returns to labor and capital. Observations at a given moment in time, rather than over time, must be interpreted cautiously. Finally, if our goal is economic and not political, we probably ought to concentrate our research on those facing the highest tax rates – that is, on moderate-income workers – rather than on the highest-income members of society.

General discussion

Gale noted that the increased share of wealth of the top 1 percent of wealth owners is largely accounted for by a drop in the share held by the 90th–99th percentiles; this suggests that changes in wealth distribution were driven by factors other than just taxes.

Christian observed that tax evasion may be an important dimension of the response to high taxes by high-income individuals. He noted evidence that capital gains understatement declined after 1983, at the same time tax rates were reduced.

Gravelle argued that, in looking at portfolio effects, one needs to think about the corporate tax rate and the effective tax rate on real assets. Also, the distribution of capital gains realizations by asset type over time shows a large change in the share of corporate stock. She noted that when using the Survey of Consumer Finances data there is considerable difficulty in resolving aggregates with aggregates from the Flow-of-Funds data.

Plesko commented that as tax rates on capital income and compensation fall, nonrate tax rules (such as limits on employee contributions to pension plans) become increasingly important.

McIntyre remarked that the tax treatment of capital losses is important. A person can obtain money for consumption tax-free by selling losses only. During noninflationary times, people should be taking fewer losses and so net realizations should be down.

Weiss stated that one should not assume pre-tax returns on assets to be invariant with respect to the tax system. Tax-free bonds should have highly variable pre-tax returns.

Poterba noted that most of the recent changes in income concentration occurred for the top 0.1 percent of the distribution – those with income over $500,000. Furthermore, rank reversal due to income composition shifts does not explain the trends in the 1980s. Nontax parameters, such as 401K contribution limits, can be quite important. He noted that portfolio response can be sluggish, and therefore may take time before it becomes an important factor.

Cutler stated that there is not much substitution between types of compensation; rather, it's simply that total compensation has increased for people like baseball players and CEOs.

MacKie-Mason noted that much of the wealth of high-income individuals is in the form of closely held firms. As corporate income tax rates have dropped, less labor compensation is being shielded from tax in the form of corporate retained earnings.

Slemrod responded that because high-income individuals account for so much of savings and wealth, it is important to understand simple things like the effective tax rate on high-income savings. If their principal behavioral response to higher tax rates is evasion, then the proper policy response may include increased enforcement. He noted that income concentration increased for all of the top percentile, not just the top 0.1 percent of income earners.

CHAPTER 7

Tax progressivity and household portfolios: descriptive evidence from the Surveys of Consumer Finances

John Karl Scholz

If you drive a car, I'll tax the street
If you try to sit, I'll tax your seat
If it gets too cold, I'll tax the heat
If you take a walk, I'll tax your feet

George Harrison, "Taxman"

1 Introduction

The 1980s were the "tax decade." The 1981 Economic Recovery Tax Act lowered the top marginal individual income tax rate to 50% from 70%, lowered all marginal income tax rates by an average of 23% over a three-year period, and implemented numerous tax preferences for individuals and corporations that were designed to stimulate saving and investment. Less sweeping changes to the income-tax code were made in 1982 and 1984. The Tax Reform Act of 1986 (TRA) again lowered rates substantially. The marginal tax rate on the highest-income households fell to 28% from 50%, while the top corporate rate was reduced to 34% from 46%. At the same time that marginal tax rates were reduced, both the individual and corporate tax bases were broadened. On the individual side, for example, TRA eliminated the deduction for state and local sales taxes, eliminated the exclusion for realized capital gains, and restricted

Prepared for the Conference on Tax Progressivity, September 11–12, 1992, sponsored by the Office of Tax Policy Research at the University of Michigan. I thank Stacy Dickert, Ip-Wing Yu, and Reint Gropp for excellent assistance; Bill Gale, Roger Gordon, Joel Slemrod, conference participants, and anonymous reviewers for helpful suggestions; CentER for Economic Research (Tilburg, Netherlands) and the VSB saving project, where a portion of this research was completed; the work of Robert Avery and Arthur Kennickell in developing a cleaned copy of the 1983–86 Survey of Consumer Finances and providing extensive documentation; and Andrew Samwick for help in securing a copy of the 1989 Survey of Consumer Finances.

220   John Karl Scholz

eligibility for tax-deductible Individual Retirement Account contributions. For corporations, the investment tax credit was eliminated, the corporate alternative minimum tax was stiffened, and depreciation schedules were lengthened.

The striking reduction in statutory tax rates in the 1980s does not necessarily imply that the tax system became less progressive. Prior to the rate reductions of the 1980s, wealthy households had a strong incentive to restructure their economic affairs to mitigate the effects of high tax rates by investing, for example, in tax-preferred assets. Moreover, the base broadening in TRA increases tax burdens of higher-income households, who make disproportionately heavy use of tax shelters and other tax preferences. To understand the relationship between the progressivity of tax burdens and the progression of statutory rates, one needs to know the degree to which wealthy households manipulate their portfolios to reduce or eliminate taxes.

1.1   *Do taxes affect portfolio choice?*

After the federal income tax was introduced in 1913, early literature on progressivity and portfolio choice focused on tax-exempt bonds. For example, Adams (1923) raised the concern that while the United States enjoyed unprecedented growth after the first world war, reported taxable incomes decreased because "the richest people hold all government tax-exempt securities," which he felt undermined the progressivity of the tax system.

The first comprehensive empirical study of the effects of taxes on the portfolio choice of individuals was made by Butters, Thompson, and Bollinger (1953), who used a survey taken in 1949 to examine the effects of tax-rate increases in the 1940s.[1] The authors interviewed a nonrandom sample of 746 "active" investors, defined as individuals who were in contact with security brokers and dealers at least once in the three years preceding the interview, and asked whether and how they adjusted their portfolios in response to taxes. The percentage of those investors who claimed their portfolio decisions were affected by federal taxes varied positively with income, increasing from 22% for the lowest income class to 93% for the highest. For the top 5 percent of the income distribution (who in 1949 held approximately 55% of all assets), 60% reported that taxes affected their portfolio choices. The most frequently mentioned effects were on the choice of assets owned, the timing of investments, and

[1] The top marginal tax rate rose from 79% on taxable incomes over $5 million in 1939 to 91% (with a maximum effective rate of 87%) on taxable income over $400,000 in 1950.

the distribution of property ownership among family members (including the use of trusts).

Feldstein (1976) used the 1962 Survey of Financial Characteristics of Consumers to estimate portfolio share equations that control for net worth, age, sex, and the ratio of human to nonhuman capital, along with a constructed measure of taxes based on labor income and portfolio wealth. He concluded that "the personal income tax has a very powerful effect on individuals' demands for portfolio assets."

Subsequent work (King and Leape 1984, 1986; Hubbard 1985) adopted a two-step approach to examining the factors that influence portfolio composition. This approach accounts for the fact that not all households hold every asset or liability, and allows for the possibility that factors affecting the decision to hold a given asset differ from factors affecting the decision concerning the amount to be held. These studies generally find that taxes are significantly correlated with the decision to hold particular assets and liabilities but are usually insignificantly correlated with the level of demand for the asset or liability, given that it is held. This finding led King and Leape (1984) to conclude that "contrary to much of the recent literature, taxes do not play a decisive role in explaining the differences in portfolio composition across households." Similar results were found by King and Leape (1987), who looked at portfolio composition over the life cycle; by Dicks-Mireaux and King (1982), who looked at the effects of pension wealth on portfolio composition; and by Ioannides (1990), who looked at dynamic aspects of portfolio choice using data from the 1983 and 1986 Surveys of Consumer Finances.

Evidence from related literatures suggests that most taxpayers do not aggressively exploit provisions of the tax code to reduce or eliminate capital income taxes. Constantinides (1983, 1984) and Stiglitz (1983) describe portfolio strategies that can, in theory, reduce or even eliminate capital gains taxes. The elements of these strategies include: defer gains; realize losses to offset ordinary income or realized gains; borrow to generate interest deductions and purchase assets yielding capital gains; and buy and sell highly correlated securities, realizing the portion that yields a loss. Poterba (1987) and Seyhun and Skinner (1991) examine tax-return data and conclude that there is little evidence that investors actually follow these dynamic, tax-optimal trading strategies. Miller and Scholes (1978) discuss ways in which the investment interest limitation of Internal Revenue Code section 163(d), along with tax-deferred investments, can be used to eliminate taxes on dividends. Feenberg (1981) and Chaplinsky and Seyhun (1990) examine tax-return data and find that most investors do not fully use such tax-reduction strategies.

It is not surprising that factors other than taxes affect portfolio and investment decisions. Many tax-reduction strategies, particularly of the type described by Constantinides and Stiglitz, involve frequent buying and selling of securities. These transactions are costly, which limits their adoption. It is also expensive to gather information about investment opportunities and about the often arcane associated tax rules. In addition, concerns about liquidity and risk undoubtedly affect portfolio decisions.

Although there is little systematic evidence since Feldstein (1976) that taxes have a strong influence on portfolio composition, previous studies faced three major problems: few data sources contain detailed information on household balance sheets; prior to the 1980s, statutory marginal tax rates changed infrequently and by relatively small amounts; and investment decisions are affected by a host of nontax factors that make it difficult to isolate empirically the role of taxes. The 1983 and 1989 Surveys of Consumer Finances, developed by the Board of Governors of the Federal Reserve System in conjunction with other federal and Congressional agencies, contain unusually detailed household balance-sheet data that span the 1986 tax reform; this largely addresses the first two concerns. I adopt a particularly simple descriptive approach to address the third concern. Namely, I see whether household portfolios change in a manner that is consistent with what would be expected following TRA if taxes are an important determinant of portfolio composition.[2] Before discussing these changes, I briefly turn to two other issues.

1.2   *Portfolio composition and the measurement of tax progressivity*

Tax progressivity is most commonly measured by comparing the ratio of taxes paid to a broadly defined measure of income for households in different income classes. When statutory marginal tax rates are very high, upper-income taxpayers may expend considerable resources to reduce their tax liabilities by investing in tax-preferred assets such as municipal bonds and tax shelters. Wealthy taxpayers may also benefit from high marginal tax rates by deducting the interest expense of borrowing, so long as the after-tax cost of borrowing is less than the after-tax return on investment. If portfolio responses are widespread, measured progressivity may be substantially lower than that implied by the progression of statutory tax rates.

---

[2] Although this approach does not isolate the effect of taxes on portfolio choice, assessing data quality and providing a broad set of stylized facts about portfolio changes in the 1980s is a prerequisite to a more structured analysis of portfolio choice and the 1986 tax reform.

At the same time, measured progressivity may be substantially higher than that implied by average tax rates because "implicit" taxes are often borne when households adjust their portfolios to minimize taxes (see e.g. Scholes and Wolfson 1992, chap. 5). Returns on municipal bonds, for example, are exempt from taxation. This tax exemption increases their attractiveness relative to fully taxed instruments, which implies, in equilibrium, that their before-tax returns are lower than those on equally risky fully taxed assets. This lower before-tax return is referred to as an "implicit tax."[3]

Considering implicit taxes may alter measures of tax progressivity. Galper, Lucke, and Toder (1988) simulated the effects of the 1986 tax reform using a numerical general equilibrium model that incorporates endogenous portfolio responses to tax changes. In a simulation with no portfolio responses, households with incomes exceeding $100,000 received a tax reduction of $16.6 billion (or roughly 5.2% of income) as a consequence of TRA. When portfolio responses were incorporated this tax reduction fell to $2.1 billion. High-income households in this simulation pay the government an additional $14.5 billion after adjusting portfolios because, with lower marginal tax rates, the benefits of holding more heavily taxed assets (which have higher pre-tax returns and lower implicit taxes) outweighs the burden of increased tax payments. The additional tax payments by high-income households in the simulation increase measured progressivity. At the same time, bearing fewer implicit taxes increases reported income, which lowers average tax burdens. In principal, the net effect of these changes for standard measures of progressivity – which do not incorporate implicit taxes – is ambiguous.

With the descriptive approach taken in this paper, it is impossible to identify the counterfactual equilibrium against which implicit taxes and portfolio responses are to be measured. However, if it is assumed that lightly taxed assets and assets and liabilities commonly used in tax shelters are associated with higher implicit taxes, the descriptive data herein can be helpful in making a qualitative assessment of the effect that portfolio changes surrounding TRA had on implicit taxes and tax progressivity.

1.3   Taxes and the allocation of risk

Economists have long been concerned about the effects of taxation on risk taking. Domar and Musgrave (1944) showed that a proportional income tax with full loss offset could increase household risk taking. Subsequent work by Stiglitz (1969) and others showed that with more realistic

---

[3] Poterba (1989) calculates the magnitude of implicit taxes for municipal bonds of different maturities over time.

features of the tax system (such as incomplete loss offsets) and combinations of assets with varying riskiness, the theoretical effect of the individual income tax on risk taking is ambiguous.[4] Using their general equilibrium simulation model, Galper et al. (1988) suggest that as much as 85% of the substantial welfare gain enjoyed by upper-income households from the 1986 tax reform would come from changes in the riskiness of households' portfolios. The authors argue that the pre-TRA tax system encouraged high-income households to invest in riskier assets. The rate reduction in TRA allowed households to reduce portfolio risk, which led to welfare gains that more than offset the effect of any reduction in after-tax income received by households.

To the extent that interest deductibility of debt causes households to carry more debt, or that progression in statutory tax rates causes households to restructure portfolios to lower tax burdens, the tax system may inefficiently alter the riskiness of households' portfolios. Given data on household balance sheets, however, it is difficult to assess this possibility because I know neither the specific securities that compose households' portfolios nor the risk associated with households' pensions.

2   Data

The 1983 Survey of Consumer Finances (SCF) contains interviews from a sample of 3,824 U.S. households selected by multistage area-probability sampling methods, along with a supplemental sample of 438 high-income households. In 1986, 2,822 of these households were re-interviewed through a less detailed telephone survey. In 1989, 2,277 households were selected by standard sampling methods, along with a supplemental sample of 866 high-income households.[5] At this time, the publicly available 1989 data do not maintain any common household links with the 1983–86 panel.[6] The SCFs are designed specifically to collect data on household balance

[4] Through the tax system, the government becomes a "partner" in risky investments. By sharing part of the downside risk, the tax system may encourage risk taking; by reducing the return to successful ventures, the tax system may discourage risk taking. Assessments of the effects of taxes on risk taking are further complicated by the interaction of inflation and the partially indexed tax system.

[5] See Avery and Elliehausen (1988) for additional details about the 1983 SCF; see Kennickell (1992) for additional details about the 1989 SCF. Using the 1983 SCF, Avery et al. (1984a,b) present tabulations of asset and liability distributions, and Avery and Elliehausen (1986) describe characteristics of high-income households. Avery, Elliehausen, and Kennickell (1987) discuss the burden of installment debt using the 1983–86 SCF panel. Kennickell and Shack-Marquez (1992) present data on asset and liability holdings from the 1983 and 1989 SCFs.

[6] The 1989 SCF was designed to have a panel component, but the households followed from the 1983–86 panel have not yet been identified in the publicly available data. Data

sheets, though they also contain detailed information on demographic characteristics, income, and other variables. Because I want to focus on portfolio changes surrounding TRA, the analysis focuses on the 1983 and 1989 surveys.

Juster and Kuester (1991) argue that just as the CPS (Current Population Survey) is used as the "standard of comparison" for demographic statistics because it is the benchmark household survey in the United States, the 1983 SCF is the standard of comparison for financial characteristics. They compared data from the SCF with the National Longitudinal Survey of Mature Men (NLS-MM) and the Retirement History Survey (RHS) and find that both the NLS-MM and RHS appear to underrepresent both tails of the wealth and income distributions. Curtin, Juster, and Morgan (1989) conclude that the 1983 SCF wealth data appear to be somewhat more accurate than similar data from the Panel Study of Income Dynamics and the Survey of Income and Program Participation.

Avery, Elliehausen, and Kennickell (1988) provide a detailed comparison of the 1983 SCF and the household sector Flow of Funds Accounts (FoFs) and a good discussion of the many pitfalls that arise when comparing household surveys with the Flow of Funds. In Table 1 I replicate and extend the Avery et al. (1988) analysis using the 1983 and 1989 SCFs and FoFs.[7] There is a wide discrepancy between the SCF and FoF savings-account totals (row 2 of Table 1). Curtin et al. (1989) suggest that the discrepancy may arise because of difficulties in the FoF of distinguishing household from business holdings of liquid assets. Although the reported levels of savings accounts are much lower in the SCFs than in the FoFs, the percentage changes in the asset balances between 1983 and 1989 are similar.

Large discrepancies appear in the SCF and FoF growth rates for some assets and liabilities. The growth rate in aggregate bond holdings (the sum of rows 4–7) in the FoFs is 131% between 1983 and 1989; the comparable SCF growth rate is 55%. The discrepancy between the SCFs and FoFs is even more striking for equity: the FoFs household sector accounts indicate that equity holdings increased by 86%, while personal holdings as reported in the SCFs fell by 16%.[8]

have been blurred in the 1989 SCF, particularly for 300 selected households, to minimize the possibility of identifying survey respondents. Steps were taken when blurring data to preserve key population statistics; see Kennickell (1992) for further details.

[7] The 1983 SCF figures are quite close to the totals reported in Avery et al. (1988). The largest discrepancies occur for money market mutual funds (12%), insurance reserves (−20%), and mutual funds (−14%), where the deviation from Table 1 and the previously reported figures are given in parentheses. The first two discrepancies appear to be due to differences in the way IRAs and Keogh accounts are allocated between categories.

[8] The data reported in Kennickell and Woodburn (1992) and Kennickell and Shack-Marquez (1992) are also consistent with large discrepancies between the SCF and FoF for stocks and bonds.

Table 1. *Comparison of selected SCF asset and liability categories with Flow of Funds estimates (billions of dollars)*[a]

	1983 SCF	1982 FoF[b]	1989 SCF	1989 FoF[b]	Percentage change SCF	Percentage change FoF
Assets						
Currency and checking[c]	271.3	316.9	539.9	496.8	99.00	56.77
Savings accounts[d]	667.6	1,413.8	1,210.5	2,375.4	81.32	68.02
MMMF[e]	140.2	189.4	390.0	391.9	178.17	106.92
Savings bonds[f]	27.3	68.3	86.9	117.7	218.32	72.33
Other federal bonds[g]	115.0	184.7	145.6	313.8	26.61	69.90
State and local bonds[h]	204.6	153.2	305.4	526.6	49.27	243.73
Corporate and foreign bonds[i]	47.4	37.6	75.0	64.7	58.23	72.07
Mortgage assets[j]	117.1	126.1	169.7	212.9	44.92	68.83
Corporate stock[k]	931.5	1,184.0	782.2	2,205.1	−16.03	86.24
Mutual funds[l]	109.7	66.7	276.1	480.6	151.69	620.54
Insurance reserves[m]	295.2	232.8	393.1	351.8	33.16	51.12
Owner-occupied real estate[n]	4,330.4	3,768.3	6,391.3	5,954.2	47.59	58.01
Debt						
Mortgages[o]	978.3	1,059.7	1,615.9	2,350.0	65.17	121.76

[a] Data are from the 1983 and 1989 surveys of Consumer Finances and the *Balance Sheets for the U.S. Economy 1960–91* (March 1992), Board of Governors of the Federal Reserve System.

[b] The 1983 SCF was conducted early in 1983 so these data are compared with the 1982 Flow of Funds. The 1989 SCF was conducted from August 1989 through March 1990 so these data are compared with the 1989 Flow of Funds. Both the 1982 and 1989 FoF household sector figures include charitable and other nonprofit organizations, personal trusts and estates, as well as households. Avery et al. (1988) present adjusted 1982 FoF figures that exclude nonhousehold holdings.

[c] All accounts with banks, thrifts, or credit unions with checkwriting privileges.

[d] All noncheckable deposits at banks, thrifts, and credit unions, including large and small time deposits, certificates of deposit (CDs), and individual retirement accounts (IRAs) and Keoghs at depository institutions.

[e] All money market mutual fund accounts (MMMFs) held outside of banks, thrifts, and credit unions. This includes broker call accounts as well as IRAs and Keoghs at brokerages.

[f] Face value of U.S. Government Savings Bonds.

[g] All other U.S. Government notes, bills, and bonds at face value.

[h] State and local government bonds, bills, and notes at face value.

[i] All other bonds at face value.

[j] Outstanding principal on mortgage assets, including land contracts and notes. Unlike Avery et al. (1988), I do not include business notes owed to households in this category.

[k] Market value of publicly traded stock.

[l] Market value of all mutual fund holdings.

[m] Cash value of whole-life insurance policies and IRAs held with insurance companies.

[n] Market value of principal and secondary residences.

[o] Principal outstanding on home mortgages.

Some of the difference between the SCF and FoF totals may be due to differences in the populations covered by the two data sources. The FoF household sector figures include charitable and other nonprofit organizations and personal trusts and estates, as well as households, while the SCFs include only households. Avery et al. (1988) make use of unpublished Federal Reserve worksheets to present both the published FoF aggregates and the household sector aggregates less the amounts held by nonprofit organizations and personal trusts and estates in 1983. The differences range from 27% for aggregate bond holdings to 0% for money market mutual funds, insurance reserves, owner-occupied real estate, and mortgages. If nonprofit organizations and personal trusts and estates became relatively more important from 1983 to 1989, growth rates in the FoFs would be larger than those found when comparing the 1983 and 1989 SCFs. This might have occurred, for example, if individual investors withdrew from the equity market following the October 1987 stock market crash, while nonprofits and personal trusts and estates did not. Further research is needed to resolve the discrepancies in Table 1. Until such research is completed, the differences should serve as an important caveat to studies making use of the 1989 SCF.

Table 2 provides information on the detailed categories of assets and liabilities found in the SCFs. Checking accounts, homes, and savings accounts are the most prevalent assets, while housing, businesses, other property, and equity are, in aggregate, the largest. It is clear from a comparison of conditional means and medians that the ownership distribution of some assets is highly skewed. Among the most striking examples are equity, trusts, and tax-exempt bonds. In general, there are few dramatic changes in the asset amounts between 1983 and 1989. The largest percentage increase occurred in money market accounts and individual retirement accounts (IRAs) and Keogh accounts. Gale and Scholz (1992) show that contributions to IRA accounts equaled 18% of personal saving between 1982 and 1986, and that tax-deductible contributions equalled 10% of personal saving in 1987.

The summary statistics on liabilities show a large amount of variation. One of the major changes of TRA was a restriction on the deductibility of debt not secured by property. The data in Table 2, however, show that debt for automobiles and credit cards – which lost favorable tax treatment – still increased substantially. At the same time, there appeared to be a shift away from nondeductible general lines of credit into deductible home-equity lines of credit. These patterns are examined in more detail in Section 3.3. Tables 3a and 3b give cumulative distributions for assets and liabilities listed in Table 2 by income percentile and exogenous tax rate.

The typical household in the United States has very little wealth. The median level of financial assets in 1983 was less than $2,500, generally split between a checking account and perhaps savings accounts, CDs, or savings bonds.[9] Median net worth in 1983 was $34,260, with housing by far the largest nonfinancial asset.[10] To examine more varied portfolios, the data must have an adequate representation of high-income households. The SCFs are potentially useful in this respect because they oversample wealthy households.

Figure 1 shows cumulative distributions for the ownership of selected assets held disproportionately by lower-income households, by income percentile in 1983 and 1989. Households in the bottom 60 percent of the income distribution have roughly 21% of net worth (the solid bar), but hold roughly 37% of the certificates of deposit in 1983 and 1989. To a lesser extent, these households also hold a disproportionate share of checking accounts, savings accounts, and savings bonds. These assets are liquid and safe, but receive no special tax preferences.

Figure 2 shows similar distributions for assets held disproportionately by higher-income households. Households in the top 5 percent of the income distribution hold roughly 42% of net worth. They hold disproportionate shares of taxable bonds (58%), trust balances (65%), equity (66%), and tax-exempt bonds (77%), where the average 1983 and 1989 share is given in parentheses. Equity and tax-exempt bonds are tax-preferred. Trusts, too, are often established as part of estate-tax planning for high-income households (Scholes and Wolfson 1992, chap. 27).

3   Do taxes affect portfolio decisions?

If taxes significantly affect household portfolios, two patterns should be apparent in the data. Within the cross section, the composition of portfolios should be systematically related to the tax rates facing the household. For example, high marginal tax–rate households should be more likely to hold tax-exempt bonds. Over time, portfolios should also vary in a manner consistent with the dramatic tax changes in the 1980s. For example, we should expect to see a shift away from forms of credit whose

---

[9] Kane (1986) examines wealth data from 1962, 1970, and 1977, and discusses how transactions costs, minimum denomination requirements, and difficulties in arranging credit inhibit low-wealth households from holding stocks, bonds, and investment real estate.

[10] In 1989, the median level of financial assets was $3,980 while net worth was $41,220. Financial assets include checking accounts, money market accounts, savings accounts, IRAs, Keoghs, CDs, savings bonds, other bonds, equity, mutual funds, and trusts. Net worth includes financial assets, property, and businesses, less all liabilities. Pension assets are not included in these or any other tabulations in the paper.

Table 2. *Conditional mean and median asset and liability holdings, 1983 and 1989ᵃ*

	1983 (in 1989 dollars)				1989			
	% that hold	Conditional mean ($1000s)	Conditional median ($1000s)	Total (billions)	% that hold	Conditional mean ($1000s)	Conditional median ($1000s)	Total (billions)
Assets								
Homes	63.5	87.3	64.7	4,697.4	64.7	106.1	70.0	6,391.3
Business assets	14.3	237.6	57.0	2,869.2	11.4	309.8	50.0	3,288.3
Other propertyᵇ	18.8	132.9	46.6	2,114.3	19.3	160.3	43.0	2,878.4
Equityᵇ	20.1	72.7	5.6	1,237.3	20.5	47.7	7.0	910.7
CDs	20.0	28.5	12.4	483.8	20.0	30.9	13.0	573.4
Trusts	4.0	113.2	12.4	385.2	3.6	105.7	18.0	350.3
Dollar cash value of whole life insurance	34.1	12.4	4.3	358.6	35.6	10.6	3.6	350.7
Money marketsᶜ	14.9	27.3	11.0	345.0	22.7	30.9	6.0	652.0
Tax-exempt bondsᵈ	3.3	113.0	24.9	313.8	4.4	98.7	22.2	407.4
Savings accountsᵉ	61.7	4.6	1.4	241.6	43.8	7.1	1.9	291.4
IRAs and Keoghs	17.3	14.0	5.0	205.3	24.5	26.4	11.0	602.8
Taxable bondsᶠ	3.0	79.1	12.4	202.2	4.7	65.8	15.0	286.8
Checking accountsᵍ	78.7	2.2	0.6	149.3	75.2	3.0	1.0	207.8
Land contracts or notes	3.8	45.4	22.8	145.8	2.5	60.6	28.0	141.2
Savings bonds	20.2	2.0	0.4	34.0	24.0	3.9	0.7	86.9

Liabilities

Mortgages	37.1	34.7	27.0	1,091.0	38.7	44.8	32.0	1,615.9
Debt on other properties	7.6	58.9	23.3	381.9	7.0	114.5	28.0	741.7
Miscellaneous other debt	29.8	7.7	1.6	193.4	32.2	8.1	2.0	241.5
Car loans	28.9	4.7	3.8	115.0	35.1	7.5	6.0	243.7
Other lines of credit	11.2	5.4	1.2	51.6	3.3	10.1	2.0	30.9
Credit cards	37.2	1.1	0.6	34.0	40.8	1.8	0.9	69.7
Debt on real estate, land contracts, and notes	0.8	36.8	21.3	24.0	0.2	26.9	12.0	5.8
Home-equity lines of credit	0.5	22.1	7.5	9.8	3.2	26.7	18.0	79.2

[a] The data for this table are taken from the 1983 and 1989 Surveys of Consumer Finances.
[b] The market value of publicly traded stock plus equity held in mutual funds.
[c] All money market accounts, including money market accounts with checkwriting privileges at banks and thrifts and brokerage cash and call accounts.
[d] All tax-exempt bonds and tax-exempt mutual funds.
[e] Passbook savings accounts, share accounts, Christmas Club accounts, and other types of savings accounts.
[f] Includes taxable-bond mutual funds.
[g] Unlike Table 1, this category does not include money market accounts with checkwriting privileges at banks and thrifts. Here, all money markets are classified together regardless of the type of depository institution.

Table 3a. *Cumulative distribution of assets and liabilities, by income percentiles, 1983 and 1989*[a]

	Income percentile									
	0–60		60–80		80–90		90–95		95–100	
	1983	1989	1983	1989	1983	1989	1983	1989	1983	1989
Assets										
Homes	31.3	28.9	22.1	22.5	15.8	16.1	10.7	12.2	20.0	20.3
Businesses	13.2	16.3	9.2	9.3	7.4	6.6	16.5	5.7	53.8	61.9
Other property	14.6	9.0	13.5	14.1	10.2	11.0	10.5	12.0	51.2	54.0
Equity	4.8	8.4	5.8	15.4	6.4	9.1	8.3	9.1	74.7	58.0
CDs	35.0	39.6	24.5	18.9	11.4	9.5	10.5	9.5	18.5	22.5
Trusts	5.2	12.1	11.3	13.0	5.2	8.0	5.1	10.5	73.2	56.4
Whole-life[b]	25.5	16.5	22.9	23.1	16.2	15.1	7.7	17.1	27.6	28.3
Money markets	16.6	28.4	16.0	14.7	10.7	10.5	12.2	6.0	44.5	40.4
Tax-exempt assets	3.3	4.2	1.9	10.0	2.1	4.2	8.5	10.9	84.1	70.7
Savings	34.7	32.8	24.3	22.0	13.6	9.7	13.6	22.9	13.8	12.6
IRA/Keoghs	13.1	15.7	10.4	18.7	12.3	14.3	12.1	18.9	52.1	32.4
Taxable bonds	4.7	7.2	4.0	12.2	17.0	7.1	18.7	13.0	55.6	60.5
Checking	32.4	30.8	16.7	28.8	12.1	9.6	11.5	8.4	27.3	22.3
Land contracts	28.5	13.3	9.2	15.7	25.6	14.0	9.5	26.4	27.2	30.6
Savings bonds	26.5	33.1	29.4	29.8	15.0	8.7	13.5	10.8	15.6	17.6

Liabilities

Mortgages	22.5	17.3	26.6	26.6	19.3	20.4	13.5	15.2	18.1	20.5
Debt on other property	8.3	6.7	12.5	10.2	11.4	7.8	9.7	9.4	58.2	65.9
Miscellaneous other loans	28.7	33.7	12.9	23.7	10.1	8.4	7.1	5.8	41.2	28.5
Auto loans	33.9	26.4	28.0	34.0	18.1	22.4	11.3	8.1	8.7	9.1
Other lines of credit	18.5	3.7	13.5	9.9	11.8	29.9	3.9	4.8	52.3	52.1
Credit cards	34.4	30.3	29.5	29.2	17.5	19.2	9.5	11.7	9.0	9.6
Debt on real estate and										
land contracts	12.4	3.3	3.7	12.3	38.9	13.5	18.0	6.7	27.0	64.2
Home-equity credit	27.2	12.2	11.4	25.1	2.2	16.8	38.2	12.2	20.9	33.7

Other totals

Income	27.5	23.3	22.3	22.9	15.5	16.1	10.9	10.5	23.8	27.2
Net worth	20.5	20.8	14.5	15.9	10.9	10.6	11.6	10.6	42.5	41.8

[a] Data are from the 1983 and 1989 Surveys of Consumer Finances.
[b] Dollar cash value of whole-life insurance policies.

Table 3b. *Cumulative distribution of assets and liabilities, by exogenous marginal tax rate, 1983 and 1989[a]*

	Marginal tax rate									
	0%–10%		10%–20%		20%–30%		30%–40%		40%–50%	
	1983	1989	1983	1989	1983	1989	1983	1989	1983	1989
Assets										
Homes	2.1	4.5	9.4	24.4	15.8	49.3	18.8	21.8	53.9	—
Businesses	0.0	0.5	0.6	2.9	1.8	80.2	4.4	16.4	93.1	—
Other property	0.2	0.9	2.1	7.7	4.2	71.4	8.0	20.1	85.6	—
Equity	0.4	1.2	1.2	7.3	2.2	74.6	3.6	16.9	92.6	—
CDs	1.5	5.5	12.0	32.9	15.6	43.2	17.2	18.4	53.6	—
Trusts	0.4	4.5	1.2	6.0	2.4	74.0	1.7	15.5	94.3	—
Whole-life[b]	1.9	3.5	6.7	16.0	14.4	59.2	18.5	21.3	58.4	—
Money markets	0.6	1.6	3.6	14.2	9.5	58.1	14.3	26.0	72.0	—
Tax-exempt assets	0.8	0.0	0.2	1.9	1.0	77.5	0.9	20.6	97.2	—
Savings	2.7	5.3	12.3	28.1	18.4	46.3	17.6	20.4	48.9	—
IRA/Keoghs	0.4	1.3	1.0	13.3	5.5	56.7	7.7	28.7	85.3	—
Taxable bonds	1.2	0.6	0.7	7.6	1.9	77.3	1.7	14.6	94.6	—
Checking	4.8	4.3	9.6	25.4	14.2	56.1	12.3	14.2	59.1	—
Land contracts	0.4	1.9	5.2	12.3	18.3	50.8	10.4	35.1	65.6	—
Savings bonds	0.9	3.5	10.5	37.0	16.0	44.6	19.0	15.0	53.7	—

234

Liabilities									
Mortgages	1.5	1.8	7.2	23.0	17.8	52.7	24.4	22.4	49.1	—
Debt on other property	0.1	0.4	1.2	3.5	5.4	77.6	9.1	18.5	84.2	—
Miscellaneous other loans	8.8	9.2	8.8	26.7	12.5	46.0	15.5	18.1	54.3	—
Auto loans	2.1	5.7	11.5	35.4	22.8	48.0	28.6	10.9	35.0	—
Other lines of credit	0.4	0.5	4.3	6.5	8.8	69.5	9.7	23.6	76.8	—
Credit cards	3.3	7.2	11.5	31.3	22.8	47.7	29.5	13.8	32.9	—
Debt on real estate and land contracts	—	—	2.8	12.3	5.4	47.1	12.8	40.6	78.9	—
Home-equity credit	2.8	7.0	1.5	23.6	31.1	39.7	4.8	29.6	59.9	—
Other totals									
Income	3.9	5.0	9.4	25.4	17.2	52.3	19.7	17.3	49.7	—
Net worth	1.0	2.5	4.9	13.5	8.2	63.4	10.1	20.6	75.9	—

[a] Data are from the 1983 and 1989 Surveys of Consumer Finances. The exogenous marginal tax-rate calculation is described in the text. Dashes denote "not applicable."

[b] Dollar cash value of whole-life insurance policies.

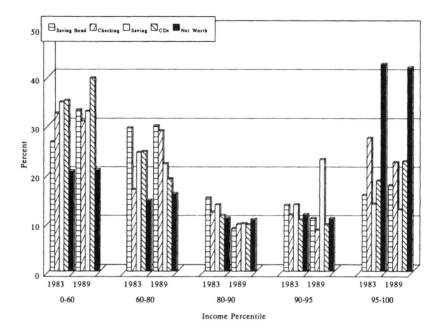

Figure 1. Cumulative distribution of assets held disproportionately by households in the 0–60th income percentiles, by income percentile, 1983 and 1989. *Source:* 1983 and 1989 Surveys of Consumer Finances.

deductibility was limited by TRA. In the following sections I highlight the tax treatment and tax changes most relevant to a given asset and liability category, and then present data on assets and liabilities by incomes and tax rates within the cross section and across time.

3.1   *Overview of assets, liabilities, and marginal tax rates*

Two households with identical wealth and labor income may have different tax rates depending on the composition of the households' portfolios. In this sense, tax rates are affected by portfolio composition. To account for this potential source of endogeneity, I constructed an exogenous marginal tax-rate measure for 1983 and 1989 by first calculating modified adjusted gross income, defined as the sum of labor and capital income assuming capital income comes from investing the household's entire net worth in fully taxable Aaa corporate bonds. Exemptions and filing status are then determined by the household's age, marital status, and number of children. Modified taxable income is calculated by subtracting

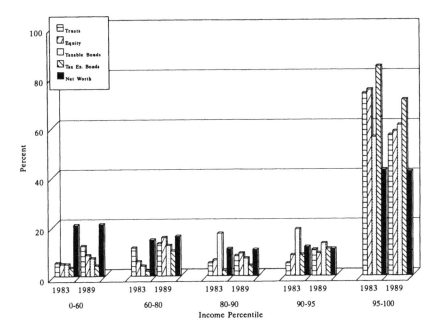

Figure 2. Cumulative distribution of assets held disproportionately by households in the top 5 income percentiles, by income percentile, 1983 and 1989. *Source:* 1983 and 1989 Surveys of Consumer Finances.

exemptions and the standard deduction from modified adjusted gross income.[11] The exogenous marginal tax rate is calculated by applying the appropriate rate schedule to modified taxable income. This calculation is similar to one used in King and Leape (1984) and provides an indication of the incentive a household faces to invest in tax-preferred securities.

Table 4 shows the patterns of constructed "exogenous" marginal tax rates faced by households holding each category of asset and liability in 1983 and 1989. The first and third columns show the average exogenous marginal tax rates for households holding the listed asset or liability using the SCF sample weights. The second and fourth columns show exogenous marginal tax rates weighted by the household's share of the total holdings

---

[11] Assuming that all households take the standard deduction is extreme, in that it ignores the ability of households to deduct state income and property taxes, sales taxes in 1983, medical expenses above some threshold, and casualty losses. The simulations do not incorporate the effect of the alternative minimum tax, tax on social security benefits, or floors on itemized deductions.

238   John Karl Scholz

Table 4. *Exogenous marginal tax rates, by asset and liability*[a]

	1983		1989	
	MTR[b]	Portfolio-weighted MTR[c]	MTR	Portfolio-weighted MTR
Assets				
Tax-exempt bonds	44.5%	49.1%	27.8%	28.8%
Taxable bonds	41.6	47.1	25.2	27.6
IRAs and Keoghs	40.4	46.2	25.1	27.4
Business assets	40.1	48.4	25.1	28.3
Money market accounts	37.6	43.4	23.1	27.9
Equity	37.2	48.1	24.7	27.7
Other property	36.9	46.4	22.7	27.8
Land contracts or notes	35.4	41.4	23.1	27.6
Trusts	35.0	48.5	25.3	26.7
U.S. Savings Bonds	33.4	38.4	22.1	23.0
Certificates of Deposit (CDs)	32.8	38.1	20.2	23.1
Dollar cash value of whole-life insurance	31.4	39.8	21.1	26.0
Homes	30.8	38.4	20.1	24.7
Savings accounts	29.3	36.3	19.8	23.9
Checking accounts	29.1	38.1	19.6	24.2
Liabilities				
Debt on real estate, land contracts, and notes	40.5	44.3	29.5	28.4
Debt on other properties	39.8	46.2	25.6	28.4
Mortgages	34.2	38.2	22.6	25.6
Other lines of credit	33.4	44.2	23.7	28.2
Credit cards	31.0	33.8	20.6	22.6
Auto loans	30.7	34.5	20.8	22.3
Home-equity lines of credit	30.5	39.9	24.8	24.5
Miscellaneous other loans	26.3	36.9	17.4	23.0
Full sample	25.7	43.8[d]	17.9	26.6[d]

[a] Data are from the 1983 and 1989 Surveys of Consumer Finances.
[b] MTR is the average marginal tax rate on the holders of the listed asset or liability.
[c] The portfolio-weighted marginal tax rate is the average marginal tax rate on the average dollar held in the listed asset or liability category.
[d] Weighted by shares of net worth.

of the listed asset or liability.[12] The table illustrates the substantial differences in tax rates faced by investors in different assets and liabilities. Not surprisingly, given the widespread ownership of checking and savings accounts, the average exogenous marginal tax rate on owners of these assets is only slightly higher than the samplewide average. Marginal tax rates on owners of taxable bonds, tax-exempt bonds, and IRAs and Keogh accounts are considerably higher.[13] Tax-exempt bonds, IRAs, and Keoghs enjoy substantial tax preferences, which is consistent with the idea (at least at this level of detail) that taxes may be an important factor shaping the structure of household portfolios.

With the flattening of tax rates in TRA, there is considerably less variation in tax rates by asset and liability in 1989. Depending on the weighting system, the variation between the highest and lowest taxed assets in 1983 is 13% to 15% for savings accounts compared to tax-exempt bonds. In 1989, the variation is 6% to 8%. The reduction in tax-rate differentials across assets raises the question of whether high-income, high-wealth households responded to the more uniform marginal rates by substituting tax-favored assets for others with higher returns, lower risk, or fewer implicit taxes.

3.2   Assets and TRA

3.2.1 *Tax-exempt bonds.* Tax-exempt-bond yields are lower than taxable bonds with equivalent risks and maturities, owing to their tax-free status.[14] Even with lower before-tax yields, however, after-tax returns on tax-exempt bonds can be higher than those on other investments for investors with high marginal tax rates. Within a cross section, holdings of tax-exempt bonds should be positively related to tax rates and factors correlated with tax rates, such as income.

Over time, the expected relationship is more complicated. Several factors, including the relative tax treatment of debt versus equity, affect the demand for municipal bonds. Gordon and MacKie-Mason (1990) suggest

---

[12] This asset- or liability-weighted marginal tax rate is similar to tax rates calculated in Skinner and Feenberg (1990). These tax rates represent marginal rates on a "representative" or average dollar of income in the given asset or liability.

[13] Feenberg and Poterba (1991) report, based on tax-return data, that the weighted average marginal tax rate on tax-exempt municipal bonds is 27.6%, which is almost identical to the 27.8% rate reported in Table 4.

[14] The yield spread between taxable and tax-exempt bonds implies that municipal bonds carry an implicit tax τ, where $\tau = 1 - r_m/r_f$; r_m is the return on municipal bonds, and r_f is the return on fully taxed bonds of equivalent risk and maturity.

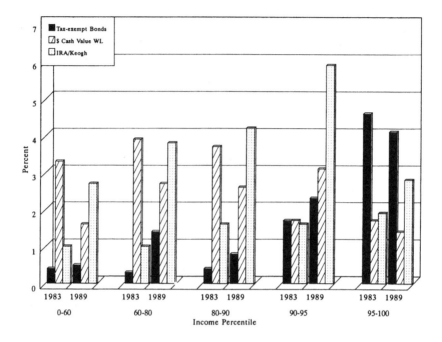

Figure 3. Portfolio shares of tax-exempt bonds, life insurance, and re-tirement accounts, by income percentile, 1983 and 1989. *Source:* 1983 and 1989 Surveys of Consumer Finances.

that TRA provided a modest increase in the attractiveness of debt relative to equity, which should lead to an increase in the demand for debt.[15] In the absence of any corresponding change in yields, demand for munici-pal bonds would nevertheless fall because of the reduction in tax rates. Poterba (1989), however, shows that personal tax rates appear to affect the yield spread between taxable and tax-exempt bonds. Feenberg and Poterba (1991, table 1) show that implicit taxes on tax-exempt bonds of 1-year maturity fell sharply in the 1980s, to 26.1% in 1990 from 48.5% in 1980; at the same time, the supply of tax-exempt debt increased. As shown in Figure 3, the net effect of these changes has been to increase the importance of tax-exempt bonds in the portfolios of households with income below the 95th percentile of the income distribution. The portfolio

[15] Although the reduction in personal and corporate taxes reduced the tax cost of both debt and equity, Gordon and MacKie-Mason (1990) suggest that the tax cost of debt fell more, because the rate reduction on corporate equity was mitigated by changes in depreciation rules and the elimination of the investment tax credit.

share devoted to tax-exempt bonds fell for the highest-income house-holds. However, ownership of tax-exempt bonds is still heavily concen-trated in high marginal tax–bracket households. Of the tax-exempt bonds held by individuals, roughly 97% were held by households with tax rates of 40% or higher in 1983;[16] in 1989, 98.1% were held by households with tax rates of 28% or higher. Portfolio shares for the complete set of assets and liabilities are given in Table 5.

3.2.2 *Life insurance and retirement accounts.* A February 1987 article in *Money* magazine, "Investments That Can Save You Taxes," begins, "Tax reform took the zing out of the high write-off deals that once quickened the heart rates of investors looking for ways to cut or defer taxes." Never-theless, the article goes on to describe a number of remaining tax-favored investments. Insurance and annuities receive the following backhanded compliment, "Thanks to the new tax law, these old gray mares of the investment world ain't what they used to be." Life insurance offers tax-free accumulation of return (the "inside buildup") and a death-contingent benefit, but – unlike IRA accounts between 1982 and 1986 – insurance contributions are not tax deductible. Figure 3 shows that whole-life insur-ance is a fairly popular investment for households in all income classes, accounting for 1.4% to 3.9% of assets. The portfolio share devoted to the cash value of whole-life insurance fell for households other than those with incomes in the 90th to 95th percentile between 1983 and 1989. By low-ering marginal tax rates, TRA reduced the attractiveness of tax-preferred investments.

As with other tax-deferral instruments such as life insurance, interest on an IRA accumulates tax-free. TRA eliminated the tax deductibility of IRA contributions for married couples with incomes over $50,000 and single taxpayers with incomes over $35,000, so long as these households are covered by an employer-provided pension plan. For households with in-comes below these thresholds or without a pension, IRAs remain a highly subsidized asset. Keogh plans offer similar benefits to the self-employed, but with potentially higher contribution limits: 20% of self-employment income up to an annual contribution of $30,000, as opposed to the $4,000 ($2,250) limit for married (single) IRA contributors.

Figure 3 shows that the portfolio share devoted to IRAs and Keoghs has increased dramatically for households in all income percentiles be-tween 1983 and 1989. Data from tax returns show that IRA participation

---

[16] Households with marginal tax rates above 40% also hold 95% of taxable bonds. House-holds with incomes in the top 5 percent of the income distribution hold a considerably greater share of their assets in tax-exempt bonds than in taxable bonds, though this share fell between 1983 and 1989.

Table 5. *Portfolio shares of assets and liabilities, by income percentile, 1983 and 1989*[a]

	Income percentile										All households	
	0–60		60–80		80–90		90–95		95–100			
	1983	1989	1983	1989	1983	1989	1983	1989	1983	1989	1983	1989
Assets												
Homes	52.8	52.1	49.5	48.8	47.1	50.0	31.5	40.5	16.4	18.7	34.1	36.7
Business assets	13.6	15.2	12.5	10.4	13.4	10.6	29.5	9.8	27.0	29.3	20.8	18.9
Other property	11.1	7.3	13.6	13.8	13.7	15.4	13.9	17.9	18.9	22.4	15.3	16.5
Equity	2.1	2.0	3.4	4.3	5.0	3.7	6.4	3.9	16.2	6.9	9.0	4.7
CDs	6.1	6.4	5.7	3.7	3.5	2.6	3.2	2.8	1.6	1.9	3.5	3.3
Trusts	0.7	1.2	2.1	1.5	1.3	1.4	1.2	1.9	4.9	2.8	2.8	2.0
Whole-life[b]	3.3	1.6	3.9	2.7	3.7	2.6	1.7	3.1	1.7	1.4	2.6	2.0
Money markets	2.1	5.7	2.6	3.5	2.3	3.6	2.6	2.2	2.7	4.1	2.5	4.1
Tax-exempt assets	0.4	0.5	0.3	1.4	0.4	0.8	1.7	2.3	4.6	4.1	2.3	2.3
Savings	3.0	2.7	2.8	2.2	2.1	1.4	2.1	3.5	0.6	0.5	1.8	1.7
IRA/Keoghs	1.0	2.7	1.0	3.8	1.6	4.2	1.6	5.9	1.9	2.8	1.5	3.5
Taxable bonds	0.3	0.6	0.4	1.2	2.2	1.0	2.4	1.9	2.0	2.5	1.5	1.6
Checking	1.7	1.8	1.2	2.0	1.1	1.0	1.1	0.9	0.7	0.7	1.1	1.2
Land contracts	1.5	0.5	0.6	0.8	2.4	1.0	0.9	1.9	0.7	0.6	1.1	0.8
Savings bonds	0.3	0.8	0.5	0.9	0.3	0.4	0.3	0.5	0.1	0.2	0.2	0.5

Liabilities (as a fraction of total assets)

Mortgages	8.8	7.9	13.8	14.6	13.4	16.1	9.2	12.8	3.5	4.8	7.9	9.3
Debt on other property	1.1	1.4	2.3	2.6	2.7	2.8	2.3	3.6	3.9	7.0	2.8	4.3
Miscellaneous other loans	2.0	2.2	1.2	1.8	1.2	1.0	0.9	0.7	1.4	0.9	1.4	1.3
Auto loans	1.4	1.8	1.5	2.8	1.3	2.7	0.8	1.0	0.2	0.3	0.8	1.4
Other lines of credit	0.3	0.0	0.3	0.1	0.4	0.4	0.1	0.1	0.5	0.2	0.4	0.2
Credit cards	0.4	0.6	0.5	0.7	0.4	0.7	0.2	0.4	0.1	0.1	0.2	0.4
Debt on real estate and land contracts	0.1	0.0	0.0	0.0	0.6	0.0	0.3	0.0	0.1	0.1	0.2	0.0
Home-equity credit	0.1	0.3	0.1	0.7	0.0	0.6	0.2	0.5	0.0	0.4	0.1	0.5

[a] Data are from the 1983 and 1989 Surveys of Consumer Finances. The figures represent the value of the given asset or liability as a percentage of household assets.

[b] Dollar cash value of whole-life insurance policies.

dropped off sharply after TRA.[17] Thus, the growth in IRA and Keogh accounts disproportionately reflects a combination of new contributions to IRAs made between 1983 and 1986, and growth in the value of IRA accounts established before TRA.[18] There is sharp disagreement in the literature about whether these contributions reflect net increases in wealth.[19] Gale and Scholz (1992) present evidence suggesting that these contributions result largely from a re-allocation of asset accumulation that would otherwise have occurred in the absence of IRA provisions. Venti and Wise (1992) and Feenberg and Skinner (1989) present and describe other analyses that suggest these contributions reflect mainly new savings. Joines and Manegold (1991) report intermediate results.

3.2.3 *Real estate and housing.* The tax treatment of real estate investments was tightened by TRA. The February 1987 *Money* magazine article stated: "Their write-offs pinched, these deals no longer tower above the tax-favored pack. Blessed be the tax-shelters, for they are not meek indeed." The important restrictions included eliminating the investment tax credit; eliminating the exclusion of 60% of long-term capital gains, which increased the top marginal tax rate on long-term capital gains to 28% from 20%; lengthening the depreciation provisions for real estate; and limiting the ability to use losses earned on passive investments to offset income from other investments.

Scholes and Wolfson (1992, p. 448) note that sales of public limited partnership interests, a common vehicle for tax shelters, fell from more than $8 billion in 1986 to roughly $3 billion in 1989.[20] Although it would be inappropriate to attribute all of the decline in real estate partnerships to the effects of tax laws – because at the same time the economy started showing signs of slipping and in many locations the real estate market was saturated – taxes presumably played some role in the falloff of investment.

[17] In 1985, 16.2 million taxpayers made deductible IRA contributions worth $38.2 billion. In 1988, 6.4 million taxpayers made deductible contributions worth $11.8 billion.

[18] An inherent difficulty in this study is that 1989 portfolio holdings presumably reflect both a continuing adjustment to the tax rules put in place in the early 1980s and adjustments to TRA. It is impossible to disentangle these changes with cross-sectional data from 1983 and 1989.

[19] Taxpayers have a great deal of flexibility, including borrowing or transferring existing financial assets, when investing in an IRA. If IRAs are not financed by reductions in consumption, they will not increase national saving. Slemrod (1990) gives a hierarchy of economic responses to tax reform: changes in the timing of transactions, financial and accounting responses, and the real decisions of individuals and firms. The IRA figures may simply reflect a financial response to the 1981 tax changes that made all households eligible for deductible IRAs.

[20] At the same time that the tax treatment of real estate investments was tightened, incentives for conducting business in the form of partnerships or sole proprietorships was increasing (as discussed in Section 3.4.2).

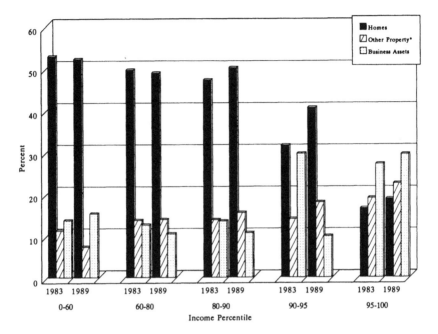

Figure 4. Portfolio shares of homes, other property, and business assets, by income percentile, 1983 and 1989. *Note:* "Other property" includes land contracts and notes. *Source:* 1983 and 1989 Surveys of Consumer Finances.

Housing is by far the largest asset in the typical household's portfolio.
In the United States, housing benefits from a number of tax preferences,
including the fact that the implicit rental value of the home is untaxed
while mortgage interest payments are deductible, and special capital gains
preferences are available to homeowners. The reduction in marginal tax
rates in TRA lowered the value of both preferences, which should have
reduced the demand for housing because the user cost of homeownership
increased (Poterba 1990). Of course, a number of other factors might be
expected to affect housing demand, including demographic changes, inflation, change in construction costs, and the tax treatment of alternative
assets. Thus, without more systematic investigation (see e.g. Ioannides
1989 or Poterba 1991) it is very difficult to assess the specific role of taxes
in housing investment decisions.

Figure 4 suggests that other property and land contracts and notes
constitute a larger share of the highest-income households' portfolios,
despite a significant tightening of the tax treatment of real estate by TRA.
There has also been an increase in the share of housing as a percentage of

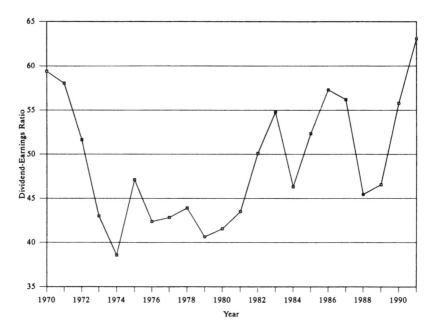

Figure 5. Percentage of dividend payouts to earnings, 1970–91. *Source:* CEA (1992, table B-91).

assets in the upper end of the income distribution. The increase in portfolio shares devoted to property-backed assets is consistent with an increase in the demand for such assets induced by the curtailment in TRA of tax preferences for many nonhousing assets. The tax reform also eliminated the deductibility of the interest expense of debt not backed by real estate. As discussed in Section 3.3, this restriction appears to have had a substantial effect on the composition of liabilities held by households. It may also have affected the composition of assets, as households must now use property-backed assets for collateral in order to deduct the interest expense of borrowing.

3.2.4 *Equity.* For households investing in equity, the reduction in marginal tax rates associated with TRA substantially increased the attractiveness of dividends relative to corporate retentions.[21] Figure 5 shows that

[21] Retentions were made less attractive by the increase in capital gains tax rates, tightening of depreciation schedules, and elimination of the investment tax credit. The reduction in corporate tax rates increased the attractiveness of retentions.

the percentage of dividends to earnings is volatile, but has maintained an upward trend following TRA.[22]

When examining disaggregated data on equity holdings, one might expect to see high–marginal tax rate households holding equity in firms with low dividend yields and low–marginal rate households holding equity in firms with high dividend yields. This conjecture, first raised by Miller and Modigliani (1961), is called the "dividend clientele" hypothesis. By investing in low-yield securities, high–marginal tax rate investors can defer personal income taxes on capital income. When the investor wishes to receive income from the equity, shares may be sold to generate the desired level of income.

Table 6 shows dividend yields by income percentile and marginal tax rates for households with equity.[23] In both years, households in the highest two ranges of the income distribution have yields below the sample average. In addition, when classified by marginal tax rates, the highest-income households (facing marginal tax rates of 50% in 1983 and 28% in 1989) have below-average portfolio yields.[24] These tabulations are consistent with the dividend clientele hypothesis, and with more formal econometric results presented in Scholz (1992) that suggest taxes play a significant role in explaining the yield characteristics of household equity portfolios, even after conditioning on factors associated with risk and transactions costs.

3.3   Liabilities and TRA

The 1983 and 1989 SCFs show that household debt as a percentage of assets increased substantially in the 1980s. Data on credit-market debt as a percentage of financial assets and homes from the Flow of Funds household sector accounts, plotted in Figure 6, also show a large and steady increase in debt over the 1980s.[25]

[22] In 1992, the average dividend/price ratio (as opposed to the dividend/earnings ratio graphed in Figure 5) was at its lowest level since 1972.

[23] The 1983 average yield of 4.5% in Table 6 is quite close to the 4.4% yield reported in the *Economic Report of the President* (CEA 1992, table B-91). The average yield of 5.0% in 1989 is much higher than the yield of 3.45% in the ERP, which is additional evidence that equity – the denominator of the dividend yield – is understated in the 1989 SCF.

[24] The highest statutory marginal tax rate in 1989 was 33%, but once exemptions and deductions were "clawed back" by the 33% bracket, the marginal tax rate fell to 28%. Hence the marginal tax rate on the highest-income households in 1989 was 28%.

[25] Adding consumer durables to the asset base lowers the y-axis coordinates by roughly 2 percentage points, but does not alter the graph's shape.

Table 6. *Average dividend yields for equity holders, by income percentile and marginal tax rate, 1983 and 1989*[a]

	1983	1989
Income percentile[b]		
0–20	4.6	5.0
20–40	6.6	3.8
40–60	4.8	5.7
60–80	5.2	5.5
80–90	5.0	7.0
90–95	3.8	4.3
95–100	4.3	4.7
Exogenous marginal tax rate (%)		
0–10	14.6	4.5
10–20	7.6	6.6
20–30	4.3	4.7
30–40	6.8	5.6
40–50	4.3	—
All households	4.5	5.0

[a] Figures are from the 1983 and 1989 Surveys of Consumer Finances and author's calculations.
[b] Income percentiles are calculated based on the sample of equity holders.

When looking at descriptive data, one of the best ways to illuminate the role that taxes play in portfolio composition is to look at changes in the composition of debt. The following, for example, appeared in the *Wall Street Journal:* "Want to finance a car, pay college tuition or take an expensive vacation? If you're like a growing number of Americans, you're looking at a home-equity loan. . . . [T]he fact that interest remains generally tax deductible makes home-equity loans and credit lines more attractive than ever. As a result, homeowners are using them for everything from making investments to paying medical bills" (Lynn Asinof, 10 June 1991, p. C-1). The article then points out that interest on borrowing up to $100,000 is still tax deductible with a home-equity loan. In contrast, interest on credit cards, auto loans, and other types of consumer credit can no longer be deducted. If taxes play a role, one would expect to see more borrowing in those liability categories that remained tax-deductible and less borrowing in those categories whose interest deductions were

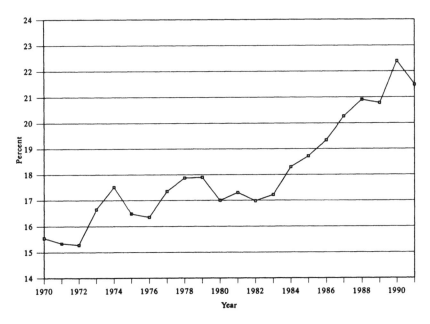

Figure 6. Credit-market debt as a percentage of financial assets and homes, 1970–91. *Source:* Board of Governors of the Federal Reserve System (March 1992), *Balance Sheets for the U.S. Economy, 1960–1991.*

limited by TRA, relative to what would have occurred in the absence of tax reform.

Figure 7 graphs debt not secured by property as a percentage of assets by income class in 1983 and 1989. Of the two categories of debt balances that fell in the SCF data – other lines of credit and miscellaneous loans – both had their deductibility curtailed by TRA. At the same time, credit-card and automobile loan balances grew sharply.[26] As shown in Figure 8, the categories of debt secured by property – mortgages, debt on other property, and home-equity lines of credit – increased substantially for households with incomes above the 60th percentile of the income distribution.

If tax changes affected these patterns then one would expect to see sharper differences between homeowners, who still have opportunities for tax-deductible borrowing, and households without homes, who no longer have such opportunities. Table 7 shows household leverage (liabilities as a percentage of assets) for homeowners and households without

---

[26] The trend in automobile loans is reflected in the households sector FoF accounts, where installment consumer credit grew to $730.9 billion in 1989 from $330.4 billion in 1982.

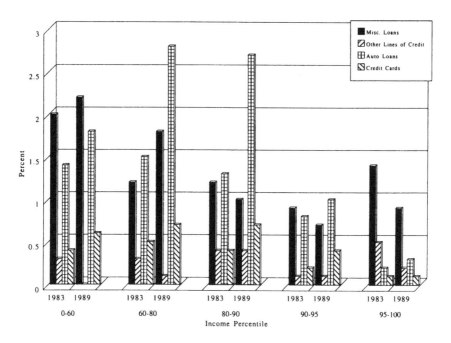

Figure 7. Portfolio shares of nondeductible loans as a percentage of assets, by income percentile, 1983 and 1989. *Source:* 1983 and 1989 Surveys of Consumer Finances.

homes by income percentile. Because more households own homes, the top panel of Table 7 is similar to the leverage ratios shown in Figures 7 and 8. There are sharp increases in property-backed debt, particularly for households in the top 10 percent of the income distribution, though leverage increased for households throughout the income distribution. In contrast to the homeowner sample, leverage fell for households without homes in the bottom 60 percent of the income distribution, even though households typically accumulate debt over expansionary periods of the business cycle. Because the tabulations condition only on income, and other factors (such as age, wealth, and marital status) presumably affect the use of debt, strong conclusions require further analysis. These results suggest that households with the ability to receive tax-subsidized borrowing may have increased their leverage at rates faster than those who had their access restricted. In addition, there is a shift in the composition of debt that is consistent with the incentives provided by TRA.

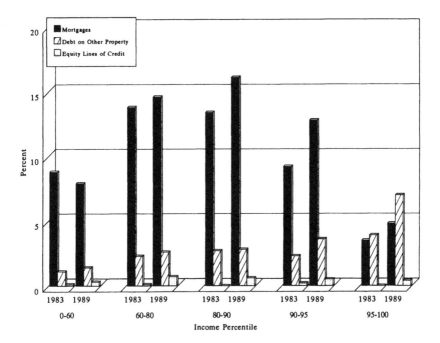

Figure 8. Portfolio shares of deductible loans as a percentage of assets, by income percentile, 1983 and 1989. *Source:* 1983 and 1989 Surveys of Consumer Finances.

3.4   *Other effects of TRA*

3.4.1 *Interest-rate arbitrage.* The phrase "interest-rate arbitrage" is used to describe transactions where households borrow, deduct the interest expense, and then invest in (generally) tax-preferred assets.[27] As long as the (tax-subsidized) rate of interest paid on borrowing is less than the return received from the tax-preferred asset, transactions of this type will be attractive. Because the value of the interest-expense deduction increases with a household's marginal tax rate, the incentive to engage in interest-rate arbitrage increases with the marginal tax rate.

The tax system imposes restrictions on taxpayers' ability to engage in tax arbitrage. Code section 163(d) allows the tax deduction for interest expense only to the extent that taxable investment income – which includes

---

[27] To the extent "arbitrage" refers to a riskless transaction, I am using the term loosely.

Table 7. *Liabilities as a percentage of assets for households with and without homes, 1983 and 1989*[a]

	Income percentile									
	0–60		60–80		80–90		90–95		95–100	
	1983	1989	1983	1989	1983	1989	1983	1989	1983	1989
Homeowners										
Mortgages	9.8	9.4	15.1	15.5	13.8	16.6	9.9	13.5	3.6	5.0
Debt on other property	0.6	1.0	2.1	2.3	2.6	2.7	2.3	3.6	3.8	7.1
Miscellaneous other loans	1.1	1.5	1.1	1.5	1.1	1.1	0.8	0.6	1.4	1.0
Auto loans	0.8	1.3	1.3	2.4	1.2	2.4	0.8	1.1	0.2	0.3
Other credit lines	0.3	0.0	0.3	0.1	0.3	0.3	0.1	0.1	0.4	0.2
Credit cards	0.3	0.4	0.4	0.5	0.3	0.5	0.2	0.4	0.1	0.1
Debt on real estate and land contracts	0.1	0.0	0.0	0.0	0.6	0.0	0.3	0.0	0.1	0.1
Home-equity credit	0.1	0.3	0.1	0.7	0.0	0.7	0.3	0.5	0.0	0.4
PB debt[b]	10.6	10.7	17.3	18.5	17.0	20.0	12.8	17.6	7.5	12.6
Non–PB debt	2.5	3.2	3.1	4.5	2.9	4.3	1.9	2.2	2.1	1.6
Non-homeowners										
Mortgages	—	—	—	—	—	—	—	—	—	—
Debt on other property	6.3	3.3	4.1	5.9	6.1	4.9	2.5	4.3	5.5	4.6
Miscellaneous other loans	9.6	5.8	1.9	6.1	4.7	2.8	2.2	1.6	2.5	2.2

Auto loans	6.4	4.9	3.5	9.5	4.6	11.2	1.4	0.2	0.1	0.8
Other credit lines	1.2	0.1	0.8	0.6	1.7	3.8	0.2	0.5	2.4	0.5
Credit cards	1.9	1.5	1.0	2.8	1.2	3.8	0.2	0.8	0.1	0.1
Debt on real estate and land contracts	—	—	—	—	—	—	—	—	—	—
Home-equity credit	—	—	—	—	—	—	—	—	0.2	0.1
PB debt	6.3	3.3	4.1	5.9	6.1	4.9	2.5	4.3	5.7	4.7
Non–PB debt	19.1	12.3	7.2	19.0	12.2	21.6	4.0	3.1	5.1	3.6

[a] Data are from the 1983 and 1989 Surveys of Consumer Finances. All variables are defined as the given category as a percentage of total assets.
[b] Property-backed debt is the sum of mortgage debt, debt on other property, debt on real estate and land contracts, and home-equity lines of credit.

Table 8. *Reasons for borrowing and median amount outstanding,
1983 and 1989*[a]

	1983		1989	
	Percent	Conditional median ($)	Percent	Conditional median ($)
Home purchase, repair	3.4	1,267	5.9	4,000
Car or durable good	20.9	469	20.9	744
Indoor hobby	8.3	473	5.3	420
Outdoor hobby	5.5	1,618	0.3	1,000
Saving and investment	10.6	3,735	7.0	11,000
Special expenses	36.5	1,245	45.8	2,000
Miscellaneous needs	14.8	871	14.7	900
Fraction of loans taken for investment purposes, by income, 1983 and 1989				
Income percentile				
0–20	3.0	373	1.9	2,000
20–40	3.5	2,100	4.7	1,794
40–60	5.0	1,245	5.0	10,000
60–80	7.0	1,925	9.0	22,000
80–90	20.2	4,980	9.1	8.000
90–95	28.7	2,863	8.6	24,000
95–100	39.9	12,450	25.7	28,000

[a] Data are from the 1983 and 1989 Surveys of Consumer Finances.

interest, dividends, rents, royalties, and capital gains – is equal to or exceeds the interest-expense deduction. Prior to TRA there was an extra $10,000 cushion to this limitation. In addition, Code section 265 prevents deduction of interest on loans used to purchase or hold assets, like municipal bonds, whose returns are exempt from federal income tax. This provision, however, has been interpreted so that a taxpayer can both borrow and purchase tax-exempt bonds in the same fiscal year, as long as he or she can demonstrate that the loan was used for some purpose other than to purchase or hold tax-exempt bonds.

In both the 1983 and 1989 SCFs, questions are asked about the reasons a household borrowed. In 1983, general questions were asked about the purpose of credit for a large set of consumer loans. In 1989, separate questions were asked about the purpose of consumer loans, home-equity lines of credit, and other lines of credit. The 1983 and 1989 responses are tabulated in Table 8 and provide direct evidence on the degree to which households borrow for investment purposes.

The top panel of Table 8 gives a frequency distribution of reasons households gave for borrowing in 1983 and 1989. In both years the "special expenses" category is the most common response; these loans are primarily for educational expenses. The conditional medians indicate that the largest balances on loans outstanding are on loans for investment purposes, but across the sample these account for fewer than 11% of all loans.[28]

The second panel of the table shows that high-income households are much more likely than the typical household to borrow for investment purposes. These are the households for whom interest-rate arbitrage is most profitable. By lowering marginal tax rates and restricting interest deductibility, TRA attempted to reduce the incentive for high-income taxpayers to engage in tax-related interest arbitrage. Comparing figures for 1983 and 1989 in Table 8 shows that there was a relatively large drop in the fraction of loans taken by high-income taxpayers for investment purposes, which is broadly consistent with the proposition that TRA reduced tax arbitrage.[29]

3.4.2 *Organizational form.* For the first time in many years, the top corporate tax rate exceeds the highest personal income-tax rate following TRA. Businesses now have a greater incentive to organize as partnerships, proprietorships, or subchapter S corporations (collectively referred to as "pass-through forms") rather than as schedule C corporations, because income earned in these pass-through forms is taxed only at the personal level (see e.g. Gordon and MacKie-Mason 1990). The 1983 and 1989 SCFs provide fairly detailed information on the financial status and organizational form of closely held businesses.

Table 9 shows that 8.9% of households had either a partnership or a proprietorship in 1983. As expected, by 1989 the percentage of households with partnerships or proprietorships has increased, though only to 9.4%. The fraction of households holding a business in a pass-through form increases steadily with income and the exogenous tax rate. While the fraction of households holding a business in a pass-through form was increasing, there was a 1.3–percentage-point decline between 1983 and 1989 in the number of households owning a business that was *not* in a

[28] The saving and investment category is composed of the following specific responses: invest in businesses, invest in financial assets, invest in real assets, purchase insurance or pay taxes, or make other investments.

[29] Restricting interest deductibility makes interest-rate arbitrage less attractive. In 1989, only 5.2% of consumer loans (with a median amount of $6,000) and 9.0% of other lines of credit (with a median amount of $17,000) were taken for investment purposes. In contrast, 25.5% of generally deductible home-equity lines of credit were taken for investment purposes; the median amount outstanding on these loans was $46,000.

Table 9. *Percentage of population with a closely
held business, by income percentile, 1983 and 1989*[a]

	% owning a partnership or proprietorship		% owning a partnership, proprietorship, or closely held corporation	
	1983	1989	1983	1989
Income percentile				
0–20	3.1	2.4	3.6	2.6
20–40	4.6	6.7	5.4	7.1
40–60	8.2	9.2	10.5	10.2
60–80	12.1	9.9	15.6	11.7
80–90	11.9	15.4	16.7	17.7
90–95	16.9	17.1	25.9	22.0
95–100	25.0	25.4	41.7	38.9
All households	8.9	9.4	12.1	11.3
Exogenous tax rate (%)				
0–10	0.2	2.0	0.3	2.0
10–20	2.8	6.3	3.2	6.7
20–30	7.3	13.9	8.8	17.6
30–40	9.7	24.4	12.5	31.3
40–50	22.3	—	32.5	—

[a] Data are from the 1983 and 1989 Surveys of Consumer Finances.

pass-through form.[30] The increase in closely held businesses organized as partnerships and proprietorships and the reduction in the number of closely held schedule C corporations is consistent with tax incentives provided by TRA.

3.4.3 *Implicit taxes.* In Table 10, exogenous and actual marginal tax rates are given by income percentile.[31] The difference between these marginal

[30] The 1983 SCF does not distinguish between subchapter S and other corporate forms, but only 1.1% of all households owned subchapter S corporations in 1989. Gordon and MacKie-Mason (1990, p. 120, fig. 4.2) present figures showing that subchapter S elections appear to have risen slightly between 1983 and 1988.

[31] Recall that the exogenous tax-rate measure is calculated assuming the household's entire net worth is invested in taxable Aaa bonds.

Table 10. *Average exogenous and actual marginal tax rates, by income percentile, 1983 and 1989*[a]

Income percentile	1983		1989	
	Exogenous MTR	Actual MTR	Exogenous MTR	Actual MTR
0–20	6.1	4.0	8.2	7.8
20–40	16.7	13.3	11.3	9.8
40–60	25.2	20.8	17.3	15.7
60–80	34.6	27.0	22.5	18.1
80–90	42.9	34.1	28.3	23.3
90–95	47.4	40.7	30.2	25.8
95–100	49.1	47.6	29.9	27.9
All households	25.7	20.9	17.9	15.4

[a] Data are from the 1983 and 1989 Surveys of Consumer Finances and author's calculations.

tax rates gives a crude indication of the degree to which portfolio responses affect the measurement of tax progressivity (measured by average marginal tax rates). As expected given the compression of statutory marginal tax rates in TRA, portfolio responses reduce marginal tax rates by a considerably smaller amount in 1989 than in 1983, except in the highest income percentiles. To the extent that households lessened the effect of progressive rates prior to TRA by accepting greater portfolio risks and lower before-tax returns, TRA may have reduced implicit taxes. This result would not be surprising because by lowering marginal tax rates TRA reduced the benefits – and by restricting opportunities for reducing tax rates raised the costs – of restructuring portfolios to lessen tax payments. Unfortunately, it is extremely difficult to provide a quantitative measure of the degree to which TRA reduced implicit taxes.

4   Descriptive evidence on other factors affecting investment decisions

Many other factors play some, and perhaps more important, roles in portfolio decisions than do taxes. In this section I briefly describe tabulations from the 1983 and 1989 SCFs related to transactions and information costs, liquidity, and risk and the influence the tax system has on risk taking.

4.1   *Transactions and information costs*

The 1983 and 1989 SCFs provide information about the reason a particular institution was chosen for households' checking accounts. In both years responses associated with transactions costs – convenient location of offices and being able to combine financial services – are the most important reasons for choosing a particular institution. One would expect transactions costs to be a critical factor in determining the location of checking accounts, because the money foregone when choosing an institution with a higher interest rate or lower required minimum balance is presumably small. In fact, roughly four times as many households gave transactions-cost reasons, as opposed to direct monetary reasons such as "low service charges" or "high interest rates," for choosing an institution. The proportion of households giving "time" reasons versus "money" reasons varied little with income.

King and Leape (1987) argue that information costs play a very significant role in portfolio decisions. To support this claim, they present a tabulation from a survey on household balance sheets taken by SRI International. The responses are to the question: "Why doesn't anyone in your household hold any stocks (or stock mutual funds, or bonds, or bond funds)?" For each of these instruments, between 34% and 47% percent of the respondents answered "Don't know enough about it." The authors then present probit estimates for the ownership of "information-intensive" assets and show that the probability of ownership increases with age, even after controlling for a wide array of other attributes.[32] They interpret these results as supporting a model where information barriers play an important role in investment decisions. However, in a similar analysis using the 1986 SCF, Ioannides (1990) finds few significant age effects. He interprets his evidence as not being supportive of the hypothesis that households' portfolio decisions are significantly affected by the slow accumulation of information about investment opportunities.

There are no direct questions on the cost and importance of information in the 1983 and 1989 SCFs. Questions are asked in 1983, however, about sources of advice in making financial decisions. On average, 27.1% of households seek professional advice when making financial decisions. This percentage increases from 22.5% for households in the bottom 60 percent of the income distribution to 58.8% for households in the top 5 percent of the distribution. Figure 9 disaggregates these percentages into the source of investment advice by income category. Across the sample,

---

[32] King and Leape (1987) define information-intensive assets as corporate equity, municipal bonds, corporate bonds, saving certificates, Treasury bonds, money market instruments, and single-premium annuities.

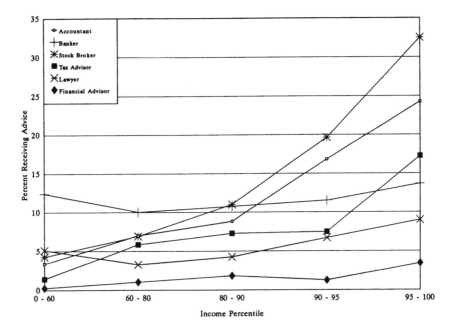

Figure 9. Percentage of households receiving professional investment advice, by income percentile, 1983. *Source:* 1983 Survey of Consumer Finances.

the most common sources of advice are bankers (11.8%), brokers (7.7%), and accountants (6.4%). Four percent of the population report receiving investment advice from a tax adviser, but this percentage rises sharply with income.

4.2 *Liquidity*

Concerns about liquidity may also affect portfolio decisions. For example, a young household knowing with reasonable certainty that they will be wanting to make a down payment on a house may be unwilling to contribute to an IRA despite their tax-preferred status, owing to penalties on withdrawals before age 59. The 1983 SCF contains the attitudinal question, "Which of the following statements on this card comes closest to how you feel about tying up your money in investments for long periods of time?" The possible responses are: Tie up money for a long, intermediate, or short period of time to earn substantial, above-average, or average returns. A fourth category is that the household was not willing

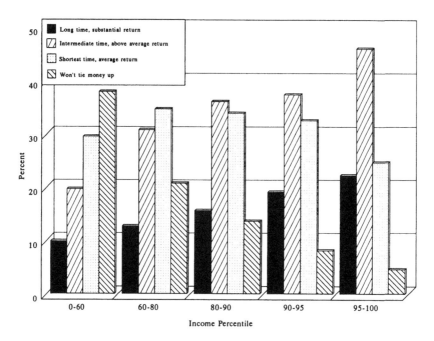

Figure 10. Attitude toward liquidity, by income percentile, 1983.
Source: 1983 Survey of Consumer Finances.

to tie up money at all. Interpretation of this question is clearly difficult because one household may view tying up money for six months to be a very long time, while another may view this as not tying money up at all.

Despite the difficulties involved in making cross-person comparisons of attitudes toward liquidity, there is evidence that this variable has some predictive power for analyzing financial decisions (Ioannides 1990). Figure 10 shows that the attitude toward liquidity responses varies systematically with income, with the highest-income households being the most willing to tie money up for a substantial period of time. The fact that attitudes toward liquidity vary systematically with income may complicate attempts to identify the effects of taxes on portfolio choice.

4.3   Risk

Risk and investor attitudes toward risk undoubtedly play an important role in investment decisions. It is not possible to determine the inherent riskiness of a household's portfolio in the 1983 and 1989 SCFs, because the specific assets that compose the holdings in a particular asset or liability

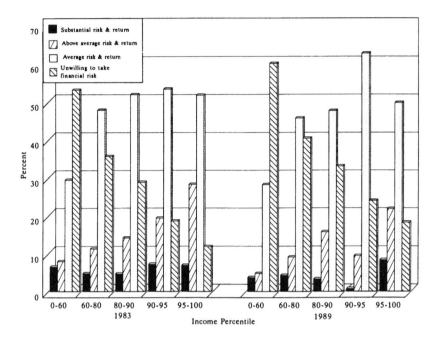

Figure 11. Attitude toward risk, by income percentile, 1983 and 1989.
Source: 1983 and 1989 Surveys of Consumer Finances.

category are not known. Nevertheless, some information is available in the surveys on attitudes toward risk.

The 1983 and 1989 SCFs contain the attitudinal question, "Which of the following statements on this card comes closest to the amount of financial risk you are willing to take when you save or make investments?" The possible responses are: Take substantial, above-average, or average financial risks expecting to earn substantial, above-average, or average returns. A fourth category is that the household was not willing to take any financial risks. There is some evidence that this variable has predictive power when analyzing financial decisions (see e.g. Scholz 1992 and Ioannides 1990), but interpretation of this question is plagued by a similar difficulty that arises with the liquidity question. As shown in Figure 11, the percentage of households reporting that they are unwilling to take any risks falls sharply with income, while willingness to take above-average and average risks generally increases with income. These figures vary only slightly when tabulated by the source of investment advice households receive, though those receiving professional advice from bankers appear to like risk somewhat less than do other households.[33] As with the liquidity question, the close relationship between risk attitudes and income may complicate efforts to identify the portfolio effects of taxation.

A more objective measure of risk is the degree of diversification of the household's portfolio. A number of papers – including Uhler and Cragg (1971), King and Leape (1984, 1986, 1987), and Ioannides (1990) – show that households' portfolios rarely span the complete set of assets, even accounting for mutual funds. However, this observation may reveal little about diversification because households may be well-diversified within a particular asset category, rendering further diversification into other asset types unnecessary (particularly when transactions and/or information costs are important). The 1983 and 1989 SCFs provide additional information on the diversification of households' equity portfolios. Specifically, households are asked about the number of companies in which they own equity.

Blume, Crockett, and Friend (1974) present tabulations of portfolio diversification of households in 1971, based on Internal Revenue Service tax-return data. In Table 11 these tabulations are compared to similar tabulations from the 1983 and 1989 SCF.[34] In each year, households with mutual funds (which presumably are well-diversified) are dropped from the sample, leaving only households with equity but no mutual funds in Table 11.[35] Just as in 1971, the typical household owning equity in the 1980s was poorly diversified, holding equity in slightly more than three companies. Even very high–income households held fewer than the 30–40 securities that Statman (1987) suggests are needed for a well-diversified portfolio.[36] When equity portfolios are weighted by the share of equity held by the household, however, portfolios appear to be significantly more well-diversified. Specifically, the average dollar of equity is held in a portfolio with 15 other securities in 1983 and 14 securities in 1989.

[33] Those who receive investment advice from their spouse have by far the most conservative attitudes toward risk, followed by those who obtain their advice from the media.

[34] Incomes in 1983 and 1989 were deflated to 1971 levels using the all-items consumer price index (CEA 1992, table B-56). The index was 40.5 in 1971, 99.6 in 1983, and 124.0 in 1989.

[35] On average 12.4% of equity holders in 1983 and 11.5% of equity holders in 1989 are excluded from the sample because they have shares in mutual funds. Households with few securities in their equity portfolios may still be well-diversified through pension holdings.

[36] Best and Grauer (1991) suggest that a passive investor should not deviate too far from an index fund. They also show that extremely large portfolio changes may be required for active investors who wish to maintain efficient portfolios with fewer securities than suggested by Statman (1987).

Table 11. *Average number of companies held by households with equity: 1971, 1983, and 1989*[a]

AGI class[b]	1971[c]	1983	1989	Value-weighted[d] 1983	Value-weighted[d] 1989
0–5	3.2	2.4	2.8	9.4	5.3
5–10	3.8	2.5	2.9	5.5	12.3
10–15	4.0	3.2	2.5	10.5	6.7
15–25	4.3	3.6	3.9	12.3	14.3
25–50	6.7	5.7	4.6	18.5	12.1
50–100	9.2	10.3	5.5	20.0	13.0
100–200	13.2	11.3	6.5	22.9	13.3
200–500	16.8	15.9	4.9	18.6	12.2
500+	18.7	18.2	13.3	14.0	29.6
All households	4.5	3.2	3.5	15.2	13.8

[a] Data are from the 1983 and 1989 Surveys of Consumer Finances and author's calculations.
[b] Thousands of 1971 dollars.
[c] Data are from Blume et al. (1974, p. 31, table 7).
[d] Each household is weighted by the proportion of total equity held by the household.

The tabulations and papers cited in this section indicate that risk is important to investors, and that the typical household has not fully diversified their equity portfolio. This statement says nothing, however, about whether the tax system affects the riskiness of households' portfolios. As noted when I discussed implicit taxes, TRA presumably reduced the incentives households faced to accept greater portfolio risk in order to lessen tax payments, but measuring the precise effect the tax system has on risk taking is extremely difficult.

5   Conclusions

This paper began by asking whether taxes affect the composition of household portfolios and, if so, how these changes affect the measurement of tax progressivity. To pursue these issues I examined several aspects of portfolio choice using data from the 1983 and 1989 Surveys of Consumer Finances.

Across households within a period, we would expect portfolio composition to vary with income. High-income households in high tax brackets should hold a larger share of their portfolios in tax-favored or tax-exempt assets. These assets are indeed held disproportionately by high-income households. Households with high marginal tax rates also have a stronger incentive to engage in tax arbitrage. I find that upper-income households report a considerably higher fraction of loans taken for investment purposes than is the case for lower-income households. High-income households also appear to hold a disproportionate share of equity with low dividend yields, as would be expected if taxes mattered in investment decisions.

Over time, the 1986 tax reform provides a good opportunity for examining changes in households' portfolios. The intertemporal analysis, however, is complicated by a host of other factors. TRA was so wide-ranging that the combined effects of the tax changes rarely lead to unambiguous incentives to hold one asset or another (Hendershott 1990). In addition, general equilibrium responses will in all likelihood attenuate responses. Higher taxes on equity relative to debt, for example, should increase demand for bonds, which in turn will lower bond yields, muting some of the expected first-order effects on portfolio choice. It is also very difficult to separate tax effects from other factors (such as risk aversion) that may affect portfolio choice. Further research examining the effects of taxes on risk-taking and measuring the magnitude of various implicit taxes would clearly be valuable.

Despite these caveats, tax changes appear to matter in some circumstances. TRA decreased statutory marginal tax rates significantly for higher-income households. This caused the yield spread between taxable and tax-exempt bonds to narrow, which – along with an increase in the supply of tax-exempt bonds – led to increased holdings of tax-exempt bonds by households with incomes below the 95th percentile of the income distribution. The portfolio share devoted to life insurance fell for most households. Lower marginal tax rates also increased the incentive for closely held businesses to organize in pass-through forms, which is also observed in the data.

More dramatic changes have occurred on the liability side of households' balance sheets. There was a striking increase in the amount of debt held by households between 1983 and 1989. Debt backed by property, which retained its deductible status in TRA, grew rapidly; some forms of nondeductible debt rose, while others fell. However, lower-income households without homes, who have considerably fewer opportunities to deduct interest payments on borrowing, reduced their debt over the period. In addition, fewer high-income households reported taking loans for investment purposes in 1989 than in 1983. Given the significant changes in the tax treatment of debt in TRA, further examination of the determinants of household borrowing is likely to be a promising avenue for research on the influence of taxes on household portfolios.

REFERENCES

Adams, T. S. (1923), "Tax-Exempt Securities," *Proceedings of the National Tax Association, 1922*, vol. 15, pp. 261–83.

Avery, Robert B., and Gregory E. Elliehausen (1986), "Financial Characteristics of High-Income Families," *Federal Reserve Bulletin* 72: 163–77.

(1988), "1983 Survey of Consumer Finances: Technical Manual and Codebook," Mimeo, Board of Governors of the Federal Reserve System, Washington, DC.

Avery, Robert B., Gregory E. Elliehausen, Gregory Canner, and Thomas Gustafson (1984a), "Survey of Consumer Finances, 1983," *Federal Reserve Bulletin* 70: 679–92.

(1984b), "Survey of Consumer Finances, 1983: a Second Report," *Federal Reserve Bulletin* 70: 857–68.

Avery, Robert B., Gregory E. Elliehausen, and Arthur B. Kennickell (1987), "Changes in Consumer Installment Debt: Evidence from the 1983 and 1986 Surveys of Consumer Finances," *Federal Reserve Bulletin* 73: 761–78.

(1988), "Measuring Wealth with Survey Data: an Evaluation of the 1983 Survey of Consumer Finances," *Review of Income and Wealth* 34: 339–69.

Best, Michael J., and Robert R. Grauer (1991), "On the Sensitivity of Mean-Variance-Efficient Portfolios to Changes in Asset Means: Some Analytical and Computational Results," *Review of Financial Studies* 4: 315–42.

Blume, Marshall, Jean Crockett, and Irwin Friend (1974), "Stockownership in the United States: Characteristics and Trends," *Survey of Current Business* 54: 16–40.

Butters, J. Keith, Lawrence E. Thompson, and Lynn L. Bollinger (1953), "Effects of Taxation: Investments by Individuals," Monograph, Division of Research, Graduate School of Business Administration, Harvard University, Cambridge, MA.

Chaplinsky, Susan, and H. Nejat Seyhun (1990), "Dividends and Taxes: Evidence on Tax Reduction Strategies," *Journal of Business* 63: 239–60.

Constantinides, George M. (1983), "Capital Market Equilibrium with Personal Tax," *Econometrica* 51: 611–36.

(1984), "Optimal Stock Trading with Personal Taxes: Implications for Prices and Abnormal January Returns," *Journal of Financial Economics* 13: 65–89.

Council of Economic Advisors (1992), *Economic Report of the President.* Washington, DC: Government Printing Office.

Curtin, Richard T., F. Thomas Juster, and James N. Morgan (1989), "Survey Estimates of Wealth: an Assessment of Quality," in R. E. Lipsey and H. S. Tice (eds.), *The Measurement of Saving, Investment, and Wealth.* Chicago: University of Chicago Press, pp. 473–551.

Dicks-Mireaux, Louis, and Mervyn A. King (1982), "Portfolio Composition and Pension Wealth," Working Paper no. 903, National Bureau of Economic Research, Cambridge, MA.

Domar, Evsey D., and Richard A. Musgrave (1944), "Proportional Income Taxation and Risk Taking," *Quarterly Journal of Economics* 58: 388–422.
Feenberg, Daniel (1981), "Does the Investment Interest Limitation Explain the Existence of Dividends?" *Journal of Financial Economics* 9: 265–9.
Feenberg, Daniel R., and James M. Poterba (1991), "Which Households Own Municipal Bonds? Evidence from Tax Returns," *National Tax Journal* 44: 93–103.
Feenberg, Daniel R., and Jonathan Skinner (1989), "Sources of IRA Saving," in Lawrence Summers (ed.), *Tax Policy and the Economy.* Cambridge, MA: MIT Press, pp. 25–46.
Feldstein, Martin (1976), "Personal Taxation and Portfolio Composition: an Econometric Analysis," *Econometrica* 44: 631–50.
Gale, William G., and John Karl Scholz (1992), "IRAs and Household Saving," Mimeo, The Brookings Institution and University of Wisconsin–Madison.
Galper, Harvey, Robert Lucke, and Eric Toder (1988), "A General Equilibrium Analysis of Tax Reform," in H. Aaron, H. Galper, and J. Pechman (eds.), *Uneasy Compromise: Problems of a Hybrid Income-Consumption Tax.* Washington, DC: Brookings, pp. 59–108.
Gordon, Roger H., and Jeffrey K. MacKie-Mason (1990), "Effects of the Tax Reform Act of 1986 on Corporate Financial Policy and Organizational Form," in J. Slemrod (ed.), *Do Taxes Matter: The Impact of the Tax Reform Act of 1986.* Cambridge, MA: MIT Press, pp. 91–131.
Hendershott, Patric H. (1990), "Comments on Skinner and Feenberg," in J. Slemrod (ed.), *Do Taxes Matter: The Impact of Tax Reform Act of 1986.* Cambridge, MA: MIT Press, pp. 80–8.
Hubbard, R. Glenn (1985), "Personal Taxation, Pension Wealth, and Portfolio Composition," *Review of Economics and Statistics* 67: 53–60.
Ioannides, Yannis M. (1989), "Housing, Other Real Estate, and Wealth Portfolios: an Empirical Investigation Based on the 1983 Survey of Consumer Finances," *Regional Science and Urban Economics* 19: 259–80.
(1990), "Dynamics of the Composition of Household Asset Portfolios and the Life Cycle," Mimeo, Department of Economics, Virginia Polytechnic Institute and State University, Blacksburg.
Joines, Douglas H., and James G. Manegold (1991), "IRAs and Saving: Evidence from a Panel of Taxpayers," Mimeo, Department of Finance and Business Economics, University of Southern California, Los Angeles.
Juster, F. Thomas, and Kathleen A. Kuester (1991), "Differences in the Measurement of Wealth, Wealth Inequality, and Wealth Composition Obtained from Alternative Wealth Surveys," *Review of Income and Wealth* 37: 33–62.
Kane, Edward J. (1986), "Wealth-Based Engels Curves for Financial and Real Estate Assets," *Research in Finance* 6: 233–45.
Kennickell, Arthur (1992), "Description of the First Public Release of the Full 1989 SCF Cross-Section Dataset and 1989 Survey of Consumer Finances Codebook," Mimeo, Board of Governors of the Federal Reserve System, Washington, DC.
Kennickell, Arthur, and Janice Shack-Marquez (1992), "Changes in Family Finances from 1983 to 1989: Evidence from the Survey of Consumer Finances," *Federal Reserve Bulletin* 78: 1–18.
Kennickell, Arthur B., and R. Louise Woodburn (1992), "Estimation of Household Net Worth Using Model-Based and Design-Based Weights: Evidence

from the 1989 Survey of Consumer Finances," Mimeo, Board of Governors of the Federal Reserve System and Statistics of Income Division, Internal Revenue Service, Washington, DC.

King, Mervyn A., and Jonathan I. Leape (1984), "Wealth and Portfolio Composition: Theory and Evidence," Working Paper no. 1468, National Bureau of Economic Research, Cambridge, MA.

  (1986), "Wealth, Taxes, and Portfolio Composition: an Econometric Study," Mimeo prepared for the International Seminar on Life-Cycle Theory (Paris), London School of Economics.

  (1987), "Asset Accumulation, Information, and the Life Cycle," Working Paper no. 2392, National Bureau of Economic Research, Cambridge, MA.

Miller, Merton H., and Franco Modigliani (1961), "Dividend Policy, Growth, and the Valuation of Shares," *Journal of Business* 34: 411–33.

Miller, Merton, H., and Myron S. Scholes (1978), "Dividends and Taxes," *Journal of Financial Economics* 6: 333–64.

Poterba, James M. (1987), "How Burdensome Are Capital Gains Taxes?" *Journal of Public Economics* 33: 157–72.

  (1989), "Tax Reform and the Market for Tax-Exempt Debt," *Regional Science and Urban Economics* 19: 537–62.

  (1990), "Taxation and Housing Markets: Preliminary Evidence on the Effects of Recent Tax Reforms," in J. Slemrod (ed.), *Do Taxes Matter: The Impact of the Tax Reform Act of 1986.* Cambridge, MA: MIT Press, pp. 141–60.

  (1991), "House Price Dynamics: The Role of Tax Policy and Demography," *Brookings Papers on Economic Activity* 2: 143–83.

Scholes, Myron S., and Mark A. Wolfson (1992), *Taxes and Business Strategy: A Planning Approach.* Englewood Cliffs: NJ: Prentice-Hall.

Scholz, John Karl (1992), "A Direct Examination of the Dividend Clientele Hypothesis," *Journal of Public Economics* 49: 261–85.

Seyhun, H. Nejat, and Douglas J. Skinner (1991), "How Do Taxes Affect Investors' Stock-Market Realizations? Evidence from Tax-Return Panel Data," Working Paper no. 91-39, Mitsui Life Financial Research Center, School of Business Administration, University of Michigan, Ann Arbor.

Skinner, Jonathan, and Daniel Feenberg (1990), "The Impact of the 1986 Tax Reform on Personal Saving," in J. Slemrod (ed.), *Do Taxes Matter: The Impact of the Tax Reform Act of 1986.* Cambridge, MA: MIT Press, pp. 50–79.

Slemrod, Joel (1990), "The Economic Impact of the Tax Reform Act of 1986," in J. Slemrod (ed.), *Do Taxes Matter: The Impact of the Tax Reform Act of 1986.* Cambridge, MA: MIT Press, pp. 1–12.

Statman, Meir (1987), "How Many Stocks Make a Diversified Portfolio?" *Journal of Financial and Quantitative Analysis* 22: 353–63.

Stiglitz, Joseph (1969), "The Effects of Income, Wealth, and Capital Gains Taxation on Risk-Taking," *Quarterly Journal of Economics* 83: 262–83.

  (1983), "Some Aspects of Capital Gains Taxation," *Journal of Public Economics* 21: 257–94.

Uhler, R. S., and J. G. Cragg (1971), "The Structure of Asset Portfolios of Households," *Review of Economic Studies* 38: 341–57.

Venti, Steven F., and David A. Wise (1992), "Government Policy and Personal Retirement Saving," in J. Poterba (ed.), *Tax Policy and the Economy.* Cambridge, MA: MIT Press and National Bureau of Economic Research, pp. 1–42.

Comments

Roger H. Gordon

The U.S. Tax Reform Act of 1986 (TRA) included many provisions changing the taxes due on capital income received by both individuals and corporations. Measuring the distributional effects of these tax changes is not as straightforward as it might appear. What is easily reported is the change in tax payments on capital income for each individual resulting from the tax reform, holding constant this individual's portfolio and the rate of return earned on the portfolio. These calculations were done originally when projecting the distributional consequences of the legislation; the equivalent exercise could now be done using current portfolio choices.

What we would like to measure, however, is the change in welfare of individuals in different parts of the income distribution resulting from the 1986 tax reform, taking into account the option individuals have to change their behavior in response to the reforms as well as the impact of the resulting price changes. When behavior does change in response to a tax reform, the gain to each class of taxpayers will be underestimated when measured by changes in tax liabilities holding fixed their behavior at their ex ante values, because such a measure ignores the benefit these taxpayers derive from altering their behavior. In contrast, any measure of the gain based on ex post data will normally be overestimated, because this measure ignores the nontax costs that ultimately limit the extent to which people are willing to change their behavior to save on taxes. The more important are these behavioral changes, the larger are the respective biases. Both measures also ignore the welfare effects of price changes that occurred in response to the tax reform.

The objective of the paper by Scholz is to compare data from two surveys of individual wealth holdings – one done in 1983, before TRA; the other done afterward in 1989 – to assess the importance of portfolio re-adjustments in response to the changes in the tax treatment of capital

268

income under TRA.[1] To the degree that these portfolio re-adjustments were important, biases in standard measures of the distributional effects of the tax reform are important.[2]

In principle, behavioral changes should occur in response to any tax reform, since any reform changes the general equilibrium in the entire economy. However, TRA focused in particular on the tax treatment of capital income, making Scholz's paper particularly valuable. As a general rule, shifts in portfolios and other financial re-adjustments (e.g. changes in debt/equity ratios), holding the real allocation of resources constant, require little time or real costs and so should take place very quickly in response to a tax change. Capital gains liabilities provide one inhibition to portfolio re-adjustment, but the huge capital gains realizations preceding TRA suggest that substantial re-adjustments occurred anyway.

What changes would have been expected in response to TRA? To begin with, personal tax rates were cut relative to corporate tax rates, creating an incentive for profitable firms to shift from a corporate to a noncorporate form of ownership. In addition, the legislation restricted an individual investor's ability to deduct tax losses, by imposing passive-loss restrictions and eliminating the deductibility of nonmortgage interest payments. Since the aggregate income from partnerships was negative prior to the tax reform, either these deductions would be lost or they would need to be shifted to the corporate sector. In addition, there were a variety of other more detailed changes – for example, eliminating the partial exemption of long-term capital gains and eliminating the "General Utilities" doctrine that allowed corporations to avoid corporate taxation on their capital gains.

Data sources on individual portfolio choice are extremely limited. The comparison of the 1983 and 1989 Survey of Consumer Finances (SCF) should in principle provide an extremely valuable source of information about the behavioral effects of TRA. What portfolio changes does Scholz actually find using these data? Of what consequence are these observed changes for the measurement of the distributional effects of the legislation? Several expected changes do show up clearly in the data. First, individual debt holdings shift dramatically toward mortgage debt, as the tax reform limited the deductibility of nonmortgage interest payments. Does

---

[1] These portfolio re-adjustments include both shifts in the ownership of a given supply of financial and real assets among different investors as well as changes in the relative supplies of various assets.

[2] Measures of the pattern of behavioral changes resulting from the tax reform would also be needed in assessing the efficiency consequences of the tax reform – the information resulting from this study is of broader interest than the immediate objective of the paper.

an investor bear any offsetting nontax losses as a result of this reclassification of debt, losses that would be ignored in standard distributional studies? Individuals would certainly bear some transactions costs, in the form of any new surveys, title searches, and appraisals that may be required before a mortgage is approved. These costs would seem to be minor, however, when amortized over the life of a mortgage of typical length. If so, then measures based on ex post data on interest deductions, or based on ex ante data but assuming full reclassification of debt, would be reasonably accurate.

Yet, not all debt was in fact reclassified as mortgage debt. Transactions costs must be important enough to prevent individuals from reclassifying at least small or temporary loans as mortgage debt, suggesting that such costs could well have been important for some of the debt that was reclassified; just how important remains an open question.

The restrictions on interest deductibility would also be expected to lead to a reduction in indebtedness for those whose total debt exceeded the maximum mortgage allowed under TRA. Although Scholz does not look at this subgroup in particular, he finds that indebtedness generally went up. I find it hard to attribute this change in behavior to the tax reform. As argued in Gordon and MacKie-Mason (1990), the cut in personal relative to corporate tax rates should have caused corporate borrowing to replace personal borrowing. The narrowing of personal tax rates and the reduction in nominal interest rates should also have lessened the arbitrage gains of those in high tax brackets borrowing from those in low brackets to invest in more lightly taxed assets. Some other changes in the economy probably led to this increasing indebtedness.

Another clear change evident in the data is the increased amount invested in IRA and equivalent accounts. Because IRA provisions were tightened under TRA, this increase presumably occurred mainly prior to the tax change. To what degree are the distributional consequences of IRAs mismeasured simply by looking at the resulting change in tax payments? If IRAs are not marginal savings but rather a shift of assets from a taxable account into an IRA, and if their illiquidity is of no consequence, then the welfare effect for the individual of the option to invest funds in the IRA in a given year simply equals the resulting increase in the present value of the income earned from the investments. Assume the individual's tax rate is constant over time. When an individual invests \$1 in a taxable bond, the present value of the resulting income must be worth just \$1, so that the investor breaks even. When an individual invests \$1 in a taxable bond held in an IRA, withdrawing the funds after N years, then the present value of the resulting income is $-(1-t) + (1-t)e^{rN}e^{-r(1-t)N} = (1-t)(e^{rtN}-1)$, where r is the interest rate and t the individual's tax rate.

Given our assumption of a constant tax rate, this expression measures the present value of the gains from the option to invest \$1 in an IRA that year.

Existing studies of the distributional consequences of the tax reform would normally measure the gain from access to IRAs simply by the savings t obtained due to the deductibility of each \$1 contribution to an IRA. Although the measure t certainly differs from the theoretically appropriate measure $(1-t)(e^{rtN}-1)$, the difference becomes small when $rN(1-t) \approx 1$, a not implausible approximate value for the typical holding period.[3] The true welfare gain to the individual contributor would be smaller to the extent that contributions come from new savings, the liquidity loss is costly, or the individual's tax rate is higher when the funds are withdrawn from the IRA.

One other change that shows up clearly in the data is an increase in the dividend payout rate. Given the increase in the capital gains tax rate and the cut in the ordinary tax rate on dividend income, this change should not be surprising. What nontax factors are traded off with tax considerations in setting the dividend payout rate is much debated, however, making it difficult to evaluate the needed correction to standard distributional measures. The normal presumption would be that nontax benefits of dividends offset the extra taxes due on dividend payments at the margin, so that the extra taxes paid as a result of the higher payout rate are at least partially offset by the nontax benefits of the added dividends. This would be the implication of the Poterba–Summers (1985) model of dividends, in which investors value the liquidity provided by dividends; or of the Easterbrook (1984) story, in which dividends are paid in order to force firms to seek outside financing for any new investment project (to prevent firms from undertaking value-reducing investments). However, if dividends serve the role of a signal, as in Gordon and Malkiel (1981), then dividend payments impose nontax liquidity costs on the firm paying the dividends. Better firms face lower liquidity costs, making dividends an effective signal. When the tax penalty to dividend payments is cut, dividends are a cheaper signal for all firms, so that all firms must signal more aggressively in equilibrium. The result is an increase in nontax costs, adding to the costs already borne through the tax penalty on the increased dividends.

Many other changes in behavior that would have been expected as a result of TRA do not show up clearly in the data. Were these changes less important than expected, or are the data inadequate? For example, after TRA the corporate tax rate exceeded the top personal tax rate for the

---

[3] Note, though, that the bias from using the simpler measure t varies with t.

first time, giving profitable corporations an incentive to shift to a non-corporate form. At the same time, the tax change gave noncorporate firms with tax losses an incentive to shift to the corporate form, due to the higher corporate tax rate and the newly introduced restrictions faced by noncorporate owners with respect to passive-loss deductions. The SCF data, as reported in this paper, show relatively little change in noncorporate assets as a whole. This is not inconsistent with the theoretical forecast, given the conflicting incentives faced by firms with profits versus losses. However, this lack of change in net assets may hide the forecasted shift of taxable income into the noncorporate form and of tax losses into a corporate form. For example, Scholes and Wolfson (1988) note that there was a sharp increase in the number of subchapter S corporations around the time of TRA, a corporate form which is treated the same for tax purposes as noncorporate firms. Similarly, IRS Statistics of Income figures show that aggregate partnership income declined steadily during the 1980s prior to TRA, reaching −$17.4 billion in 1986, but jumped to $14.5 billion by 1988. I am not sure why these changes did not show up more clearly in the SCF data.

This shifting of taxable income from corporate returns to personal returns certainly requires some correction when tabulating the distributional consequences of TRA. From the individual shareholder's perspective, combined corporate and personal tax payments may change little, yet reported personal income and personal tax payments of corporate shareholders may change substantially. Corporate compensation schemes may also shift toward straight wage payments and away from deferred and other more complicated forms of compensation, given the higher tax rate faced on funds accumulating within the corporation. Again, any welfare calculations that ignore changes in either corporate or personal tax liabilities could be badly biased. The cuts in personal relative to corporate tax rates in the early 1980s also encouraged a shift of income out of the corporate sector. The declining corporate profits rate noted by Auerbach and Poterba (1987) in the early 1980s is certainly consistent with this forecasted shift of taxable income out of the corporate sector.

Another expected effect of TRA was a drop in the amount of capital invested in owner-occupied housing, and in real estate more generally. To begin with, the cut in personal tax rates lowered the value of the tax-exempt status of the return on owner-occupied housing. In addition, slower depreciation schedules, the end of tax incentives encouraging resale of assets in order to redepreciate them, and limits on the deductibility of passive losses all made rental property less attractive. Yet, according to the SCF data, there was no noticeable decline in the amount of wealth invested in real estate. This should not really be surprising, in spite of the substantial slowdown in new construction, given the long life of real property. One consequence of the slow adjustment of the stock of real property to changes in tax incentives, however, should be sizeable windfall losses to the owners of this property at the time when expectations changed regarding future tax law. In principle, windfall gains and losses should be important for a variety of other assets whose supply can adjust only slowly in response to tax-law changes. For example, Auerbach and Kotlikoff (1983) note that existing corporate capital should experience an important windfall gain when the investment tax credit is eliminated and the corporate tax rate is cut. These various windfalls could well have played an important role in the overall distributional effects of TRA, yet could not easily be measured using SCF data sources.

Many other price changes that occurred in response to TRA may have had important distributional effects. For example, to the extent that (in spite of the slow adjustment) the supply of rental real estate dropped in response to TRA, rents should have increased, imposing added costs on tenants. As another example, the increase in the municipal bond rate imposes added borrowing costs on municipal residents, in addition to providing a higher rate of return to lenders. Again, these are effects that cannot be captured using SCF data sources.

Therefore, although the SCF evidence does help in clarifying some of the distributional implications of the changes in capital income taxes effected by TRA, there is much that such a survey cannot reveal. The inconsistencies between the SCF and the Flow of Funds data also raise questions about the interpretation of some results. In spite of this, Scholz's paper has shown that further work using the SCF data should help shed light on at least some of the behavioral responses to the Tax Reform Act of 1986.

REFERENCES

Auerbach, Alan J., and Laurence J. Kotlikoff (1983), "Investment Versus Savings Incentives: the Size of the Bang for the Buck and the Potential for Self-Financing Business Tax Cuts," in L. H. Meyer (ed.), *The Economic Consequences of Government Deficits.* Boston: Kluwer-Nijhoff, pp. 121–54.
Auerbach, Alan J., and James M. Poterba (1987), "Why Have Corporate Tax Revenues Declined?" *Tax Policy and the Economy* 1: 1–28.
Easterbrook, Frank H. (1984), "Two Agency–Cost Explanations of Dividends," *American Economic Review* 74: 650–9.
Gordon, Roger H., and Jeffrey K. MacKie-Mason (1990), "Effects of the Tax Reform Act of 1986 on Corporate Financial Policy and Organizational Form," in J. Slemrod (ed.), *Do Taxes Matter? The Impact of the Tax Reform Act of 1986.* Cambridge, MA: MIT Press.

Gordon, Roger H., and Burton G. Malkiel (1981), "Corporate Finance," in Henry
  J. Aaron and Joseph A. Pechman (eds.), *How Taxes Affect Economic Be-
  havior.* Washington, DC: Brookings.
Poterba, James, and Larry Summers (1985), "The Economic Effects of Dividend
  Taxation," in E. I. Altman and M. G. Subrahmanyam (eds.), *Recent Ad-
  vances in Corporate Finance.* Homewood, IL: Irwin.
Scholes, Myron S., and Mark A. Wolfson (1988), "The Effects of Changes in Tax
  Laws on Corporate Reorganization Activity," Mimeo, Graduate School of
  Business, Stanford University.

General discussion

Metcalf noted that as TRA eliminated most tax shelters, it increased demand for state and local securities. He also argued that the prevalence of
holding stocks through a pension implies more diversification than counting the number of different stocks held.

McIntyre noted that auto leasing increased in the years after tax reform as well.

Gravelle commented that there is ambiguity about how TRA affected
the taxation of real assets. It certainly affected whether firms operate as
corporations or not. Gravelle claimed that it is not true that TRA made
debt more attractive.

Steuerle argued that since portfolio responses can take place over a
long period of time, it can be quite difficult to pinpoint what behavior has
changed in response to recent tax-policy changes.

MacKie-Mason noted that taxable income and marginal tax rates are
endogenous to tax-motivated financial manipulations. For example, people in the 0-percent tax-rate bracket own a large share of noncorporate
assets.

Shackelford remarked that because a majority of large firms are now
on the alternative minimum tax or in a loss position, the average marginal corporate tax rate might in fact still be lower than the marginal personal tax rate.

Poterba suggested that it would be an interesting exercise to apply the
portfolio elasticities estimated in Feldstein's 1976 *Econometrica* paper to
Scholz's data, and compare the predicted results to actual behavior. He
also noted that publicly traded partnerships in 1991 are only 10% of what
they were before 1986.

CHAPTER 8

Progressivity of capital gains taxation with optimal portfolio selection

Michael Haliassos & Andrew B. Lyon

1   Introduction

The debate over capital gains taxes has served as a focal point for the larger debate over the desired progressivity of the tax system. Some argue that a reduction in the capital gains tax rate predominantly benefits upper-income taxpayers. Others argue that taxpayers in all income groups receive capital gains, and that once-in-a-lifetime gains artificially distort the concentration of gains by income class. In addition to the concern over progressivity, there are debates on the efficiency consequences of capital gains taxes: the degree to which they hinder or promote saving and investment and their effects on portfolio behavior.

In this paper we present new data from the Internal Revenue Service on capital gains realizations between 1985 and 1989 as well as data from the Federal Reserve Board Survey of Consumer Finances (SCF) on stockholding. These data show a high concentration of stockholding and capital gains realizations in the highest income groups.

Next, we draw upon these data to examine distributional effects and portfolio responses to changes in the tax treatment of capital gains. A simple analysis of tax burden focusing only on tax payments is not an accurate indication of the burden of a tax. Taxes generally create costs beyond the dollar value collected by causing persons to change their behavior to avoid the tax. Economists have long noted the "lock-in" effect as one of these additional costs. Taxes also reduce the variance in after-tax returns; for risk-averse investors, this reduction is a benefit.

We wish to thank Carol Bertaut for data from the Survey of Consumer Finances and helpful discussions, and Bill Gale, Jim Poterba, Joel Slemrod, Eric Toder, and conference participants for helpful suggestions. We owe special thanks to John O'Hare of the Joint Committee on Taxation for providing us with tabulated data from the Sales of Capital Assets studies.

275

We examine capital gains taxes using a model based solely on utility-maximizing behavior. Econometric estimates of realization behavior in response to changes in tax rates are frequently criticized for relying on artificial or ad hoc specifications of the realization response. Kiefer (1990) presents a simulation model that demonstrates how the realization response can be modeled endogenously. This model, however, is atemporal: risk-neutral agents maximize the expected value of terminal wealth. Intertemporal models of risk-averse agents are modeled by Slemrod (1983), Cook and O'Hare (1992), and Galper, Lucke, and Toder (1988). This latter model is modified to estimate changes in portfolios and trading behavior by Hendershott, Toder, and Won (1991, 1992). This model has a considerable amount of disaggregation, including 147 separate households, five financial assets, owner-occupied housing, and consumer durables. A corporate sector is modeled; its financial behavior with respect to debt/equity ratios and dividends versus retained earnings is endogenous. One cost of working with a model of this size is that portfolio selection and capital gains–realization decisions must be simplified.[1]

We have opted instead to use a smaller, stylized model, but allow asset demands and realizations to be derived as solutions to the households' maximization of intertemporal utility of consumption. For this purpose, we incorporate alternative systems of capital gains taxation into a consumption-based model of portfolio selection. We consider a three-period model with two financial assets: a risk-free bond and a risky stock. Our model is in the spirit of Auerbach's (1992) analysis based on a similar model. We differ from his analysis by explicitly allowing for a dividend component to stock returns, which analyses of historical data have found to be sizeable. We also differ by providing a capital gains asset which is risky in both periods that it may be held, rather than only in the second. This seemingly slight difference is important, because the possibility of a capital loss affects initial asset holdings and realizations. A shortcoming of our model is that the constant *relative* risk-aversion parameter, though popular for analysis of portfolio behavior, does not distinguish between risk aversion and elasticity of intertemporal substitution.[2] We hope in

[1] For example, exponential utility functions are used because they allow derivation of explicit solutions. This utility function, however, displays constant *absolute* risk aversion (i.e., no change in the amount of risky asset holdings for different wealth levels). In addition, changes in taxation induce realizations in an ad hoc way, and the dependence of realizations on other factors such as income and risk aversion is ignored.

[2] The same parameter in this utility function affects the willingness both to substitute consumption across states of the world (within a single time period) and to substitute consumption over time periods. Hall (1987) has noted the difficulty in separating these parameters in common utility functions. Epstein and Zin (1991) investigate a class of utility functions for which the effects of these parameters on behavior are better separated.

future research to incorporate other forms of the utility function where this feature is not present.

We find that reforms whose reductions in the capital gains tax rate are offset by increases in the tax rate on other investment income are efficiency-*reducing*. Surprisingly, we find that for taxpayers for whom loss limits are not binding, a move to accrual taxation is *also* efficiency-reducing. These results are partly attributable to a reduction in risk-sharing effected by these reforms. We find that for those taxpayers for whom loss limits are potentially binding, large efficiency gains can be achieved by increasing the amount of capital losses that may be deducted against ordinary income.

In the next section we present data on capital gains realizations from tax-return data. In Section 3 we outline our model, and in Section 4 present calculations of portfolio holdings and realizations under the benchmark tax system. Section 5 examines the effects of alternative capital gains tax cuts, and Section 6 examines accrual taxation. The final section presents our conclusions.

2 Distribution of capital gains income

This section presents data on the distribution of capital gains income using the Sales of Capital Assets panel data set for 1985–89. Presently, the panel contains tax information on 11,452 taxpayers for each of the years between 1985 and 1989 (57,260 tax returns).[3] These data are stratified to oversample high-income taxpayers based on their income in 1985. Taxpayers in the highest income decile represent approximately 70% of the sample.

Two recent studies have examined capital gains realizations using a panel of tax-return information in the public domain. Feenberg and Summers (1990) use a nonstratified panel of returns covering the period 1979–84. Slemrod (1992) uses a more recent version of the nonstratified panel that includes 1985 and 1986. These studies find that capital gains realizations in any given year are highly concentrated among taxpayers in the highest income groups. Capital gains tend to be much more heavily concentrated among these high-income taxpayers than are other forms of income.

The studies of Feenberg and Summers (1990) and Slemrod (1992) also examine one standard criticism of studies based on cross-sectional analyses

---

[3] The data set is not available in a public-use format. Data presented in this section are based on computations by John O'Hare and Cathy Koch of the Joint Committee on Taxation. The authors greatly appreciate the cooperation of these individuals and the Joint Committee on Taxation in performing these calculations.

of capital gains: If capital gains are realized only infrequently, a taxpayer of moderate income who has a large one-time realization of capital gains will be classified as "rich" in a study focusing on only a single year's income and realizations. With a single year's data, one could address this problem only by classifying taxpayers by an income concept that excludes capital gains. This approach, however, would understate the concentration of gains among taxpayers who have large recurring realizations.

The availability of panel data allows these studies to follow a taxpayer for a number of years to compare cumulative realizations to the taxpayer's average income over this extended period. Slemrod (1992), using the seven-year panel ending in 1985,[4] finds that a one-year study does overstate the concentration of capital gains income accruing to high-income taxpayers. However, even using cumulative capital gains over the seven-year period for each taxpayer and classifying each taxpayer by average income over this seven-year period, Slemrod finds that capital gains still are heavily concentrated among the highest income groups. The highest income percentile received 52% of all capital gains using the single-year approach, while using income measured over the seven-year period this percentile accounted for 44% of all capital gains earned. In contrast, the highest income percentile accounts for 8% of income from all sources using either the single-year or seven-year measure.

The findings that we report in this section are based on the most recent data available. Our ability to use a stratified random sample of returns reduces sample variance, since previous studies have shown capital gains to be concentrated among high-income taxpayers. Our analysis generally confirms earlier findings of Feenberg and Summers (1990) and Slemrod (1992). In fact, we find an even slightly greater concentration of gains among the highest income decile than in earlier studies. This may be due to our use of a stratified sample of returns or may reflect a change in concentration over time.

We first examine the extent to which gains realizations tend to be a recurring event for taxpayers during the 1985–89 period. Sales of stock, other securities, and partnerships constitute about one-half of capital gains. Except for the market crash of October 1987, this period was generally one of rising stock prices. By the close of 1989, the Standard & Poor's 500 composite index had increased by more than 100% relative to 1984 and by over 200% since June 1982.[5]

---

[4] Slemrod omits 1986 from his study to avoid possible anomalous results due to the large quantity of capital gains realized in advance of the new provisions contained in the 1986 Tax Reform Act.

[5] An important legislative event in this period was the enactment in September of the Tax Reform Act of 1986. This Act eliminated the 60% long-term capital gains exclusion effective January 1, 1987, and may have given some taxpayers an incentive to accelerate the

Table 1. *Frequency of net capital gains realizations, 1985–89*

Number of years in which taxpayer reported net gains (1)	Percent of all taxpayers by frequency of net gains (2)	Percent of taxpayers reporting gains by frequency of net gains (3)	Percent of reported net gains (4)
No years	77.59	—	—
One year	9.11	40.65	7.78
Two years	4.84	21.60	14.60
Three years	3.10	13.83	11.15
Four years	2.89	12.90	24.41
Five years	2.48	11.07	42.06
All taxpayers	100.00	100.00	100.00

Note: Frequency tabulated for taxpayers reporting only net capital gains (sum of net gains reported on schedule D and other distributions reported on form 1040).
Source: Sales of Capital Assets Panel, 1985–89.

Table 1 presents data on the frequency with which net gains were realized by taxpayers between 1985 and 1989. Capital gains for this purpose include net capital gains reported on schedule D, the excluded portion of long-term gains (for 1985 and 1986), and other distributions listed directly on form 1040.[6] Over three-fourths of all taxpayers had no realized net gains over this period. Of those who reported a gain in at least one year, nearly 60% also reported a net gain in at least one other year. Thus, to some extent gains realizations appear to be a recurring event. Only 2.5% of taxpayers reported positive net gains in each of the five years, yet these taxpayers accounted for 42% of all net gains. For these taxpayers, capital gains realizations are not only a frequent but also a quantitatively important recurring source of income.

Table 2 examines the distribution of capital gains income across income groups. Capital gains are defined here to include both net gains and net losses.[7] Income is defined to equal adjusted gross income (AGI) plus

realization of gains in 1986. Because realizations in 1986 may be unusual, all findings reported in the text were also examined for the four-year period excluding 1986. The exclusion of this year does not affect the annual rate of realizations across taxpayers; nor does it alter the general distribution of gains.

[6] Taxpayers who receive capital gain distributions from mutual funds and who engage in no other transactions may report these gains directly on form 1040.

[7] Reported net capital losses in any year are limited to $3,000. Excess losses may be carried forward and reported in subsequent years by the taxpayer. Certain losses on the stock of

Table 2. *Distribution of capital gains income and total income: snapshot versus time exposure, 1985–89*

Income percentile (1)	Single-year average capital gains (2)	Five-year capital gains (3)	Single-year average income (4)	Five-year income (5)
0–10	3.25	3.70	0.17	0.78
10–20	0.10	0.34	2.66	2.86
20–30	0.35	0.98	3.78	4.01
30–40	0.62	0.52	4.97	5.12
40–50	0.76	1.07	6.28	6.43
50–60	1.08	2.17	7.99	8.04
60–70	0.81	1.34	9.94	9.93
70–80	2.27	1.83	12.28	12.30
80–90	3.21	5.59	15.69	15.43
90–95	5.49	6.48	10.14	10.04
95–99	15.76	17.87	12.72	12.45
99–100	66.30	58.12	13.38	12.61

Note: Income consists of AGI plus excluded gains and excluded dividends (1985–86), and statutory adjustments. Capital gains are those reported on schedule D and other distributions reported on form 1040.
Source: Sales of Capital Assets Panel, 1985–89.

(i) excluded gains and dividends (for 1985 and 1986) and (ii) statutory adjustments.[8] The panel data are used to examine the discrepancy between annual measures of the distribution of capital gains income and those based on longer periods of observation. In column 2, the data in the panel are treated as if they represented five different single-year observations. In column 3, the data are properly treated as a panel and the five-year distribution of capital gains income is examined relative to five-year income of the taxpayer. Columns 4 and 5 of Table 2 show the distribution of the income measure across income percentiles using the single-year average and the five-year measure, respectively.

qualifying small businesses that would otherwise be classified as capital losses are allowed as ordinary losses up to $100,000. These losses are reported as other income and not on schedule D.

[8] These adjustments consist mainly of IRA and Keogh contributions and alimony paid. For 1985 and 1986, they additionally include moving expenses, employee business expenses, and the two-earner deduction.

Examining the highest income percentile, one can observe how the single-year measure of the distribution of capital gains income overstates the concentration of gains in this group. Column 2 shows that, on average, a single-year study over this period would have estimated that the highest income percentile received 66% of all capital gains reported in a given year. When the same taxpayer is followed for each of the five years, column 3 shows that taxpayers in the highest five-year income percentile received 58% of all gains reported over the five-year period. Column 5 shows that this highest income percentile received 13% of income from all sources over the five-year period.[9]

Although we would prefer to use a longer time period to approximate permanent income, the high concentration of gains in this income percentile and the other groups comprising the top decile (accounting for 82.5% of all gains over the five-year period) leads one to conclude, as Slemrod (1992) does, that capital gains income is "largely a phenomenon of the upper-income classes."[10]

Table 3 presents an alternative examination of the distribution of capital gains income across income groups. In this table, income is defined to exclude all capital gains or losses. Thus, the realization of a large capital gain will not cause a taxpayer to be classified in a higher income group. Although this understates the true income of taxpayers with recurring gains, it may be a closer measure of the permanent income of taxpayers with infrequent gains than the measure used in Table 2. Because we exclude capital gains from this income measure, we also increase income by the amount of losses claimed by the taxpayer on business or partnership activities. Losses claimed from these activities may be associated with gains received in other years. For example, an active particpant in real estate may claim operating losses on some properties while simultaneously receiving capital gains on other properties (or on the same property in a future year). Eliminating these losses gives a better understanding of gains realizations among taxpayers with low permanent income as opposed to large business losses.

[9] Excluding 1986 data from the panel, the highest income percentile accounts for 55.5% of all capital gains.

[10] One notable exception to the general tendency for gains to be concentrated among higher-income groups is the concentration of gains in the lowest decile (less than $8,000 of income in 1989). This group of taxpayers receives 3.7% of five-year capital gains while accounting for less than 1% of total income. In what follows we note that the concentration of gains in this income group is substantially eliminated when individuals with other tax losses are removed from the group. Even without this adjustment, most taxpayers in this decile are unaffected by the tax treatment of capital gains, since either they have negative income or the standard deduction and personal exemption eliminate all of their tax liability.

Table 3. *Distribution of capital gains income and total positive income: snapshot versus time exposure, 1985–89*

Positive income percentile (1)	Single-year capital gains (2)	Five-year capital gains (3)	Single-year average positive income (4)	Five-year positive income (5)
0–10	0.84	1.05	1.23	1.65
10–20	0.97	0.65	2.79	3.00
20–30	2.26	0.31	3.86	4.11
30–40	1.23	2.20	5.11	5.27
40–50	2.96	2.26	6.48	6.61
50–60	2.16	1.76	8.24	8.20
60–70	4.00	5.09	10.22	10.23
70–80	6.52	5.49	12.58	12.53
80–90	5.86	5.57	15.94	15.58
90–95	6.62	6.32	10.29	10.05
95–99	20.37	20.16	12.43	12.31
99–100	46.21	49.15	10.81	10.46

Note: Positive income consists of AGI plus excluded dividends (1985–86) and statutory adjustments, less: (i) net capital gain or loss; (ii) schedule C losses; (iii) schedule E losses; (iv) schedule F losses; (v) form 4797 business property losses; and (vi) negative other income. Capital gains are those reported on schedule D and other distributions reported on form 1040.
Source: Sales of Capital Assets Panel, 1985–89.

Using this measure of income, column 3 of Table 3 shows that the highest income percentile receives 49% of five-year capital gains and the highest decile cumulatively receives 75.6% of gains, down from 82.5% in Table 2.[11] Income groups between the 60th and 80th percentiles show a modestly higher amount of capital gains. Removal of losses from the definition of income substantially reduces the amount of gains reported among those in the lowest income decile.

Finally, in Table 4 we present data on the realization of capital gains by age group. The Internal Revenue Service matched taxpayer social security numbers for returns included in this panel with social security records to determine the age of the taxpayer as of January 1 in the year covered by

[11] Excluding 1986 data from the panel, the highest income percentile continues to receive 49% of all gains, and the highest decile receives 72.4% of gains.

Table 4. *Age distribution of capital gains, 1985–89*

Age in 1985 (1)	Percent of all returns (with or without gains) (2)	Percent of all taxpayers with gain or loss (3)	Percent of taxpayers with gain or loss in 4 or more years (4)	Percent of 5-year net gain or loss (5)	Percent of age group with gain or loss in at least 1 year (6)
Less than 30	31.83	15.99	10.95	4.01	12.82
30–49	38.55	40.56	31.61	29.35	26.84
50–54	6.60	7.78	7.96	14.45	30.10
55–59	6.36	8.93	14.74	12.81	35.86
60–64	5.14	8.91	8.52	12.87	44.23
65–69	3.92	7.14	11.68	10.62	46.45
70 and older	7.60	10.68	14.53	15.91	35.84
All taxpayers	100.00	100.00	100.00	100.00	25.52

Source: Sales of Capital Assets Panel, 1985–89.

the return.[12] The data show that most capital gains are received by tax-payers who are under age 60, but that taxpayers over age 60 account for a sizeable proportion of gains. Taxpayers age 60 and older in 1985 accounted for only 16.7% of all tax returns (column 2) but 26.7% of all taxpayers claiming gains or losses (column 3) in the five-year period. These older age groups also accounted for 39.4% of all gains claimed over the five-year period (column 5). Despite the heavier concentration of gains among older taxpayers, less than half of the taxpayers in these older age groups realized capital gains in at least one of the five years examined.

Taken together, Tables 2 and 3 show that while all income groups receive some capital gains, the largest part of gains is received by those in the highest income decile of the population. We also find that – although it is not true that most capital gains are received by the elderly, or that most elderly receive capital gains – some elderly account for a sizeable portion of gains relative to their numbers in the taxpaying population. Although this section has focused primarily on the distribution of capital gains across income groups, the finding that only one-fourth of all

[12] Public-use data sets provide only data reported on the return, and therefore do not include this variable.

taxpayers received any capital gains suggests that examination of the heterogeneity of taxpayers within income groups would be an interesting area for future research.

3   The model

The results examined in the previous section indicate that high-income taxpayers realize most capital gains. As a result, most capital gains taxes are paid by high-income taxpayers. The distributional effects of capital gains taxes are incompletely described, however, by focusing only on tax payments. In examining the burden of a tax, one would like to examine both the burden borne directly through the payment of a tax and the burden borne indirectly by altering one's behavior to avoid the tax. These indirect costs are frequently ignored in distributional analyses, but they are potentially significant in magnitude. As an extreme example, consider the effects of two alternative taxes on the purchase of a good: a small tax and a tax so large that none of the good is purchased. The large tax in this case collects no revenue. Of course, no one would claim that the large tax is less burdensome than the small tax. A distributional comparison of tax payments under the two alternative taxes would be uninformative. Because the indirect costs of a tax system are as fundamental to any system of taxation as the direct tax payments, we believe that distributional analyses should incorporate these costs.

By modeling the decision to save and allocate savings among various assets, we can begin to measure these indirect costs of taxation. In this section we describe our model, which is used to examine both the direct and indirect costs of capital gains taxation. We compute the total burden of the capital gains tax by finding the lump-sum tax that would give an individual the same level of utility as the existing capital gains tax. If the capital gains tax creates indirect net costs to the individual, the hypothetical lump-sum tax will collect more revenues than the existing tax. In this case, tax payments understate the burden of the capital gains tax. If the capital gains tax creates indirect net benefits – for example, by reducing the riskiness of an asset – then the lump-sum tax will collect smaller revenues than the existing capital gains tax.

An advantage of modeling capital gains behavior in a utility-maximizing framework is that we can also examine the distributional effects of alternative tax schemes, after taxpayers have modified their behavior in response to the new system of taxation. This allows us to examine, for example, the claim that a lower rate of tax can result in more tax revenues *and* make individuals better off. Such a claim is dependent on the alternative scheme imposing smaller indirect costs than the current tax system.

Our model economy consists of four types of agents: two groups of expected utility maximizers, the firm that employs them and issues stock, and the government that issues fiat money and riskless bonds. Households live for three periods (each period representing 20 years), and may choose between four different assets: currency, government bonds, private loans, and stock. Currency bears zero nominal interest; it is dominated in return by other riskless assets and is therefore optimally held in an amount just sufficient to cover purchases of the consumption good. Since we do not intend to study the monetary transmission mechanism, money is assumed in our "cash-in-advance" economy to be neutral; its only function is to define the nominal price level. We consider a simple version, where the inflation rate is taken to be known with certainty and to occur at an annualized rate of 3%.

Government bonds and private loans are perfect substitutes in agents' portfolios. Perfect substitutability implies a common riskless interest rate. We thus abstract from liquidity constraints in the form of a wedge between the borrowing rates available to the government and to households. This simplifies the portfolio selection problem by allowing us to consider one "riskless asset" and a real riskless rate set at a historically based level. We assume an annual real riskless rate of 3.13%, equal to Siegel's (1992) estimate of the average real rate on bonds in the United States over the period 1800–1990. Our simplifying assumption – that changes in tax rates do not affect the pre-tax real rate – is tantamount to considering a small open economy with a real rate tied to the world interest rate through capital mobility. In view of the absence of inflation uncertainty, constancy of the real rate on bonds does not require the assumption that debt is indexed.

The historical average of annual pre-tax real rates of return on stocks over the period 1800–1990 was calculated by Siegel (1992) as 7.77% per annum. Our procedure for calculating appropriate 20-year stock returns for use in our numerical solutions is as follows. First, we compute equiprobable "high" and "low" annual stock returns that match both the average annual return computed by Siegel and its standard deviation (18.36%). Because each annual outcome can occur with probability 0.5, we compute the expected value and standard deviation of the return over a 20-year period from this binomial process. Finally, we choose a "high" and a "low" 20-year return that match these two moments. The 20-year cumulative return is thus set to roughly 7.39 in the good state and −0.46 in the bad state.

The return on stocks consists of capital gains and dividends. We model each of these components separately, given their potentially different tax rates and the ability of the taxpayer to defer capital gains taxes but not dividend taxes. Schwert (1990) has found that dividend yields (i.e., the ratios of end-of-period dividend to beginning-of-period stock price) represent about half the total average stock return in his 1802–1987 sample. Their standard deviation is about one-twentieth as large as that of capital gains returns, and there is no evidence of a secular increase in dividend yields since 1800. We have chosen dividend yields for the "high" and "low" states so that their expected value is half the total expected pre-tax return on equity. Although it would be natural to assume zero variance of dividend yields, this causes a technical problem: in a two-state world, the total return in the low state is so low relative to the average dividend yield that it would require impossibly large capital losses, implying negative stock prices in the low second-period state. To avoid this, we allowed for essentially minimum variability in dividend yields consistent with positive stock price in the low state. The resulting coefficient of variation over each 20-year period was 0.84.

Households choose portfolios of these assets to maximize expected lifetime utility of consumption, which is assumed to be time separable.[13] Utility in each period exhibits constant relative risk aversion, with degree of relative risk aversion denoted by A.[14] The range of A values considered by Mehra and Prescott (1985) as plausible for representative-agent models was between 2 and 10, and this is the range we consider. In general, how "plausible" a particular risk parameter is depends on the size (coefficient of variation) of the gamble considered (Kandel and Stambaugh 1991). Evidence from the SCF suggests strongly that the proportion of highly risk-averse individuals is much larger among low-income households than among high-income groups, based on their responses to direct questions about attitudes toward risk.[15] Column 2 of Table 5 shows that the percentage of households who responded that they are not willing to undertake any financial risk is virtually a monotonically declining function of income: it ranges from 67% for very low incomes to 6% of households

[13] The Appendix provides more detail on the model.
[14] Utility in a given state of nature may be written as: $U(c) = (c^{(1-A)} - 1)/(1-A)$, $A > 0$, where c represents consumption in that state. Utility in each period is time separable. We set the discount factor to 0.818 for each 20-year period.
[15] Indeed, Shaw (1989) suggests that high risk aversion discourages individuals from investing in risky firm-specific human capital and reaching high income levels. It is interesting to note that limited stockholding among low-income households could also be observed if low- and high-income agents had the same degree of risk aversion but those with low incomes faced more income uncertainty. Kimball (1989) derives conditions under which increased background (income) risk reduces exposure to a risky asset in an atemporal model, even though it is uncorrelated with stock returns; he terms this property "standard risk aversion." This is a possibility we cannot explore in the present paper, since we do not incorporate nondiversifiable individual risk.

Table 5. *Risk preferences and portfolio holdings*

Income percentile (1)	Percent desiring no financial risk (2)	Percent holding riskless assets (3)	Percent holding stock (4)	Average riskless financial assets (1992 $) (5)	Average stock holdings (1992 $) (6)
0–10	67	37	6	1,284	664
10–20	70	48	3	2,607	247
20–30	59	52	7	4,959	760
30–40	54	68	14	10,068	1,587
40–50	44	72	13	8,031	2,127
50–60	47	77	15	12,218	2,895
60–70	42	84	19	12,041	1,094
70–80	34	84	26	14,335	6,346
80–90	34	92	30	19,493	6,504
90–95	21	94	44	25,612	20,675
95–99	17	93	55	48,770	68,169
99–100	6	96	78	147,467	801,276

Note: Riskless financial assets are defined to include savings accounts (other than checking), money market funds, CDs, and bonds. Stock ownership includes mutual funds. Holdings in pension funds and IRAs are not included. Income is the sum of all income reported by the respondent.
Source: 1983 Survey of Consumer Finances.

in the 99th percentile. Although we present a number of model predictions for the entire range of degrees of risk aversion, we will often contrast results for high-income households at low values of A to those for low-income households with A values at the high end of the spectrum.

After-tax labor income is taken to be exogenous in the model. In our simulations, high-income households are assumed to earn (net of tax) twice as much as low-income households in each period of their life. An element of life-cycle behavior is built into the model by assuming that after-tax labor income in the third period drops to one-fourth of what it was in the first two periods. This generates an incentive to save for the final period of life. In the third (and final) period of life, all assets are liquidated and consumed.[16]

[16] We assume that all asset sales occur while the individual is alive. Thus, we do not consider bequest motives and the possible advantages of deferring realizations until death to allow heirs a step-up of basis.

The model incorporates taxation at two rates, t_{ib} and t_{is}, for each group of households $i = 1, 2$. Rate t_{ib} is applied to interest earnings on loans to the government and to other households, as well as to dividends received on stocks.[17] The tax rate on capital gains is t_{is}, and it is applied at realization. The U.S. tax code imposes a limit of $3,000 on the net capital losses that can be declared for tax purposes; we incorporate a loss limit equal to 5% of the after-tax labor income received by high-income households.[18] This constraint turns out to be binding only for high-income households with degrees of risk aversion of 4 or less. The IRS Sales of Capital Assets panel data indicate that just 4.5% of taxpayers with gains or losses had $3,000 or more in net capital losses in 1985 and 1986. This portion increased to 12.9% in 1987, 11.9% in 1988, and 14.9% in 1989.[19] Of course, what matters from a utility-maximizing perspective is not whether the limits are binding for *all* states of nature but whether they are potentially binding for at least *one* state of nature.

In our simulations of the benchmark case, tax rates for high-income households are equal to 30% on both capital gains and interest income, while those for low-income households are set at 15%. We consider several policy experiments involving reductions in t_{is} (and endogenously determined increases in t_{ib}) that preserve the expected utility of the corresponding household group at the benchmark level. We also consider a switch to accrual taxation. Each of these policy changes is assumed to occur in the first period, before any savings and portfolio decisions have been made. The excess burden in the benchmark case is compared to that under the different policy experiments. All computations take into account optimal portfolio responses to the tax rates facing the household.

The policy experiments that we examine preserve either the expected utility of each class of agents or the expected present value of tax collections, on the basis of information available at the beginning of the first period. In effect, we are considering cases where decreases in investor risk resulting from higher tax rates are absorbed by the government. The government's ability to reduce risk has received considerable attention in other research dealing with risk sharing.[20]

---

[17] We do not consider a differential tax rate for long-term versus short-term gains. Constantinides (1984) suggests trading strategies involving realization of gains immediately upon their eligibility for long-term treatment. Lyon (1990) finds this strategy to be successful only for high-variance stocks and to offer only slight benefits over a deferral strategy.

[18] Because each period in the model represents 20 years, this percentage was chosen to approximate the effects of the $3,000 limit applied on an annual basis.

[19] Poterba (1987) finds that in 1982 11.2% of taxpayers with gains or losses had more than $3,000 in capital losses.

[20] Examples in the context of income taxation include Eaton and Rosen (1980), Gordon and Varian (1988), and Varian (1980).

A frequently adopted alternative assumption is to focus on policies that preserve the amount of real tax collections in each future time period and state of the world.[21] The motivation for considering such policies is that they leave the government budget constraint unaffected, though this presumption is not strictly accurate to the extent that policy changes influence interest rates on government debt.[22] We intend in future research to investigate the consequences of this and of a range of alternative assumptions about government finance.

The alternative assumption just described supposes that the government has access to lump-sum taxes or transfers that are imposed in an amount necessary to preserve tax revenues *after* returns on risky assets are realized in the future. What is particularly interesting for assessing effects of capital gains taxation on risk taking is that such policies are revenue neutral but not portfolio neutral. Households are faced both with risky asset returns and with risky lump-sum taxes and transfers. Because lump-sum taxes and transfers are by definition independent of the amount of risky investment undertaken by the household, the government imposes risk even on those who would not have chosen to bear any asset-return risk. Tax-rate changes result in re-allocation of private-sector risk between these two sources. The rational response to this risk re-allocation is to alter portfolios in order to hedge against unwanted risk. Conditions under which our conclusions would be modified by alternative modeling assumptions remain to be examined. The present paper shows that such modifications would not arise from the cut in capital gains tax rates per se, but from the assumption that the government maintains a given level of tax revenue risk by redistributing risk among households.

We make no attempt to predict the short-term effects of changes in tax regime. Unanticipated changes in tax rates during an investor's lifetime have contemporaneous lump-sum tax or subsidy effects that depend on accumulated capital gains or losses up to that point. It is then optimal for investors to respond to the new tax regime by rebalancing their portfolios in directions suggested by our analysis. The magnitude of these portfolio changes is sensitive to the amount of accrued gains at the time of the legislative change. In this paper, we focus on the permanent effects of such tax changes by comparing regimes in which there are no unanticipated changes in tax rates throughout the investment horizon of each household.

[21] For example, this assumption is used in Slemrod (1983) and in Galper et al. (1988).

[22] The assumption ensures that the primary budget deficit in each period and state of the world is the same across policy regimes. However, a change in interest rates resulting from the tax-policy experiment still affects the total budget deficit and the time path of government monetary and nonmonetary debt.

4   The benchmark tax system

Under the benchmark system, capital gains are taxed at the same rate as dividend and interest income, but not until realization. High-income households face a tax rate of 30%, which is twice that of their low-income counterparts. Because stocks offer higher expected returns than riskless assets and – starting from a portfolio with no stocks – have zero covariance with consumption, it is always optimal for expected utility maximizers to hold some stocks.[23] The extent of stockholding, however, does depend on both income and risk aversion.

In their first period of life, both high- and low-income households hold stocks and bonds in relative amounts that depend crucially on risk aversion. At low levels of the risk-aversion parameter A, it is optimal to engage in arbitrage by borrowing at the low (riskless) rate to invest in stocks. At slightly higher risk-aversion levels (around 3 in our simulations), it is optimal for both types of assets to be held in positive amounts, with optimal stockholding still dominating holdings of riskless assets. At $A \approx 5$, the covariance of stock returns with consumption becomes an important consideration, the equity premium notwithstanding; investors characterized by these or higher levels of risk aversion want to hold more riskless assets in their portfolios than stocks.

The levels of risk aversion separating each of these three regimes are slightly lower for the low-income group. This is a consequence of the asymptotic behavior of marginal utility as consumption approaches zero. Households with constant relative risk aversion are disproportionately interested in marginal utility at low states, and this concern limits their exposure to stockholding risk. As shown in columns 5 and 6 of Table 5, data from the SCF show that households in the 95th percentile of income or above hold on average more stocks in their portfolios than riskless assets; the opposite is true for all other income groups examined. Thus, low risk aversion among high-income households is corroborated not only by their responses to attitudinal questions (column 2), but also by their portfolio behavior.

In the second period of life, portfolio behavior is state dependent. In our simulations, the "good" state involves capital gains for stockholders

---

[23] Despite their idiosyncratic risk, stocks have zero covariance with a nonstockholder's consumption. As a result of this and of the equity premium, a household increases expected utility by at least marginally increasing stockholding above zero. This attitude of expected utility maximizers toward divisible risky projects was first noted by Arrow (1970), termed by Segal and Spivak (1990) "second-order risk aversion," and explored in the context of stockholding behavior by Haliassos and Bertaut (1992) and Bertaut (1992). As stockholding increases, the progressively larger covariance of stock returns with consumption serves to limit stockholding to a finite amount.

while the "bad" state involves capital losses. In the bad state, it is optimal for both groups to realize their losses (up to the allowable limit) in order to receive an immediate reduction in tax liability provided by the capital loss, and then to purchase anew all the stocks they want to hold until the third period.[24] In the good state, unconstrained expected utility maximizers find it optimal never to realize capital gains but to engage in short sales of stocks instead, in order to reduce their net stock holdings and smooth their consumption over time. Such a transaction results in the same net stock position as an outright sale, but defers tax liability. We limit the extent by which taxpayers may defer taxes through short sales by imposing quantity constraints on such sales. For the results presented in this paper, short sales are ruled out completely. As a result, households are encouraged to realize some capital gains in the second period of their life even in a "good" state. We regard this restriction as bringing the model closer to actual trading behavior.

The proportion of capital gains realized in the second period of life is fairly similar across income groups for any given risk aversion parameter, but is heavily dependent on that parameter. Households whose A is at the low end of the spectrum realize slightly more than 65% of their gains (Figure 1). The proportion increases at a decreasing rate, reaching 85% for $A = 10$. This, in conjunction with the SCF self-reported data on risk aversion, implies that the proportion of capital gains which is deferred on average by high-income households should substantially exceed the corresponding average proportion for low-income households.[25] In our solutions, the proportion of deferrals by high-income households with $A = 3$ is about 50% larger than for low-income households with $A = 10$. Combined with the much larger stockholding by high-income, less risk-averse households, this implies a very substantial difference in the size of unrealized capital gains across the two income groups.

In computing the burden of the benchmark system, we compare it to one of lump-sum taxation on (first-period) income. The *equivalent variation* is the lump-sum tax on first-period income that results in the same expected utility as the benchmark system of proportional taxation. Alternatively, it is the amount that households faced initially with no taxes would be willing to pay the government to prevent it from imposing proportional

[24] Technically, such a "wash sale" is disallowed under the U.S. tax law; only if more than 30 days elapse between buy and sell dates is the tax loss permitted. Because our model features 20-year trading periods, we do not believe that inclusion of this constraint would alter our results. Stiglitz (1983) discusses strategies for avoiding wash-sale and various other legal restrictions pertaining to capital gains taxes.

[25] The 1989 SCF includes questions allowing one to calculate directly unrealized gains by household and to test this implication of the model. Unfortunately, a property weighted data set is not yet publicly available.

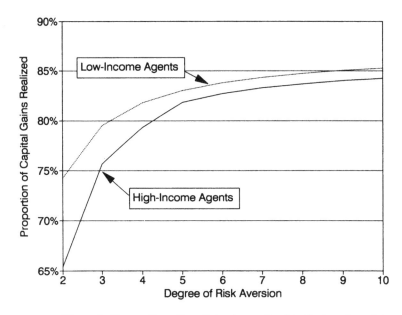

Figure 1. Proportion of capital gains realized in the benchmark tax system. The percentage of accrued capital gains that are realized in the second period of life is an increasing function of risk aversion.

taxation (and the associated loss limits). This measure may be the best yardstick to use in comparing the burden of alternative tax instruments. Naturally, the equivalent variation measure is positive, since taxation reduces households' feasible set of consumption opportunities. *Excess burden* is a comparison of the equivalent variation to the present value of tax revenues that are collected from the proportional tax system.[26] An interesting finding in the context of the expected utility model is that tax revenues far outweigh the amount households would be willing to pay to avoid proportional taxation, so that excess burden is negative. In other words, tax payments on capital gains, dividends, and interest collectively overstate the burden of these taxes relative to lump-sum taxation. Further, excess burden is more negative for those with low risk aversion, even when expressed as a fraction of tax revenues from that group.

The negative excess burden of the proportional tax system arises primarily from two related factors: (i) the desirable effects that capital gains

---

[26] The present value of government tax revenues is computed at the rate relevant for government borrowing, namely, the riskless rate on government bonds. In the absence of borrowing constraints for individuals, the excess burden is independent of the period in which the equivalent variation is computed.

taxation has on stockholding risk (even in the presence of loss limits); and (ii) the portfolio response of households to the introduction of proportional taxation. Although capital gains taxation lowers the expected return on stocks, it also reduces its variance by taxing realizations in the good state and subsidizing losses in the bad one.[27] As explained previously, we assume in this model that the government can absorb the risk associated with a risky flow of tax revenues. The finding that excess burden is most negative for households with a low risk-aversion parameter and high incomes arises primarily from the fact that both high incomes and low risk aversion are associated with more substantial stockholding.

In our model, we find capital gains taxation generally encourages stockholding, relative to lump-sum taxes that provide the same expected utility.[28] Households make full use of tax-loss opportunities in the bad state by holding more stocks to begin with and selling as many as the loss limit allows in order to reap the immediate reduction in tax liability. They then repurchase a (larger than otherwise) amount of stocks to hold to the third period. Recalling that households' concern with bad states is disproportionate, one can understand why the amount they are willing to pay to eliminate (or reduce) the distorting proportional taxation is less than the tax revenues collected from them.

The increased stockholding associated with proportional taxes yields substantial tax revenues to the government. Interestingly, the increase in taxes collected under proportional taxation does not arise simply from higher tax collections in the last period of life; even the amount of capital gains realizations in the second period is higher owing to the higher overall stockholding. Movement to the lump-sum tax system would cause tax liabilities to fall by 50% for high-income taxpayers ($A = 3$) and by 23% for low-income taxpayers ($A = 10$). These changes in tax liability are noted in the first row of Table 6. Of course, the true burden of the proportional tax system is identical to that of the lump-sum tax system, since equal utilities are attained. Again, this illustrates the shortcoming of focusing only on tax payments to assess the distributional effects of taxation. Because of the risk-sharing element of the tax system, a simple analysis of the burden of capital gains taxes based solely on the amount of taxes collected particularly overstates the utility cost of taxation for higher-income taxpayers.

[27] This utility-increasing feature of proportional taxation was first noted by Domar and Musgrave (1944). Atkinson and Stiglitz (1980) provide a more recent exposition in an atemporal model.

[28] The one exception is for high-income taxpayers with $A = 2$ (for whom the loss limit binds); replacement of proportional taxation with lump-sum taxation increases stockholding by 2.5% in the first period. Excess burden, however, is still negative for this group.

Table 6. *Summary of effects of policy experiments on tax liabilities*

	Percentage change in actual tax liability	
Policy change	High-income group $(A = 3)$	Low-income group $(A = 10)$
(1) Replace benchmark with lump sum tax	−49.7	−22.9
(2) Remove loss limits; increase capital gains tax rate	+28.9	0
(3) 20% reduction in capital gains tax rate; increase in t_{ib}	−5.6	−3.0
(4) Accrual taxation; remove loss limits	+15.7	−1.7

Note: Each policy change holds the utility of each group constant.

The importance of risk-sharing considerations can also be demonstrated by comparing our benchmark system to one without loss limits. High-income taxpayers subject to a 30% tax rate on capital gains and a loss limit can achieve the same utility with a *higher* capital gains tax rate if the loss limit is removed. At $A = 3$, high-income taxpayers would be indifferent between the benchmark system with a loss limit and a counterfactual situation in which the loss limit is eliminated and the capital gains tax rate increased to 40%. As shown in the second row of Table 6, tax revenues from these taxpayers would increase by over 25% at this higher rate. This indicates that there is a range of feasible tax rates for which both utility and revenue can be increased by eliminating loss limits (or increasing the amount of losses that may be deducted).[29] In a distributional analysis, of course, these higher tax payments by high-income investors would not be an indication of an increased tax burden.

In the next section we examine a policy experiment involving a reduction in capital gains tax rates, and in Section 6 we consider a switch to accrual taxation.

5   Effects of a reduction in capital gains tax rates

In this section, we examine the effects of a simultaneous reduction in capital gains tax rates and an increase in tax rates on dividend and interest

[29] In a model with multiple capital gains assets (especially negatively correlated ones), this result might not hold. If two negatively correlated assets existed then an investor could

income which preserves the expected utility each income group has under the benchmark system. These simulations also allow us to draw implications for the utility effects of alternative revenue-neutral tax schemes. We assume these tax changes take place at the beginning of the first period, before any portfolio decisions have been made. For the main body of our analysis, we consider a 20% reduction in capital gains tax rates (reducing the rate to 24% for high-income households and to 12% for low-income households). The increase in t_{ib} required to maintain the expected utility of income group i differs across income groups and depends on risk aversion. We carry out sensitivity analyses by considering the entire range of risk aversion parameters from $A = 2$ to $A = 10$.

For the high-income group, the utility-preserving tax rate t_{1b} ranges from 31.6% for low risk aversion ($A = 2$) to 30.2% for highly risk-averse households ($A = 10$), given a 20% cut in capital gains tax rates. This is to be compared to a rate t_{1b} of 30% assumed under the benchmark system without differential taxation. For low-income households, the utility-preserving t_{2b} is slightly above 15% – rising to just 15.5% for households with $A = 2$. For both groups, the utility-preserving t_{ib} is inversely related to risk aversion, primarily because holdings of the riskless asset are smaller (often negative) among the less risk-averse.

We find that this differential taxation entails an *increase* in excess burden relative to the benchmark, for both income levels, for the entire range of risk-aversion parameters, and for varying sizes of capital gains tax cuts. In Figure 2, we express this increase in excess burden as a proportion of the present value of tax revenues collected from each group in the new equilibrium. In the region where loss limits are not binding ($A > 4$), this measure is uniformly higher for high-income households than for low-income households; it is inversely related to the degree of risk aversion for any given income level. For the cases we focus on – namely, high-income households with $A = 3$ and low-income households with $A = 10$ – the changes in excess burden relative to tax revenues are 6.0% and 3.1%, respectively. Tax revenues fall for these groups by 5.6% and 3.0%, as shown in the third row of Table 6.

Because the cut in capital gains tax rates induces some undesirable effects on the risk properties of capital gains assets, the tax rate on alternative sources of income, t_{ib}, cannot increase substantially if it is to preserve the same expected utility of each group. Although holdings of riskless assets by the least risk-averse are also increased, the increase in t_{ib} is insufficient to make up for the loss in capital gains tax revenues.

always sell the asset that declined in value and defer gain on the asset that appreciated. The portfolio could be partially rebalanced by increasing investment in the asset that was sold, rather than by selling shares of the appreciated asset.

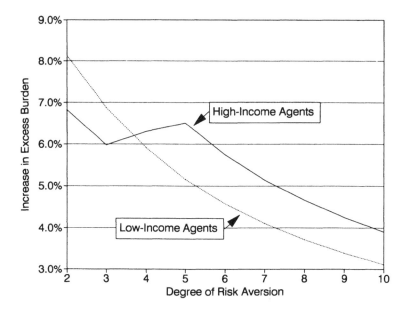

Figure 2. Increase in excess burden from capital gains tax cut as a percentage of tax revenues. A 20% capital gains tax cut increases excess burden (measured here as a fraction of initial tax revenues from a taxpayer) most for agents with low degrees of risk aversion.

To illustrate the importance of portfolio adjustments for our findings, consider how they affect total capital gains realizations. Total realizations depend on both the level of stockholding and the proportion of gains realized. We examine the effects of the capital gains rate reduction on both components. Among taxpayers for whom loss limits are not initially binding, a cut in capital gains taxes induces increased bondholding and discourages stockholding. In the region where the loss limit is binding, only for the least risk-averse ($A = 2$ and $A = 3$) does stockholding increase. Even here, the increase in stockholding is less than 0.5%.

As expected, at the lower capital gains tax rates the proportion of capital gains realized by each group in the "good" state of the second period of life increases. However, this increase is relatively small. In our benchmark simulation, low-income households (with $A = 10$) realize 85.3% of their capital gains in the second period. If capital gains tax rates are reduced by 20% of their benchmark level, this proportion increases, as expected, but by less than 0.5%. The proportion realized by high-income households is only slightly more sensitive. But even for these high-income taxpayers (with $A = 3$), 75.7% of capital gains are realized under the benchmark system in the second period, and this amount increases by only 2.7% when capital gains taxes are reduced.

As a result, for taxpayers for whom the loss limits are not binding, total realizations decline with the cut in capital gains taxes. For taxpayers for whom the loss limits *are* binding, total realizations increase but by a far smaller percentage than the tax-rate reduction. In either case, tax revenues fall substantially compared to the benchmark system.

In view of the evidence of an inverse relationship between income and risk aversion, our findings suggest that the increase in excess burden resulting from a utility-preserving shift to differential taxation will be larger for high-income households than for those with low incomes. Portfolio size turns out to matter significantly for the change in tax revenues and hence for excess burden. The implication is that if the government wants to cut capital gains taxes without affecting welfare, it will suffer a large reduction in tax revenues. If, on the other hand, it decides to raise t_{ib} sufficiently to preserve tax revenues, then expected utility drops and both income groups are worse off than under the current system.

Although the findings we discuss relate primarily to permanent effects of tax changes, our model is consistent with a short-run increase in capital gains realizations following a capital gains tax cut. To see this, consider households who have accumulated capital gains and are now at the beginning of the second period of life. Their optimal portfolios at the current capital gains tax rate would dictate realizing a fraction of capital gains in the second period. If it is announced that the applicable tax rate has been reduced, this is a welcome bonus to these households: First, they experience a lump-sum tax bonus on the accumulated gains they were already planning to realize; second, the lower tax rate induces a portfolio response that makes them better off from that point on. Because this portfolio response generally implies lower stockholding than at the higher tax rate, the tax cut will actually generate larger capital gains realizations in the second period than what households had planned for at the beginning of their lifetime.

This should reconcile our findings with the observation that households with accumulated capital gains tend to favor a reduction in gains tax rates, and with the common perception that such a reduction should encourage realizations in the short run. What appears questionable is the notion that a permanent move to lower capital gains tax rates will promote stockholding and gains realizations enough to provide larger tax revenues over the long run.

6   Accrual taxation of capital gains

Using our model, we now calculate the change in excess burden that results if capital gains were taxed on an accrual basis rather than at realization.

We assume that the accrual tax system has no limit on the amount of losses that may be claimed against ordinary income.[30] As in our previous experiments, the policy change holds utility constant. The resulting accrual tax rate thus differs conceptually from the traditional measure that holds the present value of tax payments constant, assuming unchanged realizations and portfolios. For taxpayers whose loss limits are not binding, we find that a move to accrual taxation increases excess burden. In contrast, if loss limits are binding constraints then we find that a move to accrual taxation, together with the elimination of loss limits, can reduce excess burden. This latter reform is dominated, however, by the one considered in Section 4: taxation at realization without loss limitations.

It may at first appear surprising that we find cases where the movement from realization taxation to accrual taxation generates excess burdens. Public-finance economists have long emphasized the excess burden created from the lock-in effect on capital gains. As our results presented earlier show, the lock-in effect exists in our model, too. It must be remembered, however, that the lock-in occurs only when stocks have appreciated in value. When stocks decline in value, shareholders can claim these losses immediately in the absence of loss limitations. In our model, these taxpayers then repurchase stock after claiming their losses.

For taxpayers not constrained by the loss limits, the accrual tax rate required to make them as well-off as under the benchmark system must be lower than the rate under realization taxation. Allowing for behavioral response to the accrual tax system, taxpayers become better-off from the elimination of the lock-in effect but worse-off by the increase in the variance of returns caused by the lower tax rate. In theory, either effect can dominate. In our simulations, we find that the accrual tax rate necessary to hold utility constant must be sufficiently low that tax revenues fall relative to the benchmark case.[31] Among taxpayers for whom the loss limits are binding, the switch to accrual taxation together with the removal of loss limits can generate greater risk-sharing in the bad state than under the benchmark case. These taxpayers benefit from the advantages of both greater risk-sharing and elimination of the lock-in effect.

The loss limitation in our model is binding only for high-income taxpayers with risk-aversion coefficients of 4 or less. For taxpayers with the

---

[30] If an accrual tax system were enacted then retention of loss limits would appear to be less justified, since a taxpayer could no longer claim losses on some assets while deferring gains on other assets.

[31] Our results differ from those of Auerbach (1992), who finds that the move to accrual taxation generates efficiency gains. Our results differ, in part, because stock returns in the first period of Auerbach's model are certain; therefore, the reduction in the accrual tax rate has no effect on variances in returns earned in this period.

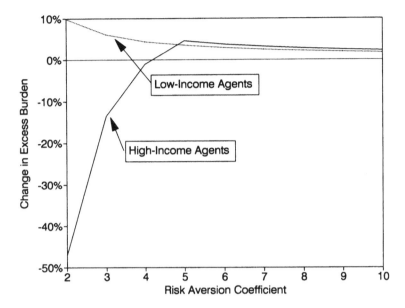

Figure 3. Change in excess burden from accrual taxation as a percentage of tax revenues. Accrual taxation results in higher excess burdens
than the benchmark tax system for taxpayers not constrained by the loss
limit. Lower excess burdens result for taxpayers previously constrained
by the loss limits.

lowest risk-aversion coefficients, desired stockholding is large and the inability to deduct all losses in the event the bad state occurs results in a
large utility loss. These taxpayers are willing to accept a very high accrual
tax rate in exchange for removal of the loss limitations. For the least risk-
averse ($A = 2$), an accrual tax rate of 50% leaves them the same utility as
in the benchmark case. At higher rates of risk aversion, stockholding is
smaller so that the inability to deduct losses is less costly. At $A = 4$, the
accrual tax rate falls to 27.4%. In each case, the accrual tax rate results
in higher tax revenues than in the benchmark, so that excess burden is
reduced. As shown in the fourth row of Table 6, tax payments for high-
income taxpayers (with $A = 3$) are 16% greater than in the benchmark.

Figure 3 shows the change in excess burden that results from the shift
to accrual taxation. The change in excess burden is expressed as a fraction of tax payments made by each group in the new equilibrium. At low
levels of risk aversion and high income, the welfare gain from switching
to accrual taxation appears quite large, approaching 50% of tax revenues
for the high-income group at $A = 2$. These gains appear to arise entirely

from the elimination of the loss limit. As noted above, the switch to accrual taxation is dominated by the elimination of loss limits and the retention of taxation at realization.

For taxpayers for whom the loss limit is not binding, the increase in excess burden declines with risk aversion. The change in excess burden ranges from 10% of revenues for low-income taxpayers at $A = 2$ to less than 2% of tax revenues for low-income taxpayers at $A = 10$.

7   Conclusions

In this paper we have examined new data on capital gains realizations by taxpayers in the 1985–89 period. These data show a high concentration of capital gains among taxpayers in the highest income groups. More than half of all capital gains are realized by the richest 1 percent of the population. As a result, reductions in capital gains tax rates would reduce tax payments the most for these taxpayers.

We present a stylized model of savings and portfolio behavior. We caution the reader that this model makes a number of simplifying assumptions; however, these simplifications allow us to explore in full detail the changes in behavior that occur in response to permanent changes in the taxation of capital gains. Our model suggests that reductions in capital gains tax rates will lead in many cases to a reduction in stockholding. This occurs partly because of the increase in risk that results as capital gains tax rates are lowered. For these taxpayers, even though the lock-in effect is reduced slightly, the increase in the proportion of gains realized is not sufficient to offset the decline in stockholding, so total realizations decline. Only for taxpayers currently constrained by loss limits do we find an increase in stockholding when capital gains tax rates are reduced. The resulting increase in realizations, however, is not sufficient to make up for the much larger reduction in tax rates, so total revenues decline. We find that a revenue-neutral reduction in capital gains tax rates, offset by increases in taxes on risk-free investment income, results in a decline in taxpayer utility. In future research we seek to examine the sensitivity of our results to alternative assumptions about the extent to which the government absorbs fluctuations in tax revenues.

We find that the elimination of loss limits offers a potential welfare gain. The removal of loss limits increases the risk-sharing characteristics of the tax system. With greater risk sharing, taxpayers in our model respond by holding greater amounts of stock. The removal of loss limits causes the government to collect less tax revenue (in expectation) on stocks that would have been held anyway, but additional tax revenue is collected by the increase in stockholding. Taxpayers would be better-off with the elimination of loss limits, and so would be willing to accept slightly higher tax rates on capital gains in return. As a result, net tax revenues can increase and still leave these taxpayers better-off.

This example of an efficiency-enhancing reform, and our other examples of efficiency-decreasing tax changes, illustrate the trouble with conducting traditional distributional analyses based on the tax payments collected from a household. Table 6, which summarizes the effects of the various policy changes, indicates substantial variation in tax liabilities for each income group. Yet in each experiment, the utility of each group is held unchanged. Traditional distributional analysis, which focuses only on tax revenues, would give quite different impressions of the distributional effects of these reforms. As models of taxpayer behavior improve, better distributional analyses of taxes should include measures of excess burden (whether positive or negative) when evaluating the true costs of a tax.

For the case of capital gains taxation considered in this paper, we find that the dollar amounts of capital gains taxes paid overstate the burden of these taxes relative to lump-sum taxation. Our results suggest that distributional analyses of the overall progressivity of the tax system based on tax payments probably overstate progressivity, because capital gains tax payments are concentrated in the highest income brackets. Our results further suggest that reductions in the tax liability of capital gains realizations are likely to benefit taxpayers less than equal-size reductions in other taxes.

Appendix: the formal model

We consider two classes of households, high- and low-income, each of which solves:

$$\max_{\substack{N_0, B_0, N_{1i} \\ Q_{1i}, B_{1i}}} E_0 \sum_{t=0}^{2} \beta^t U(C_t), \quad i = H, L, \tag{1}$$

where i indexes states of the world in period $t = 1$, defined by whether divided yields are high (H) or low (L). N denotes stock purchases, Q denotes stock sales, and B denotes purchases of one-period riskless bonds. The discount factor is β, $U(C_t)$ is utility of consumption at time t, and E_0 is the mathematical expectations operator. The budget constraint for the first period is

$$C_0 = Y_0 - N_0 \frac{P_{s0}}{P_0} - \frac{B_0}{P_0}, \tag{2}$$

where Y_t denotes real labor income, P_t is the price of the good, and P_{st} is the nominal stock price. In the second period, state-dependent consumption is

$$C_1 = C_{1i} = Y_1 + N_0 d_{i1}(1 - t_b) + Q_{1i} \frac{P_{s1i} - (P_{s1i} - P_{s0})t_s}{P_{1i}}$$

$$+ \frac{B_0(1 + I_1(1 - t_b))}{P_{1i}} - N_{1i} \frac{P_{s1i}}{P_{1i}} - \frac{B_{1i}}{P_{1i}}, \quad i = H, L, \qquad (3)$$

where real dividends are denoted by d_i, the tax rate on nominal capital gains by t_s, that on dividend and interest income by t_b, and the pre-tax nominal riskless rate by I. In each period, the high- and low-dividend states are equiprobable, but the size of realizations has been chosen to match the first two moments of the data. In the third period, consumption levels are

$$C_2 = C_{2ij}$$

$$= Y_2 + (N_0 - Q_{1i} + N_{1i})\left(\frac{P_{s2ij}}{P_{2ij}} + d_j(1 - t_b)\right) - (N_0 - Q_{1i})t_s \frac{P_{s2ij} - P_{s0}}{P_{2ij}}$$

$$- N_{1i} t_s \frac{P_{s2ij} - P_{s1i}}{P_{2ij}} + \frac{B_{1i}}{P_{2ij}}(1 + I_2(1 - t_b)), \quad (i, j) \in (H, L) \times (H, L).$$

$$(4)$$

The use of two state subscripts, i and j, allows us to keep track of the history of dividend realizations, which is relevant for consumption.

There are several inequality constraints. Consumption must be non-negative:

$$C_0 \geq 0, \; C_{1i} \geq 0, \; C_{2ij} \geq 0, \quad i = H, L, \; (i, j) \in (H, L) \times (H, L). \qquad (5)$$

The short-sales constraints on stocks are

$$N_0 \geq 0, \; N_{1i} \geq 0, \quad i = H, L. \qquad (6)$$

The first part of the following double inequality ensures that stock sales are nonnegative; the second, that households do not attempt to sell more stocks than they own:

$$0 \leq Q_{1i} \leq N_0, \quad i = H, L. \qquad (7)$$

The following two equations impose a limit θ on the amount of losses that may be claimed for tax purposes:

$$Q_{1L} \frac{P_{s0} - P_{s1L}}{P_{1L}} \leq \theta; \qquad (8)$$

$$(N_0 - Q_{1i}) \frac{P_{s0} - P_{s2jL}}{P_{2jL}} + N_{1i} \frac{P_{s1i} - P_{s2jL}}{P_{2jL}} \leq \theta \quad \text{for all } i, j. \qquad (9)$$

In our model, pre-tax real stock returns in each state are state- but not time-dependent, and are exogenously determined (asset supplies are infinitely elastic). Bonds are riskless and are assumed to offer constant real returns. Goods prices are exogenous in the model:

$$P_0 = \bar{P}_0, \quad P_{1i} = \bar{P}_{1i}, \quad P_{2ij} = \bar{P}_{2ij}, \quad i = H, L, \quad (i, j) \in (H, L) \times (H, L). \quad (10)$$

Finally, dividend yields are calibrated to match their historical expected value and variance:

$$k_i \equiv \frac{d_i}{P_{s0}/P_0} = \bar{k}_i, \quad i = H, L; \quad (11)$$

$$k_{ij} \equiv \frac{d_j}{P_{s1i}/P_{1i}} = \bar{k}_{ij}, \quad (i, j) \in (H, L) \times (H, L). \quad (12)$$

Stock prices at $t = 0$ are set equal to unity.

REFERENCES

Arrow, Kenneth (1970), *Essays in the Theory of Risk Bearing.* Chicago: Markham.
Atkinson, Anthony B., and Joseph E. Stiglitz (1980), *Lectures on Public Economics.* New York: McGraw-Hill.
Auerbach, Alan J. (1992), "On the Design and Reform of Capital Gains Taxation," *American Economic Review* 82: 263-7.
Bertaut, Carol (1992), "Who Holds Stocks in the U.S.? An Empirical Investigation," Mimeo, Board of Governors of the Federal Reserve System, Washington, DC.
Board of Governors of the Federal Reserve System, *1983 Survey of Consumer Finances.* Washington, DC.
Constantinides, George M. (1984), "Optimal Stock Trading with Personal Taxes: Implications for Prices and the Abnormal January Returns," *Journal of Financial Economics* 13: 65-89.
Cook, Eric W., and John F. O'Hare (1992), "Capital Gains Redux," *National Tax Journal* 45: 53-76.
Domar, Evsey D., and Richard A. Musgrave (1944), "Proportional Income Taxation and Risk Sharing," *Quarterly Journal of Economics* 58: 388-422.
Eaton, Jonathan, and Harvey S. Rosen (1980), "Labor Supply, Uncertainty, and Efficient Taxation," *Journal of Public Economics* 14: 365-74.
Epstein, Larry G., and Stanley E. Zin (1991), "Substitution, Risk Aversion, and the Temporal Behavior of Consumption and Asset Returns: an Empirical Analysis," *Journal of Political Economy* 99: 263-86.
Feenberg, Daniel, and Lawrence Summers (1990), "Who Benefits from Capital Gains Tax Reductions?" in Lawrence H. Summers (ed.), *Tax Policy and The Economy,* vol. 4. Cambridge, MA: MIT Press, pp. 1-24.
Galper, Harvey, Robert Lucke, and Eric Toder (1988), "A General Equilibrium Analysis of Tax Reform," in Henry Aaron, Harvey Galper, and Joseph Pechman (eds.), *Uneasy Compromise: Problems of a Hybrid Income-Consumption Tax.* Washington, DC: Brookings, pp. 59-108.

Gordon, Roger H., and Hal R. Varian (1988), "Intergenerational Risk Sharing," *Journal of Public Economics* 37: 185–202.

Haliassos, Michael, and Carol C. Bertaut (1992), "Why Do So Few Hold Stocks? The View from Asset Pricing Theory," Mimeo, Department of Economics, University of Maryland, College Park.

Hall, Robert E. (1987), "Consumption," Working Paper no. 2265, National Bureau of Economic Research, Cambridge, MA.

Hendershott, Patric, Eric Toder, and Yunhi Won (1991), "Effects of Capital Gains Taxes on Revenue and Economic Efficiency," *National Tax Journal* 44: 21–40.

(1992), "A Capital Gains Exclusion and Economic Efficiency," *Tax Notes* 54: 881–5.

Kandel, Shmuel, and Robert F. Stambaugh (1991), "Asset Returns and Intertemporal Preferences," *Journal of Monetary Economics* 27: 39–71.

Kiefer, Don (1990), "Lock-in Effect with a Simple Model of Corporate Stock Trading," *National Tax Journal* 43: 75–94.

Kimball, Miles (1989), "Standard Risk Aversion," Mimeo, Department of Economics, University of Michigan, Ann Arbor.

Lyon, Andrew B. (1990), "Capital Gains Tax Rate Differentials and Tax Trading Strategies," Mimeo, Department of Economics, University of Maryland, College Park.

Mehra, Rajnish, and Edward C. Prescott (1985), "The Equity Premium: A Puzzle," *Journal of Monetary Economics* 15: 145–61.

Poterba, James M. (1987), "How Burdensome Are Capital Gains Taxes?" *Journal of Public Economics* 33: 157–72.

Schwert, G. William (1990), "Indexes of U.S. Stock Prices from 1802–1987," *Journal of Business* 63: 399–426.

Segal, Uzi, and Avia Spivak (1990), "First Order versus Second Order Risk Aversion," *Journal of Economic Theory* 51: 111–25.

Shaw, Kathryn L. (1989), "An Empirical Analysis of Risk Aversion and Income Growth," Mimeo, Department of Economics, Carnegie Mellon University, Pittsburgh, PA.

Siegel, Jeremy J. (1992), "The Real Rate of Interest from 1800–1990: a Study of the U.S. and U.K.," *Journal of Monetary Economics* 29: 227–52.

Slemrod, Joel (1983), "A General Equilibrium Model of Taxation with Endogenous Financial Behavior," in Martin Feldstein (ed.), *Behavioral Simulation Methods in Tax Policy Analysis.* Chicago: University of Chicago Press, pp. 427–54.

(1992), "Taxation and Inequality: a Time Exposure Perspective," in James M. Poterba (ed.), *Tax Policy and The Economy,* vol. 6. Cambridge, MA: MIT Press, pp. 105–27.

Stiglitz, Joseph E. (1983), "Some Aspects of the Taxation of Capital Gains," *Journal of Public Economics* 21: 257–94.

Varian, Hal R. (1980), "Redistributive Taxation as Social Insurance," *Journal of Public Economics* 14: 49–68.

Comments

James M. Poterba

This paper has two parts. The first provides new empirical evidence on the pattern of capital gains realizations, both across households and over time for a given set of households. The second develops a simple multi-period model where households divide their portfolios between a risky asset and a safe security, and uses it to analyze the welfare consequences of various capital gains tax reforms. Both sections provide interesting new insights on capital gains taxation.

The first part of the paper presents new results from a very recent data set, the 1985–89 IRS Sales of Capital Assets Panel. The findings show that most capital gains are realized by the same households, year after year. In this five-year data set, only one-fifth of all net gains were realized by households reporting gains in only one or two years. In contrast, two-thirds of all gains were reported by households with gains in at least four of the five sample years. These statistics confirm findings with similar data sets for earlier periods. Such confirmation is welcome, since the mix of capital gains has changed over time. Gains on equities became a larger share of total gains in the 1980s, while gains on real estate and other physical assets declined relative to previous decades.

The results for the 1985–89 period are also of somewhat special interest, however, because of the major change in realization incentives that was legislated in 1986. The aggregate time series for gain realizations shows a remarkable spike in 1986, as individuals rushed to realize gains before the capital gains tax rate increased in 1987. The findings in this paper suggest that most of the rise in realizations was the result of taxpayers with chronic gains realizing more gains than usual, rather than taxpayers with a few appreciated assets making once-and-for-all realizations.

The second part of the paper presents a simple model of multiperiod portfolio choice; this section generalizes a recent model developed by Alan Auerbach. Households choose how much of their portfolios to hold in a risky asset, as well as whether or not to realize their gains or losses. The model captures one important aspect of portfolio lock-in, since households may hold suboptimal quantities of the risky asset, but it does not allow for distortions among various risky assets. It also simplifies actual realization decisions by suppressing all uncertainty about the time path of consumption needs. More realistic life-cycle analyses would permit random fluctuation in the amount of spendable resources that households need in each period.

The model illustrates a number of effects associated with capital gains tax changes, but it is probably not yet ready to be used for detailed policy recommendations. The model needs further development to include several features of the actual economy that are currently omitted. First, there is no explicit discussion of how the government re-allocates the risk it acquires via the capital gains tax. A key point of the paper is that the risk-sharing effects of this tax are important, and that loss-offset provisions can have important welfare effects. This claim depends critically on the way the government re-allocates the risk it bears through the capital gains tax. The model has an awkward characteristic: when the government accepts a share of the risk associated with returns on risky assets, it reduces the riskiness of taxpayers' after-tax income but does not increase the risk of any other after-tax income flow. Yet the government cannot, in general, *eliminate* risk. This modeling approach could be justified if there were a world insurance market that the government could use but which private households could not access, but there is no obvious analog to this situation in reality. If the imposition of a capital gains tax forces the government to levy other state-contingent taxes to satisfy its revenue requirements, then the present model does not fully describe the risk-sharing properties of the tax code. There is even a presumption that the government will be less efficient at sharing risks than the private market will be, since it is forced to reallocate risks through the tax system rather than explicit insurance markets.

A second issue that bears further attention is the transaction cost of trading securities. The present model ignores ﹍rading costs, so households pursue textbook strategies of realizing losses and holding appreciated securities. Data on actual investor behavior usually calls these assumptions into question, since investors appear hesitant to realize losers for "behavioral" or other reasons. Transaction costs are one variable that could be added to the model to induce divergences between optimal and observed behavior; this could have important effects on welfare calculations. The general precept that tax distortions are larger when they reinforce pre-existing distortions suggests that adding trading costs would increase the welfare cost of realization-based taxes.

The third feature of reality that the model could usefully be expanded to recognize is the absence of constructive realization of gains at death. The model developed here is a life-cycle model, so households neither leave bequests nor receive inheritances. For very high-income and high-wealth households, however, intergenerational transfers are potentially quite important. Households at the very top of the wealth distribution, who tend to receive most of the capital gains in the economy, do not satisfy the lifetime budget constraint: they tend to leave substantial bequests. Because gains that are held at death escape taxation entirely, there are powerful incentives that distort portfolio or perhaps even consumption decisions at advanced ages. The present framework could be expanded to allow for such intergenerational transfers, and the resulting model would almost certainly provide more insight on the incentives facing investors.

Finally, this paper does not address the issue of whether capital gains and losses can be generated through various activities labeled "tax shelters." All of the gains (and losses) in this analysis are the result of genuine investments. In practice, enterprising citizens may find ways to transform wages, interest, or dividends into capital gains, and the capital gains tax then becomes a "backstop" for the rest of the tax code. In this situation the welfare analysis of capital gains–tax changes is more complex, and could even involve changes in other aspects of behavior such as labor supply.

General discussion

Metcalf noted that the aged are receiving a disproportionate amount of the capital gains. He also questioned if it is risk-sharing or rather the lock-in effect that causes reduced stockholding in the model in response to a reduced tax on capital gains.

Sansing commented that in this model, government has no access to a means of eliminating risk that is not available to private capital markets. Overall risk in the model only appears to decrease, because the government produces no goods with the tax revenue it raises. If the model includes goods provided by government with the tax revenues, the adverse consequences of risk borne by government would show up in the variance of public good production.

Gravelle remarked that for the model to be useful for policy analysis, it needs to extend the treatment of loss offsets to better reflect reality. She suggested comparing the indexation of gains to percentage exclusion in terms of risk. In addition, she suggested adding more periods and a bequest motive to create a more complete model.

MacKie-Mason observed that short-sales constraints matter critically for the wealthy because they aren't as limited as others. He noted that tax shelters are extremely hard to model because there are so many possible forms of sheltering and tax arbitrage.

Christian suggested modeling progressivity directly, because it has implications for risk-sharing and the optimal portfolio.

Haliassos noted that while the data they used are not in the public domain, there is some possibility that other researchers could gain access to them through the Joint Committee on Taxation. In response to the comments about whether the government can absorb tax-revenue risk, he argued that it may be able to do so by altering the time path of its expenditures and/or deficits. The welfare implications of alternative schemes depend on how the particular adjustments affect the expected utility of households; these alternatives need to be explored in future research and compared to revenue-neutral schemes. There is no reason to believe that the latter are in general neutral with respect to the amount of risk faced by households or to the portfolios they choose.

CHAPTER 9

Perceptions of fairness in the crucible
of tax policy

Steven M. Sheffrin

1   Introduction

The dramatic changes in U.S. tax laws in the 1980s naturally lead one to
inquire into the forces that shape and change tax policy. Two views are
often implicit in informed discussions of tax policy; at the risk of simpli-
fication, these may be termed the "idealist" and the "political" view.

According to proponents of the idealist view, major changes in tax policy are driven by deep-seated normative theories or ideologies about the
tax system. The 1981 tax changes were based on incentive-based supply-
side theories whose antecedents range from Andrew Mellon to Arthur
Laffer to the optimal-tax theorists. The 1986 tax reform, on the other
hand, traces its origins to Robert Haig, Henry Simons, Joseph Pechman,
Richard Musgrave, and other "tax reformers." A possible future major
shift toward consumption-based taxation would owe its allegiance to the
tradition of Irving Fisher and Martin Feldstein. Proponents of this view
of the formation of tax policy adhere to the dictum of John Maynard
Keynes that practical men are the slaves of "defunct economists."

The political view of tax policy emphasizes special interests, influential
committee chairmen, and the pursuit of political advantage by catering
to the latest reading of volatile public opinion. Birnbaum and Murray
(1987) highlight the full apparatus of lobbyists and special interests in the
formation of tax policy. But the best single statement of the pursuit of
political advantage through tax policy comes from maneuvers between
President Bush and the Democrats in the winter of 1992. Dan Rostenkowski, Chairman of the House Ways and Means Committee, described

Hayden Williams provided valuable research assistance on this project. I benefited from
tips on the literature from Peggy Hite, Alan Lewis, Julie Nelson, and Michael Roberts.
Valuable comments were received from Jane Gravelle, Jay Helms, Joel Slemrod, Ellen
Worcester, and conference participants.

309

how public opinion is used for political advantage: "We do focus groups and take polls . . . and you can bet that we'll be in the 92 percentile when we get our bill out."[1]

This is one cynical view of the role of public opinion in tax policy. But there is an alternative perspective that suggests that deep-seated public opinions and attitudes may have a more profound role to play in the formation of tax policy, perhaps akin to the influence of ideologies. Perceptions of fairness in tax policy can influence actual tax policy in a number of ways. First, there may be deep-seated preferences over how progressive the tax system should be. These preferences could in turn be translated through the political system, operating perhaps as constraints on the political actors in the system. Second, the public may have characteristic perspectives or perceptual "windows" on taxation which also affect the formation of tax policy. For example, some economic psychologists have suggested that status-quo bias, "framing" of alternatives, and "mental accounts" are important determinants of public attitudes toward economic phenomena.[2] These characteristic perspectives may profoundly influence the actual course of tax policy.

This paper explores whether the public has deep-seated attitudes and perceptions that influence the formation of tax policy. It draws on a wide variety of studies by economists, tax lawyers, accountants, and psychologists, as well as on some original survey research. We begin by first assessing the extent of public knowledge about the tax system and how well-founded public opinions are. We then turn to the topic of progressivity and review several surveys and experiments designed to uncover public preferences toward distribution of the tax burden. Some evidence is also presented about perceptions of the desirability and incidence of corporate taxes.

One area in which there appear to be distinct differences between the preferences and attitudes of the public and those of economists is that of tax incentives and tax preferences. These attitudes are explored through the use of a survey, a discussion of perceptions of implicit taxation, and a case study of a controversial tax incentive. The paper concludes with some suggestions of how public attitudes do in fact influence the formation of tax policy.

To this point, the term "public" has been used rather loosely. This is intentional. The broad public that influences tax policy includes the average

---

[1] As quoted in the *Sacramento Bee* (14 February 1992, p. A-4). Despite Rostenkowski's claims, the Democratic bill did not survive a White House veto and failed to carry a majority in the House on the override vote.

[2] I refer here to the work of Kahneman, Thaler, and Tversky. For a good introduction to this work, see Thaler (1992).

taxpayer as well as the high-paid lobbyist or tax attorney. If there are deep-seated attitudes that influence tax policy, they should be held by a wide range of participants in society.[3]

2   How deep is public knowledge about taxation?

Attitudes about the tax system and perceptions of fairness will naturally be influenced by what the public actually knows about the tax system. The tax system is one of our most complex social contrivances and, realistically, one can only expect there to be limited knowledge about it. Biases, however, may arise with incomplete information or incomplete knowledge. Moreover, the public may not have the conceptual apparatus to address certain policy questions. Each of these defects – bias and inadequate conceptual frameworks – appears to be present in public attitudes and perceptions about taxation.

The first bias concerns awareness of actual rates of taxation. A number of independent experiments have concluded that taxpayers underestimate either their tax liabilities or marginal tax rates. Enrick (1963, 1964) conducted several surveys during an August–December period in which respondents were first asked to estimate the federal taxes they paid and then to look up their actual taxes. Taxpayers appeared to underestimate their taxes; in fact, the number of taxpayers underestimating their taxes was roughly twice the number overestimating their taxes. Roughly 45% of taxpayers made errors of greater than 10% in estimating their tax liability.

Lewis (1978) found that British taxpayers tended to underestimate *marginal* tax rates. He asked the following question to a sample of 200 Bath residents: "In the first column please put what you think the income tax rates are for people in each income bracket: this means if people in each income bracket earned an extra pound how many pence do you think would go in income tax?" He found that mean estimates of marginal tax rates were 11% below those prevailing at the time. His results appear in the first three columns of Table 1. However, individuals were more accurate in assessing marginal rates close to their own brackets.

Finally, in a Canadian survey, Auld (1979) also found substantial underestimates for taxpayers in higher income brackets. However, at lower incomes they overestimated their taxes. The discrepancies reported were

---

[3] Although we will typically include tax attorneys and accountants in our definition of the public, we will make a distinction between views of economists *qua* economists and those of the general public. This is quite common in the economic psychology literature, which (for example) will comment on the differences in perception by the public of transactions that are identical in the economic sense but are "framed" differently.

Table 1. *Perception of and preference for marginal rates in the United Kingdom*

Taxable-income bands (£)	Actual marginal rate (summer 1977)	Estimates (mean)	Preferences (mean)
0–6,000	35%	32%	23%
6,000–7,000	40	36	26
7,000–8,000	45	40	28
8,000–9,000	50	44	32
9,000–10,000	55	47	34
10,000–12,000	60	52	38
12,000–14,000	65	57	42
14,000–16,000	70	62	47
16,000–21,000	75	68	51
Over 21,000	83	75	56

Source: Lewis (1978, table 1).

so large that Auld raised the question of whether income was accurately reported by the participants.[4]

A second form of bias concerns the relative visibility of taxes. The public is more aware of some taxes than others. As a general rule, income and property taxes are more visible than payroll or indirect taxes. Cullis and Lewis (1985) conducted a survey of 900 adults in the United Kingdom. One of their questions was: "Do you know where the government gets the money to pay for services?" Respondents were given a free response and then probed for additional ones. Although 93% mentioned the income tax only 56% mentioned taxes on goods, despite the importance of the VAT (value-added tax) in the British tax structure.[5]

The relative visibility of income taxes and property taxes (often paid in a few installments directly by the taxpayer) may explain why they are always the two most disliked taxes in yearly surveys of the Advisory Commission for Intergovernmental Relations (ACIR).[6] It also explains why conservatives who wish to limit government are suspicious of value-added

[4] In an errors-in-variable framework, if both income and taxation were reported subject to independent random errors then a regression of tax liability on income would yield a flatter slope and higher intercept than the true tax schedule relating taxes to income. This is precisely what is found.

[5] Cullis and Lewis also report similar findings in other studies on taxpayer awareness.

[6] Attempts to explain the survey results in terms of predicted economic incidence have not been very successful; see e.g. Fisher (1985).

taxes, despite their general preference for consumption taxes as opposed to income taxes.

Lawmakers appear to be aware of visibility in the design of tax law. Coop and McGill (1992) note the tendency in recent years for tax increases to be hidden in terms of "bubbles" and phase-outs of deductions and exemptions, as opposed to statutory rate increases. On the other hand, tax decreases proposed for the middle classes have been highly visible, taking the form of credits against income taxes.

Whereas taxpayers may underestimate rates and be overly conscious of "visible" taxes, they may simply not have well-informed views on complex issues. Keene (1983, p. 374) worries that "survey researchers have begun to try to measure the unknowable and untappable." Keene reviews three surveys taken in the late summer and early fall of 1982 by reputable pollsters about the desirability of the flat tax. Depending on the precise questions, support for the flat tax ranged from a high of 62% to a low of 27%. Keene argues that these wide differences are not totally due to the wording of the questions but arise because opinion in this area is not firm, at least with regard to responses to questions by pollsters.

The apparently straightforward notion of tax progressivity is actually fairly complex and can pose problems for taxpayers. Consider taxes as a function of income, $T = T(y)$. There are at least three different measures pertinent to measuring the tax burden:

> *Measure 1:* Taxes increase with income – $T(y)$ is monotonically increasing.
>
> *Measure 2:* Taxes paid as a share of income rise with income – $T(y)/y$ is increasing in y.
>
> *Measure 3:* The tax on incremental income, or marginal tax rates, increases with income – $T'(y)$ is increasing in y.

In a 1963 preface to a re-publication of their classic book *The Uneasy Case for Progressive Taxation,* Blum and Kalven note that when they started their project they were determined to probe public attitudes toward progressive taxation. They report that they were warned off by colleagues in the social sciences.[7] In their initial experiments they found that respondents had difficulty distinguishing between measure 1 and measure 2. Blum and Kalven (1963, p. x) viewed this as a mathematical barrier. Recent evidence by Roberts, Hite, and Bradley (1992) confirms this conjecture.

Many writers on progressivity often make another mathematical mistake in believing that a tax structure must satisfiy measure 3 if it is to satisfy measure 2 as well. Yet increasing tax burden with income does not

---

[7] Blum and Kalven were at the University of Chicago Law School. Chicago economists were among the least receptive to survey approaches.

require rising marginal rates throughout the tax code: a flat tax with an exemption has constant marginal rates above the exemption, but taxes paid rise as a share of income. Even Blum and Kalven, who were clearly aware of this distinction, spent most of their book discussing measure-3 as opposed to measure-2 progressive taxes.

Another example of extended confusion of marginal and average rates was the "bubble" introduced in the 1986 Tax Reform Act. To maintain a top 28% statutory rate, lawmakers phased out the personal exemption and the benefits of being taxed at the lower 15% rate for taxpayers above certain incomes. For example, a married couple would have a 33% marginal tax rate between $78,400 and $162,770 while income above this latter amount would be taxed at the 28% rate. This was immediately attacked as unfair, even though the average tax rate would monotonically increase to 28% for those taxpayers in the bubble. It is always difficult to separate confusion from political posturing, but it did seem that large numbers of congressmen and citizens fell into the former category.[8] This bubble was burst in the 1990 tax law, but new bubbles emerged in the tax code.

Finally, the 1986 Tax Reform Act provides an interesting test case of how public opinion compares with expert views. In April of 1989, the American Institute of Public Opinion asked the following question: "Do you think the 1986 tax reform bill has made for a fairer distribution of the tax load among all taxpayers, one that is less fair, or hasn't made much difference from the previous system?"[9] The response (in percentages) for the total population and college-educated were as follows.

Respondents	More fair	Less fair	No dif-ference	Don't know
Total	13	39	32	15
College-educated	20	46	25	9

It is clear that, on average, those with opinions felt that 1986 law made the tax system less fair. In fact, the 1986 law did lower rates but simultaneously broadened the base. Most experts felt that tax reform made the system more fair. Steuerle (1992, p. 122) wrote: "In the end, tax reform was probably mildly progressive or at least distributionally neutral." Expert opinion clearly differed from public opinion on this issue.[10]

[8] The bubble could, of course, create adverse incentive effects, but this was not the cause of perceived unfairness.

[9] The source is *Index to International Public Opinion,* 1989–90, "Economic Affairs," p. 85. Polls taken just before passage of the law did indicate mild support.

[10] Gravelle (1992) argues that the wealthy may benefit because some of the capital-income increases were transient, and that the rich may gain utility from more preferred portfolio positions.

This review suggests that we should be cautious in assessing public attitudes. There may be biases, lack of firm opinions, conceptual barriers to understanding, and a general lack of awareness of key events. However, there are better and worse ways of trying to measure attitudes and perceptions. Sophistication in survey research has increased since the initial pilot experiments of Blum and Kalven in the early 1950s. What does this more recent work reveal?

3   Direct evidence on attitudes toward progressivity

There have been several serious studies of preferences for income-tax progressivity. In addition to examining knowledge of the tax system in the United Kingdom, Lewis (1978) also surveyed preferences for marginal rates. Hite and Roberts (1991) and Porcano (1984) conducted surveys in the United States. The most illuminating contrast is between the Lewis and the Hite and Roberts studies.[11]

In 1977, Lewis surveyed 200 Bath residents about their knowledge concerning marginal tax rates and their preferences for marginal rates. The question used to ascertain knowledge was discussed in Section 2; the question for preferences was: "In the second column please put what you think would be fair income tax rates for each income tax bracket. There are no right or wrong answers, just put what you think is fair. This means how many pence do you think ought to go in income tax for each extra pound earned for people in each of the income brackets presented?" The survey was conducted in the summer of 1977 after a presentation of a summer budget, so Lewis thought that marginal tax rates may have been fresh in people's minds.

The results from Lewis's survey are shown in Table 1. Actual marginal rates ranged from 35% to 83%. Preferred marginal rates were lower, ranging from 23% to 56%. Preferred rates were 27% below estimated rates and 35% below actual rates. (The latter number is larger because taxpayers underestimated rates.) These percentages were relatively uniform across brackets. In a separate question, 65% of taxpayers agreed that individuals with higher incomes should pay a higher percentage of their incomes in tax than should individuals with lower incomes. Note that this is a question concerning average tax rates.

The clear conclusion from Lewis's study is that these U.K. taxpayers believed strongly in income-tax progressivity. "Fair" marginal rates

---

[11] The sample that Porcano used was small (approximately 80) and contained many students. Moreover, he was primarily interested in the type of rules used to assign the tax burden as opposed to detailed information on marginal rates. The Hite and Roberts work was more comprehensive on the topic of rates. In any case, the rates chosen in Porcano's work were close to those in the Hite and Roberts study.

were about 35% below those actually prevailing at the time. Nonetheless, even preferred rates of taxation were fairly high, reaching 56% marginal rates.

In a carefully executed and comprehensive study, Hite and Roberts (1991) received responses to an eight-page questionnaire booklet from nearly 600 individuals out of a total sample of 900. Their respondents closely corresponded to the overall population of the United States in terms of age and income. Among the topics they examined were: preferred average rates, preferences over alternative tax structures, differences in preferred rates when dollar amounts were used instead of percentages, sensitivity of progressivity to revenue requirements of the government, and the relation of self-interest to reported rates. The survey was conducted subsequent to the Tax Reform Act of 1986.

Table 2 contains some of their most important results. Preferred average tax rates for married couples ranged from 2.36% for the lowest bracket to 27.16% for the highest bracket. However, there was a large standard deviation for the responses in each category. For example, at the highest income level, the standard deviation was approximately 14, indicating wide dispersion in preferences.

The respondents were also asked to comment on the fairness of alternative rate schedules. There were five different schedules. Schedule A was the statutory rate structure after the 1981 act; schedules B and C were drawn from earlier periods of progressive rates; schedule D was the rate structure that emerged from the 1986 Tax Reform Act; and schedule E was a flat tax with an exemption. One difficulty in comparing these rate schedules is that they appear to raise different amounts of revenue. For example, statutory rates for schedules B and C are higher at all levels of income than for schedule A.

The bottom part of Table 2 reports the results of respondents asked to judge the fairness of these alternative rate structures and to choose the most preferred one. By a slim plurality, the flat-rate structure (alternative E) was chosen by 34% of the respondents. However, this meant that 66% chose progressive rate structures. Respondents were also asked if each schedule was fair; responses were measured on a scale of 1 (strongly agree) to 5 (strongly disagree). Only alternative A, a progressive tax schedule, received an overall mean response below 3.

In other results in the study, the degree of progressivity (based on relative tax burdens) was not sensitive to the revenue requirements of the government. Self-interest did play a role, as higher-income individuals advocated lower top tax rates than did lower-income individuals. When respondents were asked for assessments in dollars rather than rates, the effective rates (converted from the dollar responses) were substantially lower, reaching a top limit of only 20.1%.

Table 2. *U.S. attitudes toward progressivity*

Family income[a] ($)	Preferred average rate (%)	
	Mean	Standard deviation
5,000	2.36	4.82
10,000	4.74	5.65
15,000	8.31	5.73
20,000	11.67	5.91
25,000	13.87	5.94
30,000	16.08	6.79
40,000	19.11	8.17
50,000	23.67	10.45
100,000	27.16	14.20

Income ($)	Choice of rate structures				
	A	B	C	D	E
5,000	0%	0%	0%	0%	0%
10,000	14	18	23	15	20
20,000	18	24	31	15	20
30,000	28	37	40	28	20
100,000	45	59	66	33	20
Most preferred by:	33%	4%	1%	28%	34%
Fairness[b]	2.97	3.96	4.22	3.20	3.41

[a] With no children.
[b] 1 = strongly agree; 5 = strongly disagree.
Source: Hite and Roberts (1991, tables 1 and 2).

What is most striking is the difference in desired progressivity between the studies of Lewis and of Hite and Roberts. As a means of comparison, consider alternative tax schedules B and C in Table 2. These two are the closest to the preferences expressed by the British taxpayers, yet only 4% of the Hite and Roberts sample chose these as the most preferred! It is true that these rates raised more revenue than others. But depending on whether dollars or percentages were used, top average rates in the Hite-Roberts study were still between 20% and 27%, substantially below the average rates implied in Lewis's survey.

What can account for these differences? One obvious difference is the country. Perhaps British taxpayers prefer more graduated rate schedules than U.S. taxpayers. A second possibility is that the structure or progressivity of other taxes in the economy may affect responses to surveys about income-tax progressivity. For example, if non-income taxes in Great Britain are less progressive than non-income taxes in the United States, then British taxpayers may prefer a more progressive income-tax structure even though their overall preference for progressivity is the same. No evidence is available for this conjecture.

A more likely possibility concerns the structure and level of tax rates at the time the survey was taken. Lewis's survey was conducted during a time of high marginal rates in the United Kingdom, before the rate reductions of the 1980s. There is a nagging suspicion that the same survey conducted in 1992 would show a preference for distinctly lower rates among British taxpayers, particularly since the top marginal tax rate was reduced to 40% in the 1980s.

Preferences for progressivity may be context dependent. Note that in both studies, preferred rates were somewhat below actual rates. Preferences seem to be heavily influenced by the current structure of rates. A study of Swedish taxpayers provides evidence in favor of this hypothesis. Wahlund (1989) discusses survey evidence during a period in which marginal income rates decreased in Sweden; preferred marginal rates decreased along with actual rates. The idea that the current economic environment can influence perceptions and opinions has become an important theme in research in economic psychology. Tversky and Kahneman (1991) discuss a number of experiments in which individual choices are biased by the status quo. The current initial position appears to matter substantially in a wide range of choice situations. Moreover, the variability of rate structures in the United States itself suggests that preferences may be malleable. After all, as recently as 1980 the top marginal rate on income in the United States was 70%.[12] It is hard to believe that this could have been sustained for very long with only 4% approval (the sum of alternatives B and C).

Another possible approach to measuring attitudes toward tax progressivity would be to begin with the assumption that the public believes that individuals in similar circumstances should be treated similarly and not face rates of taxation which are too disparate. Granting this strong assumption, can we find reliable measures of individuals in "similar circumstances"?

Recent discussion and debate about the composition of the middle class suggests that this may be a difficult task. The Congressional Budget Office

---

[12] Steuerle (1992, pp. 24–7) discusses the changes in average and marginal rates in the era before 1980, emphasizing the sharp increase in effective marginal rates on wealthier individuals in the late 1970s.

(CBO) uses a rule of thumb that the middle 60 percent define the middle class which, for a family of four, thus ranges from $19,000 to $78,000 in annual income. From their survey, Hite and Roberts found that 90% of respondents felt that they were middle-class or below, indicating a smaller percentage of individuals who describe themselves as higher than the middle class.[13] Political definitions by congressional staffers are even more variable: one staffer suggested the 20th–95th percentile ($19,000–$137,000) while another specified a much narrower range of $20,000–$50,000.[14] Taking the CBO range as a compromise, historically we have had a wide range of tax rates applying to the middle 60 percent of the income distribution.[15]

A second alternative to measuring individuals in similar circumstances is to rely on the research by several European economists on "individual welfare functions." In this literature, subjects are asked to respond to the following question:

> Taking into account your own situation with respect to family and job, you would call your net family income (including fringe benefits and with subtraction of social security premium) per year

excellent	if it were above	_____
good	if it were between	_____
amply sufficient	if it were between	_____
sufficient	if it were between	_____
barely sufficient	if it were between	_____
very insufficient	if it were between	_____
bad	if it were between	_____
very bad	if it were below	_____

The nine verbal qualifications ("very bad," etc.) were placed on a 0–1 scale by assigning the numbers $0.11, 0.22, \ldots, 0.89$ in ascending order.[16] Let the income for each category be given by z_i. It is then assumed that there is a function $U(z)$ that maps income levels onto the 0–1 interval.

Specifically, a functional form of $U(z)$ is specified such that the logarithm of income follows a cumulative normal distribution, with mean u and standard deviation σ. From the answers to each questionnaire, the mean and standard deviation of the welfare function can be estimated for each individual. The results of responses yielding over 12,000 individual welfare functions have been reviewed by Van Herwaarden, Kapetyn, and Van Praag (1977).

---

[13] Peggy Hite provided me with this unpublished information from their survey.

[14] "Definition of Middle Class Varies Widely," *Washington Post* (9 January 1992).

[15] Steuerle's work (1992, table A.3) contains marginal and average tax rates for families of four at one-half median income, median income, and twice median income.

[16] This procedure can be justified under the very strong assumption that individuals try to convey as much information about their welfare ranking as possible. This leads to equal division of the intervals. See Van Praag and Kapetyn (1973).

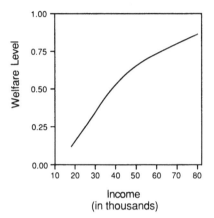

Figure 1. Individual welfare function.

From their results, it is possible to specify ranges over which individuals may consider themselves in similar circumstances. Suppose the middle class is defined to be those in the range between "very insufficient" and "good." Under this definition, the middle class spans those who struggle (but are not desperate) to those who are comfortable (but not affluent). This definition includes the range between 22% and 89% on the welfare scale. With a choice of parameters, we can then find the ranges of incomes that fall in this category. The value for the parameter u depends on the units of measurement; $\exp(u)$ is the income level that gives a utility level of 0.5, or halfway in the satisfaction scale. Fix this income level at $37,403, which is the average family income in 1990.

The value of β, which determines the spread in the distribution, varies somewhat in the reported research. It tends to be highest for those individuals with a volatile income history or in a peer group with wide variation in income. Because the studies were performed in Belgium and the Netherlands, which have more stable income distributions than the United States, we chose a high value of 0.61 that corresponds to the mean reported for those working independently.[17] With these parameters, the welfare function is plotted in Figure 1. Recall that we are considering individuals to be similar if they are within the range of "very insufficient" and "good"; this corresponds to 0.22–0.89 on the welfare scale. Carrying out the calculations for these parameters yields a range for this definition of "similarly situated individuals" of $23,300–$79,226. This is very close

[17] Van Praag and Kapetyn (1973, p. 49). The results are not that sensitive to other values of σ, such as that associated with an overall mean of 0.51.

to the 60-percent range of the Congressional Budget Office. But it also corresponds in Belgium and the Netherlands to very progressive income taxation for those taxpayers falling within this definition of similarly situated individuals.[18]

In summary, large numbers of individuals consider themselves to be of the middle class, and individual welfare scales can also be interpreted to suggest that individuals over a wide range of incomes consider themselves to be in similar circumstances. But historically we have witnessed large differences in the progressivity of the tax system within this group. The idea of a coherent middle class does not seem to be useful in explaining tax policy. At least in the United States, the term "middle class" refers primarily to class characteristics and a shared sense of values. There are, however, clear differences in economic well-being within this group. It is these perceived differences in well-being, rather than an abstract notion of a middle class, which are more likely to drive tax policy.

4   Perceptions of the corporate income tax

When asked their opinions about corporate taxes, the public on average sees no harm, and indeed sees virtue, in raising them. The results of two polls illustrate this nicely. In October of 1985, the Gallup Poll asked whether individuals approved or disapproved of "Raising more tax revenues from corporations and less from individuals."[19] The responses were: approve, 77%; disapprove, 11%; no opinion, 12%. In terms of public opinion about taxation, this response is as one-sided as (although opposite to) the responses to questions about whether personal income taxes should be increased.

In April of 1987, after decisions had been made to levy additional taxes on corporations in the 1986 Tax Reform Act, the Harris Poll attempted to determine which taxes the public would prefer to see raised in order to close the deficit.[20] Their specific question was: "Now let me ask you about some of the possible federal taxes that have been proposed as a way to reduce the federal deficit. In answering, please assume that there would be a guarantee that the money collected from the taxes would have to go towards reducing the deficit and would not be used for new spending programs. How much would you object to (each item read) – a great deal, some but not a lot, only a little, or not at all?" The alternatives and responses were as follows.

---

[18] Pechman (1987) provides a description of the very progressive personal income-tax system in the Netherlands.

[19] *The Gallup Poll, Public Opinion* (1985, p. 145).

[20] *Index to International Public Opinion* (1987, p. 112).

Alternative	Object a great deal	Object not a lot	Object only a little	No objections	Not sure
A 20 cent a gallon tax on gasoline	60%	14%	12%	13%	1%
Putting a 10 percent federal income tax surcharge on the current taxes individuals pay	59%	15%	15%	10%	1%
A national sales tax of 2 percent on all purchases, excluding purchases of drugs or food	36%	19%	22%	22%	1%
A $5 a barrel tax on oil imports into the U.S.	31%	22%	19%	25%	3%
Increasing excise taxes on tobacco and alcoholic products	22%	11%	12%	54%	1%
Putting a 10 percent income tax surcharge on the current taxes corporations pay	20%	17%	19%	41%	3%

Individuals would object most strongly to increased gasoline and income taxes, but view increased taxes on corporations as a minor nuisance – less objectionable even than increased sin taxes.

Not only do individuals feel that the corporate tax burden can probably be raised, they also become outraged when they learn that corporations pay no corporate income taxes to the government. Birnbaum and Murray (1987, p. 12) describe the public outcry following the publication of a Citizens for Tax Justice study by Robert McIntyre in 1984 that 128 out of 250 of the largest corporations paid no federal income taxes for at least one year between 1981 and 1983. They note that "In a particularly embarrassing revelation, the study showed that among the corporate free-loaders was W. R. Grace & Company, whose chairman, J. Peter Grace, had headed a commission for President Reagan that concluded that wasteful government spending was 'sending the country down the tubes for future generations of Americans.'"

This quote from Birnbaum and Murray inadvertently reveals some of the source of anger when corporations do not pay federal income taxes. Note their use of the word "freeloader"; this clearly personalizes the corporation, placing it on the same moral plane as an individual. It is a moral failing of a corporation not to pay taxes – a defect in its character. This anthropomorphic language is used in many contexts, for example, "greedy, environmentally polluting corporations."

But as economists always point out, taxes may be levied on corporations but ultimately individuals somewhere bear the burden. This burden may fall on the owners, managers, or workers of the corporation, or may be passed on through a wide variety of channels to other individuals in the economy. Ultimately, the burden does fall on individuals. Yet much public discussion ignores this point. Incidence is a very subtle concept. Unless probed, the public will assume that taxes are paid by the entity on which they are levied. Even important public documents ignore the incidence of the corporate tax when it is clearly relevant. As Gravelle (1992) points out, the pamphlet explaining the 1986 Tax Reform Act issued by the Joint Committee on Taxation contains tables showing the change in the tax burden without including any effects from the corporate tax, despite the fact that 1986 law shifted the nominal burden to corporations.[21]

We often do hear, in public discussion and commentary, the idea that corporations "shift" the tax. In order to obtain some information on public views of tax incidence, as part of a survey (detailed in Section 5) I asked the following question of 150 students in an introductory macroeconomics course:[22]

> Who do you think really ends up paying the taxes that are assessed on corporations?
>
> (a) Owners, that is, shareholders of corporations.
> (b) All investors in the economy.
> (c) Consumers, because corporations simply raise prices.
> (d) Workers, because corporations reduce wages.

The responses were: (a) 9%, (b) 30%, (c) 55%, (d) 6%.

Surprisingly, the respondents did not see the owners of corporations bearing the tax; rather, to the extent that they believed capital bore the tax, they shared the Harberger perspective that it was passed on to all capital in the economy. The most frequent answer was that consumers bore the tax in terms of higher prices.

Note that these respondents were forced to identify the party on whom the tax truly falls, and were not permitted to say simply that the corporation pays the tax. In daily life, however, they are not forced to draw these

---

[21] Difficulties in agreeing on the incidence of the corporate tax may have been the reason behind this exclusion.

[22] The question was added to both versions of the survey described in Section 5. The percentage responses from both versions were quite similar. About half of the students had taken a prior introductory microeconomics course, but incidence of the corporate tax is not a topic typically covered in that course. It should be noted that UC–Davis students are not representative of the larger public. One potential bias is that most students do not work full-time and so may not be sensitive to taxes passed on as lower wages. A high percentage of UC–Davis students do, however, work part-time.

connections. Separate mental compartments are more likely the rule: In one compartment, corporations can be attacked as freeloaders for not paying taxes; in the other compartment, it is recognized that corporations shift the burden.

This mental dichotomy provides the best explanation of the poll and survey findings. Based on the Harris poll, the public loves to raise corporate taxes. However, if forced to think through the ultimate incidence, a majority (at least of students) believes the tax falls on consumers, and fewer than 40% believe it falls primarily on capital income. One could possibly argue that these responses on tax incidence do support a preference for corporate taxation. The evidence could be read that the corporate tax is viewed as a mixture of a tax on capital income and a value-added or sales tax. This might even be viewed as strongly preferable to an income tax. But the general animosity toward nonpaying corporations (as witnessed by the reaction to McIntyre's study and the popularity of corporate minimum taxes), coupled with the strong poll results in favor of increased corporate taxation, suggest that the public compartmentalizes its views: entities should pay taxes even if they ultimately pass them on.

5   Economists versus the public

Economists generally do not have strong opinions *qua* economists on the subject of progressivity. In general, different rate structures will produce different distributions of after-tax income and different values of excess burdens. There may be some rate structures that dominate others on both grounds – that is, producing more equal incomes and less excess burden – but, in general, different distributional preferences will lead to different rate structures. Economists can provide only limited guidance on this issue.[23] While economists may be somewhat more sensitive to excess burden, in principle there need not be any major conflicts between the public and economists regarding progressivity.

With respect to the tax base and, in particular, to tax subsidies and preferences, there do appear to be sharp differences in perspectives. To understand these differences, it will be useful to review two basic principles that economists tend to carry into the analysis of tax subsidies and preferences.

The first principle is that government funds should be allocated efficiently. If the government wishes to subsidize a particular investment activity, then the direct or tax-subsidy program should be designed so that competition will lead to equal pre-tax rates of return for alternative activities

[23] Slemrod (1983) provides an accessible and balanced discussion of the lessons and limitations of optimal income-tax theory.

within this class of investments. For example, if the government wishes to produce more energy conservation, the pre-tax rate of return on all conservation investments should be equal. If not, it would be possible to re-allocate funds toward projects with a higher rate of return in order to produce more energy conservation. To accomplish the goal of efficient promotion of energy conservation, direct subsidies or tax credits should be made available to all parties on an equal basis. If some parties are arbitrarily denied benefits then rates of return will generally not be equalized.

The second principle is that purchasers of tax-favored securities do not generally benefit to the full extent of the nominal tax subsidy. Competition among purchasers tends to "compete away" at least a portion of the security's tax benefits, leading to lower pre-tax yields. The classic example is tax-exempt bonds. If certain classes of bonds are exempt from tax then investors will bid for these bonds, which increases their price and lowers their pre-tax yield. This reduction in yield is called *implicit taxation*. As an example, suppose that the yield on taxable bonds were 10% and the yield on (identical) tax-exempt bonds were 7%. The rate of implicit taxation in this case would be 30%. Investors with tax rates of 30% would be indifferent between purchasing the taxable and tax-exempt bonds; investors with higher tax rates would prefer the tax-exempt bonds; and investors with lower tax rates would prefer the taxable bonds. The same basic principle applies also to other tax-favored securities.

These two principles of economic analysis – efficiency and implicit taxation – are not generally held by the public; in particular, they collide sharply with the "entity" view that all entities should pay tax. To illustrate the collision with the economic efficiency principle, an experiment was conducted with 150 students in a class on economic principles.

Students were given descriptions of two programs designed to stimulate investment, together with questions about these programs. The descriptions and programs are reproduced here as Figure 2 and Figure 3. One program, "Investment First," involved direct subsidies of 10% for any investment. The second program, "Investment Credit," offered a tax credit of 10% for any investment. The students were given information about a fictitious firm, Lincoln Computer, that paid $2 million in taxes last year and planned to invest $10 million. Under the subsidy program, it would therefore receive a payment of $1 million; under the tax-credit program, it would receive tax credits of $1 million. The students were asked to express their opinion on the desirability of these programs on a scale of 1 to 5 (strongly approve to strongly disapprove). They were then told that the program was successful and the company would double its investment; this would lead to a subsidy of $2 million and zero taxes under the tax-credit plan. Students were then asked whether their impressions

Please read the following paragraphs and then answer the questions that follow. There are no "right" or "wrong" answers—we are just asking for your opinion.

The U.S. government wishes to increase productivity by increasing investment spending by firms. The government proposes a new plan "Investment Credit" which will subsidize investment spending in the following manner: for each dollar of investment spending, the government will reduce the firm's taxes by ten cents. That means for every dollar spent, the true cost to the firm is only ninety cents because it receives a ten cent tax rebate.

The Lincoln Computer firm paid $2 million dollars in taxes last year. It plans to expand rapidly and increase its investment. It is currently planning to invest $10 million next year. Under the "Investment Credit" plan, the firm would thus reduce its taxes to $1 million.

Questions:

1.   What are your general feelings about the "Investment Credit" plan?

    a.   Strongly approve
    b.   Approve
    c.   Indifferent
    d.   Disapprove
    e.   Strongly Disapprove

2.   Under the current plan, Lincoln Computer pays $1 million in taxes if it invests $10 million. Suppose the investment credit program was successful in stimulating investment and Lincoln doubled its investment to $20 million and thus reduced its taxes to zero. Would your impressions of the program:

    a.   Become more favorable?
    b.   Remain the same?
    c.   Become less favorable?

Figure 2. Stimulating investment via tax subsidy.

of the program became more favorable, remained the same, or became less favorable.

Before discussing the results, it is important to note that these programs are absolutely identical for the corporation described. The only difference is that in the case of the subsidy there are two separate accounts with the government – tax payments and direct subsidies – while there is only one account for the investment credit program.

The results of the survey appear in Table 3. Confronted with the initial data, the respondents mildly approved of both programs, with near identical mean responses of 2.62 and 2.64 for the subsidy and credit program, respectively. This placed the mean responses between approve (2) and indifferent (3). (The small difference between the two mean responses was statistically insignificant.) On the other hand, when the firm doubled its investment, the responses diverged dramatically. The mean for the subsidy

Please read the following paragraphs and then answer the questions that follow. There are no "right" or "wrong" answers—we are just asking for your opinion.

The U.S. government wishes to increase productivity by increasing investment spending by firms. The government proposes a new plan "Investment First" which will subsidize investment spending in the following manner: for each dollar of investment spending, the government will pay the firm ten cents. That means for every dollar spent, the true cost to the firm is only ninety cents because it receives a ten cent subsidy.

The Lincoln Computer firm paid $2 million dollars in taxes last year. It plans to expand rapidly and increase its investment. It is currently planning to invest $10 million next year. Under the "Investment First" plan, the firm would thus receive a $1 million dollar payment.

Questions:

1.   What are your general feelings about the "Investment First" plan?

     a.   Strongly approve
     b.   Approve
     c.   Indifferent
     d.   Disapprove
     e.   Strongly Disapprove

2.   Under the current plan, Lincoln Computer receives $1 million for the $10 million investment. Suppose the subsidy program was successful in stimulating investment and Lincoln doubled its investment to $20 million and received a $2 million dollar payment. Would your impressions of the program:

     a.   Become more favorable?
     b.   Remain the same?
     c.   Become less favorable?

Figure 3. Stimulating investment via tax credit.

response was 1.94, indicating that the opinion of the program improved slightly. However, the mean for the investment credit program was 2.44, indicating that the program was viewed much less favorably than at the lower level of investment. The difference in these means was significant at the 0.01 level.

Thus, the fact that the firm receiving the investment credit paid no taxes was clearly troubling to the respondents. Entities should pay taxes. Subsidies equal to taxes paid were not as troubling. These results are similar to the phenomenon of "mental accounts" and "framing" discussed by Thaler (1992).

The entity view accounts for the outrage against individual or corporate taxpayers who have true income but pay no tax. This view is not totally irrational, and public outrage may have some merit given the phenomenon of tax arbitrage. With differing marginal tax rates, opportunities for

Table 3. *Response to survey* ($N = 150$)

	Investment-stimulating programs	
	Subsidy	Credit
Initially favored by:	84	66
Mean responses		
Question 1 (1–5 scale)[a]	2.62	2.64
Standard deviation	(1.00)	(0.95)
Question 2 (1–3 scale)[b]	1.94	2.44
Standard deviation	(0.64)	(0.68)

[a] 1 = strongly approve; 5 = strongly disapprove.
[b] 1 = more favorable; 2 = same; 3 = less favorable. Difference between the two listed means is statistically significant at the 0.01 level.

borrowing and lending, and tax-favored investments, there are strategies that higher-bracket individuals can engage in to reduce their tax. The classic example is for high-income individuals to borrow from lower individuals to purchase tax-exempt bonds or other tax-favored assets. Interest deductions are taken against a high tax rate and the proceeds from the investment are sheltered. As Steuerle (1985) emphasizes, these opportunities were ubiquitous before the Tax Reform Act of 1986, and still exist in many forms today. They also are exacerbated by inflation, since nominal rates do not rise to the extent necessary to offset tax arbitrage.

The average taxpayer knows that these strategies exist, and senses that sophisticated taxpayers are taking advantage of them while the average taxpayer has much fewer opportunities for similar actions. Corporations are examples of sophisticated taxpayers that can take advantage of tax arbitrage possibilities. Reaction against this phenomenon can partly explain the entity view of taxation. Nonetheless, as our experiment illustrates, even an efficient subsidy plan with no element of tax arbitrage would meet public disfavor. The political response to this disfavor will be policies that limit the subsidy, such as the various incarnations of the minimum tax. These limitations can interfere with economic efficiency.

A recent television commercial for a tax-exempt–bond fund illustrates an example of neglecting implicit taxation. The commercial shows water (income) being poured into a vessel, but leaks in the vessel (taxes) prevent the water level (wealth) from rising; the tax-free–bond fund plugs up the holes, allowing the water level to rise. However, the flow of water into the vessel is depicted in the commercial to be as rapid with the tax-free fund as with taxable funds. To be accurate, the flow of water should be decreased for the tax-free account.

Probably the best evidence concerning the difficulty the public has with the concept of implicit taxation comes from an article by a noted tax lawyer. Bittker (1980) agonizes over the different perceptions of what he terms "equity theorists" and "efficiency theorists" over tax preferences. Equity theorists, including himself, generally believe that tax-favored investments lead primarily to horizontal inequities between those who purchase them and those who do not. As an example, purchasers of tax-exempt bonds do not pay tax whereas purchasers of taxable bonds do pay tax. Efficiency theorists argue that yields on tax-exempt bonds fall sufficiently for horizontal inequalities to be eliminated, and that all that remains is a preferred borrowing rate (thus economic inefficiency) for states and municipalities that can issue tax-exempt securities. However, horizontal inequities will remain if the tax rate of some investors exceeds the market rate of implicit taxation. Bittker emphasizes that the efficiency view of tax subsidies was not held by the equity theorists.

The reason this article is especially interesting is because Bittker is in the same tradition as Stanley Surrey and part of the general tax-reform movement. Bittker argues that the moral thrust toward tax reform based on equity considerations alone is sharply diminished once the efficiency view of tax subsidies is understood. It is also clear that the equity-based tax-reform movement, dominated by lawyers, did not really focus on implicit taxation. For example, in his famous book *Pathways to Tax Reform,* Surrey (1973) discusses the minimum tax as a corrective to tax expenditures that allow individuals or corporations to dramatically reduce their tax. No mention of the concept of implicit taxation can be found in the chapter of his book that deals with the minimum tax. However, it is clearly relevant to Surrey's discussion of whether the minimum tax should be flat or progressive and other aspects of vertical equity. A full treatment of vertical equity must recognize implicit taxation.

An excellent example of both the entity view of taxation and the lack of understanding of implicit taxation comes from a notorious episode in modern tax history: the case of "safe-harbor" leasing, a provision of the 1981 Economic Recovery Tax Act. The investment incentives in the 1981 law – accelerated depreciation and investment credits – were very extensive, and effectively reduced the tax rate on equipment to zero *if* these credits and deductions could be used. Many large corporations, however, did not have positive taxable income and so could not take advantage of these benefits. Moreover, small start-up firms would also be limited in their use of these benefits. The tax benefits that could not be used were effectively "dead souls."[24]

The Reagan Administration's solution to this problem was to liberalize leasing rules so that corporations which could not utilize these benefits could effectively sell them to other corporations. The merits of this policy were sharply debated among tax experts.[25] Many tax experts who were critical of the law focused on two points. First, corporations with persistent tax losses would have a zero effective tax rate on investment in any case, and so did not need further subsidies. Second, the market could have excessive transactions costs.

But it was clear that the public was perturbed primarily by those corporations that *purchased* tax credits, not by the ones that sold them, and by "profitable" corporations that engaged in leasing. The Joint Committee on Taxation (1982, p. 22) noted the controversy created when General Electric purchased so many credits that it obtained a refund on past taxes. Occidental Petroleum sold tax benefits because they had domestic losses that prevented them from taking depreciation and credits in spite of their positive worldwide income.

General Electric surely benefited when it purchased the tax benefits, but only to the extent that they got them for a good price. If the market were perfect and sellers of benefits were much fewer than potential buyers, then $1 of benefits would sell for $1. The Treasury estimated that tax-benefit buyers paid only 85¢ for $1 of benefits, so in this case profits were made by the buyers. Purchasers of benefits paid a very high rate of implicit taxation in the stream of payments that constituted the safe-harbor lease. Yet more outrage was directed at buyers than sellers, and U.S. Senators questioned whether limitations should be made on purchases.[26]

The case of Occidental Petroleum was also revealing. If we were interested in stimulating domestic investment, why should we treat Occidental Petroleum differently than Chrysler? The fact that Occidental was profitable on a worldwide basis should be even more reason to subsidize them rather than Chrysler, because their profitability might indicate that they were highly efficient. But Occidental Petroleum attracted public outrage, while Chrysler was held up as a good example of safe-harbor leasing.

The Joint Committee also raised the issue that the public may find transactions unfair whenever nontaxable companies can make money by selling excess tax benefits. But, if columnists are a guide, more fun was made of potential purchasers of benefits. For example, it was suggested that a well-off journalist should be able to purchase tax credits from a

[24] With apologies to Gogol, I pursue this analogy in Sheffrin (1982).
[25] Steuerle (1985, pp. 142–4) discusses the alternative positions of tax experts on the issue.
[26] See comments by Senator Grassley in Senate Finance Committee (1981, pp. 70–1).

welfare mother.[27] Presumably the journalist would have had to pay $1 for $1 worth of tax benefits. Implicit taxation is generally overlooked in public discussions.

6   Is there feedback from perceptions of fairness?

An important final issue is whether feedback exists from perceptions of fairness in the economy and the tax system. The most obvious channel is through tax compliance. Perceptions of gross unfairness in the tax system may lead to a loss of faith in the system, increased cheating, and a general reduction in the level of compliance or increased administrative costs for the same level of compliance.

Although this certainly appears to be a plausible channel, existing research has not been fully successful in documenting and quantifying this effect. The essential problem is that the relationship between compliance and subjective attitudes toward the tax system is very subtle and works through a number of channels other than perceived fairness. Beliefs about tax morality and the perception of the honesty of others have also been found to be correlated with compliance.

In Sheffrin and Triest (1992) we review existing evidence on the relationship of subjective attitudes toward the tax system and compliance, and provide additional microeconometric evidence based on an analysis of survey data. With regard to the issue of perceived fairness, some surveys and experimental evidence find a link between perceptions of fairness and compliance, but others do not. In our econometric work, we used a framework in which responses to survey questions served as indicators of unobserved variables that determine compliance. The unobserved explanatory variables in our compliance model corresponded to measures of (1) attitudes toward compliance, (2) perception of the honesty of others, and (3) the probability of detection. The first variable was most closely related to perceptions of fairness, and included as an indicator a question concerning whether the government spends too much. From our experience with this study, we believe it would be difficult to isolate and separate precise effects of perceptions of fairness from other attitudinal variables in econometric or survey research. In particular, we found that the significance of some of the attitudinal variables in our equation explaining compliance were sensitive to the precise econometric assumptions necessary to identify structural parameters in the model.

But assuming there is a link between perceptions of gross unfairness and compliance, what would constitute "gross unfairness?" From the work

---

[27] Richard Cohen, "Tax Credits," *Washington Post* (29 November 1981, p. B1).

surveyed in Section 3, it appears that perceptions of gross unfairness would not arise from a tax schedule that was only modestly progressive. Perceptions of desired progressivity appear to be context dependent – that is, closely related to the current degree of progressivity. Recent surveys indicate only a moderate desire for progression. It is not clear whether a flat tax with an exemption level would be perceived as unfair; this would largely depend on the context in which it was introduced. Current surveys do not indicate an overwhelming public demand for progressivity.

The public does find it unfair when profitable entities pay little or no tax. There is no better polemical device for tax reform than to show entities paying little tax. That the public holds firmly to the entity view of taxation strongly implies that there are limits to the extent to which subsidy and incentive programs can operate through the tax system.

This in turn yields two important consequences. First, even if subsidies and incentives do operate through the tax system, they are not likely to operate fully efficiently in the sense of leading to identical pre-tax returns. Inevitably, the subsidies and incentives will run into limitations imposed by the entity view of taxation (such as the minimum tax), which effectively limit expenditures in ways that do not necessarily lead to economic efficiency. Even efficient subsidy programs with no possibility for tax arbitrage will encounter limits, leading to differences in pre-tax returns for identical activities; our experimental evidence with the "Lincoln Computer" company illustrates this point. This is an additional consideration that must be taken into account when weighing the merits of subsidies awarded through the expenditure process versus subsidies awarded through the tax system.

A second consequence is that as long as incentives and tax subsidies remain in the tax law (and it is unlikely they will ever fully disappear), the result will be continued complexity in the tax system. The minimum tax is a classic example of this phenomenon. Since its inception the minimum tax has undergone numerous changes and variations, both for individuals and for business. One of its purposes is to protect the entity view of taxation – taking away with one hand the subsidies and incentives given out by the other. Two-handed tax law will always be complex.

One overriding impression from this analysis of perceptions of fairness and progressivity is the public's limited knowledge and its tendency to view aspects of the tax code with separate mental compartments. Evidence of limited knowledge includes a tendency to underestimate rates, a dislike for more visible taxes, difficulties in understanding different notions of progressivity, and a general unawareness of implicit taxation. Taxpayers appear to use separate mental compartments for views on personal and corporate taxation, and seem also to use separate mental compartments for their views on corporate tax incidence and the desirability of increasing corporate taxes.

These two factors imply that the public does not hold a single, comprehensive view of tax progressivity that applies to the entire tax system. Treating corporate taxes apart from individual taxes and failing to recognize implicit taxation places important limits on the public's grasp of overall tax progressivity. Could the public be educated to the nature of corporate and implicit taxation? One could perhaps imagine a public debate over corporate tax integration which would lead *some* of the public to begin thinking about corporate and individual taxation together. Currently, however, such recognition is far removed from the public consciousness.

REFERENCES

Auld, D. A. L. (1979), "Public Sector Awareness and Preferences in Ontario," *Canadian Tax Journal* 27: 172–83.

Birnbaum, Jeffrey H., and Alan S. Murray (1987), *Showdown at Gucci Gulch.* New York: Random House.

Bittker, Boris I. (1980), "Equity, Efficiency, and Income Tax Theory: Do Misallocations Drive Out Inequities?" in Henry J. Aaron and Michael J. Boskin (eds.), *The Economics of Taxation.* Washington, DC: Brookings, pp. 19–31.

Blum, Walter J., and Harry Kalven, Jr. (1963), *The Uneasy Case for Progressive Taxation.* Chicago: University of Chicago Press (Phoenix Edition).

Coop, Cindy A., and Gary A. McGill (1992), "Visibility and Perceptions for Fairness: a 'Now You See It, Now You Don't' Tax Policy for the 1990s?" *Tax Notes* 20: 1013–16.

Cullis, John, and Alan Lewis (1985), "Some Hypotheses and Evidence on Tax Knowledge and Preferences," *Journal of Economic Psychology* 6: 271–87.

Enrick, Norbert Lloyd (1963), "A Pilot Study of Income Tax Consciousness," *National Tax Journal* 16: 169–73.

(1964), "A Further Study of Income Tax Consciousness," *National Tax Journal* 17: 319–21.

Fisher, Ronald C. (1985), "Taxes and Expenditures in the U.S.: Public Opinion Surveys and Incidence Analysis Compared," *Economic Inquiry* 23: 525–50.

The Gallup Poll, Public Opinion (various issues). Wilmington, DE: Scholarly Resources.

Gravelle, Jane G. (1992), "Equity Effects of the Tax Reform Act of 1986," *Economic Perspectives* 6: 27–44.

Hite, Peggy A., and Michael L. Roberts (1991), "An Experimental Investigation of Taxpayer Judgments on Rate Structures in the Individual Income Tax System," *Journal of the American Taxation Association* 13: 47–63.

Index to International Public Opinion (various issues). New York: Greenwood.

Joint Committee on Taxation (1982), *Analysis of Safe-Harbor Leasing* (June 14). Washington, DC: Government Printing Office.

Keene, Karlyn (1983), "What Do We Know about the Public's Attitude on Progressivity?" *National Tax Journal* 36: 371–6.

Lewis, Alan (1978), "Perceptions of Tax Rates," *British Tax Review* 6: 358–66.

Pechman, Joseph A., ed. (1987), *Comparative Tax Systems: Europe, Canada and Japan*. Arlington, VA: Tax Analysts.

Porcano, Thomas M. (1984), "Distributive Justice and Tax Policy," *Accounting Review* 59: 619–36.

Roberts, Michael L., Peggy A. Hite, and Cassie F. Bradley (1992), "Understanding Progressivity: an Experimental Investigation Using Abstract and Concrete Framing," Mimeo, Culverhouse School of Accountancy, University of Alabama, Tuscaloosa.

Senate Finance Committee (1981), *Hearing on Safe Harbor Leasing* (December 10). Washington, DC: Government Printing Office.

Sheffrin, Steven M. (1982), "What Have We Done to the Corporate Tax System?" *Challenge* 25: 46–52.

Sheffrin, Steven M., and Robert K. Triest (1992), "Can Brute Deterrence Backfire? Perceptions and Attitudes in Taxpayer Compliance," in Joel Slemrod (ed.), *Who Pays Taxes and Why? Tax Compliance and Enforcement*. Ann Arbor: University of Michigan Press.

Slemrod, Joel (1983), "Do We Know How Progressive the Income Tax System Should Be?" *National Tax Journal* 36: 361–9.

Steuerle, C. Eugene (1985), *Taxes, Loans and Inflation*. Washington, DC: Brookings.

(1992), *The Tax Decade*. Washington, DC: Urban Institute.

Surrey, Stanley S. (1973), *Pathways to Tax Reform*. Cambridge, MA: Harvard University Press.

Thaler, Richard H. (1992), *The Winner's Curse*. New York: Free Press.

Tversky, Amos, and Daniel Kahneman (1991), "Loss Aversion in Riskless Choice: a Reference Dependent Model," *Quarterly Journal of Economics* 106: 1039–61.

Van Herwaaden, Floor, Arie Kapetyn, and Bernard Van Praag (1977), "Twelve Thousand Welfare Functions," *European Economic Review* 9: 283–300.

Van Praag, M. S. Bernard, and Arie Kapetyn (1973), "Further Evidence on the Individual Welfare Function of Income: an Empirical Investigation in the Netherlands," *European Economic Review* 4: 33–62.

Wahlund, Richard (1989), "Perception and Judgment of Marginal Tax Rates after a Tax Reduction," in K. G. Grunert and F. Olander (eds.), *Understanding Economic Behavior*. Dordrecht: Kluwer, pp. 135–79.

Comments

Jane G. Gravelle

Steve Sheffrin's paper suggests some disturbing, but perhaps unsurprising, findings about public perceptions of taxes. The findings indicate that the public has a limited knowledge of the subtleties of economics. Indeed, there appears to be little understanding of notions such as incidence and tax shifting, economic efficiency, and implicit taxation. For this reason, the public seems particularly willing to accept corporate taxes, although economic analysis of these taxes – whose incidence is uncertain and whose efficiency costs are large – does not tend to give them high marks. More fundamentally, the public has poor factual knowledge about the tax system (e.g., they inaccurately estimate rates) and seems unusually swayed by the visibility of taxes.

At the same time, there is evidence of public support for progressive taxation, although this view does not seem to be reflected in fundamental attitudes toward specific taxes reported on surveys. I might add, by the way, that the part of the paper I found least satisfactory is the notion of a broad middle class where "equals" would be defined and equally treated to proportional tax rates. I don't find it plausible to suggest that those with incomes ranging from (say) $20,000 to $80,000 should be thought of as similar. We may all think of ourselves as middle-class, but I suspect the vast majority of individuals would characterize these income groups as highly unequal.

Sheffrin's findings of limited information should not be so surprising. It is reasonable to expect that individuals, given the cost of acquiring and retaining information, would be unlikely to amass significant detail about a subject in which they have no direct decisionmaking power. I suspect that one would find similar results in many other areas. The public, for example, probably does not possess accurate information about the disposition of government revenues, and – if constituent mail to Congress is any indication – believe that much larger shares of the budget are devoted

335

to welfare and to foreign aid than is actually the case. Nor, I suspect, would they be found to have a clear understanding of many other technical fields (besides economics) that are relevant for public policy.

In fact, up to a point, this paper tells a consistent story about economics and about policymaking. Individuals are not well informed about tax policy, but this is simply an aspect of "rational ignorance." When information is costly to obtain and retain, and when that information concerns areas where individuals are not actually making decisions, then it is perfectly rational to be uninformed. At the same time, these surveys suggest that individuals support the notion of progressive taxation – although their views appear somewhat influenced by the current tax environment. The implications thus far are that policy should be made to reflect these tastes for progressivity, and that policy choices should be made presuming that individuals are not well informed but have fundamental preferences that should be considered.

The difficulty in this assessment, however, is that despite the limited information individuals have, they appear to hold very strong views about taxes – views that are not necessarily consistent with preferences for progressivity, and often not consistent with formulation of an efficient tax system. For example, there appears to be a preference for taxes that are less visible, such as the corporate income tax and general sales taxes.

The major question that the author leaves unanswered is what we are to make of his findings. Does it tell us something about the influence of public attitudes on collective decisionmaking? Does it provide a guide for policymakers as to what they should do to formulate a desirable tax policy?

With regard to the first question – how have public attitudes affected decisionmaking – there are two issues: perceptions and knowledge of policymakers, and the influence of public attitudes on the structure of the present tax system.

It would be most interesting, but probably quite difficult, to perform similar research to ascertain the knowledge and attitudes of policymakers, particularly those who must make decisions but are not trained in economics. From my own perspective of answering questions posed by Congressional staff, there is plenty of anecdotal evidence of shortfalls in the understanding of the economic effects of taxation. One recent example is the proposal to stimulate the economy, in the midst of a recession, by cutting taxes that were argued by proponents to increase savings. Another example that crops up again and again is the argument that business taxation hampers international competitiveness (a term whose meaning is unclear in the first place) because it adds to the cost of doing business. Economists are well aware that any price increase that does occur would be offset by exchange-rate adjustments, but this notion is not clearly understood by many policymakers.

This question of just how knowledgeable policymakers are blurs the already difficult question of how public attitudes have shaped the tax law. The public apparently finds corporate taxes quite acceptable, yet corporate taxes constitute a small and (in recent years) declining share of receipts. Despite the apparent taste for hidden consumption taxes, these taxes are also small and virtually non-existent at the Federal level. Are these outcomes the result of policymakers who do not hold the same views as the public, or who recognize the characteristics of inefficiency in the former case and regressivity in the latter? Or are there other forces – special interests, for example – that carry the day?

We do have some anecdotal evidence that specific instances of public reaction to taxes shape tax policy. The Tax Reform Act of 1969 was fueled in part by public reaction to the disclosure that very high–income individuals were paying no taxes. The alternative minimum tax enacted in 1986 was likewise largely in response to reports of large corporations paying little or no taxes. But whether there is a more persistent and systematic relationship between public attitudes and tax policy decisions is unclear, and perhaps incapable of being clarified.

It is with respect to the second point – implications for the design of tax policies – that the results of this study may yield some insights. The presence of poor information on the part of the public presents some difficult issues in public policymaking. Should one attempt to educate the public on why such proposals might be desirable, or should one try to arrange tax revisions that are otherwise deemed desirable so that they will be acceptable to the public? The success of educating the public seems doubtful; indeed, it is not even clear that economists can get their message across to policymakers. To design tax policies so that they seem more acceptable to the public is the alternative.

Consider, for example, the recent study of corporate tax integration by the Treasury Department. Were it not for some practical difficulties, the most straightforward approach to full integration would be to tax shareholders on a partnership basis. If relief is restricted to dividends, it is a simple matter to allow for the deduction by corporations of dividends. Another approach would be to impose a corporate tax but allow a credit against the tax for shareholders, either under full integration or a dividend-relief scheme; yet another alternative would be a dividend exclusion. If we believe that the public would find nonpayment of tax by corporations unacceptable, then the credit method or an exclusion of income at the individual level would be more likely to meet with success. Note that the two proposals actually highlighted in the Treasury study were the Comprehensive Business Income Tax (CBIT) and dividend exclusions; both of these proposals would maintain collection of corporate taxes. Indeed, by simultaneously disallowing corporate interest deductions while excluding from the personal income–tax base interest, dividends, and capital gains on corporate stock, the CBIT would actually increase corporate revenue collections. Of course, such a choice runs the risk that some high-income taxpayers whose income is primarily composed of corporate dividends (or dividends, interest, and capital gains in the case of the CBIT) will pay low taxes. But that outcome might be the lesser evil in the public's mind.

Some additional examples come to mind. If a policy to tax earnings on pension investments were to be considered, the more visible approach (attributing contributions and earnings to individuals and taxing them) may be considerably less attractive than the less visible approach (taxing the earnings of pension trusts directly). Investment incentives might be offered with an eye to revenue patterns. For example, adoption of direct expensing would initially wipe out tax liabilities of many firms; investment credits could also have significant effects on taxes for some firms. An alternative would be to allow expensing in excess of depreciation. If this change were coupled with a disallowance of interest deductions and no taxes on interest receipts then most firms would still be paying substantial taxes, yet the tax burden (abstracting from the taxation of dividends and capital gains at the personal level) would be zero.

Public perceptions also have important implications for a concept that has been circulating for some time – the return-free income tax system. With some revisions in the tax laws, it would be possible for the vast majority of individuals to be assessed tax (and either billed or sent a refund) without filing an income-tax return. Such an approach could make the income tax much more palatable, particularly if there is some tendency to over-withhold.

General discussion

Gale raised another example of public misperception of tax policy – the payroll tax. Because the statutory incidence is shared equally between employer and employee, the general public seems to think that the economic burden is shared equally, too. Most economists, however, believe that laborers bear most or all of the burden of the payroll tax. Noting that economists' views and public opinions diverge most strongly on optimal tax questions, such as poll taxes, he wondered about who needs to educate whom.

Lyon believed that there are many examples of apparent taxpayer irrationality, including taxpayer complaints about the taxation of IRA withdrawals (which offsets the deductibility of contributions). For that reason, he advocated that economists educate the general public, not the other way around.

Cutler argued that people tolerated taxes if revenues are not wasted and the benefits are apparent. He observed that more closely knit societies have higher tax rates, as they see benefits more easily. Because of the inability to get good survey response, he suggested looking instead at behavior with respect to taxes (e.g., voting), as is done in measuring the value of environmental public goods.

Gold questioned whether people are cognizant of the benefits from federal, state, and local government and where the revenue for these benefits is obtained. For example, they are unaware that local governments generally spend much more than they raise. Given how ignorant the public is regarding fiscal matters, it is surprising that policy responds to economic incentives as much as it does. He concluded that term limits are undesirable because the small number of state legislators with a good grasp of state tax policy have a significant positive influence on the quality of tax legislation enacted.

David wondered whether expressed preferences are motivated by altruism or self-interest. In a 1981 paper of his, survey data collected in the state of Wisconsin were analyzed to determine the extent of altruistic motivation relative to self-interest in the choice of preferred tax structure. The analysis shows two results clearly. (a) The population is divided into two groups: one group has little knowledge of the tax system and expresses random opinions; the other has well-formed opinions, which were modeled to determine the balance between self-interest and altruism. (b) Among the population identified as informed responders, self-interest (as measured by responses consistent with tax minimization) did not explain variation in attitudes, and many more educated high-income persons expressed altruistic opinions that implied progressive taxation.

The implication of this research is that it is necessary to distinguish informed and uninformed responses to typical polls. Sheffrin's report of lack of consistency in the population data does not go deeply enough to find the opinion that will be influential in making political choices on progressivity issues.

Roberts remarked that, in his own work, when people are asked to report preferences on statutory tax rates, they have preferences that would give them higher effective tax rates than what they currently face, meaning that they overestimate the real burdens they currently face.

Moreland would like to see the same attitude surveys applied to nontax economists.

Toder remarked that because most people don't understand incidence, discounting, and other elements of the tax system, those who do can thereby exploit a system designed for the majority who do not understand.

Steuerle commented that ignorance about taxes is no different from ignorance about any good or service. He wondered what people would be willing to pay for a certain rate structure. Can they then think about taxes as a final good?

Holtz-Eakin argued that although people are bad at analyzing hypothetical situations, they learn as they gain experience and need to know about particular issues.

Hite believed that the public isn't so terribly ignorant and that apparent ignorance is often rational, given that information is costly to obtain. People often focus on that part of the tax system which affects them most.

Sheffrin was surprised by the deep-seated biases about things like incidence. He expressed a belief that Congress generally has a better grasp on tax issues than the general public, and believes there is a case for praising lobbyists in their role as informants of Congress. Finally, he noted that although the property tax is closest of all taxes to being a benefit tax, it is also one of the most unpopular.

CHAPTER 10

Progressive taxation, equity, and tax design

Richard A. Musgrave

Beginning in 1981, repeated and major changes in the federal tax structure have taken place. At the same time, its overall level remained practically unchanged, with a revenue/GNP ratio of 23.3% in 1980 and 23.2% in 1993. Did this stability extend to the degree of progressivity as measured by the pattern of effective rates? Spanning the entire income scale, the ratio of effective rates payable by the top to that payable by the bottom quintile dropped from 3.41 in 1980 to 3.17 in 1993, suggesting a slight flattening of progression. But a closer look at what happened over various ranges in the scale is needed to understand what went·on.

For this we may draw on data presented earlier in this volume (Kasten, Samartino, and Toder, Table 1). Beginning at the top, the ratio of effective rates for the fifth to the fourth quintile dropped from 1.21 in 1980 to 1.01 in 1993. With benefits accruing mostly to the highest 2 percent of income recipients, this flattening reflected the drastic cutback in top income and corporate tax rates under the 1980 legislation. Moving down from the fourth to the third and from the third to the second quintile, the ratios changed but little, falling from 1.16 to 1.14 and from 1.27 to 1.26, respectively. This stability over the middle range reflected the offsetting effects of rate reduction and base broadening under the tax reform of 1986. The pattern of stability continues as we drop from the second to the bottom quintile, with ratios of 1.93 in 1993 and 1.84 in 1980. Increases in personal exemptions, the standard deduction, and earned income credit (i.e., an enlarged zero-rate bracket) raised progressivity while increased payroll tax rates lowered it. The picture changes if social security is viewed as a contributory system. Without also allowing for benefits, it may then be appropriate to exclude payroll taxes. When moving down from the third to the second quintile, the ratio now rises from 1.4 in 1980 to 1.6 in 1993, followed by a sharp climb from 2.8 to 7.5 from the second to the bottom quintile. Middle to lower-end progressivity, excluding payroll tax, thus

341

increased substantially. This, however, only reflected a return of exemptions and standard deductions to their earlier real-value levels, levels that had been eroded by inflation.

How should these developments be interpreted? Do they merely reflect changes in political fortune, in the ups and downs of class and special interests, and in efficiency considerations, or do changing views on equity enter? My concern here is with the latter, beginning with a brief anatomy of the rationale for and against progression as it developed in the context of tax theory. This is followed by a look at public perceptions and at progressivity as an overriding determinant of tax structure design.

1   Approaches to tax equity

Like it or not, fairness in taxation is an age-old issue that cannot be avoided, especially in a seminar on progressive taxation. Such is the case even though the ultimate determinants of equity fall outside the bounds of Pareto optimality. But so do other factors, such as the state of technology or consumer tastes, which economists also must accept as inputs into their analysis. Though economics cannot establish the "correct" equity norm, it can explore the implications of alternative norms, implications that must be weighed in the balance if an intelligent choice among them is to be made. Moreover, economists – especially those dealing with the public sector – cannot disregard the social setting in which fiscal policies operate, including the central issue of distributive justice and its bearing on tax equity. How this issue has been dealt with offers a fascinating piece of intellectual history, one that needs to be understood in interpreting the ongoing debate of the '80s and '90s. Three tracks in the approach to tax equity may be distinguished: the benefit rule, the ability-to-pay rule, and the least-total-sacrifice (or maximum-welfare) rule. All bear on the case for and against progressive taxation, but in different ways.

Benefit rule and quid pro quo

The principle of benefit taxation as a fairness rule derives from an underlying concept of fairness in exchange, or quid pro quo. Though early on directed at the benefits from defense, the principle was later extended to encompass the entire expenditure side of the budget, offering a rule of fair budgeting rather than of taxation alone. In this respect it differs from the ability-to-pay approach, which is limited to fairness in taxation. Based on fairness in exchange, benefit taxation naturally fits the framework of a market economy and an entitlement view of distributive justice. Individuals, according to that view, are entitled to dispose of their earnings, as stipulated by John Locke's "natural order" (1690, p. 327) and Adam Smith's premise of "providential design" (1759, p. 304).

With factor and product prices set in a competitive market, the virtue of the "invisible hand" is extended to yield an outcome that is not only efficient but also just. Benefit-tax finance of public goods fits that pattern. Consumers pay for public services in line with their preferences, as they do for private goods. If preferences were known then government could simply impose benefit taxes to match marginal evaluations. But they are not. Nonrival consumption of public goods calls for their free availability, so that consumers are not compelled to bid. A political process is needed, therefore, to secure preference revelation and to replace bidding in the market. The resulting tax price, as formulated by Lindahl (1919, p. 170), will approximate what consumers would offer if the benefit were provided in the form of a private good. Accordingly, benefit taxation shares the twofold virtue of competitive market pricing: it enables government to provide public goods in a manner which is both efficient and just.

In practice, benefit taxes cannot be assigned individually, so that some index must be used. For street cleaning, a property tax based on road frontage may serve, but for general benefits (e.g. defense) a general index such as aggregate income or expenditures is needed. By the logic of benefit taxation, the appropriate rate schedule will be progressive, proportional, or regressive depending on whether the income elasticity of demand for the public service is above, equal to, or below its price elasticity (Buchanan 1964). Moreover, the logic of benefit taxation calls for different tax prices or shares to be applied to various public services, depending on their demand and supply conditions. The resulting distribution of tax shares for revenue as a whole is of no particular interest in this context, since by definition benefit taxes are distributionally neutral. This is as it should be, based on the premise that individuals are entitled to what they can earn and purchase in a competitive market. Given that premise, the budget deals with the fair and efficient provision of public goods only, and has no redistributional function. Whether the overall system is to be progressive or not is simply a matter of demand elasticities and without fairness implications per se.

Individuals, though granted entitlement to use of their own earnings, may nevertheless have distributional concerns and engage in voluntary giving. To the extent that the donor's satisfaction rests on the act of giving, this remains a private activity and without relevance to taxation. But a linkage arises once A derives satisfaction from seeing B's welfare increased in response to C's giving. Giving now creates external benefits and thus assumes public-good characteristics. Subsidies through the budget – for example, tax deductions for charitable giving – then become appropriate.

This complicates matters, but still fits the essentially quid pro quo nature of equity under the benefit approach.

While benefit taxation as a fairness rule rests on an entitlement-based distributive justice, benefit taxation as an efficiency tool does not require that premise. Wicksell (1896), in what remains the most significant single contribution to fiscal literature, recognized that distributive justice may call for corrections in the distribution of earnings, but nevertheless (p. 102) gave benefit taxation a central role in his system. Benefit taxation would serve to solicit preference revelation for public goods and would thus be efficient, but would be *just* only if applied to a just state of distribution. The system, therefore, called for a two-track approach. Adjustments in the distribution of income, presumably through a tax–transfer system, would be needed to establish a just state distribution, followed by benefit-tax finance of public goods. This construct, as will be apparent, resembles my basic distinction between the allocation and distribution branches of the budget, and has set my framework for fiscal analysis (Musgrave 1959, p. 5).

Ability to pay and equal sacrifice

A second and more common approach to tax equity disregards expenditure benefits and calls for the tax burden to be distributed in a "fair" fashion. Fairness is interpreted as calling for taxation in line with ability to pay. People with equal ability should pay the same (the concept of horizontal equity), while those with higher abilities should pay more (the concept of vertical equity).[1] The distribution of the tax burden was thus to be based on a fairness norm rather than to be derived from a premise of entitlement.

Adam Smith (1776, p. 310) rather ingeniously combined both benefit and ability-to-pay considerations in one dictum: "The subjects of every state," he argued, "ought to contribute toward the support of government,

---

[1] Our conference theme of progressive taxation calls for primary attention to be given to the vertical dimension of tax equity. But it should be noted briefly that horizontal equity (the equal treatment of equals) also enters. In the context of income tax, people with equal incomes should pay the same. With income broadly defined, tax liability should be independent of particular income sources. But the system's capacity to reach various sources differs. Moreover, various sources of income differ in importance at various points in the income scale. Thus, failure to fully tax capital gains will not only cause horizontal inequity between people having the same total true income yet with different capital gains shares; it will also reduce progressivity at the upper end of the scale, where capital gains income is most important. Similarly, failure to tax imputed rent tends to lower middle-income liabilities while failure to reach pensions reduces low-income taxes. Failure to secure horizontal equity thus also distorts the vertical dimension of tax progressivity.

as nearly as possible, in proportion to their respective abilities, that is in proportion to the revenue which they respectively enjoy under the protection of the state." But this nexus, regrettably, was lost in English-language (but less so in continental) tax theory. From Mill to Edgeworth, from Marshall to Pigou, and up to the recent models of optimal taxation, public service benefits have been disregarded and tax equity viewed in isolation. This separation, in many ways, has been unfortunate. The concept of equity, on closer consideration, should include not only tax burdens but also expenditure benefits. Furthermore, the tax–expenditure linkage is needed to explain how the political process does (or, in the Wicksellian sense, should) determine the level and composition of the budget as well as who pays.

Viewed as a matter of taking, equitable taxation thus became a matter of assessing tax shares so as to secure a fair distribution of the resulting loss or sacrifice. The principle that all should be treated equally under the law called for equality of sacrifice (Mill 1849, p. 804) but views differed on whether "equality" should be interpreted in absolute or in proportional terms. With the rise of marginal analysis in the 1880s, equal marginal sacrifice was added to the roster (Edgeworth 1897). But whichever interpretation of "equal" is chosen, the resulting rate schedule would depend on the shape of the marginal–utility-of-income schedule. Based on the premise of declining marginal utility of income, equal absolute sacrifice would call for regressive, proportional, or progressive taxation depending on whether the elasticity of the marginal–utility-of-income schedule falls short of, equals, or exceeds unit elasticity. Equal proportional sacrifice would leave a more complex relationship, whereas equal marginal sacrifice would require maximum progression and absorption of top incomes until the required revenue is obtained.

Least total sacrifice and maximum welfare

As the doctrine developed, the rule of equal marginal sacrifice soon won the day and with Pigou (1928, p. 60) became *the* correct solution. Viewed from the perspective of fairness, this was hardly persuasive. Why should only the marginal sacrifice be considered, rather than the entire loss as called for by equal-absolute, equal-proportional, or still other sacrifice rules? The answer, it appears, is that equal marginal sacrifice was chosen not so much as a matter of fairness but as an efficiency-based prescription for securing least total sacrifice. The move from Mill's equal absolute or proportional sacrifice to Pigou's enshrinement of equal marginal sacrifice thus involved a paradigm shift from equity to Pareto efficiency as the basic criterion. Equal marginal sacrifice, and with it least total sacrifice, fitted neatly into the economist's utilitarian goal of welfare maximization. The case for distributing the burden of a given tax revenue so as to minimize aggregate loss was but a by-product of the general case for distributing income so as to maximize welfare. The entitlement base for distributive justice was thereby replaced by that of utilitarian welfare maximization.

Two further problems remained. To begin with, there was the question of operational applicability. The earlier discussion of ability to pay had been based on the convenient assumption of known, comparable, and even similar marginal–utility-of-income schedules, an assumption that later was discarded as unwarranted (Robbins 1932). At first this seemed to shatter the very foundation of the utilitarian approach to fair burden assignment, but not for long. The earlier construct was soon replaced by the concept of a social welfare function, based on individual perceptions of distributive justice (Bergson 1938). These subjective welfare functions were then seen to coalesce into a social norm (a "social" welfare function) determined as the outcome of a political process. By assuming the shape of that function to be thus set – or, more carefully, by deriving required tax distributions for alternative functions – the argument could then proceed much as it had before. Given the premise of a downward-sloping social welfare function, least total sacrifice (or maximum welfare) retained the presumption in favor of maximum progression.

Next, this presumption had to be qualified by allowance for adverse economic effects. Voiced from the outset by Bentham, Edgeworth, and Marshall (1890), that concern was then formalized in terms of deadweight loss and incorporated into the burden concept. Beginning with Pigou and with Ramsey (1927) and followed later by Diamond and Mirrlees (1971), the earlier measure of socially weighted income loss was replaced by a measure of welfare loss which allowed for the implicit burden of deadweight loss. With deadweight loss rising by the square of the marginal tax rate, maximum progression no longer followed from the mere premise of a downward-sloping marginal utility of income or social welfare function. Rather, the optimal distribution of the tax burden (so as to minimize the total welfare loss) would now depend not only on the shape of the social welfare function but also on market responses to the tax wedge. Calculations based on a range of elasticity assumptions showed the earlier case for progressive taxation to be weakened substantially by allowance for deadweight loss. Conclusions regarding the optimal pattern of progression, however, greatly depended on stipulated elasticities and on the social weighting system applied (Slemrod 1983). But these were refinements only. Notwithstanding its more sophisticated reformulation in the optimal taxation model, Pigou's equal-marginal- (or least-total-) sacrifice view of tax equity had remained essentially unchanged. At the same time, policy conclusions regarding the "correct" pattern of progressivity had now become contingent on (1) the postulated shape of the social welfare function and (2) empirical propositions regarding taxpayer responses.

More basically, left open was the bottom-line question of why, as a matter of fairness or distributive justice, equal marginal sacrifice and hence least total sacrifice should be the accepted criterion. The case for least total sacrifice in tax-burden distribution, as Edgeworth and Pigou saw it, derives from the broader efficiency goal of securing a distribution of income which maximizes aggregate welfare. This takes us back to Bentham's proposition that self-interested individuals, bent on maximizing their own welfare, will also wish to maximize aggregate welfare (Bentham 1789, p. 3), an heroic conclusion which hardly follows. Using superior force or bargaining from a stronger position, the self-interested and better-endowed individual would disagree, as Hobbes had put it in his "warre of everyone against every man" (1651, p. 188). To sustain acceptance, the target of maximum aggregate welfare had to be given an ethical underpinning. Based on the golden rule of valuing the welfare of others as one's own, individuals should discard envy and agree to Pareto-optimal re-arrangements, that is, re-arrangements which produce a net gain for the group as a whole, even though the individual may lose. Given this more demanding premise of impartiality, least total sacrifice or welfare maximization becomes the preferred solution.

As formulated more recently, and in line with economists' taste for maximizing behavior, impartiality has been interpreted as calling for choice under uncertainty.[2] Individuals are called upon to choose among alternative patterns of distribution from behind a veil – that is, without knowing their own capacities and what their own position in any one pattern would be (Vickrey 1945; Harsanyi 1955; Rawls 1971). Assuming a fixed pie available for distribution and stipulating declining marginal utility or postulating risk aversion, people would then agree on an equal division of income; but, allowing for deadweight losses in response to taxation, some

---

[2] As I see it, the "veil" construct and interpretation of distributive justice *qua* risk aversion, though congenial to the economist's mode of thinking, is of questionable merit. If individuals have agreed on the principle of impartiality and thereby on the least-total-sacrifice rule, they should be willing to proceed directly to a corresponding income or tax-burden distribution. The veil construct becomes roundabout and redundant. Moreover, reliance on self-interested choice following disinterested acceptance of the veil seems inconsistent. This also poses the question of how acceptance of the impartiality premise (as distinct from entitlement to earnings) can be reconciled with tax avoidance and the standing of the resulting deadweight loss (Musgrave 1992).

degree of inequality would be agreed on.[3] Applying this reasoning to the narrower problem of just taxation, tax shares to be agreed upon from behind a veil would similarly fall short of maximum progression.

Conclusion

Economists, as this brief exploration into the genesis of tax equity suggests, can be useful in setting forth the analytics that help determine the "correct" pattern of progression or vertical-burden distribution under alternative views of distributive justice, but they cannot pronounce on which is *the* correct one. This reflects not only our limitations in adequately measuring economic responses to taxation but also, and more importantly, that the outcome depends on the underlying equity norm, a choice which is not to be captured within the confines of Paretian efficiency. This choice depends on how the problem of distributive justice is viewed – for example, from a Lockean entitlement perspective, from rules of equality in sacrifice, or from the utilitarian target of maximum welfare (least total sacrifice) with its ethical anchor in the premise of impartiality. All this, to be sure, may be taken as subsumed by the stipulated shape of the social welfare function, and the young economist, eager to get on with maximizing, may be impatient with these underpinnings. But to understand what goes into the underlying reasoning, and hence the case for or against progression, the various inputs need to be sorted out. The utilitarian model, convenient though it is to the economist's toolbox, is not the only possible formulation.

2   Public perception of tax fairness

The public's perception of tax equity can hardly be expected to coincide with any of the preceding models as conceived by philosophers and economists. Attitudes, as noted before, may well reflect a desire to freeload and to let the cost be paid by others. Nevertheless, the very fact that interests in a democratic society must be reconciled by compromise carries an element of fairness. Moreover, the public and even the Ways and Means or Senate Finance Committee are not entirely callous; views of fairness also enter. The cynic's view is not the most realistic one.

To begin with, there is rather general agreement on the guiding principle of horizontal equity: people in equal positions should be treated equally. The definition of equal position, to be sure, is a matter of debate

---

[3] Viewed in this context, Rawls's rule of maximin may be interpreted as involving extreme risk aversion.

and not easily defined in a complex economy. Not surprisingly, the tax law is full of instances where special interests succeeded in securing preferential treatment. After a brave effort at loophole closing in 1986, there is now reason for concern that they will be re-opened. Nevertheless, the principle that there should be no discrimination in the treatment of equals is a basic part of our tax mores.

No such general consensus holds regarding the public's view on vertical equity, the treatment of unequals. Will that perception resemble, if only vaguely, the economist's utilitarian paradigm of aggregate welfare maximization, calling in turn for overall burden minimization? I suspect not. More likely, the public perception begins with an entitlement-based view of distributive justice, to be qualified in some respects. This includes a modest (much short of Rawlsian) correction for poverty at the lower end of the scale. Over the middle range, it calls for proportional taxation based on a rule of equal absolute sacrifice, together with an implicit premise of a generally applicable and unit-elastic marginal utility schedule. To this may be added a dislike of excessively high incomes and the power that they generate, leaving a case for upper-income tax progression. In all, the public's perception, if only gropingly so, is more likely to move in these terms than in those postulated by recent utilitarian models.

These normative issues, however, are only part of the story. The other part pertains to the choice of tax instruments and their incidence. The public's perception (note here Sheffrin's contribution to this volume) can hardly be expected to understand the technical complexities of tax design. In the context of the income tax, do we refer to exemptions and bracket rates, or to the final pattern of effective rates that result? Is it understood that exemptions constitute a zero bracket, so that a so-called flat-rate (linear) tax remains progressive in effective rates? Is the progressivity of the tax structure over the entire income range what matters to the public, or do attitudes distinguish between lower-, middle-, and upper-range progression? How do views on progression vary with the overall level of taxation? Does popular support for taxing business units suggest failure to understand that tax burdens eventually come to rest on individuals? How is the problem of shifting allowed for, and how is the perception of fairness modified by concerns over detrimental (even deadweight loss) effects of high marginal rates? Finally, to what extent are fairness views affected by the expenditure side of the budget, especially for the payroll tax and other earmarked programs?

These questions and others that could be added explain the difficulty of ascertaining the public's perception of tax fairness and its application to particular tax statutes. For someone who has followed the fortunes or misfortunes of progressive taxation for six decades (if I may claim that

as a comparative advantage), it is also evident that the public perception
is fickle and changes with the circumstances of the times. In the 1930s,
"soak the rich" meant a top marginal rate of 50%; only a small part
of the population was covered by income tax. War finance in the 1940s
turned the income tax into a mass tax with a top marginal rate of 92%.
By 1962 that rate still stood at 91%, but was then followed by a series of
cuts, to 70% in 1977, 50% in 1982, and 28% in 1986. In part, that decline
reflected recognition that high nominal rates were (or had become) largely
ineffective and could not be enforced. Concern with deadweight loss and
supply-side effects also entered. Politically speaking, Congress, while leg-
islating high marginal rates, may never have meant such rates to apply in
earnest. This is suggested by the reform of 1986, when upper-bracket base
broadening was matched by reduction in high bracket rates, rather than
permitting such broadening to raise effective rates.

Public attitudes also follow a cycle. Beginning with the New Deal in
the 1930s, the political climate favored a more egalitarian view of distributive justice, and continued to do so for some decades. That of the '70s
and '80s brought a swing of the pendulum back toward what I have referred to as the entitlement premise. A new change in direction, also supported by adverse changes in the underlying distribution of income, may
now be in the making. With the top rate already returned from 28% to
31%, a further increase is now likely; it appears that the trend of the '80s
is being reversed, albeit within moderate limits.

3   Progressivity and tax-structure design

I now leave the elusive question of whether or not the tax structure should
be progressive, and turn to the more tangible bearing of progressivity on
tax-structure design. Here tax economists find a comfortable domain.

In rem *versus personal taxation*

Whatever the choice between income and consumption as the tax base,
the desired degree of progression is fundamental to the appropriate choice
of tax instruments. If equity calls for equal amounts of tax, a head tax
will do. If taxation is to be proportional to the base then the size of the
base enters but an indirect, *in rem* approach will still do. Progression,
however, requires a global determination of the individual's tax base, and
hence direct and personal taxation. Such taxation is inevitably more complex, whether on an income or consumption base. Like all good things,
tax equity is costly, and that cost should be minimized by choosing the
appropriate tax instrument. But rather than choosing the instrument and

then deciding how progressive it should be made, efficient tax design calls for first setting the desired pattern of effective rates and then choosing the appropriate tax form. What matters, moreover, is not so much the overall degree of progression as measured by (say) changes in the Gini coefficient, but rather the desired patterns over various stretches of the income range.

Suppose first that the community's view of equity calls for a proportional tax without exemptions – that is, a constant effective rate over the entire range. Under the income base, this may be obtained in direct form by a flat-rate tax on the income recipient, an *in rem* tax on the income payer, or a value-added tax of the income type. Under the consumption base, the choice is between a flat-rate expenditure tax, a consumption-type value-added tax, or a retail sales tax. With the somewhat precarious assumption that a wages tax is in fact equivalent to a consumption tax, there is the further option of a tax on wage income, whether paid by the recipient or withheld as a payroll tax by the employer. The same result may also be approximated via a cash-flow tax where, after excluding the normal return to capital via expensing, the remaining base is largely in payroll form. Whether directed at the income or consumption base, proportional taxation can thus be accommodated more simply in *in rem* form, without requiring the more cumbersome mode of personal taxation.

More likely, the public's sense of equity will not accept an across-the-board proportional tax; at the least exempting an initial amount will be called for. A combination of exemption and flat rate will then cause the effective rate above that amount to rise over the lower- to middle-income range, tending to approach a flat rate after some midpoint is reached. This outcome may be approximated by combining the *in rem* modes of the preceding pattern with a cash payment, equal to the tax on the exempt part of the base. Allowance for family size would add a personal element but could still be accounted for by a corresponding adjustment in refunds. The need for direct and global-base taxation of the personal type may still be avoided.

Such direct taxation becomes unavoidable, however, once equity is taken to call for effective rates to rise beyond the middle range. If the call is for a rising effective rate throughout the income scale, personal taxation with rising bracket rates must begin where the exemption effect flattens out. But suppose now that the desired pattern calls for a rising effective rate over the lower range, followed by a flat rate over the middle and resumption of a rising rate at the upper end. In that case, an *in rem* flat-rate approach *cum* exemption might be used over the lower and middle ranges, with a progressive personal tax applicable to taxpayers at the upper end of the scale only. Set at (say) $100,000, this would cover a quarter of taxable income but with only some 5% of returns now required. The administrative and compliance costs involved would thus be vastly reduced, thereby permitting tighter enforcement of the remainder. My own preference is for a moderately but continuously rising effective rate, but today's public perception of equity may well fit the approach described here. If so, the prevailing tax structure is unnecessarily complex, implying as it does the headaches of direct taxation for a large number of taxpayers without imposing a significant degree of progression over the middle range of the scale.

An important caveat must, however, be added. Taxation, as noted previously in the Wicksellian context, is needed not only to provide noninflationary and equitable finance but also to secure preference revelation. To meet that function and to exert fiscal discipline, taxation should be visible to voters as the cost of public services, and here personal taxation (even if not of the benefit type) has a great advantage. Seen from this perspective, administrative ease secured by retreat to impersonal taxation may be purchased at too high a cost.

Income versus consumption base

In principle, the preceding observations may be applied to either the income or consumption base. The traditional view of income taxation as progressive and consumption taxes as regressive need no longer hold, since consumption may be taxed via a progressive and personal expenditure tax. Such is the case at least in theory, although it may not be so in practice. The option of a personalized and progressive expenditure tax has not as yet entered public awareness, with retail sales taxes or consumption-based value-added taxes (VAT) still viewed as the usual alternative to income taxation. As noted before, proposals for a cash-flow tax recently entered the fray, and based on the premise that a wage income tax and a consumption tax are equivalent, a cash-flow tax could be viewed as prepayment of a consumption tax.

Combined with an exemption, these *in rem* taxes on consumption could then form the first-bracket component of a progressive expenditure tax. Such could be the case, but most VAT or cash-flow tax plans do not make this addition. As a matter of fiscal politics, rather than of fiscal logic, the debate over income versus consumption base remains linked to that over progressive versus flat or regressive taxation.

The desired degree of progressivity may nevertheless affect the choice between the two bases. Assuming a given amount of revenue to be raised by a flat-rate tax, the traditional efficiency argument favors the consumption base. That preference might be weakened with progressive taxation.

Because consumption tends to fall with rising income, the consumption tax must be more progressive to reach the same burden distribution with respect to income; hence, resulting deadweight losses may be more severe. However, it may be countered that under a consumption tax regime, progressivity should be measured against consumption rather than income. It may also be noted that the consumption base is more stable, so that annual taxation is less distorting.

Centralized versus decentralized finance

Next, it should be noted that the feasibility of progressive taxation greatly depends on the way in which the fiscal system is organized. Any one jurisdiction within a federation, acting on its own, cannot afford to impose the higher marginal rates required under a progressive (as opposed to an equal-yield flat-rate) income tax. Unless others will follow suit, this invites a shift of residence and loss of tax base to lower-rate jurisdictions. With capital more mobile than labor, capital flight is the more likely response, and – as the weight of capital income rises when moving up the income scale – this becomes especially detrimental to progression. The feasibility of progressive taxation at the state (not to mention the municipal) level is thus severely impaired. Similar considerations also apply to central taxation in the international context, as income earned abroad cannot be readily reached.

Would these obstacles to effective progression be less severe for the expenditure tax? Perhaps so. Because consumption is linked more closely to residency than is income, tax avoidance by choosing to operate in a lower-rate jurisdiction becomes more difficult. But there is more to the problem. For a progressive expenditure tax to be assessed correctly, interjurisdictional cooperation in the reporting of financial transactions across borders would be needed – but this would be difficult to achieve.

Whichever the base, technical considerations once more carry important implications for the politics of tax policy. Implementing progressive taxation is more feasible under a system of central finance than with decentralization. The "distribution branch," as I call it, must be part of the central budget. While the debate over central versus decentralized finance does not render this aspect explicit, it is not surprising that attitudes toward progression hide in the wings.

Tax burdens versus fiscal benefits

As noted previously in the context of the payroll tax, it may not be fair to look at the burden distribution of the tax system without also considering the expenditure side of the budget. This is especially apparent in the case of social security with its earmarked and contractual base, but there is also a more general case to be made. After all, what matters is how the budget operation affects the state of distribution; it is unimportant in the end whether the impact comes from the expenditure or the tax side of the budget. It may thus well be argued that equity should be viewed in terms of net benefit or burden. This could be instituted easily with regard to transfer payments. Certain in-kind programs such as low-cost housing, highways, or education may also be imputed to their users, whereas benefit allocations from still others (such as national defense) become less manageable. Precise estimates may be unattainable, but an approximation can be made.

If this is done, the picture changes considerably. Notwithstanding many middle-class programs, the overall distribution of benefits is much more "pro-poor" than is the distribution of tax burdens "anti-rich." A net-benefit-and-burden view of distributional impact therefore yields a pattern of distribution much more favorable to the lower half of the income scale than emerges from tax-only patterns (such as those described earlier in this volume by Kasten, Sammartino, and Toder). The effective net-benefit/income ratio, it appears, falls sharply over the lower to middle range of the income scale, reaches zero somewhat above the median level, and then declines at a more moderate rate (Musgrave and Musgrave 1989, p. 246).[4]

4   Summary

Issues of tax equity, along with their underlying image of a good society, cannot be resolved by considerations of economic efficiency only. If earners are taken to be entitled to their income, fair taxes are benefit taxes with legitimate redistribution limited to voluntary giving. Absent such overriding entitlement, the issue of just distribution – and with it the issue of equity in the distribution of the tax burden – becomes one of "fairness" rules. These may call for various equal-sacrifice prescriptions. Or, based on the utilitarian target of welfare maximization, the call may be for equal marginal sacrifice and hence least total sacrifice. Whichever rule is chosen, implementation calls for a social welfare function by which to

[4] Note that this approach accounts for tax burdens and expenditure benefits only. It differs from an even broader view that would allow for such changes in private earnings as may result from public purchases or employment. The distinction, however, becomes blurred in the case of interest payments, which might be interpreted as either transfers or factor receipts. Under the latter view, interest payments are not counted, thus further increasing the more favorable position of the lower part of the income scale. Further difficulties arise in the treatment of deficit or surplus budgets, issues which need not be pursued here.

weigh the resulting burdens. Testing these principles against the reality of public perception, the concept of fairness more likely begins with an entitlement norm, modified by dislike of excessive inequality at the lower and (to a lesser extent) upper end of the scale.

Whether progression is favored or not, the desired pattern is of basic importance for tax-structure design. A target of proportional taxation permits implementation by indirect and *in rem* taxation, and (combined with an exemption) this still holds where effective rate progression is limited to the lower and middle ranges. Global-based and hence personal taxation becomes essential, however, if such progression is to extend further up. These considerations apply whether the tax base is to be defined in income or consumption terms, so that the desired degree of progression or lack thereof can be implemented in either mode. Such is the case in principle, although in practice the income base remains more amenable to progressive taxation. But whatever the goal, rational tax design calls for setting the desired pattern of effective rates first, with the choice of tax instruments to follow.

REFERENCES

Bentham, J. (1789), *The Principles of Morals and Legislation* (L. J. Lafleur, ed., 1978). New York: Hafner.

Bergson, A. (1938), "A Reformulation of Certain Aspects of Welfare Economics," *Quarterly Journal of Economics* 52: 310–34.

Buchanan, J. M. (1964), "Fiscal Institutions and Efficiency in Collective Outlay," *American Economic Review* 54: 227–35.

Diamond, P. and Mirlees, J. A. (1971), "Optimal Taxation and Public Production," *American Economic Review* 61: 8–27, 261–78.

Edgeworth, F. Y. (1897), "The Pure Theory of Taxation," *Economic Journal* 7: 46–70, 226–38, 550–71; reproduced in Musgrave and Peacock (1958).

Harsanyi, J. (1955), "Cardinal Welfare, Individualistic Ethics and Interpersonal Comparison of Utility," *Journal of Political Economy* 73: 309–21.

Hobbes, T. (1651), *Leviathan* (C. B. McPherson, ed., 1968). Baltimore: Pelican.

Lindahl, E. (1919), *Die Gerechtigkeit der Besteuerung*. Lund: Gleerupska; reproduced in Musgrave and Peacock (1958).

Locke, J. (1690), *Two Treatises on Government* (P. Lasset, ed., 1960). New York: Mentor.

Marshall, A. (1890), *Principles of Economics*. London: Macmillan.

Mill, J. S. (1849), *Principles of Political Economy* (W. J. Ashley, ed., 1921). London: Longmans.

Musgrave, R. A. (1959), *The Theory of Public Finance*. New York: McGraw-Hill.
(1992), "Social Contract, Taxation and Deadweight Loss," *Journal of Public Economics* 49: 369–81.

Musgrave, R. A., and P. B. Musgrave (1989), *Public Finance in Theory and Practice*. New York: McGraw-Hill.

Musgrave, R. A., and A. Peacock, eds. (1958), *Classics in the Theory of Public Finance*. New York: McGraw-Hill.

Pigou, A. C. (1928), *A Study in Public Finance*. London: Macmillan.

Ramsey, F. P. (1927), "A Contribution to the Theory of Taxation," *Economic Journal* 37: 47–61.

Rawls, J. (1971), *A Theory of Justice*. Cambridge, MA: Harvard University Press.

Robbins, L. (1932), *An Essay on the Nature and Significance of Economic Science*. London: Macmillan.

Slemrod, J. (1983), "Do We Know How Progressive the Income Tax System Should Be?" *National Tax Journal* 36: 361–9.

Smith, A. (1759), *The Theory of Moral Sentiments* (E. West, ed., 1969). New Rochelle, NY: Arlington.

(1776), *The Wealth of Nations* (E. Cannan, ed., 1904), vol. 2. New York: Putnam.

Vickrey, W. (1945), "Measuring Marginal Utility by Reaction to Risk," *Econometrica* 13: 319–33.

Wicksell, K. (1896), *Finanztheoretische Untersuchungen*. Jena: Fischer; reproduced in Musgrave and Peacock (1958).

General discussion

Sansing noted that traditional views regarding the distributional effects of taxation are largely incomplete because of their failure to consider the distributional effects of government expenditures.

Inman commented that Varian's 1981 paper adds income redistribution to the no-entitlement argument by considering taxation as a system of social insurance.

Hoerner noted that you arrive at essentially the same place by following the entitlement view of taxation with equality as a public good or by following the no-entitlement view.

Slemrod stated that horizontal equity is another important consideration in designing a tax system. It is difficult analytically, though, to integrate horizontal equity with vertical equity.

Spindle questioned how optimal tax theories need to be adapted to account for intergenerational equity.

Index

Aaron, Henry, 52n, 65n, 126
ability-to-pay principle or rule, 2, 8, 342
Adams, T. S., 220
adjusted family income (AFI)
  decompositions, 108-16
  defined, 98-9
  trend in Gini coefficient for, 99-107
Arrow, Kenneth J., 290n
Atkinson, Anthony B., 293n
Auerbach, Alan J., 41n, 200n, 272, 273,
  276, 298n
Auld, D. A. L., 311
Auten, Gerald, 200n
Avery, Robert B., 180t, 224n, 225, 226-7t,
  228

Ballard, Charles L., 138, 153, 156
benefit principle or rule, 2, 8, 342-4
Bentham, Jeremy, 347
bequests, as function of lifetime earnings,
  85-6
Bergsman, Anne B., 118
Bergson, Abram, 346
Berliant, M., 74n
Bertaut, Carol C., 290n
Best, Michael J., 262n
bias
  with incomplete information or
    knowledge, 311-15
  in measures of distributional effects, 269
Birnbaum, Jeffrey H., 309, 322
Bittker, Boris I., 329
Blackburn, McKinley L., 103, 124
Blank, Rebecca, 122
Blinder, Alan, 122
Bloom, David E., 122, 124, 207n
Blum, Walter J., 313
Blume, Marshall, 262

Bollinger, Lynn L., 220
Bosworth, Barry, 42n, 120n, 121, 141, 142
Bradley, Cassie F., 313
Browning, Edgar K., 137, 153, 156, 171
Buchanan, James M., 343
Burman, Leonard, 200n
Burtless, Gary, 42n, 120n, 121, 139, 141, 142,
  144n, 204n
business cycle effect, 122-3
Butters, J. Keith, 220

Cancian, Maria, 123
capital gains
  concentration of, 277
  effect of rate reduction for, 294-7
  effect of tax law changes (1980-89), 36
  implicit tax rates on, 42-7
  as share of income, 200
  as tax burden, 7
  taxed on accrual basis, 297-300
  tax treatment (1962-88), 187-8
capital gains realizations
  distribution, 7
  frequency (1985-89), 278-9
  increases in, 6
  response to marginal tax rate changes,
    40-2, 122, 200
  simulation model for, 276-7, 284-9,
    301-3, 305-7
  as source of family income, 13
  timing of, 187-8, 200-3
Case, K., 65
Caspersen, E., 74-5n
Center for the Study of the States, 62
CES or CEX, *see* Consumer Expenditure
  Survey
Chaplinsky, Susan, 221
choice under uncertainty, 347-8

For EU product safety concerns, contact us at Calle de José Abascal, 56–1°,
28003 Madrid, Spain or eugpsr@cambridge.org.

www.ingramcontent.com/pod-product-compliance
Ingram Content Group UK Ltd.
Pitfield, Milton Keynes, MK11 3LW, UK
UKHW040735250425
457623UK00033B/21